KEPHALAION

PHILOSOPHICAL TEXTS AND STUDIES
WIJSGERIGE TEKSTEN EN STUDIES

edited by / onder redactie van

C. J. DE VOGEL, L. M. DE RIJK,

A. TH. PEPERZAK O.F.M., J. P. M. GEURTS

Uitgaven van het Filosofisch Instituut der Rijksuniversiteit te Utrecht

PROFESSOR C. J. DE VOGEL

KEPHALAION

STUDIES IN
GREEK PHILOSOPHY
AND ITS CONTINUATION
OFFERED TO
PROFESSOR C. J. DE VOGEL

edited by

J. Mansfeld and L. M. de Rijk

1975
VAN GORCUM & COMP. B.V. - ASSEN, THE NETHERLANDS

ISBN 90 232 1212 6
Library of Congress Catalog Card Number: 74-84367

Printed in the Netherlands by Van Gorcum, Assen

THIS VOLUME IS OFFERED
TO PROFESSOR C. J. DE VOGEL,
WHO FOR MORE THAN TWENTY-FIVE YEARS
HELD THE CHAIR OF ANCIENT AND MEDIEVAL
(SINCE 1968 OF ANCIENT AND PATRISTIC)
PHILOSOPHY IN THE UNIVERSITY OF UTRECHT.
IN THIS WAY, FRIENDS, PUPILS
AND COLLEAGUES HAVE WISHED,
ON THE OCCASION OF HER RETIREMENT,
TO HONOUR HER GREAT ACHIEVEMENTS
IN THE STUDY OF THE WHOLE HELLENIC AND
CHRISTIAN TRADITION OF PHILOSOPHY.

CONTENTS

HERACLITUS' CONCEPTION
OF FIRE

W. J. VERDENIUS

In B 36 ("for souls it is death to become water") "soul occupies the position which fire might have been expected to fill"[1]. The question arises why Heraclitus used the term 'soul' instead of 'fire'. It has been suggested that the word may refer to exhalations from the sea[2], but although souls are said to be exhaled from moist things (B 12)[3], the word is never used to denote exhalations. A more obvious explanation is that Heraclitus chose the term ψυχή in order to create a paradox[4]: the word means 'soul' as well as 'life', so that the transformation of soul into water implies the death of life; but life as such cannot die.

The solution of this paradox may be found by comparing B 36 with B 30, where the world[5] is called "ever-living fire". This seems to present a new difficulty: how can fire be ever-living if it dies in its transformation into water? It has been assumed that the ever-living fire is a mere symbol for the order of the world[6], but it appears from B 31, where sea and earth are called 'turnings' of fire, that fire is regarded by Heraclitus as an actual constituent of things[7].

Another solution is the suggestion that the ever-living fire is to be taken as extra-cosmical, and the dying fire as intra-cosmical[8]. However, the wording of B 31 seems to be incompatible with the assumption of a dualism in Heraclitus' conception of fire, for the term τροπαί implies that the other elements are manifestations of the eternal fire, and not its 'substitutes'[9]. The word is usually translated by 'change'[10], but this meaning is not found before Aristotle. Heraclitus no doubt thought of the solstices and wished to illustrate the dual movement of the cosmological process by the movements of the sun[11]. The analogy between the eternal fire and the sun is only partial, for the former "never sets" (B 108), whereas the latter is "new every day" (B 6)[12]. On the other hand, they resemble each other in that they remain themselves in their 'turnings'. Consequently there is but one fire, and we have seen that this is identical with the world. The eternal fire is said to 'manage' the world (B 64)[13], but this need not imply that it operates from the outside: it is more likely to exercise an inner rule[14] similar to the one exercised in Anaxagoras' system by Mind, which "is present where all the other things are" (B 14). It is true that "the wise" (which may be taken to be identical with fire[15]) is said to be "separated from all" (B 108), but this "may imply not complete isolation but simply a great difference"[16].

The supposition that the ever-living fire is present where all the other things are seems to be contradicted by B 90, where the world is said to be an "exchange for fire", just as goods are for gold. It has been concluded from this comparison that fire completely perishes when it is transformed into the elements of the phenomenal world. When the latter return to fire, this comes to life again, and it is only in this restricted sense that it is called 'ever-living'[17]. However, the solemn formula "it always was and is and shall be" (B 30) shows that 'always' in 'ever-living' has the same full meaning. The comparison of fire with gold does not imply a complete analogy, for it is only meant to emphasize the fact that all things are one in being primarily and ultimately fire[18].

The ever-living fire has been interpreted as a cosmic bonfire which as a whole is permanently afire, although parts of it may be temporarily extinguished[19]. But ever-living is more than ever-lasting: it implies that its subject is a living being which is permanently alive in all its parts. It should further be noted that the ever-living fire is said to be "kindling and going out" (B 30): the use of the present participles shows that it is never completely extinguished[20]. The addition of "according to measure" does not suggest that extinguished parts are balanced by burning parts [21] but that the *processes* of transformation balance each other. Accordingly the fact that fire is going out does not mean that it is "*not* ever-living in its parts"[22] but that its life even manifests itself in its going out, because that process is counterbalanced by a process of kindling, just as the life of an animal consists in the balance of nutrition and excretion[23].

This brings us back to the paradox noted at the beginning: if fire as a whole is ever-living, how can its transformation into water be called its death? It has been suggested that it is not just ordinary fire but a purer kind, commonly called 'ether'[24]. However, Heraclitus does not say that "one part of the cosmos (i.e. the sky and the heavenly bodies) is more truly fire at any one time than other parts (i.e. sea and earth)"[25]; on the contrary, according to B 30 the ever-living fire is not part of the cosmos but the whole cosmos. Besides, the fragments do not suggest that Heraclitus assumed the existence of different kinds of fire[26].

It is equally unsatisfactory to call fire "the archetypal form of matter"[27], for this does not explain the relation between its living and its

2

dying: if an archetype is eternally alive, its derivatives can hardly be mortal. On the other hand, it is true that the eternal fire, although it is identical with ordinary fire, has a more fundamental character than its empirical manifestations. Heraclitus does not draw a distinction between two worlds or between different kinds of matter, but he does distinguish the 'surface' of matter from its 'root'. These terms are to be understood in a metaphysical, not in a physical, sense, i.e. in the sense of appearance and essential nature. Fire as a natural phenomenon is transformed into water. But this passing-away of fire is identical with the coming-to-be of water (the terms γενέσθαι and γίνεται in B 36 have a pregnant sense). In other words, death as a phenomenal aspect of the world is identical with birth (B 88)[28]. 'Soul' dies when it is transformed into water (B 36), but, as is apparent from its name ('life') and from the fact that it is regenerated out of water, its death does not have an absolute character[29]. Heraclitus obviously thought that behind the contrariety of death and life there must be some unity, and that this could be only a more fundamental form of life – life maintaining and renewing itself in death[30] – embodied in the most 'lively' element, fire[31].

Fire is ever-living, and this is its essential nature. However, "the essential nature of things is wont to hide itself" (B 123). Thus the true nature of fire[32] does not manifest itself on the surface of things, or rather it manifests itself in an indirect way. Just as the Delphic god "does not speak outright, nor conceals, but indicates" (B 93)[33], fire does not reveal its essential nature to the casual observer but only to the penetrating vision of a qualified interpreter such as Heraclitus. He everywhere discerns life in death and conversely, not only in the interdependence of coming-to-be and passing-away but also in the ambivalent nature of Dionysus, the god of procreation, i.e. life, and of drunkenness, i.e. death (B 15)[34], and in the paradoxical character of the bow, which brings about death but whose name means life (B 48)[35].

These and similar opposites are intimately connected: they are based on an inner tension in the very nature of things (B 51)[36]. This connection, although it is not always immediately apparent, is stronger, i.e. more fundamental, than visible connections (B 54), for it is the common tie between all things, the divine order which is stronger than all human laws (B 114)[37]. The latter are said to be 'nourished' by the divine order (B 114), which shows that the general tension governing the world is imagined to be a kind of life[38]. In fact it is life itself, embodied in the ever-living fire[39].

The tension between opposites manifests itself in war, "father of all and king of all" (B 53)[40]. However, the universal character of war seems to be contradicted by B 67, where God (who is obviously identical with fire and accordingly with strife) is said to be war and peace. This paradox resembles the paradox of fire: war is a special aspect of the world but at the same time a universal principle[41]. Just as there is but one fire, there is but one war; just as fire, war manifests its true nature in an indirect way: that it is the effect of a universal tension appears from the general character of phenomenal contrasts, one of which is the contrast between war and peace[42].

The universal tension beneath the surface of things, the hidden order of the world, is not a neutral abstraction but a positive power. It is not embodied in some indefinite matter[43] but in a concrete element, fire. This may be equated to God, and "to God all things are beautiful and good and just" (B 102), because he sees, and even constitutes, the fundamental identity of opposites. Similarly, "strife is justice" (B 80)[44], not only because "through the very conflict of the opposites the measure will be kept"[45] but also because strife is the natural condition of things[46]. The war between opposites is something positive, not because they neutralize each other but because their continuous tension is a form of eternal life[47].

It is interesting to compare Heraclitus' conception of fire with the views of his antagonist Parmenides. There we find not only justice related to real being (B 1, 28; 8, 14) as well as regulating the phenomenal world (B 1, 11-14; 12, 3)[48], and names as expressing the appearance of things (B 8, 38, 53; 9, 1; 19, 3)[49], but also light manifesting itself on two different levels of reality, on the surface of the world as the opposite of night, and beneath the surface as an aspect of real being[50].

NOTES

[1] G. S. Kirk, *Heraclitus: The Cosmic Fragments* (Cambridge 1954), 340. Kirk (*loc.cit.*) argues that "it is quite wrong to think of soul in Heraclitus as airy or vaporous". The insertion of air into Heraclitus' scheme (B 76) was due to the Stoics: cf. Kirk, 342-4, E. Zeller-R. Mondolfo, *La filosofia dei Greci nel suo sviluppo storico*, I 4 (Firenze 1961), 185-8. However, this does not imply that Heraclitus completely disregarded the existence of air but only that he did not consider it to be a special element: cf. Ch. H. Kahn, *Anaximander and the Origins of Greek Cosmology* (New York 1960), 152 n. 1, W. K. C. Guthrie, *A History of Greek Philosophy*, I (Cambridge 1962), 453. His theory of 'exhalation' (B 12, A 1, 9 and 11, A 11, A 12, A 15) seems to presuppose the recognition of vaporous forms of fire and water. This applies also to the use of πρηστήρ instead of fire in B 31. Kirk (330-1) takes this to be identical with the lightning-flash, but ancient authors distinguish it from κεραυνός, and Aristotle (*Meteor.* 371a15) defines it as a burning cloud (similarly Aët. III 3,9 = Heracl. A 14). Hesiod (*Th.* 846) speaks

4

of πρηστῆρες ἄνεμοι. See further Zeller-Mondolfo, 82-8, J. Mansfeld, Mnemos. IV 20 (1967), 18-9.

2 Kirk, op.cit., 341.
3 Cf. Mansfeld, op.cit., 14-8.
4 As is suggested by M. C. Nussbaum, Phron. 17 (1972), 153.
5 That κόσμος has the meaning of 'ordered whole' has been shown by G. Vlastos, A.J.P. 76 (1955), 344-6 and J. Kerschensteiner, Kosmos (München 1962), 99 and 104.
6 Kahn, op.cit., 225 and Am. Philos. Q. 1 (1964), 8: "fire symbolizes not only the paradoxes, but their solution as well. For it represents life in death, identity in change, pattern in transience". Conversely, and even more strangely, the phenomenal order of the world is taken to be a symbol for its inner order: "The periodic order of sun, stars, and seasons, with the related meteorological sequence of elemental change, has itself become the symbol for that cyclical community of life and death which forms the innermost content of Heraclitus' logos". Cf. also Zeller-Mondolfo, op.cit., 70-1.
7 Cf. Kirk, op.cit., 306, 316-7. Guthrie (op.cit., 461) argues that fire "is not a permanent substratum", because "such a permanent physis would contradict the law of flux". However, this objection does not apply to an ever-living, i.e. ever-changing, substratum. It is not correct to say that for Heraclitus "the only permanent thing is form" (Guthrie, 467).
8 M. Marcovich, RE Suppl. X (1965), 294. Similarly Guthrie, op.cit., 471, who thinks that there is a "Logos-fire surrounding the cosmos".
9 As is held by Marcovich, Heraclitus (Merida 1967), 287.
10 E.g. by Kirk, op.cit., 306, 325, 329.
11 So rightly B. Snell, H. 61 (1926), 359-60 = Gesammelte Schriften (Göttingen 1966), 134, H. Boeder, Grund und Gegenwart als Frageziel der früh-griechischen Philosophie (Den Haag 1962), 77. Kirk (op.cit., 329) refers to Snell's article for the meaning 'sudden and complete change', but this applies only to the verb τρέπομαι. The analogy between fire and the sun shows that the 'way up and down' (B 60) is to be taken in the sense of 'to and fro', as was argued by K. Reinhardt, H. 77 (1942), 19 and n. 2. For this meaning of ἄνω κάτω cf. Mnemos. IV 17 (1964), 387.
12 Cf. Kirk, op.cit., 363, Boeder, op.cit., 75-6.
13 For the question why Heraclitus used the word κεραυνός cf. Kirk, op.cit., 354-6, whose suggestion that it "is simply a symbol for fire" does not seem plausible. Heraclitus chose this special term because (1) the thunderbolt is the strongest kind of fire, (2) it is the weapon of Zeus, whose rule parallels that of fire (a) in being eternal (B 32 and Zeller-Mondolfo, op.cit., 163-4, L. Ph. Rank, Etymologiseering en verwante verschijnselen bij Homerus [Assen 1951)], 44 and n. 35) and (b) in keeping things within their natural limits (Boeder, op.cit., 79).
14 G. Vlastos, A.J.P. 76 (1955), 366 = D. J. Furley-R. E. Allen (ed.), Studies in Presocratic Philosophy, I (London 1970), 426, rightly observes that "for Heraclitus the creative source of the world is wholly within the world". Guthrie (op.cit., 471) thinks that "for Heraclitus as a child of his time it would not be illogical but natural to think of the divine principle as immanent as well as external". Cf. also G. E. R. Lloyd, Polarity and Analogy (London 1966), 273-4.
15 Cf. B. 32 and Phron. 11 (1966), 92-3.
16 Kirk, op.cit., 399. H. Gundert, Gnom. 27 (1955), 480 rightly paraphrases the text by "von jeder vereinzelten Gestalt geschieden". Marcovich (Heraclitus, 441-2) translates κεχωρισμένον by 'is different from' but takes this to refer to absolute transcendence.
17 J. Klowski, Arch. Gesch. Phil. 48 (1966), 17.

¹⁸ Accordingly, it is unnecessary to suppose that "some of the goods exchanged for gold might themselves contain a proportion of gold" (Kirk, *op.cit.*, 348). It is equally wrong to conclude from the fact that money and goods cannot be reduced physically to one another that individual things cannot be regarded as consisting of fire, as is done by M. C. Stokes, *One and Many in Presocratic Philosophy* (Cambridge, Mass. 1971), 104-6.

¹⁹ Kirk, *op.cit.*, 317, Mind 69 (1960), 334-5 = Furley-Allen, *op.cit.*, 172-3. Similarly Stokes, *op.cit.*, 104.

²⁰ This disposes of Stokes' argument (*op.cit.*, 104) that "what has been extinguished is no longer fire".

²¹ Kirk (*op.cit.*, 317) supposes that parts of the bonfire "are temporarily dead, parts are not yet alight", although he writes himself: "note the present participles". Cf. also G. S. Kirk-J. E. Raven, *The Presocratic Philosophers* (Cambridge 1957), 96, 198.

²² Kirk, *loc.cit.*

²³ The fact that the ancients assigned an important part to heat in the process of digestion (πέψις) may have contributed to Heraclitus' choice of fire. For the connection between heat and life cf. Guthrie, *op.cit.*, 61 and n. 1, 92, 101-2, 291-2, F. Solmsen, J.H.S. 77 (1957), 119-20 and *Cleanthes or Posidonius? The Basis of Stoic Physics*, Meded. Kon. Ned. Akad. v. Wet., Afd. Lett. N.R. 24 (1961), 263-89.

²⁴ Kirk, *op.cit.*, 316, 356, 365, Kirk-Raven, *op.cit.*, 200.

²⁵ Kirk, *op.cit.*, 356.

²⁶ Cf. Vlastos, A.J.P. 76 (1955), 361-2 = Furley-Allen, *op.cit.*, 421-3, who rightly observes that "no Ionian philosopher thought of 'cosmological' fire, air, etc. as different in kind from that we see and handle every day". Guthrie (*op.cit.*, 432) argues that fire "must not be imagined as a visible flame or glow, but rather a kind of invisible vapour". But Heraclitus did not make a distinction between visible fire and invisible fire, but only between a visible connection and an invisible connection (on which see below).

²⁷ Kirk-Raven, *op.cit.*, 200. In Mind 69 (1960), 335 n. 1 = Furley-Allen, *op.cit.*, 172 n. 2, Kirk admits that "the choice of word may not be the best possible".

²⁸ B 88 does not refer to alternating processes, as is maintained by Lloyd, *Polarity and Analogy*, 100-1, for μεταπεσόντα does not mean 'having changed' but 'changing'. For the coincident use of the aorist participle cf. Kühner-Gerth, I, 199, Schwyzer, II, 301, Broadhead on Aesch. *Pers.* 325, Barrett on Eur. *Hipp.* 289. It is not correct to say that the verb μεταπίπτειν as such "tends to emphasize the accomplished change and not the process" (Kirk, *Heraclitus*, 146): the meaning is that a thing *is becoming* the opposite of what it originally was. See further K. Reinhardt, H. 77 (1942), 240-4.
The interpretation of passing-away as dying is not a metaphorical use (as is held by Kirk, *op.cit.*, 341), for Heraclitus was a true hylozoist. The hylozoist character of Milesian philosophy has been rightly stressed by Guthrie, *op.cit.*, 62-5, 127-30, *In the Beginning* (London 1957), 19-20, 46 ff. This view has been criticized by G. A. Seeck, Gnom. 35 (1963), 535-6, who is right in maintaining that "wir dürfen nicht, nachdem sich einmal die Meinung gebildet hat, eine Unterscheidung werde erst später vorgenommen, jeden Ansatz negieren". On the other hand, his suggestion, "Anaximander sei den sprachlichen Möglichkeiten seiner Zeit, was den Gedanken betrifft, voraus und bediene sich nur der Formen der Zeit, um seine Gedanken auszudrücken", opens the door to all kinds of allegorical interpretation.

²⁹ Boeder (*op.cit.*, 90) wrongly thinks that souls "bleiben, zu Wasser geworden, keineswegs in einer anderen Hinsicht am Leben. Sie lösen sich gänzlich zur reinen Gegenseite des belebenden Feuers auf".

6

[30] Vlastos, A.J.P. 76 (1955), 366 = Furley-Allen, *op.cit.*, 427, rightly observes that Heraclitus chose the term 'ever-living' rather than 'immortal' "since for him the condition of life everlasting is not deathlessness but life endlessly renewed by death".

[31] For the conception of fire as a living being and a power of life cf. Hom. E 4 etc. ἀκάματον πῦρ, *h.Dem.* 239-42 and Allen *ad loc.*, Aesch. *Ag.* 597, *Prom.* 358, Eur. *Ba.* 8, Ar. *Lys.* 306, Arist. *De iuv. et senect.* 470a3, Theophr. *De igne* 1. See further H. Usener, *Kleine Schriften*, IV, 471 ff., L. Radermacher, W.S. 49 (1931), 115-8, L. Séchan, *Le mythe de Prométhée* (Paris 1951), 2-5, who observes that the renewal of the hearth-fire was intended to renovate life. Cf. also C. F. von Weiszäcker, *Die Geschichte der Natur* (² Göttingen 1954), 89: "Nehmen Sie ein so einfaches Ding wie eine Kerzenflamme. Niemand leugnet, dass wir sie physikalisch-chemisch verstehen. Aber sie hat Stoffwechsel bei gleichbleibender Form, sie stellt ihre Gestalt nach äusserer Störung wieder her, sie vermehrt sich, wenn man andere Kerzen mit ihr anzündet, ja man kann das Driesch'sche Seeigelexperiment mit ihr anstellen: spaltet man den Docht, so entstehen zwei ganze, aber schwächere Kerzenflammen... Mit Grund ist das Feuer seit der Urzeit das Symbol des Lebens. Sollten zwei so ähnliche Erscheinungen im Wesen so verschieden sein?". It is interesting to add that the Swedish expression for 'candle-light', 'levande ljus', properly means 'living light'. For other motives why Heraclitus chose fire as the substance of the world cf. Vlastos, A.J.P. 76 (1955), 364-5 = Furley-Allen, *op.cit.*, 425-6.

[32] For this meaning of φύσις cf. Kirk, *op.cit.*, 227-31.

[33] Guthrie (*op.cit.*, 414) thinks that in B 93 Heraclitus characterizes his own style of writing. But this style has been chosen because it reflects the true nature of things. For the double character of Heraclitus' λόγος (system of reasoning and system of the world) cf. Phron. 11 (1966), 90-3.

[34] Cf. Mnemos. IV 12 (1959), 297.

[35] Cf. Kirk, *op. cit.*, 117-22, whose scepticism with regard to a wider implication of this fragment ("a fragment which only incidentally involves these terms [viz. life and death]") I do not share. – For the name as a partial revelation of the nature of a thing cf. B. Snell, H. 61 (1926), 369-70 = *Ges. Schriften*, 141-3, Kirk, *op.cit.*, 67-8, 117-20, 198, Zeller-Mondolfo, *op.cit.*, 341-7, M. C. Nussbaum, Phron. 17 (1972), 10-3.

[36] Whether we read παλίντονος or παλίντροπος (Vlastos, A.J.P. 76, 1955, 348-51), the fragment refers to the tension between opposites. Cf. Guthrie, *op.cit.*, 437, 439. For the meaning of ἁρμονίη cf. Vlastos, A.J.P. 76 (1955), 350, Stokes, *op.cit.*, 96-7.

[37] Cf. O. Gigon, *Untersuchungen zu Heraklit* (Leipzig 1935), 29, *Der Ursprung der griechischen Philosophie* (Basel 1945), 203-4, F. Heinimann, *Nomos und Physis* (Basel 1945), 65-7.

[38] Kirk (*op.cit.*, 54) wrongly thinks that Heraclitus "would also have been aware that τρέφονται was in some degree a metaphor".

[39] This makes the use of τρέφω especially appropriate, as nourishment was thought to be brought about by heat (see above n. 23).

[40] Cf. Guthrie, *op.cit.*, 446-7, who rightly compares B 80, where strife is called 'common', i.e. universal. Kirk (*op.cit.*, 187) wrongly takes 'war' to be a mere "symbol for the predominance of change". It is true that "all change... could be resolved into change between opposites" (241), but in that case war does more than "symbolize the interaction between opposites" (*ibid.*): it *is* that interaction.

[41] For the pregnant meaning of ξυνός cf. Vlastos, A.J.P. 76 (1955), 347-8 n. 23, 357 n. 43 (= Furley-Allen, *op.cit.*, 418 n. 7).

[42] Accordingly, we need not assume that Heraclitus lacked "precision of vocabu-

lary", as is done by Kirk, *op.cit.*, 187. Guthrie (*op.cit.*, 444) suggests that "war itself is the true peace" and refers to B 84a ("changing it rests"). But B 53 emphasizes the dynamic character of the world (cf. B 125), and B 84a has the same meaning, for ἀναπαύεται does not imply standstill, as appears from its opposite κάματος (cf. Gigon, *Heraklit*, 94, Kirk, 252-3).

[43] Heraclitus implicitly disputes the view of Anaximander. Cf. Vlastos, A.J.P. 76 (1955), 365-6 = Furley-Allen, *op.cit.*, 426-7, but also Guthrie, *op.cit.*, 469 n. 1.

[44] Another criticism of Anaximander. Cf. Kirk, *op.cit.*, 240, Vlastos, *op.cit.*, 356-9 = Furley-Allen, *op.cit.*, 417-20, Guthrie, *op.cit.*, 447-8.

[45] Vlastos, C.P. 42 (1947), 164 = Furley-Allen, *op.cit.*, 67.

[46] Cf. Gigon, *Heraklit*, 117. For this meaning of δίκη cf. H. Fränkel, *Wege und Formen frühgriechischen Denkens* (²München 1960), 171-3. This explains the fact that Dike superintends the course of the sun (B 94).

[47] Cf. Fränkel, *op.cit.*, 249-50, Kirk, *op.cit.*, 181-2, Rev. philos. 82 (1957), 297.

[48] Cf. Phron. 12 (1967), 100-1.

[49] Cf. Heracl. B 32, 48, 67, 93.

[50] Cf. Phron. 12 (1967), 106-10. The objections raised by C. W. Müller, *Gleiches zu Gleichem* (Wiesbaden 1965), 21 n. 19, 23 n. 27, and W. Burkert, Phron. 14 (1969), 15 are not decisive.

HÉRACLITE JUGÉ PAR PLATON

RENÉ SCHAERER

> Que peut-on bien vouloir dire en af-
> firmant que tout se meut?
> (Platon, *Théétète* 181c)

C'était à Mexico, en septembre 1963, lors du XIIIème congrès international des sociétés de philosophie. J'eus alors l'agréable surprise de
rencontrer Mlle de Vogel dans un des couloirs de l'université. Connaissant par expérience la ferveur de son engagement spirituel et l'insatiable
curiosité de sa pensée, je lui demandai quel était alors l'objet de ses
recherches. Elle me répondit en anglais: «Heraclitus' flux». Je compris
phlox au lieu de *flux* et, la présence de ce mot, rare chez Platon, m'éton-
nant un peu chez Héraclite, je lui demandai quelques explications.
«Comment, me répondit-elle d'un air scandalisé, vous ne connaissez pas
le flux d'Héraclite? » Le malentendu fut vite dissipé mais cette petite
scène est restée vivante dans ma mémoire et c'est pourquoi j'ai choisi
Héraclite et son flux comme thème du sincère hommage que j'ai l'honneur
d'adresser à cette savante collègue[1].

Je me propose de réhabiliter, contre certains critiques, l'existence
authentique d'une théorie du flux héraclitéen telle qu'elle est présente
dans les fragments et telle que Platon et Aristote l'ont développée ensuite. J'en profiterai pour signaler les dangers où peut conduire une
utilisation trop étroite de la méthode historico-critique.

Platon a-t-il lu, a-t-il compris Héraclite? «Je suis convaincu du
contraire» me disait récemment un jeune collègue. Je lui fis remarquer que
cette opinion n'était pas nouvelle et qu'elle me paraissait insoutenable,
mais la raison qu'il fit valoir pour la justifier me parut digne d'être prise
en considération, car elle se fondait sur une réaction personnelle d'intuition et de goût à laquelle on ne saurait refuser, en cette matière, un
certain crédit. Entre les fragments du poème de Parménide, me dit-il, et
les commentaires qu'en donne Platon, il y a une consonance et une
continuité évidentes. En revanche, passer des fragments d'Héraclite à
leur interprétation dans les *Dialogues*, c'est vraiment passer d'un monde
dans un autre.

Il semblerait donc que Platon, fidèle interprète de son «père» Parménide,
n'ait ni lu ni compris Héraclite. Des historiens, et non des moindres, se

sont faits les avocats de cette thèse. A les en croire, l'auteur des *Dialogues* aurait interprété dans le sens d'un écoulement (*rheuma*) ce qui serait expressément affirmé par Héraclite comme un repos résultant de forces contraires qui s'annulent réciproquement. Il aurait trahi Héraclite en substituant le mouvement à la stabilité. «The dominating idea in Heraclitus is rest in change, not change in apparent stability», écrit Kirk, et de toute évidence ces mots visent Platon[2].

Reprenons le problème en examinant séparément les deux philosophes, l'auteur des fragments et son illustre commentateur.

Héraclite ne met pas en doute la réalité objective des choses sensibles ni la valeur du mode empirique d'information qui se fonde sur elles (fr. B 55). Mais ces choses sont soumises au devenir, même celles dont la stabilité paraît le plus assurée. Les permanences offertes à nos sens par les objets sensibles ne sont donc nullement illusoires, pas plus que les données phénoménales ne le seront pour Kant (*Erscheinung* n'est pas *Schein*); mais les sens sont de mauvais témoins, et seuls s'y laissent prendre ceux «qui ont une âme barbare» (fr. B 107). Le vrai philosophe leur accordera donc une confiance limitée, et se méfiera particulièrement de l'ouïe, sans doute parce que c'est par elle que se transmettent, de maître à élève, les opinions fausses. Les sens n'en sont pas moins les canaux, les fenêtres par lesquels nous entrons en contact avec le réel extérieur (fr. A 16): ils nous ouvrent sur le monde. Lorsque ces pores se ferment durant le sommeil, nous nous retirons alors dans l'univers privé de nos rêves, nous sommes absents bien que présents (fr. B 26, B 89, cf. B 34).

Témoins véridiques et superficiels, les sens signalent des permanences relatives: eau, air, terre, bois, arc, lyre. *Une vision plus profonde* révèle l'instabilité de ces mêmes données: la nuit devient jour, l'hiver été, l'eau terre etc. (fr. B 31, B 36, B 67). La loi du devenir s'impose à toutes selon l'ordre du temps. C'est exactement ce qu'affirme Aristote dans la *Physique* (253b9): «Certains vont jusqu'à dire que le mouvement n'appartient pas qu'à certaines choses et non aux autres, mais à toutes et toujours, sauf que cela échappe à notre perception». Kirk remarque avec raison à ce propos qu'Aristote exprime ici de manière explicite ce qui est implicitement affirmé par Platon, à savoir que les objets stables subissent d'invisibles changements, mais on s'étonne de lire ensuite, sous la plume du même auteur, cet étrange commentaire: «Can Heraclitus really have thought that a rock or a bronze cauldron, for example, was invariably undergoing invisible changes of material? Perhaps so; but nothing in the extant fragments suggests that he did, and his clearly-expressed reliance on the senses, provided they be interpreted intelligently, suggests that he did not»[3]. Guthrie a raison de réagir ici contre son collègue de Cambridge en lui objectant: «That the rock is changing every instant we cannot see with our eyes, but it is what their evidence suggests if we apply "minds that understand the language"[4]. Car c'est précisément une interprétation intelligente des fragments d'Héraclite qui oblige à admettre, au sein du roc et du chaudron, l'existence d'un changement imperceptible. Dès l'instant où la pierre et le bronze existent, ils subissent l'action de forces destructrices; dès leur naissance ils portent en eux leur propre mort: le chaudron s'oxyde, le roc s'effrite, l'arc et la lyre s'usent et tomberont en poussière. Prétendre donc avec Snell, Kirk et Rivier que la doctrine du flux est étrangère à Héraclite, bien plus qu'elle lui aurait semblé 'repulsive'[5], ce n'est pas seulement faire fi de témoignages intérieurs aux fragments eux-mêmes et à la doxographie, mais encore traiter l'autorité de Platon et d'Aristote avec une désinvolture choquante.

Est-ce à dire qu'il faille en rester là, que la doctrine d'Héraclite se réduise à la théorie du flux? Non certes. Admettre une telle simplification serait commettre une faute non moins grave que l'erreur contraire. Il ne suffit pas, en effet, de percevoir le fluent sous le stable, *il faut aller plus profond* et comprendre d'un esprit moins «endormi» (fr. B 75, B 57) que cette dissolution progressive implique dès le départ et à part égale la présence du négatif au sein du positif, du néant au cœur de l'être. Il appartient à l'essence du chaudron et de l'arc de disparaître, de même qu'il appartient à ma nature de vivre en mourant ma vie. Je ne puis être que sur le mode d'une négation radicale et constante de moi-même.

A ce niveau de réflexion, l'image du flux n'a plus de sens. Elle cède la place à l'opposition d'un pour et d'un contre qui s'annulent en se posant. Et ce qui est vrai de l'arc, de l'homme, de ce breuvage (*kukeon*) qui «se décompose si on ne l'agite pas» (fr. B 115), est également vrai du Principe suprême, de Zeus, qui ne peut être qu'en acceptant et refusant à la fois le nom qu'il porte (fr. B 8). Héraclite, devançant de loin Heidegger, a compris que, réduire le stable au fluent, c'est aller au delà du fluent, c'est admettre le contradictoire comme fondement de ce qui coule.

On se tromperait en considérant ici Héraclite comme un ilot de génie dans la suite des penseurs présocratiques. Sa doctrine apparaît bien plutôt comme l'aboutissement, peut-être inévitable, des théories antérieures. Cette *archè* qui, chez les Milésiens et les pythagoriciens se présente comme un intermédiaire, un arbitre et un juge entre des opposés qui, sans elle, se détruiraient l'un l'autre, qui oblige les contraires à «expier, au temps fixé d'avance, leur réciproque injustice» (Anaximandre, fr.

11

B 1), cette *archè* descend de son tribunal et se résout en une loi immanente de renvois et d'équilibre. Quant à l'image du flux, elle ne se pose – mais elle se pose nettement – que pour s'évanouir au profit d'une identité qui n'est pas réduction des contraires mais affirmation radicale de leur antagonisme. Ce qu'Héraclite reproche à ses prédécesseurs – comme le feront les plus grands philosophes après lui, Descartes, Spinoza, Leibniz, Kant, Husserl – c'est de n'être pas allés assez loin dans leur effort d'analyse, d'être demeurés en deçà de la vérité, dans un état de demi-sommeil.

Tout se résout donc en une «harmonie invisible» (fr. B 54), qui est lutte constante et parfaitement équilibrée de contraire à contraire. Gardons-nous de tomber dans l'erreur des pythagoriciens en résolvant la dissonance au sein d'un accord fondamental, dans une paix définitive qui, mettant fin à la guerre, ne serait qu'une forme de mort. Le *dia* de la distinction ne s'abolira jamais au profit du *sun* de la conciliation (fr. B 10, B 51). La balance n'est plus entre les mains de Zeus, comme dans l'*Iliade*, elle est entrée en Zeus, elle est Zeus lui-même, mais elle ne cesse d'osciller, elle est la loi du monde. La simultanéité et l'équivalence naissent du renvoi: tout est *sullapsis* ou *sunapsis* (fr. B 10, le texte est douteux).

Reste la seconde question: Platon a-t-il réellement trahi Héraclite en réduisant la guerre à un flux, *polemos* à *rheuma*? Pour oser l'affirmer, il faut avoir lu le texte des *Dialogues* comme on le lit, hélas, trop souvent aujourd'hui, en le fixant et l'immobilisant sur quelques formules. On sait que l'admirable examen du *Théétète* s'attaque aux prétentions de la connaissance empirique à constituer l'unique source du savoir[6]. La thèse de l'homme-mesure (Protagoras) conduit les interlocuteurs à une réfutation du mobilisme, attribué aux «compagnons d'Héraclite» (179d). Cette théorie «héraclitéenne» se fonde elle-même sur une tradition très ancienne, qui a sa source en Homère et dans les vieux mythes. Héraclite aurait donc reçu d'un passé lointain la théorie du flux universel. Le seul changement que cette théorie aurait subi en passant du mythe à la philosophie eût été de s'affirmer démonstrativement «au grand jour» (*anaphandon*) afin que les savetiers eux-mêmes pussent s'en pénétrer et comprendre que tout se meut, même ce qui semble immobile (179d-181b).

Platon attribue donc à Héraclite une théorie du flux universel qui serait venue à lui de fort loin. En cela, nous venons de le voir, il ne trahit nullement la pensée de l'Ephésien mais il n'en retient qu'un aspect, ou plutôt un niveau. S'il en restait là, on pourrait lui adresser un juste reproche; mais il va plus loin, et ceux qui s'en prennent à lui feraient mieux de lire attentivement les dernières lignes de la démonstration du *Théétète*. Platon pose cette question fondamentale: «Que peut-on bien vouloir dire en affirmant que tout se meut?» (181c). La réponse, c'est que la théorie du mouvement universel, sous ses deux formes de translation et d'altération, conduit à l'évanouissement de toute couleur, de toute sensation et, par voie de conséquence, à l'annulation de tout sujet et de tout objet. Le réalité devient radicalement inexprimable; les mots n'ont plus de sens. *«Ainsi»* équivaut à *«non-ainsi»*, et réciproquement. Couler et non-couler sont interchangeables. Il faut forger un «nouveau langage»: *allèn phônèn*[7].

La théorie du flux a donc sa place chez Héraclite, mais elle ne s'affirme que pour s'annuler en se renversant sur elle-même. Tel est l'avis de Platon. et c'est à la même conclusion que nous conduit l'examen des fragments dans la mesure où nous les comprenons. L'explication par l'écoulement général n'est pas fausse mais insuffisante, et c'est ainsi qu'Aristote l'entendra[8]. Admettre avec Protagoras la thèse de l'*homo-mensura*, fondée elle-même sur le mobilisme, c'est être inévitablement conduit à immobiliser ce qui coule en retournant le courant sur lui-même, à identifier l'aval à l'amont, le chemin qui descend à celui qui monte (Hér. fr. B 27). Certes Platon ne dénonce pas, sous cette théorie, une violation du principe d'identité, comme Aristote, mais il n'avait pas à le faire. La mention d'Héraclite est ici subordonnée au mouvement général du dialogue. Il n'y en a pas moins une concordance remarquable entre les interprétations données par Platon et Aristote. Platon ayant écrit au sujet des mobilistes: «Ils n'ont plus aucun terme qui s'ajuste à leur hypothèse, sauf, peut-être, que le «pas même ainsi» leur serait encore le mieux adapté dans son acception infinie», Aristote reprend la même idée et presque les mêmes mots: «Ils en arrivent enfin à la négation pure: ni ainsi ni pas ainsi. Sans quoi il y aurait quelque chose de déterminé»[9].

C'est donc bien sur l'authentique thèse héraclitéenne que s'achève la critique du mobilisme dans le Théétète. Elle conclut sur une condamnation, non sur une incompréhension. Ce renvoi de contraire à contraire que le penseur d'Ephèse conçoit comme un principe de vie apparaît à Platon, héritier de Pythagore, comme une réduction ruineuse de la vie à la mort, de l'être au néant. C'est la voie ouverte au nihilisme de Gorgias résumé dans cette formule: «Il n'y a rien». Si donc on éprouve l'impression en lisant les *Dialogues* que Platon s'inscrit dans la continuité de Parménide – quelles que soient ses réserves sur le problème du non-être – et qu'il rompt délibérément avec Héraclite, ce n'est pas qu'il ait mieux compris le premier que le second mais qu'il donne raison à l'un et tort à l'autre. Et c'était bien son droit.

13

Il convient donc de s'élever, avec Guthrie, contre une méthode trop encline à rejeter les témoignages des anciens et à condamner ceux-ci «aussi longtemps qu'ils n'ont pas pu prouver leur innocence»[10]. Certains critiques modernes se rendent ici coupables d'une étrange aberration: pour avoir consacré des mois ou des années à analyser les fragments du philosophe «obscur», ils en viennent à mesurer la certitude des résultats obtenus à la durée de l'effort accompli. S'il leur apparaît alors que les commentaires de Platon ne s'accordent pas avec ces résultats, ils concluent: Platon n'a donc pas compris Héraclite. Quant à l'hypothèse selon laquelle Platon n'aurait pas lu Héraclite, se serait contenté du «miroir» déformant et anonyme de l'héraclitéisme à la mode, elle est si aventureuse et gratuite qu'on ne saurait la retenir. Comment admettre que le fondateur et maître de l'Académie, qui enseigna durant près de quarante ans devant des disciples tels qu'Aristote (surnommé «le liseur»), Speusippe, Xénocrate et beaucoup d'autres venus de près et de loin pour l'entendre, ce Platon dont les cours et les entretiens devaient porter principalement sur le stable et le mouvant, l'identique et le contradictoire, l'un et le multiple, comment admettre qu'il ait pu développer devant un tel auditoire des théories illustres entre toutes sans les avoir ni comprises ni vérifiées dans le texte. Certes nous n'avons aucune preuve que l'ouvrage d'Héraclite sur *La nature* figurât parmi ceux que comptait la bibliothèque de l'Académie mais il serait bien étrange qu'il n'eût été à la portée de personne et que nul n'en eût fait usage.

NOTES

[1] Mlle de Vogel a présenté au même congrès une communication intitulée: *The topic of eternal change in Greek and later western philosophy compared with Indian thought* (Vol. IV-375).

[2] Cité par Guthrie: *A history of Greek philosophy*, I, Cambridge 1962, 452, n.1. Cette question est entièrement reprise dans le même ouvrage aux p.449-454 et 448-492. Aux auteurs cités par Guthrie comme adversaires de la théorie du flux attribuée à Héraclite (Kirk, Snell, Reinhardt), il convient d'ajouter notre regretté collègue, M. André Rivier qui, dans un article de la Revue de théologie et de philosophie (Lausanne, 1973, 93-107), pousse à l'extrême cette interprétation et, reprenant une hypothèse de Kirk, admet comme ayant valeur de preuve que l'image authentique d'Héraclite s'est réfractée, au IVème siècle, "dans le miroir déformant tendu par ses continuateurs". Il conviendrait donc, selon M. Rivier, de revenir, à travers ces intermédiaires anonymes, à l'Héraclite original, bien différent du compte-rendu que nous en proposent Platon et Aristote.

[3] G. S. Kirk-J. Raven, *The Presocratic Philosophers*, Cambridge 1966, 197.

[4] Guthrie, *op.cit.* 451.

[5] Le mot est de Kirk, cité par Guthrie, *op.cit.* 451, n.1.

[6] «The whole dialogue examines the claim of the world of external sensible objects

to be the sole source of knowledge», écrit justement F. M. Cornford (*Plato's theory of knowledge*, London 1935, 129).

[7] *Théét.* 183a-c. Selon Aristote, Cratyle, disciple d'Héraclite, «en venait finalement à penser qu'il ne faut rien dire, et il se contentait de remuer le doigt» (*Métaph.* 1010a10-15).

[8] Sur Aristote interprète d'Héraclite, voir la remarquable étude de G. Romeyer-Dherbey: *Le discours et le contraire. Notes sur le débat entre Aristote et Héraclite au livre IV de la Métaphysique.* Etudes philosophiques, octobre-décembre 1970, 475-496.

[9] *Métaph.* 1008a30-36. Le rapprochement est fait par Diès dans son édition du *Théétète*, 218.

[10] Guthrie, *op.cit.*, 404.

NAMING IN PARMENIDES

JOSEPH OWENS

I

What Parmenides meant by naming is a problem that has loomed rather large in recent studies[1]. Four times in the extant fragments the notion makes its appearance (Diels-Kranz Fr. B 8,38 and B 8,53; B 9,1; B 19,3). In all four instances it is met in contexts that seem to offer special help for grasping what Parmenides understood by the *doxa*, the world of human experience[2]. Accordingly the topic offers a challenge of considerable importance for those interested in the Parmenidean physical universe and its relation to the Eleatic being.

The first three of these texts have been read in widely varying ways. They have not met with any general agreement in regard to their immediate meaning. The fourth, however, seems straightforward enough. At least, it has not evoked controversy about its prima facie sense. After describing how according to appearance (*doxa*) things were born and now exist, and after growing will come to an end, the fragment concludes: "For them men have established a name distinctive of each" (Fr. B 19,3).

At first reading this clause appears to be an ordinary statement about the way things in the perceptible universe, or at least living things, are given their names. Conventionally men agree upon a certain name for each type, such as shoes and ships and sealing wax, or, in the case of the living, cabbages and kings. Moreover, individual kings and individual domestic animals are given their individually distinctive names. The name marks off each from the other. It is a sign that distinguishes in human discourse. It is given in the ordinary process of naming with which all people are familiar. It means that different positively characterized objects are set off one from another in mental and verbal expression.

So far there are no problems. But if that is all the line signifies, it would be of little interest or help. It has no important textual variants or textual difficulties, and would have only a commonplace meaning. Yet it apparently had a location in the poem that would suggest it was meant to recapitulate succinctly Parmenides' basic explanation of the *doxa*. It occurred, according to the statement introducing it in Simplicius (*In De*

Cael., p. 558,8), after the account of the perceptible cosmos had been given. Simplicius, in excerpting parts of the poem because copies of it were becoming rare, apparently had the whole work before his eyes. The presumption, then, that it concluded the section on the *doxa* if not the whole poem, seems fairly safe³. In this light two expressions in the line give rise to the suspicion that something much deeper lies beneath its placid phrasing.

One of these is the notion of 'establishing'. In conjunction with 'naming', this notion had been used in the course of the poem (Fr. B 8, 38-39 and B 8,53) in the meaning that human convention had set up the whole of the *doxa*. Against that background, establishing names should suggest something more than an innocent giving of names to things already presupposed as positively distinct from one another. It would imply that the process of naming was involved in the factor that set the various things up as distinct units. Establishing the name would somehow mean giving the thing its specific character and individuality. In a word, naming would be implicit in what makes one thing distinct from another. It would not be the mere labeling of a distinctive status already recognized for the thing in priority to the naming. What is recapitulated by Fr. B 19,3 would have been a detailed explanation of the perceptible universe as a construct set up by human convention.

The other expression 'distinctive' (ἐπίσημον) confirms this suspicion. In the *doxa*, the distinguishing marks (σήματα) of the two basic constituents of the cosmos were established or instituted (ἔθεντο) by men (Fr. B 8,55). They were not merely recognized as marks already there. As distinguishing marks they are first established by human convention. So established, they provide two opposites of equal force (Fr. B 9) that give rise to a universe of differentiation and change. Earlier the same term for "distinguishing marks" was used also in the case of being (Fr. B 8,2). By itself it does not necessarily signify things in the *doxa*, since it can also stand for the characteristics of the undifferentiated whole. But when found in conjunction with the notion of establishing by convention, it seems to recall the process by which the perceptible cosmos was explained in the third section of Parmenides' poem.

There are indications, then, that the notion of naming in Fr. B 19 may be summing up Parmenides' own way of explaining the perceptible universe. A close study of its use in the other three fragments is accordingly in order. Do these three show that Parmenides can use the expression in Fr. B 19 in quite the same way that other people use it, and yet that he can see in it a profound philosophical meaning that other

17

people do not? If so, these fragments will have to keep their thought within the ordinarily understood sense of naming, as it appears prima facie in Fr. B 19. While respecting that sense, do the fragments penetrate philosophically into depths of meaning that are only implicit in it in its use in everyday discourse, but become known to the mortal who travels the road of the goddess?

II

The first text on naming in the fragments is found at Fr. B 8,38-42. It occurs after Parmenides had been shown by the goddess that being is unchangeable, undifferentiated and whole. The passage has been read in varying ways. In the Greek it commences τῶι πάντ' ὄνομ(α) ἔσται, with ὀνόμασται as an acceptable and seemingly better established textual variant for the last two words. Both versions have had their defenders in recent discussions.[4] The dative τῷ has usually been taken in the sense of 'therefore'. But it may be a relative (as in Fr. B 1,1, B 1,25, B 1,30, and B 8,46) or a demonstrative referring to the whole and immobile being that was mentioned in the two preceding lines. Πάντα, the subject of the clause, is continued in the ὅσσα of the following line. It may be taken either as 'things', or, internally with the verb, as 'names'[5]. In consequence the details given in the next two lines (40-41) will be understood either as things and processes in the perceptible world, or as names ("institutions of speech" – Woodbury, o.c. 146) given them by men. If read as 'things', and with the accusative and infinitive construction continued through lines 39-41, the things will be "all things, whatever mortals established (κατέθεντο) believing that they are true, that they become and perish, that they are and are not, that they change in place and vary through range of bright color" (Fr. B 8,39-41). The notion of "being true" was easily applied to things in its Greek use and etymology.

In accord with one's understanding of its grammatical elements, the passage may be explained in a number of differing ways. One definite way is to read line 38 as "for which" (or "for it"), namely for being, "all things will be a name". The meaning then becomes pregnant. All things established by human convention will be names for being. The use here of 'name' in the singular need not cause difficulty, since it is used in the singular in Fr. B 19,3 and immediately given the sense of a distinctive name for each thing. The pregnant sense is that things are given the status of names.

But what are these things that are all established by human convention

18

and become looked upon as names? They are identified with sufficient clarity by the description given. They are whatever mortals believe to be genuine things, whatever things they think come into being and perish, things they believe both are and are not, move in place and change in surface characteristics. The types of change noted here are the obvious ones, types that Aristotle will later classify as change in substance, change in place and change in quality. Everything perceptible is subject to at least one of these types of change. What is signified, accordingly, includes all the things and events in the perceptible universe.

Do ordinary mortals in fact believe in this way and speak in this way? Yes, they do. They say and believe that a fire is kindled and burns out, that an animal is born and dies, that a man walks into the market place and changes in complexion with exposure of his face to the sun. They also say and believe that each perceptible thing is and is not – not at all in the sense that bread is not bread or a fish not a fish, but emphatically in the sense that bread is not a stone and a fish is not a serpent. They think that one thing is not the other, and that in the universe there is a plurality of beings. They think that perceptible things are 'true', in the Greek sense of trustworthy and unconcealed. Mortals do talk and believe that way. The goddess is reporting correctly a factual situation.

But how does all this show that each perceptible thing will be a name for the one whole and unchangeable being? There seems to be no historical background that would substantiate this claim. It could hardly be a reaction against an accepted opposition of name to substance[6]. The notion appears to be new. Presumably it will have to be explained by analysis of the poem's assertions. Does the analysis actually bear out that claim?

The future indicative "will be" (line 38) may be taken to express "an *intended* result" (Smyth, no. 2558). The result is established only later (Fr. B 8,53-61 and B 9), after a short and understandable interlude in which the wholeness of being is vividly reiterated and the opportunity to introduce its doxastic fragmentation as deceptive is taken (Fr. B 8,42-52). The procedure is entirely normal. Accordingly, first at line 53 is there call for showing that all perceptible things are a name for being. It was presented as a future undertaking at line 38. Vis-à-vis the *doxa*, it will follow as a result of the already established tenets on being. But that result is to be shown in the future, that is, in the lines shortly to be encountered in the poem.

To say that perceptible things are names is, of course, to use a metaphor. Literally, they are not names, especially not in appearance, but are metals,

19

plants, cats, dogs, and so on. Yet each of them, as a distinct thing, will be a name for the unique and all-inclusive being already described. They appear only in the *doxa*, and not in the true account. But in the *doxa* they appear as something notably different from the names by which they are designated. What, then, is the ground of the metaphor? It has to be an analogy. The analogy, quite obviously, is that as names are to perceptible things, so perceptible things are to being. The relation is designation by conventional establishment. Perceptible things, this would mean, are conventionally established constructs that give human expression to the one whole and unchangeable being[7]. Since these lines occur in the section on truth, they may be taken to assert the legitimacy of regarding each perceptible thing as metaphorically a name for being.

The poem does in fact go on to show that perceptible things are conventional constructs. The doxastic possibility of the construction lies in the basic human decision to name two forms and conventionally establish positive characteristics for each. The goddess, speaking of human opinions, relates: "For they decided to name two forms, one of which it is not right (to name)[8] – in which they have gone astray. They divided body after the manner of opposites and established (ἔθεντο) signs apart from each other,..." (Fr. B 8,53-56). The general impression given by these lines is that mortals have set up the cosmic order in a way corresponding to their process of establishing legal, social and cultural institutions. For this their *doxai* use two basic forms. One of these forms it is not right to name. But for it as well as for the other they establish bodily characteristics set off in direct contrariety to each other.

How do these assertions fit in with the notion that perceptible things are names for being? Here the basic doxastic forms, though established as perceptible appearances, are not presented as names for anything else. On the contrary, they themselves are named. In being named, they are of course distinguished from each other on the ground of perceptible characteristics conventionally attributed to each[9]. That seems to be the function of naming in this line. It is a conventional process, like all naming. But the goddess, in stating that one of the forms should not have been named, implies that the other form is named legitimately. In her message, the only thing there is to be named is being. She had named it and its signs, obviously with all the legitimate truth of her own account. But now doxastic characteristics are established for it – etherial fire, lightness in weight, gentleness. It is still described as "in every way the same as itself, and not the same as the other" (Fr. B 8,57-58), as though fire were everywhere self-identical, just like being. The legitimately named form, though now endowed with conventionally divided signs of body, seems meant to have the status of being, as Aristotle reports: "He ranges the hot with the existent"[10].

Naming, then, seems viewed as a legitimate process as long as one names being. Otherwise the use of "it is" would be prohibited, and the whole poem placed on the forbidden list. But to establish in conventional fashion signs for being that qualify it in particular ways, such as fire or lightness in weight, is to make it doxastic, no matter how much one wishes to regard fire as in every way the same as itself. This is just as doxastic as to name illegitimately the opposite form and establish conventionally its contrary characteristics.

Shortly after these lines the poem continued: "But since all things have been named light and night and whatever accords with their own capabilities in the different instances, the whole is full at the same time of light and dark night,..." (Fr. B 9,1-3). The naming of all things as day and night along with their specific designations is given as the reason, or at least the condition, for the presence of the basic forms throughout the whole doxastic universe. But where had it been shown that all things in the universe had been named light and night? Ordinary mortals do not name things in this way, so it is not a doxastic statement. If it had been shown in the few lines between Frs. B 8 and B 9, some mention could have been expected from Simplicius in quoting the passages. However, at Fr. B 8,40 all doxastic things were said to be and not to be, according to the belief of mortals. Any "being-and-not-being" was regarded there as a name for being. Here the doxastic counterparts, light and night, have been named conventionally and in turn name all perceptible things. Doxastic things, accordingly, may be called names insofar as they are set up conventionally. What they designate is being, the only thing truly there to be designated. But they in turn are designated by "light-and-night" along with their own names, because basically they are, as particular things, combinations of those two doxastic forms. The assertion "all things have been named light and night" is consequently a truth statement by the goddess about the *doxa*, just as was the assertion that all things are a name for being.

What has been shown, then, is, in the language of truth, that mortals have named not-being by conventionally endowing it with perceptible characteristics wrongly established as positive. The use of the term "not-being" by the goddess had not named anything besides being. Being was what it had named and titled. Naming required a distinct positive object[11]. To obtain this object, mortals had to divide bodily appearance

21

and conventionally set up opposite characteristics within it. Once these have been established with equal force, they provide the constituents for the highly differentiated and incessantly changing universe set up in human cognition by the process described cryptically in Fr. B 16[12].

Positive in appearance, these characteristics are negative in truth. This need not be too difficult to understand today. Black is accepted by the psychologist, the artist and the costume designer as a positive color, though shown by the physicist to consist in the negation of light rays. Solidity is regarded as positive, though if intensified to absolute zero it would mean total lack of energy. For a philosopher who makes substance consist in energy, total inertia would mean not-being. Everywhere in the Parmenidean *doxa* black holes keep appearing and in their totality they form half the perceptible universe. The universe of differentiation and change, as it appears at the moment, is the starting point of Parmenides' thought. This is made clear enough by the proem of his work. While still on the road of the goddess he sees that the perceptible universe has to be analyzed into and explained by the two basic forms, but that of these only one could be rightfully named, and is in fact named both through words and through perceptible things.

So, if Fr. B 8,38 is taken to mean that every perceptible object will be metaphorically a name for being, it offers a rewarding sense as it looks forward to the proof in the passages shortly to follow. If, on the other hand, Fr. B 8,38 is read in the sense that all names, including those listed, have been given in reference to being, it undoubtedly expresses correct Parmenidean doctrine. All names designate being. But then the line does not carry as tellingly the distinctive Parmenidean conception of the cosmos itself as a conventional construction. Containing no future reference, however, it had in this interpretation no call to anticipate the ensuing analysis of the *doxa*.

Two other fragments enter into the discussions about the Parmenidean naming. One is "Cornford's fragment," taken from Plato (*Tht.* 180E1). Even if it is genuine, neither its location in the poem nor the construction of its opening words is known. The remaining words form a distinct clause: "the name for the All is 'to be.'" If the fragment is authentic, it confirms the legitimacy of the naming process when what is designated by the name is being[13].

The second fragment is Empedocles 31B 8. It asserts that there is no nature, but only a mixing and changing of constituents. Then it adds a clause that may be understood as either "but 'nature' is a name given them by men," or "but it is named 'nature' by men"[14]. In either case,

22

though apparently echoing Parmenidean expressions, it merely asserts that the cosmic processes are mistakenly named 'nature' by men, mistakenly in virtue of Empedocles' own doctrine. It does not seem to give any direct help towards understanding the special sense of 'naming' in Parmenides, though it may have its importance in other respects.

III

Naming for Parmenides, the texts show, is basically the conventional process by which a word or expression is established to designate a thing. Metaphorically it is extended, in one reading of Fr. B 8,38, to cover the conventional establishing of perceptible things as expressions or names for the unique immobile being. It may be either right or wrong. It is right when, either by words or by perceptible constructs it designates being, the only thing positively there to be named. Accordingly the thinking out and writing and reciting of Parmenides' poem is perfectly legitimate.

Naming, however, has always to be based on a positive characteristic or distinguishing mark. It is therefore illegitimate when conventionally applied to not-being. Not-being, having no characteristics at all, cannot be known and cannot be expressed in speech. But mortals do in fact mistakenly name not-being, on the basis of the characteristics of night, darkness, ignorance, earth, thickness, heaviness. They obtain these distinguishing marks by dividing bodily appearance – for the corporeal is the only kind of being recognized by Parmenides – into these character-istics and their opposites. This whole process is wrong, for there is no not-being to be named, and the characteristics assigned to it, though appearing positive, are in reality negations. But with the second basic form so named and its characteristics so established, and with equal force given to both, the differentiations and changes in the perceptible universe may be explained. To understand them and treat of them as in this way human conventions, is truth. To believe that the differentiations and changes are the true situation, is the *doxa*.

Naming is accordingly for Parmenides a conventional process through-out which being remains sole and sovereign both in the perceptible world and in human thought and speech. Every sensible thing and every human thought and word is being. To understand that, is to be on the road of the goddess while thinking and speaking. Recognized clearly as naming the one immobile being, human thought and language and living are thoroughly legitimate. Parmenides may legitimately continue in them,

23

even though according to *doxa* they and all perceptible things are differentiated and are engendered and perish, and "for them men have established a name distinctive of each" (Fr. B 19,3). The important philosophical consequence is that for Parmenides perceptible things can retain all the reality and beauty they have in ordinary estimation, and still function as names for the one whole and unchangeable being.

NOTES AND REFERENCES

[1] See Leonard Woodbury, *Parmenides on Names*, Harv. Stud. Class. Phil., 63 (1958), 145-160; Leonardo Tarán, *Parmenides* (Princeton, N.J. 1965), 129-143; Alexander P. D. Mourelatos, *The Route of Parmenides* (New Haven 1970), 181-189. Cf. note in W. J. Verdenius, *Der Logosbegriff bei Heraklit und Parmenides*, Phron. 12 (1967), 114 n.51.

[2] Jean Beaufret, *Le poème de Parménide* (Paris 1955), 32, exploiting the overtones of 'beauty' and 'glory' in the Greek word *doxa*, remarks that for Parmenides the things of the *doxa* "ne sont absolument pas des illusions voisines du non-être, mais les choses mêmes de ce monde-ci, telles qu'elles se laissent rencontrer, dans leur éclat et dans leur gloire, au lieu unique et central de leur manifestation". On the reality of the perceptible world for Parmenides, see Woodbury, *op.cit.* 149 and 156-157, and my paper *The Physical World of Parmenides*, to be published in the *Festschrift* in tribute to Anton C. Pegis, ed. Reginald J. O'Donnell, Toronto, Pontifical Institute of Mediaeval Studies, 1974. For the case against its reality, see G. E. L. Owen, *Eleatic Questions*, Class. Qu. 54 (1960), 84-102, and Tarán, passim.

[3] "...after them it is unlikely that the *Doxa* went any further" – Tarán, 266. A short discussion of Fr. B 19 may be found in Uvo Hölscher, *Anfängliches Fragen* (Göttingen 1968), 111-112.

[4] See Woodbury, o.c. 147-149, and Mourelatos, o.c. 181-189, for the sense of "have been named"; and Tarán, 129-136, and Karl Bormann, *Parmenides* Hamburg 1971), 42 and 170-171, for "will be a name".

[5] "...the things which mortals" – Mourelatos, o.c. 184, but understood by him as an internal subject of the verb in the sense of 'names'; "institutions of speech", Woodbury, o.c. 146, and "all the names", o.c. 149. On the other hand, the 'whatever' and its antecedent have been understood as the things named, e.g. "which all things are but a name for", Thomas Davidson, *Parmenides*, Journ. Specul. Phil. IV (1870), 6. The pejorative 'but' or 'merely' is not in the Greek text – see Woodbury, o.c. 146 and Mourelatos, o.c. 183, n.41. Davidson's translation of the τῷ in Fr. B 8, 38 as a relative is in accord with the way it was taken by some early nineteenth century editors of the *Theaetetus* to support an arbitrary emendation of their text at 180E1; see Heindorf's note in the Bekker (1826) edition of Plato, III, 494. Plato's understanding of "being and not-being" as a 'name' at *Tht.*, 185C5-6, indicates that he himself took the expression as naming "what is common to all things", introduced by the relative ᾧ. For the case against taking τῷ in the sense of 'therefore' at Parmenides Fr. B 8, 38, see Woodbury, o.c. 149. Yet even with the reading "have been named" it continues to be taken as 'therefore' (Mourelatos, o.c. 181), as well as with the reading "will be a name" (Tarán, o.c. 86; Bormann, o.c. 43). On the direct application of the Greek notion of 'true' to things, though in relation to cognition, see Heribert Boeder, *Der frühgriechische Wortgebrauch von Logos und Aletheia*, Arch. Begriffsgesch. 4 (1959), 91-100; 111-112.

24

⁶ Woodbury, o.c. 145, notes that the later contrast of name with *ousia* would be unlikely before the sophistic period. The notion of "empty names", however, continues to be accepted in Bormann, o.c. 170-171, in the interpretation of Parmenides.

⁷ Tarán, o.c. 143, remarks that the word 'name' in this context "has, for Parmenides, the connotation of human convention, and human convention is the cause of the acceptance of the phenomenal world".

⁸ This seems the natural reading of the line. It has, however, been read to mean that it is wrong to name so much as one (Cornford), only one (Verdenius), or a unity of the two (Tarán). On the controversy, see Tarán, pp.217-226. On *morphê* as "perceptible form", see Mourelatos, o.c. 220, and for the 'unscrambling' of line 53, o.c. 228-229.

⁹ For an analysis of naming, see Mourelatos, o.c. 184. The notion through which the subject is named "carries meaning prior to entering in this three-term relation" – ibid.

¹⁰ *Metaph.*, A 5, 987a1-2; Oxford trans. Cf. "...he asserts that these two, viz. *what-is* and *what-is-not*, are Fire and Earth" – *GC* I 3, 318b6-7; Oxford trans. It is of course true to say: "'Nacht' sowohl wie 'Feuer' finden sich in der Lehre der Wahrheit nicht" – J. Mansfeld, *Die Offenbarung des Parmenides und die menschliche Welt* (Assen 1964), 133. Fire and night are but the conventionally established 'signs' for the two named forms, allowing the one to be identified with being, the other with not-being.

¹¹ See supra, n.9.

¹² On this much discussed fragment, see Tarán, o.c. 169-171 and 253-263.

¹³ See F. M. Cornford, *A New Fragment of Parmenides*, Class. Rev. 49 (1935), 122-123. For the case against the line as an independent fragment of Parmenides, see Tarán, o.c. 133-136. In favor of its authenticity, see Woodbury, o.c. 148-149, and Mourelatos, o.c. 187 and 284. On arbitrary changes made to bring it into line with Parmenides Fr. B 8,38, see supra, n.5.

¹⁴ The usual translation is that 'nature' is given to *them* as a name. For explanation see Mourelatos, o.c. 183-184; 189. Though "mixing and shifting" are the subject of the singular verb 'is' at the beginning of the line, the change to the plural in referring to that subject as "to them" is not regarded as difficult. If "mixing and shifting" are continued as a singular subject for the verb 'named', the τοῖς goes with ἀνθρώποισιν. Before the tmesis the line would read φύσις δ' ἐπονομάζεται τοῖς ἀνθρώποισιν. In neither case is any doctrinal issue involved.

ALCMAEON:
'PHYSIKOS' OR PHYSICIAN?

WITH SOME REMARKS ON CALCIDIUS' 'ON VISION' COMPARED TO GALEN'S PLAC. HIPP. PLAT. VII

JAAP MANSFELD

1. Alcmaeon of Croton is generally, though not universally, represented as a physician (even a practising physician) with a philosophical turn of mind, an empiricist who based certain of his inferences upon anatomical research; his date is thought to be the first half of the 5th cent. B.C., or, at the latest, about 440 B.C. Such or similar, at least, is the opinion held by most historians of Greek philosophy[1], though some of them as well as certain historians of Greek medicine[2] have taken a more skeptical position.

Though I do not wish to deny either that Alcmaeon dealt with subjects of a medical or physiological nature, or that his influence upon certain Cnidians and Hippocratics was of paramount importance[3], I shall argue that the evidence upon which the above-mentioned view of Alcmaeon as a physician who was the pioneer of anatomical research is based does not bear it out. The crucial testimony is that of Calcidius (4th cent. A.D.) in his *Comm. on the Timaeus*, Ch. 246 = *VS* 24A10, the rest of the evidence having as a rule been interpreted in the light of this passage. It can be shown, however, that the section *On vision* in Calc. which contains this chapter is paralleled to such an extent by book VII of Galen's *On the Doctrines of Hippocrates and Plato* (second half 2nd cent. A.D.) that a common source may be postulated. The author of the exposition used by Galen and Calcidius (or rather, Calcidius' immediate source, i.e., probably, Porphyry[4]) argued that Plato's theory that the rational soul, located in the brain, is the centre of sense-perception, is correct; the Peripatetics and Early Stoics, who situated this leading part of the soul in the heart, were wrong. That Plato was right had been proved by anatomical research, which had established that the sensory nerves issue from the brain. Porphyry's and Galen's common source[5], as may still be gauged from Calcidius' version, was influenced by a work defending anatomical research (or by a defence of anatomy contained in a work of a more general nature); it is the author of this defence who referred to Alcmaeon as the pioneer of dissection. By doing so, he strengthened the case for anatomy by so to speak conferring upon it a *lettre de noblesse*.

2. Theophrastus discussed Alcmaeon in his *History of Natural Philosophy* (apart from the doxographical tradition, we have his own exposition of the theory of sensation at *Sens.* 25-26 = *VS*24A5). The Anonymus Londinensis, deriving, in part, from the *History of Medicine* by Aristotle's pupil Meno, though discussing the 'medical' views of philosophers such as Philolaus and Plato, is silent about Alcmaeon. Galen does not know Alcmaeon as a physician; he omits to mention him among the Italian men of medicine[6], and mentions his name along with those of Melissus, Parmenides and all the others who, he says, wrote *On nature* (*VS*24A2). Favorinus *ap.* Diog. Laërt. VIII, 83 (*VS*24A1) even says that he was the first to have published a treatise bearing this title; this cannot be correct, but shows in any case that Favorinus did not consider Alcmaeon a medical writer[7].

Just before quoting Favorinus, Diogenes himself, *l.c.*, says that Alcmaeon "wrote chiefly on medical subjects" (*iatrika*), "but now and again touches upon natural philosophy" (*physiologei*) "as when he says that most human things are two-fold". However, Diogenes does not say that Alcmaeon was a physician, but only that he wrote on medical subjects ("chiefly" can hardly be correct). As to the medical subjects, one may first and foremost think of his theory of health and disease (*VS*24B4), but also of his study of reproduction and embryology[8].

It is only the report in Calc. which has it that Alcmaeon was a physician (*medicus*). But not a physician pure and simple: he is cited as one of those who have dissected the human body and thereby laid bare the structure of our visual apparatus. Calcidius mentions three men by name: Alcmaeon, Callisthenes the follower of Aristotle (otherwise unknown) and Herophilus, the famous physician and anatomist who worked at Alexandria in the first decennaries of the 3rd cent. B.C. Their discovery is appealed to as the *commentum vetus... medicorum et item physicorum* (p. 256,17-18 W.), while Alcmaeon is characterized as *in physicis exercitatus quique primus exectionem aggredi est ausus* (p.256,23-257,1 W.). Calcidius speaks of "physicians and also of philosophers", and feels obliged to observe that Alcmaeon was "well-versed in natural philosophy", which, to say the least, shows that he (his source) knows Alcmaeon also as a philosopher[9]. His words afford as much ground to affirm that Alcmaeon was a physician as that Herophilus was a philosopher.

3. Accordingly, much depends upon the interpretation of Calcidius' report as a whole. The anatomical discovery it describes (p.257,2-15 W.) is as follows: two narrow pathways containing natural *pneuma* (*naturalem spiritum*) issue from the brain which contains the chief and leading power of the soul, and terminate at the eyes. At their starting-point, as anatomy reveals, they have a common root, but they divide so as to go each to one eye. The eye is contained within four membranes or "tunics" of various solidity. – Hence, Alcmaeon c.s. are credited with the discovery of the *pneuma*-conducting optic nerves and of the four 'tunics' of the eye.

This report should be studied within the context of Calcidius' section *On vision* (Ch. 236-248) as a whole. His commentary is not concerned so much with expounding Plato's doctrine (*Tim.* 45a6-e2; 67c3 ff.) as with establishing its validity. However, though Plato, in the *Tim.*, appears to locate the rational part of the soul in the brain (44d, 69d ff., 73c) and says that the homogeneous body composed of daylight and the visual ray issuing from the eye passes on the visual impressions of objects "throughout the whole body to the soul, and thus causes the sensation we call seeing" (48c8-d3), he does not explain how sensations arrive at the soul[10]. His description of the anatomical structure of the eye is rather primitive: "the pure fire within us is akin to daylight, and they" (the gods) "caused it to flow through the eyes, making... the whole fabric of the eye-ball, and especially its central part" (the pupil) "smooth and close in texture, so as to let nothing pass that is of coarser stuff, but only pure fire to filter through pure by itself" (45b6-c2).

The optic nerves, which are not in Plato, are adduced by Calcidius because dissection had proved Plato to be right (cf. p.256,18-19 W., *ad certam explorationem Platonici dogmatis*). The atomists (Ch. 236), Heraclitus and the Stoics (Ch. 237), the "geometers agreeing with the Peripatetics" (Ch. 238-242) are wrong, for these "ancients" have merely appropriated fragments of Plato's whole and perfect explanation (Ch. 243, p.255,2-9 W.). Ch. 244-245 summarize this perfect view, without, surprisingly, referring to the brain as the centre of perception; however, a reference to the structure of the eye goes beyond the text of the *Tim.* and points ahead at the anatomical description of Ch. 246: *oculos, quorum levigata soliditas et tersa rotunditas, utpote munita tunicis et nervorum subtemine* ... (p.255,12-14 W.). Ch. 246 begins by repeating the verdict of Ch. 243 and quotes the ancient discovery of Alcmaeon c.s. It is only here that the notion of the brain as the rational soul's location, lacking in Ch. 236-245, is at last introduced: *cerebri sede, in qua est sita potestas animi summa et principalis* (p.257,3 W.). Ch. 247-248 quote

28

from and comment upon Plato's exposition at *Tim.* 45a5-e2, and the Platonic text is made to agree[11] with the full anatomical description of Ch. 246. In this way, the idea that "vision flows through the eye" (*Tim.* 45b7-8, Calc. p.258,5 W.) is said to have been confirmed by the experts quoted in Ch. 246: *fluere porro visum per oculos consentiunt tam physici quam etiam medici, qui exectis capitis membris, dum scrutantur naturae providam sollertiam, notaverunt ferri bivio tramite ignis liquorem*[12] (p.258, 11-14 W.). Plato's description of the eye as a whole and of the pupil (*Tim.* 46b6-e2) is misconstrued[13] so as to yield, in translation, *leves... congestosque et tamquam firmiore soliditate probatos orbes luminum, quorum tamen est angusta medietas subtilior* (p.258,14-16 W.). The "solid protection of the eye" refers, he affirms, to the "tunics", while the "narrow middle part" through which the optic fire flows[14] refers to the optic nerve: *num aliter physici membranis vel etiam tunicis solidis* (cf. Ch. 246) *contineri oculorum orbes asseverantes de natura eorum interpretari videntur? Angusta porro illa medietas, quae pervenit usque ad oculorum cavas sedes* (cf. Ch. 246, the optic nerve), *quae alia est quam haec per quam fluit ignis serenus?* (p.258,18-21 W.). Which allows him to conclude, p.259,7-8 W., that visual impressions arrive *usque ad mentis secreta*.

The argument of the section as a whole, though not very well expounded, is comprehensible. The anatomical description in Ch. 246 is inextricably bound up with its context, as appears from the forward and backward references and from the fact that it contains the only explicit statement about the brain as the seat of the rational soul, a doctrine which is essential to the whole argument.

The reasoning in Galen, *On the Doctrines of Hippocrates and Plato*, VII, which, by the way, is much easier to follow, is strikingly similar to that in Calcidius[15].

Galen sets out to prove that the brain is the source and centre of sense-perception and bodily motion. The Peripatetics and the Stoics are no longer as bold as formerly, some of them even having come over to the true doctrine. It is generally agreed that the leading part of the soul should be situated where the nerves have their starting-point[16]; that this is the brain, is proved by anatomical research (p.582,13-14; 583,2-3; 589,2 ff.; 597,13 ff. etc. Müller). Galen quotes from the great physician and anatomist Erasistratus, Herophilus' near-contemporary[17], who describes his autopsy of the beginnings of the nerves within the brain (p.599,4-600,10 M.), and he tells us of his own vivisection and dissection of animals. From p.609 M. onwards Galen concentrates on vision[18], his own explanation being partly based upon Plato's in the *Timaeus*; as a matter of fact, his quotations (at p.627-629 M.) are far more extensive than those in Calc., as he transcribes the whole of *Tim*. 48b2-d2 which, so he observes, is about the organs of sight and about vision itself. Next (p.630-632 M.) *Tht*. 184d1-6 and 184e3-185c7 are transcribed, containing Plato's epistemological view of sense-perception: it is the soul which sees etc. by means of the senses and which relates the data offered by each separate sense to identical objects. Galen comments: "in this passage as in what follows" (sc. in the *Tht*.) "and in certain other dialogues Plato teaches us about the common faculty which, arriving from the brain at each of the sense-organs *through the nerves*"[19] (my italics) "is conscious of the change within these organs". At p. 637-641 M. Galen argues against Aristotle, at p.643,3 ff. M. he refers to Epicurus. Book VII ends with a summary of his conclusions (p.644,10-648,4 M.): Erasistratus in his old age recognized the true origin of the nerves, while Aristotle was at a loss how to explain the function of the brain. However, it is Hippocrates who really is the archegete of the true doctrine[20], as has been demonstrated elsewhere and esp. in the (lost) *Commentaries on Hippocrates' Anatomy*, which is why, as Galen says, he has refrained from again quoting Hippocrates' words; on the other hand, Plato's views have been discussed in the present work since this had not yet been done elsewhere.

4. The parallel with Calcidius is obvious (I have only mentioned the principal points of agreement and omitted some minor ones). The truth of Plato's doctrine and the total or partial falsity of other views is vindicated by the results of anatomical research. We cannot but conclude that Calcidius and Galen represent two separate versions of an argument in defence of Plato, which so to speak interpolates the sensory nerves in Plato's physiology and epistemology of perception. That Galen appropriated and, of course, worked over an original source of this nature is also revealed by the fact that his *honoris causa* reference[20] to Hippocrates is superimposed upon an argument concerned only with Plato.

It is important to note that a possible echo of and at least a parallel with the imputation of the theory of nerves to Plato made in Galen's and Calcidius' source is found in one of Galen's teachers, the Middle Platonist Albinus, *Didasc*. XVII, p.173,4 ff. Hermann[21].

There are, of course, certain differences between Galen and Calcidius. Galen attributes a knowledge of the nerves to Plato on the basis not only of *Tim*. 48, but also and especially on that of *Tht*. 184-186, which as a matter of fact is more explicit about the connection between senses and soul. Possibly this latter reference was not added by Galen, but omitted by Calcidius' immediate source which, contrary to Galen, took some pains to read everything required into the words of the *Tim.* itself[22]. Furthermore, Galen refers to Erasistratus, Calcidius to Alcmaeon, Callisthenes, Herophilus and "certain others", both references serving the same purpose, *viz.*, the vindication of Plato's explanation. Though Galen may have substituted the quotation from Erasistratus on his own initiative, it is, I think, more likely that it was already contained in the original source (cf. *plerique alii*, Calc. p.256, 23 W.) and that either Calcidius' immediate source or Calcidius himself left it out[23]. In that case, it is Galen who passed over Alcmaeon etc.; obviously, he may have rejected the reference to Alcmaeon because it conflicted with his wish to introduce Hippocrates as the archegete of dissection (see also above, p.27).

5. We may now return to Calc. Ch. 246. The philosophical and learned author of the defence of Plato reconstructed above must have adapted this passage from a medical work (or an excursus contained in such a work) written in defence of anatomical research.

Scientific anatomical research upon the human body was, in antiquity, only practised at Alexandria (with the possible exception of Antioch, if Herophilus' near-contemporary Erasistratus worked there[24]) and, it appears, only during a relatively short period, *viz.*, by Erasistratus and by Herophilus and his followers during the 3rd cent. B.C.[25] Although there is some evidence for dissection at Alexandria in later centuries, it is important to note that no anatomical discoveries made later than Herophilus and Erasistratus are on record[26]. Almost from the very start dissection was criticized by physicians belonging to the Empiricist school[27], on both epistemological and ethical grounds. The Empiricist critics were later joined by the Methodists[28]: the debate about anatomy went on, which is comprehensible when we consider that the later followers of Herophilean anatomy must at least have adhered to it theoretically. But the full and epoch-making dissection of living (!) [29] and dead human bodies as practised by Herophilus c.s. was not continued in later times.

Our sources distinguish between two kinds of anatomy, *viz.*, intentional anatomical research (*kat' epitèdeusin*) as practised by Herophilus c.s. and anatomical knowledge derived from incidental observations of wounded persons etc. (*kata periptōsin*) as practised by the Empiricists[30]. The discussion concerning the uses and abuses of anatomy is familiar from the proem to Celsus' *De medicina*, where it is part of the overall opposition between the so-called Dogmatists and the Empiricists. Celsus' own

31

position which, as has been argued[31], probably derives from the physician Themison (1st cent. B.C.) is some sort of compromise; medicine, being a conjectural art, needs both *logos* and *empeiria*[32]; the investigations of the great Early Hellenistic anatomists have provided essential information, but accidental observation, though slower, is equally indispensable (*pr.*74).

One of the Empiricist arguments had it that vivisection is too cruel, and dissection of dead bodies (*quae etsi non crudelis, tamen foeda sit,* Cels., *pr.*44) unethical. Hence the Empiricists agree with the common prejudice which is mainly responsible[33] for the fact that no human bodies were dissected before the great Hellenistic anatomists, and only to a very limited extent in later times, if at all.

When viewed against this background, the report in Calc. Ch. 246 becomes fully comprehensible. It deals with the dissection of the *human* body, p.256,17 ff. W. *commentum vetus medicorum et item physicorum... qui ad comprehendendam sanae naturae sollertiam artus humani corporis facta membrorum*[34] *exectione rimati sunt, quod existimabant ita demum se suspicionibus atque opinionibus certiores futuros, si tam rationi visus quam visui ratio concineret.* While the reference to the human body shows that we should think of Early Hellenistic anatomy, the words *sanae naturae* ('healthy', not diseased 'nature') may even be read as alluding to vivisection. That only anatomical research abolishes ignorance and guess-work was the opinion of the great Hellenistic anatomists, cf. e.g. Cels., *pr.*25 *neque enim, cum dolor intus incidit, scire quid doleat eum, qui, qua parte quodque viscus intestinumve sit, non cognoverit.* The bond between *visus* and *ratio* recalls Celsus' own epistemological position. Calcidius' *ratio* translates *logos,* while his *visus* translates *thea,* 'observation', a technical term[35] of both intentional and accidental anatomy.

When, next, we look at the way Alcmaeon is characterized (...*quique primus exectionem est ausus*) the only reasonable interpretation of the words *est ausus* within the context of the passage where they occur is that, according to this report, Alcmaeon was the first to violate the taboo bound up with the anatomical investigation of the human body. It will not do to have these words refer merely to Alcmaeon's intellectual audacity as a scientific pioneer[36], as it is not a correct interpretation of Calcidius' text either when it is affirmed that Alcmaeon, who cannot, of course, have dissected human bodies, practised dissection of animals[37].

The defence of dissection embedded within the defence of Plato calls Alcmaeon the pioneer of the dissection of the human body and credits him, together with Callisthenes and Herophilus, with the discovery of the optic nerves and the four 'tunics' of the eye. However, it has been often pointed out[38] that these discoveries belong to Herophilus. Herophilus found the sensory nerves (*neura aisthètika*) issuing from the brain[39]; these, he assumed, contained *pneuma*. He held that the brain is the centre of the nervous system[40]. To the optic nerves[41] he gave the name 'channels' (*poroi*). Galen tells us why: "because only in the optic nerves the paths of the *pneuma* can be perceived and are clear"[42], and "because only the perforation of the optic nerve is apparent"[43]. He also investigated the eye, describing its four membranes[44].

So why the reference to Alcmaeon? Some scholars, assuming it to be founded in fact, suggest that Alcmaeon arrived at conclusions antici-pating[45] those of Herophilus by dissecting animals. As confirmation Theophrastus' report on Alcmaeon's theory of sense-perception (*Sens.* 25-26 = *VS*24A5) is commonly adduced. Here we read that "all the senses" (except touch, upon which Alcmaeon is silent) "are in some way" (!) "connected with the brain, and accordingly are incapacitated when the brain is disturbed or shifts its position, for then it stops up the channels (*poroi*) through which the senses act"[46]. That it is the brain which perceives is said in relation to smells: "smelling is by means of the nostrils in connection with the act of breathing-in, when we draw up the breath to the brain". Theophrastus is silent about how visual impressions are conveyed to the brain. It should be noted that he does not tell us *what* the nature of these *poroi* is; "connected in some way" suggests that he found no specific information in Alcmaeon's book. The explanation of smelling leaves open the possibility that there was a plurality[47] of *poroi* for each individual sense, as does the remark about the "loose and yielding texture of the tongue" which enables it to readily receive and transmit the savours it has melted down. Furthermore, the information about the consequences of a disturbance of the brain is the only *proof* cited by Theophrastus for the existence of *poroi*; it is an *inference* of the type easily paralleled from many other Presocratic philosophers. Alc-maeon's explanation of hearing by resonance is based upon an ob-servational analogy which can be paralleled in Empedocles[48]. – Finally, one of Theophrastus' first observations (*Sens.* 25), *viz.*, that for Alcmaeon man is different from all other creatures in being equipped not only with sensation but *also* with understanding, should make us pause. It has often been argued that Alcmaeon's word for 'understanding'[49] refers to the synthetic activity of the brain as it combines the data of the individual senses[50]. However (if, that is, we may assume that this synthetic activity of the brain was something Alcmaeon thought about) he cannot but have observed that also in animals the perceptions are synthetised, and certainly so if he arrived at his conclusions by dissecting animals. 'Understanding' must refer to a higher function similar to the 'inferring'[51] which is said to be typical of man as distinguished from the gods, Alcm. fgt. VS24B1, and which can hardly be detected by dissection.

Consequently, the only conclusions which may legitimately be drawn from Theophrastus' account are (1) that according to Alcmaeon, the brain is the centre of sense-perception and (2) that the brain and the senses are connected by some sort of *poroi*[52].

We need only assume that the author of the defence of anatomical research[53] adduced in the defence of Plato used by Calcidius' immediate source knew Theophrastus' account. He noticed the resemblance to Herophilus' views: the brain as the centre of sense-perception, *poroi* connecting it with the senses. He jumped to the conclusion that Alcmaeon anticipated Herophilus – as, in some sense of the word, he did – and that he did so by using the same means, i.e. dissection. But this was no more than an inference. Herophilus called the nerves *neura aisthètika* and spoke of *poroi* only in relation to the optic nerves – and this for a special reason all his own, as will be recalled; Alcmaeon, on the other hand, spoke of *poroi* as connectives of the brain and all the senses (touch excepted). The terminological coincidence is only a partial one; it explains, however, why Alcmaeon is adduced precisely in connection with the optic nerve.

The anatomical apologist made Alcmaeon into the first practitioner of dissection, just as, e.g., the Empiricists made the fifth-century physician Acron of Agrigentum into the first Empiricist[54]. In the discussion about anatomical research, Alcmaeon was a welcome ally to its defenders. It has been pointed out above that Calcidius' wording still betrays that it is the well-known *philosopher* Alcmaeon who is welcomed into the company of Herophilus.

6. I conclude that the empirical[55] physician Alcmaeon is an anachronism, that it is incorrect to consider him a practising physician and the father of scientific anatomy. It is not enough to just doubt or reject the evidence which appears to favour this assumption: why it does so should also be explained. It is this explanation which has been attempted above. The net result of this investigation is that Alcmaeon, epoch-making though his theory of health and disease (VS24B4) may have been, does not differ significantly from the other philosophers of the mid-fifth cent. B.C. His 'medical' theory itself is not, as a theory, different in principle from that of his near-contemporary Philolaus[56]. It is only some decennaries later

that the first hesitating beginnings of an empirical attitude may be found among those authors of our Hippocratic corpus who were both influenced by, and critical of, Presocratic natural philosophy[57].

NOTES

[1] W. K. C. Guthrie, *Hist. Gr. Phil.* I, Cambridge 1962, 341 ff., who dates Alcmaeon between 480-440 B.C., and H. Dörrie, *Alkmaion, RE* Supp. XII, 1970, 22 ff. Both Guthrie and Dörrie are rather cautious, and quite good on Alcmaeon's *philosophy.* Far less cautious are e.g. M. Timpanaro-Cardini, *Originalità di Alcmeone*, Atene e Roma 16, 1938, 233 ff. and L. A. Stella, *Importanza di Alcmeone nella storia del pensiero greco*, Mem. Acc. Lincei, Ser. VI, Vol. VIII,4, Roma 1939. F. M. Cornford's enthusiasm for Alcmaeon's empiricism (*Principium Sapientiae*, Cambridge 1952, 31 ff.), shared to some extent by Guthrie, was pertinently criticized by G. Vlastos, rev. Cornford, repr. in: D. J. Furley - R. E. Allen (ed.), *Studies in Presocratic Philosophy* I, London 1970, 47. W. A. Heidel, *Hippocratic Medicine*, New York 1941, 42 is positive about Alcmaeon as a physician and as the pioneer of dissection (cf. also the same, *The Pythagoreans and Greek Mathematics*, AJPh 61, 1940, 3 ff.; his skepticism about Alcmaeon's relation to the Pythagoreans is not wholly justified).

[2] L. Edelstein in his review of Stella, AJPh 63, 1942, 371 ff. is skeptical and says that Alcmaeon is "a typical representative of Presocratic research" about 450 B.C. or even later. F. Kudlien, *Der Beginn des medizinischen Denkens bei den Griechen*, Zürich-Stuttgart 1967, 56, 60, 119 speaks of Alcmaeon as a philosopher of nature, and says, *Anatomie, RE* Supp. XI, 1968, 40 that it is doubtful whether he was a physician at all, though if Calcidius (*VS*24A10) is to be trusted he is the "Hauptzeuge vorsokratischer Anatomie" (but he must have dissected animals); cf. also Kudlien, *Anatomie und menschlicher Leichnam*, Hermes 97, 1969, 85 n.5. J. Schumacher, *Antike Medizin*, Berlin ²1963, 75 ff. ascribes dissection of animals to Alcmaeon but is rather skeptical as to the possible accuracy of its results. F. Solmsen, *Greek Philosophy and the Discovery of the Nerves*, Mus. Helv. 18, 1961, 151-2 (repr. *Kleine Schriften* I, Hildesheim 1968, 537 ff.) is skeptical about an early date for Alcmaeon and about the validity of Calcidius' report which, however, he tends to accept as to a possible dissection of animals (cf. the similar position of Vlastos, *Isonomia Politikè*, in: *Isonomia*, Berlin 1964, 11 (doubtful if a physician, dissection of animals not doubted)). – H. Erhard, *Alkmaion, Der erste Experimentalbiologe*, Sudh. Arch. 34, 1941, 77 ff. is wholly uncritical; so is P. Ebner, *Alcmeone Crotoniate*, in: Klearchos 1969 (25 ff.), 58.

[3] See e.g. H. Grensemann, *Die hippokratische Schrift "Über die heilige Krankheit"*, Berlin 1968, 27 ff.

[4] Calcidius' account is to a large extent paralleled by Nemesius *On the Nature of Man*, Ch. 7, which refers to Porphyry's *On Sensation* at p.182, 4 ff. Matthaei (cf. also below, n.15, n.21). According to Dörrie, *Porphyrios' 'Symmikta Zetemata'*, München 1959, 155 ff. Porphyry's *On Sens.* was contained in the *Symm. Zet.* J. H. Waszink, *Timaeus a Calcidio transl. commentarioque instr.*, Plato Latinus IV, London-Leiden 1962, XCII-XCIII argues that Calcidius derives from an abstract from *On Sens.* used by Porphyry for his *Commentary on the Timaeus.* W. W. Jaeger, *Nemesios von Emesa*, Berlin 1914, 27 ff. compared Nemesius-Porphyry, Calcidius-Porphyry and Galen, and postulated a common doxographic source dating, at the latest, from the 2nd cent. A.D. (o.c. 33).

[5] It is tempting to think of Posidonius (cf. Jaeger, o.c. 45), but this possibility cannot be pursued here. For Posidonius' interest in medical science cf. J. Mans-

feld, *The Pseudo-Hippocratic Tract* ΠΕΡΙ 'ΕΒΔΟΜΑΔΩΝ *Ch. 1-11 and Greek Philosophy*, Assen 1972, 130 n.4, 135 n.27, 181 n.141, 196, 226-227.

6 Cf. the list at X, p.6 Kühn.

7 E. Schmalzriedt, *Peri Physeōs, Zur Frühgeschichte der Buchtitel*, München 1970, has conclusively demonstrated that the collective title *On Nature* cannot be of Presocratic origin. His opinion, o.c. 42, that Alcmaeon's is the earliest medical work cannot be justified by referring to Favorinus, who mentions Alcmaeon in a Hist. of Phil. (cf. E. Mensching, *Favorin von Arelate*, Berlin 1963, 130-131).

8 Aristotle, *Sens.* 436a18 ff., *Resp.* 480b26 ff. points out that natural philosophers may treat medical subjects just as physicians may discuss principles; see Edelstein, *The Relation of Ancient Philosophy to Medicine* (1952), repr. in: *Ancient Medicine*, Baltimore 1967, 354; on lay medical writers see also J. Ilberg, *A. Cornelius Celsus und die Medizin in Rom* (1907), repr. in: H. Flashar (ed.), *Antike Medizin*, Darmstadt 1971, 310 and W. Telfer's introduction to his translation of Nemesius, in: *Cyril of Jerusalem and Nemesius of Emesa*, The Library of Christian Classics IV, Philadelphia 1955, 206 ff.

9 Cf. also p.258,12 W., *tam physici quam etiam medici*; p.258,18 W., *physici*.

10 Solmsen, o.c. 166.　　11 Cf. below, n.22.

12 Cf. Ch. 246, p.256,18-20 W. *medicorum et item physicorum,... qui ad comprehendendam sanae naturae sollertiam artus humani corporis facta membrorum exectione rimati sunt*; p.257,2 ff. W., *duas... semitas, naturalem spiritum continentes,... separatae bivii specie.*

13 Calcidius' source takes ὅσον παχύτερον not as object, but as subject of στέγειν.

14 In Plato, this optic fire filters out towards the outside world; Calcidius has it run inwards.

15 Nemesius not only used Porphyry (see above, n.4), but also added to his abstract from Porphyry by quoting from the exposition of the theory of vision in Galen's *De plac. Hipp. Plat.*, VII (*De nat. hom.* p. 180,5 ff. M.); he also used Galen's lost treatise *Peri apodeixeōs* (Jaeger, o.c. 12 ff., 27 ff.). At various places he reveals his familiarity with other works by Galen (E. Skard, *Nemesiosstudien* II, Symb. Osl. 17, 1937, 9 ff.; III, ibd. 18, 1938, 31 ff.; IV, ibd. 19, 1939, 46 ff.; V, ibd. 22, 1942, 40 ff.).

16 p.582,16-583,1 M. ἔνθα τῶν νεύρων ἡ ἀρχή, ἐνταῦθα εἶναι τὸ ἡγεμονικόν.

17 Celsus, *De med.* pr. 22-23, mentions Erasistratus together with Herophilus as protagonists of dissection and vivisection of humans. For this reason, and also in view of the fact that both Erasistratus and Herophilus recognized the existence of sensory and motor nerves (cf. Solmsen, o.c. 185 ff.) it has become customary, since Wellmann, to refer to Herophilus and Erasistratus as the great Alexandrian anatomists. It cannot be denied, however, that the (admittedly meagre) evidence concerning Erasistratus is more in favour of a connection with Antioch than with Alexandria, although Erasistratus' relations with the various Chrysippi and his prescription for Ptolemy's podagra also point to relations with Alexandria. On this whole question see P. M. Fraser, *The Career of Erasistratus of Ceos*, Rendiconti Ist. Lombardo, Cl. d. lett., 103, 1969, 518 ff. and *Ptolemaic Alexandria* I, Oxford 1972, 347. Fraser also doubts whether Erasistratus practised dissection of humans, arguing that Tertullian in his *De anima* (following Soranus) only mentions Herophilus as a vivisectionist, and that Galen invariably refers only to Herophilus', not Erasistratus', advances in the field of anatomy (*Rend.* 531-532, cf. also *Ptol. Alex.* II, p.505 n.64, p.507 n.76). This doubt, however, goes too far. The crucial passage in Galen, V p.602-604 K. = *Plac. Hipp. Plat.* p. 598-600 M. proves that Erasistratus did indeed practise human anatomy. Galen says, p.598,11 ff. M. that Erasistratus for a long time believed that the nerve issues from the cerebral membrane, since he only saw its outer part; most

36

of his works exhibit this view. Being an old man, however, with leisure for scientific research only, he made *more exact dissections* (ὅτε πρεσβύτης ὢν ἤδη καὶ σχολὴν ἄγων μόνοις τοῖς τῆς τέχνης θεωρήμασιν ἀκριβεστέρας ἐποιεῖτο τὰς ἀνατομάς, p.598,16-599,22 M.), and in this way discovered that the interior part of the nerve issues from the brain itself. Fraser, *Rend.* 529 n.28 believes that τὰ τῆς τέχνης θεωρήματα does not necessarily refer to dissection, let alone of humans (cf. also ibd., 532-533), but this cannot be correct, since the *quotation* in Galen from the work of Erasistratus' old age starts with the words ἐθεωροῦμεν δὲ καὶ τὴν φύσιν τοῦ ἐγκεφάλου, καὶ ἦν ὁ ἐγκέφαλος διμερής, καθάπερ καὶ τῶν λοιπῶν ζῴων; this proves that the θεωρήματα (cf. ἐθεωροῦμεν) refer to anatomical research (anatomy as a theoretical part of medicine was criticized by the Empiricists and rejected by the Methodists), and that Erasistratus dissected humans (otherwise his remark "the brain is bipartite, as with the other animals" is meaningless). Accordingly Celsus' report may be correct after all, though it should perhaps be assumed that Erasistratus, in his old age, was inspired by Herophilus' example and that the Seleucids provided him with facilities similar to those enjoyed by Herophilus at Alexandria (Celsus, l.c. explicitly says that Herophilus and Erasistratus were given criminals by "the kings"; cf. also Fraser, *Rend.* 531, *Ptol. Alex.* I, 549).

[18] At p.624,15-625,4 a brief reference to the geometers also discussed by Calcidius-Porphyry and Nemesius-Porphyry is found.

[19] p.632,5-6 M., ἥτις ἐξ ἐγκεφάλου διὰ τῶν νεύρων εἰς ἕκαστον τῶν αἰσθητηρίων ἀφικνουμένη...

[20] This is a favourite topic with Galen. Cf. e.g. II, p.89 K.; V, p.672 K.; and Skard, o.c. 1938, 34-35.

[21] οἱ θεοί... τὸ ἡγεμονικόν... περὶ τὴν κεφαλὴν καθίδρυσαν, ἔνθα μυελοῦ τε ἀρχαὶ καὶ νεύρων..., περικειμένων καὶ τῶν αἰσθήσεων τῇ κεφαλῇ ὥσπερ δορυφορουσῶν τὸ ἡγεμονικόν. This is a 'systematical' remark; at *Didasc.* XVIII, p.173,14 ff. H., on the other hand, Albinus closely and correctly follows *Tim.* 45b-c.

[22] Probably, this betrays the hand of Porphyry: for an example of his misguided acumen in explaining a passage of the *Tim.* see Philoponus, *De aet. mund.* p.546, 5 ff. Rabe.

[23] Cf. Ch. 246, the end, where Calcidius says that the present discussion does not permit him to go farther into these matters.   [24] Cf. above, n.17.

[25] See Kudlien, *RE* 1968, 43 ff., Hermes 1969 (above n.2), who argues, against Edelstein (*The History of Anatomy in Antiquity* (1932), repr. in: *Anc. Med.*, 247 ff., and *The Development of Greek Anatomy*, Bull. Hist. Med. 3, 1935, 235 ff.), that no human anatomy at all was practised after Herophilus and Erasistratus. Fraser, *Ptol. Alex.* I, 348 ff., 363-364 also discusses the evidence. Though he says (o.c. 350) that "it is doubtful if this knowledge of anatomy" (sc. "the study of human anatomy based upon dissection, if not vivisection") "ever passed much beyond the environment of Early Ptolemaic Alexandria", his marshalling of the evidence for the centuries to follow brings him to the conclusion that human dissection may have been practised on a limited scale by surgeons in the first cent. B.C. and in Galen's days (o.c. 363-4).

[26] As I would say when judging the evidence collected by Fraser, o.c. 363-364. The remark in Galen, II p.220 K. only refers to the anatomy of the skeleton (Fraser, o.c. 364, Kudlien, *RE* 46). Ps.-Phocylides' protest against anatomy (99-102 Diehl) may refer to this limited practice, or perhaps echoes one side of the debate which had started almost in Herophilus' days.

[27] Cf. Kudlien, Hermes 1969, 91 ff., *RE* 1968, 44 ff.

[28] Cf. Kudlien, *RE* 1968, 44-46.

[29] Fraser, *Ptol. Alex.* I, 348 ff. fully discusses the ancient reports on vivisection of humans, which he sees no sufficient reason to doubt.

30 Cf. Kudlien, *RE* 1968, 44-45.
31 O. Temkin, *Celsus' "On Medicine" and the Ancient Medical Sects*, Bull. Hist. Med. 3, 1935, 249 ff.
32 This was also Galen's methodological point of view; cf. I. v. Müller, *Ueber Galens Werk vom wissenschaftlichen Beweis*, Abh. Bay. Ak., philos.-philol. Cl. 20, 1897, 436-437.
33 Cf. Edelstein and Kudlien, above n.25.   34 Cf. p.258, 12 W. *exectis capitis membris*.
35 Cf. K. Deichgräber, *Die griech. Empirikerschule*, Berlin 1930, fgt.67, fgt.68, fgt.70.
36 As J. Hirschberg, *Alkmaions Verdienst um die Augenheilkunde*, Arch. f. Ophthalm. 105, 1921, 132-133 suggested; cf. also Stella, o.c. 246, on Alcmaeon as a scientific revolutionary.
37 So e.g. Hirschberg, l.c.; E. D. Phillips, *Greek Medicine*, London 1973, 21; and the authors quoted above, n.2.
38 By e.g. Hirschberg, o.c.; H. Oppermann, *Herophilos bei Kallimachos*, Hermes 60, 1925, 14 ff. (cf. below, n.44); Solmsen, o.c. 151-152.
39 Anon. in: Rufus p.184-185 Daremberg; Galen VII, p.212 K.
40 Galen III, p.665 ff., XIX, p.315 K.
41 As Galen, *Plac. Hipp. Plat.* p.620,9 ff. M. tells us, these are the biggest nerves.
42 III, p.813 K.
43 VII, p.89 K. – On the methodological importance attached by Herophilus to perception see An. Lond. XXI, 18-23.
44 Anon. in: Rufus p.170-171 D.; Celsus VII, 7 and 13. The material collected by Oppermann o.c. shows that before Herophilus only 2 or 3 membranes were distinguished, and that Herophilus was the first to describe a fourth.
45 Hirschberg, o.c. 132-133; Timpanaro-Cardini, o.c. 236 ff. Mrs. Timpanaro, citing Arist. *HA* 533a13 ff. as evidence, suggests a tradition connecting Alcmaeon to Herophilus. Probably, however, this passage is an interpolation in the text of *HA*, see Peck, Loeb ed. *ad l.* On Aristotle generally see Solmsen, o.c. 170 ff. Perhaps the interpolated passage in *HA* explains the reference in Calc. (above, p.27) to the otherwise unknown Callisthenes.
46 τοὺς πορούς, δι' ὦν αἱ αἰσθήσεις: I have adopted the translation of G. M. Stratton, *Theophrastus De Sens.*, 1917, repr. Amsterdam 1967, 89-90; Guthrie, o.c. 347 has "through which the sensations take place", which may be better.
47 Such a plurality is paralleled in Empedocles, *VS*31A86 = Theophr., *Sens.* 7 ff.
48 *VS*31A86 = Theophr., *Sens.* 9, 21.   49 ξυνίησι.
50 E.g. Solmsen, o.c. 151; Guthrie, o.c. 347 n.1.
51 τεκμαίρεσθαι. Cf. Guthrie, o.c. 344 n.2.   52 Cf. also Oppermann, o.c. 16.
53 If Fraser's contention (cf. above, n.17 where I argue against it) that the names of Erasistratus and Herophilus are illegitimately coupled in Celsus is right, the author of the defence can hardly be earlier than the coupling itself; if, that is to say, the quotation from Erasistratus is not Galen's personal contribution (cf. above, p.31. For the continuing debate about anatomy cf. ibd.).
54 Deichgräber, o.c. fgt. 6: θέλοντες δὲ ἀπαρχαΐζειν ἑαυτῶν τὴν αἵρεσιν... "Ακρωνα... φασιν ἄρξασθαι αὐτῆς.
55 On the assumption that Alcmaeon's method was that of empirical science, D. Lanza, *Un nuovo frammento di Alcmeone*, Maia 17, 1965, 278-280 attributes Alcman fgt. 125 Page πεῖρά τοι μαθήσιος ἀρχά to Alcmaeon. Although a confusion between the names Alcman and Alcmaeon is possible, Lanza's suggestion constitutes an interesting case of interpretation based upon preconception.
56 *VS*44A27, from the Anon. Lond.
57 See Mansfeld, *Theorie en Empirie, Filosofie en Geneeskunst in de Voorsokratische Periode*, Assen 1973.

38

THE ORACLE GIVEN TO
CHAEREPHON ABOUT SOCRATES

(PLATO, *APOLOGY*, 20e-21a)

E. DE STRYCKER, S.J.

Plato's *Apology of Socrates* has the outward form of a forensic speech. In conformity with current practice, it starts with an *exordium*. Then follows the *propositio*, in which Socrates states that the indictment of Meletus rests on a slanderous campaign carried on against him for many years and claims the right to defend himself first against those 'old accusers' and only afterwards against Meletus. In order to refute the accusations of the first group he points out that he is neither a natural philosopher nor a sophist. But, if he is not such a man, why then is he so much an object of discussion? The answer is: because he possesses a certain kind of 'cleverness' or 'insight' (σοφία), – a most peculiar one, to be sure, and quite different from that of the learned men with whom most people confuse him. About the existence and the nature of that cleverness he can call in the testimony of the Delphic god. By saying this, Socrates engages in a third traditional part of forensic oratory, the *narratio*. He first concisely tells the story of the question asked by Chaerephon and of the answer given by the Pythia; then he expatiates upon his search for the hidden meaning of the oracle and upon the examination to which he submitted three categories of his fellow citizens in order to find a cleverer man than himself; he further points to the enmity he aroused by doing so, for the people whom he tested proved to be devoid of the insight which they had the name of possessing, and therefore they felt angry with Socrates and started defaming him.

The object of this paper, which is a part of a more extensive study on the *Apology*, is to examine the oracle given to Chaerephon, its historicity, its meaning and its significance both for Socrates' life and activity and for the structure of the *Apology*. The author is glad to present it to a scholar who has contributed so much to our knowledge of ancient philosophy in general and especially to a better understanding of Socrates' thought and personality.

* * *

First of all, there is no reason to doubt the historicity of Chaerephon's question and of the Pythia's response. As a rule, definite pronouncements in Plato's works concerning the biography of Socrates ought to be considered as reliable, since, whenever verification is possible, they prove to be supported by independent evidence[1]. The prominence which the *Apology* gives to this story makes it utterly improbable that Plato might simply have invented it. If such were the case, we should reject as fictitious not only the oracle itself, but also the statements which give it its frame: that Chaerephon was a democrat, that he fled from Athens under the regime of the Thirty and that he came back with his political friends in 403; further that he had died between 403 and 399 and that he had a brother still alive at the time of the trial and able to testify in court. There was no pressing need for Plato to insert in his text all these precise details which, if false and publicly exposed by some adversary[2], would have impaired the credibility of the *Apology* as a whole. We should not forget that Chaerephon was a well-known person in Athens and that his eccentric character and appearance are not only mentioned in the *Apology* (20e8; 21a3), but also made fun of in many passages of the Comics[3]. So we have no other choice than to accept as true the story told in 20c5-21a8.

About the date of that event the *Apology* does not give any indication. Many scholars[4] have argued that, since the Pythia's answer was the starting-point of Socrates' philosophical career, it should be placed many years, at least some two decades before the trial. As will be explained below (pp.43-48), I think that the prominence given to the oracle in the narration is chiefly a literary device. If so, we are left with only two pieces of chronological information. The first is that in the original version of the *Clouds* (423 B.C.) Chaerephon was already represented as a pupil of Socrates and his associate in the direction of the φροντιστήριον[5]; at that time, we may infer, he would have considered Socrates as a man of outstanding ability and probably had thought so for several years. So there is no objection to an early date for the oracle. The second point is this: if the oracle had been very recent, that is, if it dated from the last years of the Peloponnesian war, it would not have provided Plato with an appropriate starting-point for his narrative, since Socrates' elenctic activity is depicted as starting after the oracle and as thus having indirectly launched the slanderous campaign, which, in its turn, has lasted 'already many years' (18b2). I do not mean, of course, that with these words Plato intended to give an indication about the time of Chaerephon's visit to Delphi, but simply that he places that visit in an undefined but certainly not very recent past. So we may reasonably exclude the period after the blockade of Athens by Lysander in 405. I do not think we can go further than that.

Nor is that question really so important since the oracle was not widely known. This is proved by the long preamble Plato puts before it: it fills no less then sixteen lines and a half (20d4-21a3), whereas three lines and a half (21a4-7) are all that is needed to tell about Chaerephon's journey to Delphi, his question and the Pythia's answer. If the oracle had been a matter of common knowledge, most judges would probably at once have recognized the allusion in the words ἐγὼ γάρ, ὦ ἄνδρες Ἀθηναῖοι, δι' οὐδὲν ἀλλ' ἢ διὰ σοφίαν τινὰ τοῦτο τὸ ὄνομα (that of being a σοφός) ἔσχηκα (20d6-7); and surely nobody could fail to understand the sentence μάρτυρα ὑμῖν παρέξομαι τὸν θεὸν τὸν ἐν Δελφοῖς (e7-8). Still Socrates supposes the audience not to be aware of what he is about to say, for in 21a5, just before finally formulating the question of Chaerephon, he gives a last warning: καί, ὅπερ λέγω, μὴ θορυβεῖτε, ὦ ἄνδρες. So the audience was kept in suspense till that very moment. This could not have been the case if a substantial part of them had heard about the oracle.

As for the precise wording of Chaerephon's question and of the Pythia's answer, it would be wise to keep to the narrative in the *Apology*. Chaerephon asks whether somebody is cleverer than Socrates, and the answer is that nobody is. The versified form of the oracle traditional in the imperial period, ἀνδρῶν ἁπάντων Σωκράτης σοφώτατος[6], gives the answer a positive instead of a negative form. This is actually not an important change, since a few lines below in the *Apology* Socrates acts as if both phrasings were equivalent with regard to their meaning: τί οὖν ποτε λέγει (ὁ θεὸς) φάσκων ἐμὲ σοφώτατον εἶναι; (21b5-6; cf. 23b2).

Xenophon too, in his *Apology* (§ 14), speaks about the response given to Chaerephon (he does not give the content of the question), but with him it does not concern cleverness, but three other forms of human excellence: Χαιρεφῶντος γάρ ποτε ἐπερωτῶντος ἐν Δελφοῖς περὶ ἐμοῦ πολλῶν παρόντων ἀνεῖλεν ὁ Ἀπόλλων μηδένα εἶναι ἀνθρώπων μήτε ἐλευθεριώ-τερον μήτε δικαιότερον μήτε σωφρονέστερον. This paper is not the place to discuss the whole problem of Xenophon's authority with regard to facts concerning Socrates. My opinion, which I cannot substantiate here, is that, when a passage in Xenophon is closely akin to one in Plato, Xeno-phon, as a rule, is the borrower and that the has no objection to deviating from his source in order to give the idea a turn more in conformity with his own views. Now, for the Platonic Socrates, all 'virtues' are fundament-ally one, either simply φρόνησις (= σοφία), or a particular form of it

41

applied to some special field. The Xenophontic Socrates is characterized by the fact that he has a multiplicity of practical virtues, each of which is illustrated by some passages of the *Memorabilia*. We can also find in that work enumerations of them, so in b. I ii, 1-6: σωφροσύνη, εὐσέβεια, ἐγκράτεια, καρτερία, αὐτάρκεια, ἐλευθερία, or in the concluding sentence of the whole work, b. IV viii, 11: εὐσέβεια, δικαιοσύνη, ἐγκράτεια, φρόνησις, αὐτάρκεια. It is reasonable to admit that § 14 of the Xenophontic *Apology* is just a remodelling of the Platonic formulation. To say, with Burnet[7], that Xenophon here gives 'a garbled version of the matter, prudently substituting' his own words 'for the more compromising response given' by Plato, and characterized with the mention of σοφία, seems beside the mark, for in § 16, in order to prove that what the oracle said was just plain truth, the Xenophontic Socrates asks the judges, in a series of rhetorical questions, whether they know anybody who surpasses him either as a σώφρων or as an ἐλευθέριος or as a δίκαιος, and upon that he adds the claim to be a σοφός. So when Xenophon modifies the formulation of Plato it is not because, out of prudence, he wants to avoid the mention of σοφία, but because according to his views, σοφία is just one among the virtues of Socrates, and not even the most important one.

Another problem is how Chaerephon could get the notion of asking the oracle such a question. In a substantial essay[8], Rudolf Herzog puts the fact in its right frame by pointing to similar consultations which were decided by the Pythia in the period from the sixth to the fourth century B.C. A first group of stories has to do with the question who is the most pious man. It is to be found in Porphyry's *De abstinentia* (ii 15-17), who tells about three cases, one belonging to the sixth century (the poor peasant Clearchus of Methydrion is preferred to a wealthy citizen of Magnesia on the Maeander), one to the fifth (Docimus of Delphi's offering of barley groats is more appreciated than the magnificent votive monuments dedicated by Gelon, Hieron and Polyzelus after the battle of Himera [480 B.C.]), and one to the fourth (the sacrificial beasts with gilded horns and the hecatombs which Jason of Pherae intended to present to the god of Delphi arouse his displeasure). In the second group, the question to be decided is who has achieved the highest εὐδαιμονία, the most successful or most preferable life[9]; here king Gyges of Lydia is contrasted with Aglaus of Psophis in Arcadia, and his fourth successor Croesus with the Athenian Tellus and the Argives Cleobis and Biton[10]. A third set of texts speaks about Myson of Chonae in Malis, a peasant who was judged by Apollo to be σοφώτερος than the famous Anacharsis or than Chilon, one of the Seven Sages. The story is already mentioned by

Hipponax[11]; it is on the strength of this story that Socrates, in Plato's *Protagoras* (343a4), substituted Myson's name for that of Periander, tyrant of Corinth, in the list of the Seven Sages. Such anecdotes might have given Chaerephon the idea of asking the god of Delphi to bear witness to the ability of the master he enthusiastically venerated. Perhaps he took such an audacious step precisely because Socrates emphatically disclaimed every form of cleverness; Chaerephon could have hoped that the answer of the oracle would dissuade Socrates from continuing to contradict the reputation he had with many people.

If we ask further why the oracle gave the response Chaerephon wished, two possibilities, which are by no means mutually exclusive, suggest themselves. On the one hand Socrates was not a man of an exalted social position, and it had always been to people of this condition, and not to the noble and the wealthy, that the Pythia had given the prize of piety, enviable life or intelligence. On the other hand, the fact that Socrates was critical of democracy might easily have been understood in Delphi to imply that he not only opposed, on the strength of principles, the political regime of his city, but that he was actually a Spartophile. This would be enough for the Delphians, who since the peace of Callias (445 B.C.) had recovered control over the sanctuary and who favoured Spartan policy, to give a favourable answer to Chaerephon.

* * *

We now come to the crucial question: what role did the oracle really play in Socrates' life? Was it, as most scholars seem to admit, the first and principal incentive to Socrates' choice of that kind of philosophical life which is described in the *Apology* and especially in the narration? I have already hinted (p. 40) that, in my opinion, it was not. Two arguments have led me to this persuasion: first, that the interpretation of the oracle given in the narration is not, as a whole, a natural one and that it implies some not unimportant shifts of thought, although this is effectually dissimulated by Plato's literary mastery; second, that there is no mention of the oracle in any of the other works of Plato and that in the *Apology* itself Socrates' choice and his consciousness of having been entrusted with a divine mission are partially accounted for by other facts or motives.

As to the first point, it may be useful, as a preliminary, to recognize that, when trying to define more precisely the nature of the 'knowledge' attributed to him by the Pythia, Socrates is acting exactly as was intended by the oracles we quoted above about people outstanding in piety,

43

enviable life, or understanding. What the god, here too, principally had in view was not that this or that person exceeded his fellowmen in some form of excellence; he rather wished to suggest that true piety, true success, true cleverness were not what people commonly imagined them to be. This being acknowledged, we should now notice, in relation to the problem we set ourselves to solve, that the interpretation of Socrates' knowledge as a knowledge of his ignorance supposes at the outset the Socratico-Platonic doctrine about φιλοσοφία and about the three possible attitudes towards the apprehension of total truth[12]. How could Socrates, whom his close associate Chaerephon thought to be a σοφός, have got convinced of his own ignorance if not by philosophical research? Now it was precisely this conviction that gave rise to a clash between the categorical assertion of the god of Delphi and Socrates' certainty about himself. Socrates must have been quite firmly persuaded of his lack of knowledge in order to undertake, as the narration says he did (21b9-c2; cf. 22a7-8), to test the oracle and to show him that what he had said simply was not true. Moreover the chronological sequence of the threefold investigation cannot be taken at face value. Why, indeed, would Socrates have refrained from cross-examining either a poet or a craftsman till he had exhausted the complete list of the politicians? Now, if that is so, there is no reason to admit that just *that* feature of the narration, and no other, has been introduced by Plato, and to consider the rest to be literally true to the facts.

The whole narration is built up with the most exquisite skill. Gradually, a shift takes place concerning the spirit in which Socrates represents himself as conducting his investigation. When he begins, it is with the purpose of showing the oracle to be wrong. The examination of the first group leads to a double result: on the one hand Socrates discovers that he has some superiority when compared with the politicians; on the other hand he perceives that he makes himself enemies. Since that second effect is definitely dangerous, it could induce him to stop his discussions. The topic of that menace is touched indeed as an introduction to the paragraph concerning the poets. Socrates, however, thought he could not simply drop his whole design: for 'it was a duty to attach more importance to τὸ τοῦ θεοῦ' (21e4-5). This vague phrasing suggests that what Socrates does is somehow a task he has been charged with. A few lines below, we hear that when Socrates examines people, he does that 'along the god's line' (κατὰ τὸν θεόν 22a4), as indicated by the word of the Pythia. So it appears that he is no longer trying to refute the oracle. He has perceived that he has a mission, and this makes him set out on an errand that will prove to be as difficult as the twelve labours of Hercules (22a6-7). When, by examining the third group, that of the craftsmen, Socrates discovers that, though they possess a real skill, they are in matters of much more consequence not only ignorant but conceited, he considers which would be the better for him: to partake in their knowledge *and* in their self-infatuation, or to remain as he is, without both their ability and their fault. In asking himself this question he acts 'on behalf' or 'in the name of the oracle' (ὑπὲρ τοῦ χρησμοῦ 22e1). So the assertion of the Pythia that nobody has more understanding than he, is now interpreted not only as a mandate to make *other* people see that their so-called cleverness has little or no value, but also as a warning to *himself*, not to prefer anything to the modest and realistic acknowledgement of his own insufficiency. The final conclusion is that the oracle is not about Socrates at all; it is a message directed to the whole of mankind, and Socrates' name was just used as an example, in order to show concretely the difference between divine knowledge, conceited ignorance, and ἀνθρωπίνη σοφία; the last will precisely be the recognition of one's own ignorance. Upon this first conclusion, which concerns all men, follows another that is related to Socrates alone. When he resolves to spend the whole of his life examining everybody he meets, foreigners as well as citizens, he does so κατὰ τὸν θεόν, a phrase whose meaning has now become more precise, so that we may translate it 'in obedience to the god' (23b5). If it seems to him that the man he cross-examines does not possess knowledge, he undertakes to 'help the god' (b7) and to make the man see that he is deceiving himself. This absorbs the whole of Socrates' energy and so he lives in utter poverty, because he is in 'the service of the god' (διὰ τὴν τοῦ θεοῦ λατρείαν c1).

In describing Socrates' gradual discovery of the oracle's true meaning, Plato does a magnificent literary job. But that should not prevent us from seeing that he himself puts into the words of the Pythia what he wants to find in them. Of course, he only attempts this because the oracular formula makes a comparison between the cleverness of Socrates and that of the other people, and because, on the other hand, the Socratic doctrine about ἀνθρωπίνη σοφία as φιλο-σοφία, as a *search* for understanding, implies as a prerequisite the acknowledgement of one's own ignorance. But the oracle contains absolutely no hint of a mission that it might have entrusted to Socrates. This is the very reason why Plato represents Socrates as prompted, in a first moment of his investigating campaign, by a quite different motive, that of testing and even refuting the oracle. The transition from this original motive to the other cannot easily be justified

45

in logic and Plato takes care to make it so gradual that we simply shall not notice it. He shows Socrates stirred by the oracle and starting to examine all people who are thought to be clever; then as discovering that they are not, and realizing that his consciousness of his own ignorance is to be preferred to their conceit, even if the latter might be combined with some particular ability or even reasoned skill; finally as persuaded that he should continue on that way in spite of dangerous hostility, because a divine mission has been entrusted to him by the oracle, and should devote the whole of his time to it and accept extreme poverty as a consequence. At each moment, the picture is vivid and persuasive. Still the sequence of thought is not really a natural one, because some elements are introduced that do not belong to the content of the oracle: first the idea about what makes the difference between true and false σοφία, and second the idea about a divine mission. If this be true, the oracle does not, historically speaking, constitute the origin of Socrates' specific philosophical activity.

Nor is this anywhere formally asserted in the text of the *Apology*. The narration starts from the question: how did the διαβολή originate? (20c5-d4). If Socrates was neither a cosmologist nor a sophist, what was it that attracted the attention of the public to him? The answer is: the fact that Socrates possessed some kind of σοφία. For that fact, the god of Delphi stands witness. Socrates' σοφία, however, differs widely from that which is commonly attributed to other people, as appears when he disputes with them. When closely examined, they cannot substantiate their reputation, and the fact that they have been exposed makes them angry with Socrates. In this line of thought, it is not essential that the oracle should be the *starting-point* of everything. True, Plato conveys that impression, by giving the whole section the form of a narrative, which implies some kind of chronological sequence. But he never *asserts* that everything started with the oracle, and that before the oracle Socrates was not interested in what constituted human σοφία.

My second argument is the lack of any reference to the oracle in the rest of Plato's written work. Most facts and ideas which play a role in the *Apology* are to be found at one or more places in the dialogues, not infrequently in contexts or even in formulations which are closely akin to those in that work. As an instance taken from the field of religion, we may refer to the δαιμόνιον σημεῖον, which is mentioned in such relatively late works as the *Republic* (vi 496c3-5), the *Phaedrus* (242b8-c3) and the *Theaetetus* (151a2-5). If Plato had been convinced that the oracle given to Chaerephon had truly been the origin of Socrates' philosophy, it is scarcely intelligible that he does not so much as make even the slightest

46

allusion to it elsewehere. If, however, its prominence in the *Apology* is due principally to considerations of literary technique, such a silence is not surprising. Even in the *Apology*, when Socrates speaks of his mission outside the frame of the narration, he does this in very general terms, without explicit reference to the oracle, but with emphasis on the fact that he has been given an *order* (28e4-29a1; 29d3; 30a5. e2-6; 31a7-b5). How we should understand those passages seems to appear clearly from 33c4-7. There Socrates contrasts his personal motive for examining people with that of the youths who are accompanying him. They, he says (33c2-4), enjoy it, 'for it is not unpleasant'. For him, however, the case is different: it is not a question of enjoyment, but of fulfilling a task: ἐμοὶ δὲ τοῦτο, ὡς ἐγώ φημι, προστέτακται ὑπὸ τοῦ θεοῦ πράττειν καὶ ἐκ μαντείων καὶ ἐξ ἐνυπνίων καὶ παντὶ τρόπῳ ᾧπέρ τίς ποτε καὶ ἄλλη θεία μοῖρα ἀνθρώπῳ καὶ ὁτιοῦν προσέταξε πράττειν. With μαντεῖα, Socrates certainly alludes to the answer given to Chaerephon, though not exclusively, as the plural shows[13]. The *Phaedo* supplies us with an instance of ἐνύπνιον which is particularly appropriate because it contains an explicit order that has been given to Socrates time and again and which he has always understood as directing him to practise philosophy: πολλάκις μοι φοιτῶν τὸ αὐτὸ ἐνύπνιον ἐν τῷ παρελθόντι βίῳ, ἄλλοτ' ἐν ἄλλῃ ὄψει φαινόμενον, τὰ αὐτὰ δὲ λέγον, "Ὦ Σώκρατες, ἔφη, μουσικὴν ποίει καὶ ἐργάζου." καὶ ἐγὼ ἔν γε τῷ πρόσθεν χρόνῳ ὅπερ ἔπραττον τοῦτο ὑπελάμβανον αὐτό μοι παρακελεύεσθαί τε καὶ ἐπικελεύειν, ὥσπερ οἱ τοῖς θέουσι διακελευόμενοι, καὶ ἐμοὶ τοῦτο τὸ ἐνύπνιον ὅπερ ἔπραττον τοῦτο ἐπικελεύειν, μουσικὴν ποιεῖν, ὡς φιλοσοφίας μὲν οὔσης μεγίστης μουσικῆς, ἐμοῦ δὲ τοῦτο πράττοντος (60e4-61a4). Seen in this light, the interpretation of the oracle as given in the narration seems much less contorted. If Socrates has gradually come, through different ways, to the conclusion that it was his task, and one entrusted to him from above, 'to practise philosophy and to examine himself and the others' (28e5-6), the oracle given to Chaerephon inserts itself into a broader context and can be understood in connection with other, related facts. With Socrates, divine signs and personal reflection always go hand in hand. We see that, in the case of his refusal to take an active part in politics, his 'divine sign' warns him against it, and that his own considerations show the warning to be well-founded (31d5-e1). The same holds good for the way Socrates pleaded his cause in court: though on other occasions the sign often hindered him from saying things he was on the point of saying, it did not do that at any moment in connection with Socrates' defense. So the death-sentence should not be considered as a mishap, but as leading to some blessing (40a2-c3); and, Socrates adds,

47

this is confirmed by other arguments (40c4-41d6). The case with Socrates' mission is absolutely similar. Socrates *has* divine authority for what he is doing; but his own reflections point the same way. When asked why he could not go into exile and there refrain from his endless philosophizing, he says it is very difficult to answer: 'For when I say this amounts to disobedience to God and that therefore I cannot possibly keep quiet, you will not believe me, and will think that I am trying to evade my responsibility[14]; and if I say that the highest happiness for a man indeed consists in devoting his conversations every day to human perfection and to the other subjects about which you hear me discussing and examining myself and others, still less will you accept this from me' (37e5-38a6). So there is no *single* motive and no *single* event that prompted Socrates to embrace his philosophical ἐπιτήδευμα. If the narration of the *Apology* gives that impression, this is only because Plato uses one particular fact, the oracle given to Chaerephon, as a starting-point for his *narration*. He does not want us to believe that this event was in itself of paramount importance in the life of Socrates, nor should we accept such a view.

NOTES

[1] See 'Les témoignages historiques sur Socrate', *Mélanges Henri Grégoire*, II = *Annuaire de l'Institut de Philologie et d'Histoire orientales et slaves, Université Libre de Bruxelles*, 10 (1950), pp.190-230, especially pp.224-227.

[2] We have good reasons for admitting that the personality of Socrates was an object of literary polemics about 390 B.C. Besides Plato's earlier dialogues, this was the time the Κατηγορία Σωκράτους of the Sophist Polycrates was published; the first two chapters of Xenophon's *Memorabilia* were a reply to this and might have been circulated shortly after the attack; this might also have been the case for some of the various *Apologies of Socrates* which Xenophon mentions in § 1 of his *Apology* (without, however, giving the names of their authors), for instance that by Lysias. The same years saw also a literary combat about Alcibiades, which is attested for us by Isocrates' *De bigis*, by speeches xiv and xv of Lysias and by the *Against Alcibiades* of the Pseudo-Andocides; the *Symposium* of Plato and the *Alcibiades* of Aeschines of Sphettus are probably related to the same debate.

[3] Eupolis fr. 165 Edmonds; Aristoph. fr. 291. 377. 539. 573 Edm. Among the preserved plays of Aristophanes, the *Clouds* (see below n.5) gives an important place to Chaerephon, and he is further jibed at in the *Birds* (414 B.C.) 1296. 1564 and in the *Frogs* (405 B.C.) 1335.

[4] I shall quote just two of them, since they discuss the chronological question at some length. E. Horneffer, *Der junge Platon* (Giessen 1922), pp.98-101, would date it shortly after the first *Clouds* (423 B.C.); H. W. Parke, *The Delphic Oracle*, i. *The History* (Oxford 1956), pp.401-402, thinks that the conditions of war would have precluded Chaerephon from going to Delphi from 431 to 422 and from 413 to 404 and that 'on the whole it is much more likely that the oracle was given before 431, and so influenced Socrates about the age of thirty-five'.

[5] On the role of Chaerephon in the *Clouds*, see K. J. Dover, *Aristophanes, Clouds*

(Oxford 1968), pp.xxxiii and xxxv, and on the two versions of the comedy, the second of which cannot be dated with certainty, ib. pp.lxxx-xcviii (of which xcv-xcvii deal especially with Chaerephon).

⁶ Parke, *Delph. Or.*, ii. *The Oracular Responses*, nr. 420 (p.170) gives as the oldest form that in two iambics Σοφὸς Σοφοκλῆς, σοφώτερος δ᾽ Εὐριπίδης, ἀνδρῶν δὲ πάντων Σωκράτης σοφώτατος. This, however, is to be found only with two late witnesses, the Scholiast on Aristoph. *Nub.* 144 and Arethas' scholion on *Ap.* 21a. To be sure, the first, after having quoted the two verses, adds that Apollonius Molo (the well-known master of Cicero, *flor.* ca. 100 B.C.) declared the oracle to be fictitious on the ground that the Pythian oracles were in hexameters, though this does not imply that Molon knew the form with *two* iambics. The first verse is the more suspect because it sins against an elementary rule of metrics, namely that an anapest, even in a proper name, cannot occupy the second foot. The monostich, on the other hand, is already to be found in Lucian, and further in Galen, Origen, Diogenes Laertius, Libanius and such a learned antiquarian as Porphyry (*Vita Plot.* 22, 11).

⁷ *Plato's Euthyphro, Apology of Socrates, and Crito* (Oxford 1924), note on 21a5, followed by Parke, I, p.403.

⁸ 'Das delphische Orakel als ethischer Preisrichter', an appendix to E. Horneffer, o.c. (above, n.4), pp.149-170, summarized without new materials by M. P. Nilsson, *Griechische Religionsgeschichte*, I³ (München 1967), pp.648-650.

⁹ Purposely, I avoid the word 'happiness', because this English word rather points to a state of mind, whereas in Greek τὸ εὐδαιμονεῖν is equivalent to τὸ εὖ ζῆν or to εὖ πράττειν. Thus εὐδαιμονία will be ascribed to a man whose life an objective observer will judge to be most desirable. The Greeks would say that nobody can be declared εὐδαίμων until after his death (Herod. i 32; Soph. *O.T.* 1328-1330), whereas, of course, the 'feeling happy' can only be appreciated at every moment by the individual himself.

¹⁰ To be sure, it is Solon, not Apollo, who declares (in Herod. i 32) the last three to have been most εὐδαίμων; but the story of Cleobis and Biton is beyond controversy Delphic in origin, whereas Herodotus has taken that of Tellus from another source of information. See Herzog, o.c., pp.158-160; Parke, *Delph. Or.*, i, pp.379-380.

¹¹ Fr. 63 Lasserre = fr. 61 Diehl³. According to this text, Apollo called Myson ἀνδρῶν σωφρονέστατον πάντων; this will have meant that he, as a rustic, was more sober and modest than the sophisticated and greedy town-dwellers. Later, and at least in the time of Plato, he was thought to have been proclaimed σοφώτατος; cf. F. Wehrli, *Hauptrichtungen des griechischen Denkens* (Zürich 1964), pp.56-57. − The authenticity of the fragment has been successfully defended by Fr. Pfister, art. 'Myson', *RE* XVI 1 (1933), col. 1192-1194.

¹² According to other passages in Plato (especially *Lys.* 218a and *Symp.* 203e-204a), neither the σοφοί nor the ἀμαθεῖς strive for knowledge, the former because they already have it, the latter because, in their conceit, they are not aware of their lack of insight. So just a third group, viz. those who, while not knowing, are aware of their ignorance, can and will strive for knowledge (φιλοσοφεῖν). Since perfect knowledge is a privilege of the gods (*Symp.*, l.c.; *Phaedr.* 278d; cf. *Apol.* 23a5-6), 'human knowledge' (*Apol.* 20d8 and e1) will be identical with 'philosophy'.

¹³ One should pay attention to the careful phrasing of Burnet's note on 33c5: 'ἐκ μαντείων, e.g. the Delphic oracle, which, when rightly interpreted, might be construed as a command'.

¹⁴ οὐ πείσεσθέ μοι ὡς εἰρωνευομένῳ; on the meaning of εἰρωνεύεσθαι, see Burnet's note on 38a1.

49

A GENERAL THEORY OF
LITERARY COMPOSITION
IN THE PHAEDRUS

G. J. DE VRIES

Many scholars have found fault with the structure of Plato's *Phaedrus*. The dialogue itself is said to lack the "organic unity" which it (264c) proclaims to be a necessary constituent of literary composition. Often the *Phaedrus* is judged to have two not too strictly related subjects, to wit love and writing. The criticism is mistaken. In fact, the argument of the dialogue is closely knit: love is the instigating force in the process of recollection; recollection is the basic condition for knowledge; knowledge is the presupposition of the right handling of words.

When the end of the conversation is nearing, Socrates is made to formulate explicitly the main condition for good writing. Phaedrus is bid to deliver the message that a writer must possess knowledge of the truth. He is to deliver it to "Lysias and all other composers of discourses", to "Homer and all others who have written poetry", and to "Solon and all such as are authors of political compositions under the name of laws" (278c; Hackforth's translation).

This statement implies a very general theory of literary composition in which oratory, poetry and the composition of laws are put on a par (it has been prepared in 257c ff. where it is made clear that the writing of laws may be regarded as a kind of literary composition). One wonders why P. Vicaire in his perceptive *Platon critique littéraire* (1960) has omitted to discuss it (neither 257c nor 278c are even so much as mentioned).

In the generalization, implied in the statement, a high grade of abstraction is attained. Later, explicitly, literary theory comes under it. Aristotle uses a distinction which lead to the disjunction poetry – rhetoric (this was very popular with theoreticians; for a survey of their views, cp. *e.g.* R. Escarpit, *La définition du terme littérature*, Actes IIIe Congr. Ass. Int. Litt. Comp. 1962, 77 ff.; for a quite recent defense of the disjunction, cp. W. S. Howell, *Rhetoric and Poetics; A Plea for the Recognition of the Two Literatures*, in L. Wallach, ed., *The Classical Tradition*, 1966, 374 ff.). The literary critics of Hellenistic and Early Roman times, Demetrius, Dionysius of Halicarnassus and Pseudo-Longinus, ignore the disjunction:

they take their examples from poetry, oratory and history alike. But the literary relevance of legal texts remains outside their ken (this may be said without disregarding reports like Hermippus', *ap.* Athen. 619b, on the laws of Charondas being sung in Athens; the appreciation shown in that way was not primarily literary). One has to wait till recent times to find a generalization, comparable to Plato's, in the doctrine held by Jan Mukařovský, the Czech theoretician, that literature is to be found where-ever the handling of the linguistic medium is part of the communication.

Would Plato have regarded his own writings as being implied in this generalization, too? This is what H. J. Krämer thinks (*Arete bei Platon und Aristoteles*, 1959, 23, n. 22). He argues that among Plato's published works the three types are represented: oratory in the *Gorgias*, in *Republic* I and in the *Menexenus*, the fifth discourse in the *Symposium* and the speeches in the *Phaedrus*; poetry in the myths and in the *Symposium*, taken as a whole, and "political compositions" in the *Republic*. This is rather strained; but the main objection to be made to such a classification is that it would be impossible to classify in this way works like *Crito*, *Phaedo*, *Charmides*, *Cratylus* etc. Plato may have regarded his dialogues as mimes, perhaps classifying them under poetry (for this one cannot refer to *Laws* 811cd, where the viewpoint is entirely paedagogical). Probably he did not care about it.

He certainly does not at the point in the dialogue where the "implied theory" is to be found. His passionate interest in literary matters is unmistakable. For his interest in their technical aspects, there is no need to refer to what Dionysius, Quintilian and Diogenes Laërtius tell about the variants of the opening sentence of the *Republic*, found after his death among his papers. The full discussion in the latter part of the *Phaedrus* shows his interest, as does his own literary achievement. When in *Phaedrus* 266d ff. Plato mockingly parades the technicalities of current rhetorical instruction, he is conscious both of his better theoretical insight and of his consummate artistry which can scorn the petty teachings of the rhetorical schools.

But when the conversation in the *Phaedrus* has reached the point where the "implied theory" is stated, the author's main interest is centred on the philosophical basis of writing. As so often in Plato, the "theory" is given in a passing hint.

Echoes of the *Phaedrus* are heard through the ages time and again. Nobody will wonder at hearing them in Walter Pater's work. In many respects Pater was a man as un-platonic as possible; but it was not only the 'aesthete' in him that was fascinated by Plato, and often he understood him very well ("like by like" does not always hold). In the *Essay on Style* which introduces his *Appreciations* (1889; I quote from the 5th reprint, 1900) he discusses truth in literature. Here, however, where one would have expected it, no mention is made of *Phaedrus* 278c. If it had been mentioned, Pater would have had to reject its "general theory", as he distinguishes between a literature of facts and a literature of the sense of facts, "the transcript of this sense of fact rather than the fact, as being preferable, pleasanter, more beautiful to the writer himself". But he does introduce the notion of truth: "...just in proportion as the writer's aim, consciously or unconsciously, comes to be the transcribing, not of the world, not of mere fact, but of his sense of it, he becomes an artist, his work *fine* art; and good art... in proportion to the truth of his presentment of that sense; as in those humbler and plainer functions of literature also, truth – truth to bare fact, there – is the essence of such artistic quality as they may possess... all beauty is in the long run only *fineness* of truth, or what we call expression, the finer accommodation of speech to that vision within".

Here already the use of the words 'humbler' and 'plainer' shows that the two kinds of literature are regarded as being on different levels; in the course of the essay this becomes more clear. Correspondingly, the truth which they must possess is not identical: "In the highest as in the lowliest literature, then, the one indispensable beauty is, after all, truth: – truth to bare fact in the latter, as to some personal sense of fact, diverted from men's ordinary sense of it, in the former; truth there as accuracy, truth here as expression, that finest and most intimate form of truth, the *vraie vérité*".

One wonders whether Plato would have understood what is meant by "vraie vérité" and by "truth as expression". As to the former term, he knew certainly how often despotism parades as "true liberty"; as to the second, I think it is a modern refinement which would be alien to him. Anyhow, the knowledge which is asked for in *Phaedrus* 278c is factual. Plato was decidedly not naïve about the import of the term 'fact'; but he was also certainly aware of the risks to which every philosophy that speaks condescendingly about "bare facts" exposes itself.

PLATON ET LA PURETÉ DE L'ALTITUDE

PIERRE-MAXIME SCHUHL
(*Institut de France*)

Quand on séjourne en haute montagne on est frappé par la pureté de l'air, l'éclat de la lumière, la limpidité des couleurs. C'est une des raisons de la vogue de l'alpinisme, qui connaît de nos jours un tel développement: que de chemin franchi depuis la première ascension du Mont Blanc par Saussure accompagné du guide Balmat! Littérairement, cette mode avait été préparée et annoncée par Rousseau dans la *Nouvelle Héloïse*, où il disait les bienfaits du séjour à la montagne; par Nietzsche aussi: dans *Zarathustra*, on trouve comme un reflet de l'atmosphère de Sils Maria, aussi éclatante à sa façon que celle de ses sites méditerranéens de prédilection. Certes on peut trouver de plus lointains ancêtres à l'alpinisme, tel Pétrarque faisant l'ascension du Ventoux. Mais on ne paraît pas s'être avisé que le thème de la pureté de l'air et des couleurs dans l'altitude a été abordé dans l'antiquité par Platon.

Il s'agit du mythe final du *Phédon* (pages 109a-111c). Socrate y définit le bassin méditerranéen, du Phase aux colonnes d'Hercule, comme une cuvette, dont nous habitons le fond, groupés autour de la mer qui en occupe les creux comme des grenouilles ou des fourmis autour d'une mare. Au fond de ces cuvettes se superposent l'eau et l'air; plus haut, c'est le domaine de l'éther que parcourent les astres et que respirent certains privilégiés. On retrouve ici le schème de la proportion, si cher à Platon[1]. Les poissons vivent dans l'eau; mais un «saut de carpe» les fait parfois pénétrer dans la zone de l'air[2], tellement plus pure et plus belle, car la salure de la mer ronge et gâte tout ce qui est en contact avec elle.

De même un homme qui s'envolerait[3] dans la zone éthérée verrait le vrai ciel; mais aussi la vraie terre avec ses montagnes[4], où l'on séjourne «au bord de l'air» comme nous le faisons «au bord de la mer»[5]. Aux pollutions d'ici-bas où les pierres mêmes sont corrompues par la salure et la putréfaction dues aux mélanges qui s'y déversent, apportant laideur et maladies[6], il oppose la pureté de ces régions supérieures où le climat est si bien tempéré que les maladies y sont inconnues[7]. Nos sardoines, jaspes, émeraudes ne sont que des déchets par rapport à ce qu'on voit là-bas: les pierres même y sont plus belles parce que plus pures que celles que nous appelons précieuses. Et Platon ne tarit pas sur l'éclat de leurs couleurs, leur transparence[8], mais aussi le développement proportionnel des sens et de la pensée[9]; les dieux même s'y voient face à face[10].

C'est vraiment le domaine de la félicité, dont le spectacle est fait pour des spectateurs bienheureux[11]. Ajoutons que de 109b à 111e, l'expression 'pureté' revient six fois[12], ce qui est caractéristique quand on sait l'importance que présente chez Platon la technique de la répétition[13].

NOTES

[1] Voir notre *Fabulation Platonicienne*, 2e ed., Paris, Vrin, II *Mythe et proportion*, 29 sq., 37 sq. Le thème de la proportion est souligné par Platon en 110d: ἀνὰ λόγον... ἀνὰ τὸν αὐτὸν λόγον, et 111bc.

[2] «Comme ici-bas les poissons en élevant la tête hors de la mer voient les choses d'ici-bas« (109e); cf. *Fabulation* 37-38; et M. Laffranque, *Le mythe du Dauphin*, Bulletin de l'Université de Toulouse, juillet 1946, 293.

[3] v. 109e: «supposons qu'on devienne ailé et qu'on s'envole, alors on en aurait le spectacle, parce qu'on élèverait la tête».

[4] 110d: «de même, de leur côté, ses montagnes».

[5] 111a: «les autres, au bord de l'air comme nous au bord de la mer». Il y a là des îles baignées par l'air, qui sont évidemment les îles des Bienheureux.

[6] 110e.

[7] 111b: ἀνόσους.

[8] 110d: διαφάνειαν.

[9] 111b: «par la vue, par l'ouïe, par la pensée».

[10] 111bc: «et, de la sorte, ils entrent en commerce avec eux, face à face».

[11] 111a: «un spectacle fait pour des spectateurs bienheureux», 111c: «A ces privilèges s'ajoute une félicité qui en est l'accompagnement».

[12] 109b: καθαρὰν ἐν καθαρῷ 109d: καθαρώτερα 110c: καθαρωτέραν 110e: καθαροί 11b: καθαρότητα.

[13] Cf. nos remarques *Sur la technique de la répétition dans le Phédon*, REG 61, 1948, 379, et *Etudes platoniciennes*, Paris 1960, 118-125; ainsi que *Thèmes et répétitions dans République VII*, Revue Philosophique 1960, 229 sq.

LOGICAL AND ONTOLOGICAL PRIORITY AMONG THE GENERA OF SUBSTANCE IN ARISTOTLE

ENRICO BERTI

Among the many still unsolved problems of Aristotelian exegesis is that concerning the relationship between the three types of substance which are distinguished in book XII of the *Metaphysics*, that is to say, terrestrial (mobile and corruptible), celestial (mobile and incorruptible), and supra-celestial (incorruptible and immobile) [1]. In fact some scholars supposed they could regard this relationship as an instance of *pros hen* homonymy[2], involving a priority of the immobile substance which is not only onto-logical but also logical[3]; some identified it with the relationship of succession (*to ephexes*), understood as a particular sort of *pros hen* homonymy and therefore as implying logical priority as well[4]; finally, some identified it with the relationship of succession itself, without specifying whether this should be regarded as implying not only onto-logical, but also logical priority[5]. In spite of this variety of solutions, it seems to me that the problem has not been discussed with sufficient thoroughness and, especially, that the following issues have not been definitively clarified: a) whether in fact the three above-mentioned types of substance are irreducible to a common genus, and therefore give rise to a true and proper homonymy or equivocity of the notion of substance; b) whether this homonymy, if it subsists, allows some sort of logical unification, i.e. a priority of a genus in relation to the others which is not only ontological but also logical; also, what would be the precise nature of this logical priority.

An answer to these questions seems important for the general inter-pretation of Aristotle's philosophy. As a matter of fact, since substance, for Aristotle, is what gives unity to all being, a decision concerning the type of unity which it possesses determines the conception which we must have of the very unity of being; and since, furthermore, to the unity in the object there corresponds – according to Aristotle – the unity of the science which deals with it, the discussion of the unity of substance could provide us with the data necessary to clarify the as yet also unsolved problem of the relationship between the science of the immobile substance and that of the other types of substance, that is to say, the problem of the unity, and therefore of the possibility, of the science of being *qua* being, i.e. of philosophy itself.

The present investigation does not claim, of course, to provide a definitive reply to the questions enumerated above, but merely offers itself as a contribution to their discussion, by analyzing some passages in Aristotle which have not been sufficiently taken into account in this connexion.

I

Concerning the first problem, which is that as to whether the three types of substance distinguished in *Metaph*. XII are different in genus or belong to one and the same genus, we have only one explicit statement by Aristotle, *Metaph*. X 2; "the one cannot be a genus, for the same reasons for which being and substance (*ousia*) cannot be genera"[6]. The fact that Aristotle normally asserts that neither being nor one is a genus without referring to substance could suggest that, in this passage, the mention of substance need not be taken seriously; *ousia* could have the general meaning of "essence", i.e. of "what the thing is", in which case it would be extended in its application to all the categories of being[7] and would not involve a special homonymy of substance as the first among the categories[8]. Or else, it could function as a predicate of the one, in the sense that the one cannot be either a genus or a substance (but in this case one should suppress the preceding article); or, finally, it could be a gloss[9].

However, before adopting any solution tending to diminish the doctrinal significance of our passage, it is necessary to attempt a justification of it, and to ask oneself whether the reasons why neither being nor one is a genus can be valid – as the text itself claims – for substance as well. Such reasons, as is well known, are expounded in *Metaph*. III 3 and amount essentially to the consideration that being and one are predicated of everything, therefore also of the differences existing between the various genera, while it is impossible that a genus be predicated of the differences existing between its species[10]. Now, this same reason seems valid in the case of substance. For in the case of at least one of the differences existing between the types of substance indicated in *Metaph*. XII, viz. that constituted by the terms 'corruptible' and 'incorruptible' (characterizing respectively terrestrial substances on the one hand and celestial and supercelestial substances on the other), Aristotle explicitly asserts that substance itself is predicated of it. This assertion is part of the notorious argument in *Metaph*. X 10 that the corruptible and the incorruptible are contraries which differ not only in species, but also in genus, and which – we should say – are thus contradictories rather than contraries. When, in fact, he asserts that the corruptible and the incorruptible are themselves substances or properties deriving from substance[11], he does not intend to say merely that this difference depends on the essence, i.e. the form, as any specific difference would; for that because of which a thing is corruptible or incorruptible is its matter, either as the substrate of generation and corruption or merely of locomotion, or else as the presence c.q. absence of matter. Consequently, the difference between the corruptible and the incorruptible, by excluding any common substrate and thus revealing itself as a difference not only as to species, but in genus as well[12], concerns substance in its totality.

The same could be asserted, even if Aristotle never says so explicitly, of the other difference between the various types of substance, namely that formed by the terms 'mobile' and 'immobile' (characterizing respectively terrestrial and celestial substances on the one hand and supracelestial ones on the other). As a matter of fact, this does not denote only a property accidental to the different types of substance, as if the same substance were at some moments mobile and at some others immobile, but denotes a property belonging necessarily, or *per se*, to the substance to which it belongs, and therefore constituting the very notion of substance. It is well known in fact that for Aristotle the unmoved movers are such because they are entirely in actuality, i.e. because actuality is their very substance, while terrestrial and celestial substances are mobile because their very substance is potentiality or involves potentiality[13]. For the same reason, therefore, for which corruptible and incorruptible substances are different genera of substance, mobile and immobile substances too will be different genera of substance; thus, combining these two differences, one will get three different genera of substance, and precisely those indicated by Aristotle[14].

There is, furthermore, a second reason why the three types of substance could be considered as irreducible to a unique genus, viz. that they are arranged according to an order of priority. More than once Aristotle asserts that there is no common genus for things of which one is prior and the other posterior according to the species or the form (*eidei*). Since in some cases this assertion is made in order to refute the hypostatizing of the genera accomplished by the Platonists, one could get the impression that it is introduced merely to exclude the existence of a separated (*choriston*), i.e. transcendent, genus, while it leaves open the question whether there is an immanent genus or not[15]. In fact in *Metaph.* III 3, where it is said that the predicate common to a series of terms arranged according to an order of priority is not something existing over and above the terms themselves[16], the clearly polemical intention against Plato and the formulas used by Aristotle (*ti para tauta, ta gene para ta eide*) may suggest that he wants to exclude the existence of a separated genus similar to the Platonic ideas, even if the argument probably concerns only being and the one, which, for Aristotle, not only are not separated genera, but not immanent genera either[17].

Also in the case of *Eth. Nic.* I 6, where it is said that of the good there is no idea because the goods are arranged according to an order of priority, the explicit assertion of the Platonic origin of the doctrine which excludes ideas of things ordered in this way and the use of the word 'idea' instead of 'genus'[18] suggest that what is excluded here is only the existence of a separated genus, though it is well-known that for Aristotle the good is not a genus, either separated or immanent.

However, I do not believe that the same holds for other passages, e.g. *De an.* II 3, where it is asserted that a common definition of the vegetative, the sensitive and the intellective soul does not fit any of them, because they are indivisible species arranged according to an order of succession (*ephexes*)[19]. Indeed, in this passage there seems to be no trace of the anti-Platonic polemic, and the reason why the definition common to the three species of the soul is regarded as not pertinent, viz. the fact that each of them is potentially included in the successive one, primarily serves to exclude the possibility of a common immanent genus. It is, as a matter of fact, proper to the immanent genus to be contained potentially in its species and thus to constitute their common framework[20]; but in the case of the souls, what is contained in each species and ensures their continuity is always the prior species, i.e. an indivisible species and not a common genus [21].

The case of *Pol.* III 1 is similar. Here it is said that the definition of the citizen does not equally apply to the citizens of all constitutions, since the latter, in so far as the species is concerned, are arranged according to an order of priority (the good ones are prior to the degenerate ones), and things linked by an order of priority according to species have, as such, very little or nothing in common[22]. The order of priority according to species is evidently that in which each species is included in the successive one, just as the good constitution is included in its degeneration; in this way, it assumes the unifying function which in other cases is exercised by the genus.

After all, it is exactly this exclusion of an immanent genus, which was evident in the passages mentioned above (*De an.* II 3 and *Pol.* III 1), that is at the basis of the exclusion of the transcendent genus, though only the latter is explicitly asserted in *Metaph.* III 3 and *Eth. Nic.* I 6. In fact the argument used by Aristotle in those passages is that a separated genus would have been prior to the first term of the series and therefore would have prevented the latter from really being the primary term; but the separated genus was considered by the Platonists as prior to its species only because the purely logical priority of an immanent genus in relation to its species, recognized by Aristotle himself[23], was elevated by them to the ontological priority of a transcendent genus. Hence the most fundamental reason for the incompatibility between the order of priority obtaining among different terms and the ontological priority of a transcendent genus is precisely the incompatibility between that order itself and the logical priority of the immanent genus.

It must be pointed out, however, that the existence of a common genus is not excluded by an unqualified order of priority: such a priority should be "according to the species", i.e. species has to be included in species by contributing to determine its notion, thus exercising a function replacing that normally exercised by the genus[24]. If it could be demonstrated that among the three types of substance indicated by Aristotle in *Metaph.* XII there is such a priority, not only would one introduce a further argument in favour of the – already established – thesis of their irreducibility to a unique genus, but one would definitively establish that they are connected by a priority of the logical type, thus answering the second problem examined in this note.

II

That among the types of substance there is an order of priority, at least in the ontological, i.e. causal sense, seems to be sufficiently generally agreed upon. This follows not so much, as some scholars maintain, from the two passages in *Metaph.* IV 2, where Aristotle explicitly refers to an order of succession (*ephexes*) – because in the first of these he directly refers to the sciences and only indirectly to the *ousiai*, without specifying what he means by the last term[25], and in the second he refers to entities in general[26] –, as from some other passages, in which a substance prior to the other ones is mentioned, which can only be the immobile substance. By this, of course, I do not mean to say that, whenever Aristotle uses the expression "primary substance", he is referring to the immobile substance. It is well known, in fact, that in the *Categories* it designates the ultimate subject of predication, i.e. the individual substance, and that in *Metaph.* VII it at some times designates the ultimate essence, i.e. the indivisible species, of each genus of being, and at others the ultimate essence of the genus "substance", which is in effect the form of the physical substances[27].

But there are passages where the reference of the expression "primary substance" to the immobile substance is out of the question; I have in mind primarily *Metaph.* XII 7, where it is said that, just as substance is the first among the things belonging to the list of the intelligibles *per se*, the substance that is simple and in actuality, i.e. immobile substance, is the first among the substances[28]. In the light of this passage any difficulty of identifying the "primary substance" which is mentioned in *Metaph.* IV 3 with the immobile substance disappears, even if there are some who believe they could identify it with being *qua* being[29]; as does also that of recognizing that the reason why the science of the immobile substance is said to be primary in *Metaph.* VI 1 is that the immobile substance is the first of the substances[30]. Some doubt may remain, rather, concerning the significance of the expression "primary substance" in two passages of *Metaph.* XII 8, where it could denote respectively the first among the immobile substances or else the stars[31].

Moreover, the fact that among the three types of substance there is an order of priority at least of a causal character, i.e. which is ontological, follows from the fact that the immobile substances are the causes of the circular movement of the celestial substances, which themselves, in their turn, are the causes, or accessory causes, of the more complex movements of the terrestrial substances: Aristotle in fact declares explicitly that the mover is prior to the moved[32]. That the celestial substances, i.e. the stars and the spheres by which they are carried, are moved by the immobile substances, is the best known doctrine of the entire Aristotelian metaphysics; on the other hand, that the terrestrial substances, from the elementary bodies to the most elevated of the living beings, i.e. to man, depend on the celestial substances, especially on the movement of the sun, in that which is their most intense and peculiar form of movement, i.e. generation and corruption, is perhaps a less known but equally well established Aristotelian doctrine[33]. Since, however, it does not appear that the terrestrial substances depend directly on the immobile ones, it could be asserted that among the three types of substance there is a dependence in the sense of a definite succession (*ephexes*).

But such dependence till now has become evident only with relation to movement or to generation and corruption; consequently, since for

Aristotle movement, or generation and corruption, is a mode of being, the most one could say is that a priority as to being, i.e. one of an ontological type, obtains among the immobile substance and the others, and not yet a priority as to notion, i.e. one of a logical type. Not always, in fact, do the two types of priority coincide: there are cases in which to an ontological priority in one sense there corresponds a logical priority in the exactly contrary sense, as in the case of the relationship between the individual substance and its universal predicates (genus and specific difference), or between the composite substance and the accidents which are parts of it (e.g.: "white man" and "white"), or, finally, between the sensible bodies and the geometrical forms which delimitate them[34]. In other cases, on the other hand, the two types of priority coincide, as, in general, in the case of realities that are *pros hen* homonyma, e.g. the categories of being or the forms of friendship[35].

The fact that substances are arranged according to an order of succession does not by itself show anything concerning an alleged logical priority of the first to the others: the order of succession in fact is nothing but a relationship of priority and posteriority characterized by immediacy[36]. This can take place either according to position (*thesei*) or according to species (*eidei*) or according to any other respect[37]. It will have to be considered, therefore, whether the three types of substance, apart from the ontological point of view, are successive also from the logical point of view, i.e. according to notion. To solve this problem one will first of all have to go back to the notion of substance.

The defenders of the existence of a logical priority among the three genera of substance maintain that such a notion is fundamentally that of the immobile entity or of the immaterial entity. In fact in the Aristotelian texts there is some foundation for the establishment of a hierarchy among the three types of substance according to the extent to which each of them possesses the characteristic of immobility. For instance, Aristotle asserts more than once that the terrestrial substances, i.e. those submitted to generation and corruption, imitate and to some extent partake of the eternity of the celestial substances through the continuous repetition of generation and corruption[38]. Analogously it can be supposed that the continuous and immutable movement of the celestial substances is an imitation or partial participation in the immobility of their movers[39].

In the same way it is possible to establish a hierarchy among the three types of substance according to their degree of materiality; while, in fact, the immobile substances are completely immaterial or, better, possess that minimum of materiality which multiplicity consists in, in the case of the celestial substances the matter of locomotion (*hyle topike*) is added to multiplicity, and in the case of the terrestrial substances it is the matter of generation and corruption (*hyle gennete*) which is added to multiplicity and to the matter of locomotion[40]. But neither immobility nor immateriality is ever indicated by Aristotle as the constitutive characteristic of the notion of substance, and the hierarchy grounded on such notions, in as much as it implies a relationship of imitation or participation or addition (*prosthesis*) among the genera of substance, looks more Platonic and Neoplatonic than Aristotelian.

The characteristics constitutive of the notion of substance, according to Aristotle, seem rather to be other, precisely: a) being the subject of predication, i.e. something that exists by itself and not in something else; b) being at the same time something determinate, i.e. being provided with a proper nature or essence which is very definite. These two features amount to the concept of a "separated" (*choriston*) entity or to that, equivalent to this, of "this definite thing" (*tode ti*)[41]. On the basis of these characteristics the notion of substance, which is applicable in general to all terms (genera, species and individuals) belonging to the first category of being, in that they function as subjects for those belonging to the other categories, applies in a primary sense to the individuals, which therefore in the *Categoriae* are called "primary substances", and in a derivative sense to the species and genera, which therefore are called "secondary substances"[42].

But, if one analyzes the internal structure of individual substance in relation to sensible substances, as Aristotle does in *Metaph.* VII, one finds that it is constituted by a form and a matter, and that the cause for which it is what it is, thus for which it is substance, i.e. something separated and determinate, is its form. On this ground it must be concluded that, in the case of sensible substances, the notion of substance applies to such a form in a more proper sense than to the composite individual[43]. This does not mean, of course, that the form of the sensible substances is, by itself, a substance, i.e. exists separately from its matter: on the contrary, it is substance in a primary sense precisely in that it is the form of an individual which, in virtue of it, is "separated", i.e. existing in itself and not in something else, and completely determinate[44].

Thus, one may say that the form of the sensible substances possesses a priority in relation to the composite both from the ontological point of view, in that it, as formal cause, is the cause of the being of the composite, and from the logical point of view, in that, as form, it is contained in the definition of the composite. This priority, however, is not in any way identifiable with the relationship between the immobile and the mobile substances, since the former are not at all the formal causes of the latter and therefore, even if in a certain sense, that is to say as moving causes, they are causes of their being, indeed of their generation and corruption, are in no sense contained in their definitions.

The same point has to be made concerning the priority of actuality in relation to potentiality, asserted by Aristotle in *Metaph.* IX 8: what is prior to potentiality, both from an ontological and from a logical point of view, is in fact the actuality of that which is in potentiality, not the actuality of the immobile substances, which is prior to the actuality of the mobile substances from an ontological point of view in that it is a moving cause, but is not so from a logical point of view[45].

In *Metaph.* XII 7, however, Aristotle asserts that the substance that is simple and in actuality, i.e. the immobile substance, is the first term in the list of things intelligible *per se*[46]; hence one has to suppose that it is more intelligible than any other thing, and that in this sense it must possess not only ontological but also logical priority. But this logical priority is *sui generis*: it consists exclusively in the fact that the immobile substance, being simple, coincides entirely with its own notion, i.e. is entirely intelligible. In it the substance coincides with the very cause of the substantiality and of the intelligibility, i.e. with the form; therefore it is substance; and it is intelligible as substance, not in virtue of something else, but only in virtue of itself. In this sense it is absolutely primary both from the ontological and from the logical point of view. On the other hand, the mobile substances, whether celestial or terrestrial, being composed of form and matter, do not entirely coincide with their own notion, which is identified merely with their form; hence, though having the principle of their own substantiality and of their own intelligibility in themselves, they are not identical with such a principle, and therefore they are not absolutely primary, either in the ontological or in the logical order[47].

In this sense, one may affirm that the immobile substances possess a priority to all the other genera of substance which is also of a logical nature, but differs both from that of the genus in relation to the species and from that of the term that is primary according to the species in relation to the other terms of a succession or of a relation *pros hen*. In the notion of the mobile substances, in fact, the immobile substance is not contained at all either as genus or as a term of common reference. From the logical point of view indeed there seems to be no dependence of the mobile on the immobile substances.

63

This does not mean, however, that substances are completely homonymous: it seems possible to recognize at least a relationship of analogy between the different genera. In each of them, in fact, the intelligibility depends on the form: since there is no common form, there is no principle of common intelligibility; however, since each genus has its own form, each genus has its own intelligibility[48]. The difference lies in the fact that in the immobile substance there is a full coincidence between substance and form, while in the mobile substance there is no such coincidence. Within the limits of analogy, which is a logical relationship, one can thus establish a priority, in which the *princeps analogatum* is the immobile substance; but it is a priority that is more ontological than logical, in the sense that in the immobile substance those conditions of intelligibility which are also found in the mobile substances are more perfectly realized. From the logical point of view it would seem that one could say, rather, that the *princeps analogatum* is the mobile substance. It is in fact from the analysis of the mobile substance that we get the notion of substance and it is only starting from this notion that we extend it, by analogy, to the immobile substance[49].

This curious situation is expressed by the famous Aristotelian doctrine according to which the things which are more intelligible in themselves, or according to notion, do not coincide with those more intelligible to us, or according to sensation, and we must proceed from the latter to the former[50]. That such a doctrine applies also to the three types of substance distinguished in *Metaph.* XII is shown by the very structure of book XII, which deals first with the terrestrial (chs. 2-3), then with the celestial (chs. 6-8) and finally with the supracelestial substances (ch. 9)[51]. On the basis of this treatment one can say that the immobile substances possess an absolute logical priority, since they are entirely intelligible, i.e. are entirely exhausted by their own notion, while the mobile substances possess a logical priority in relation to us, since they, though not being entirely intelligible, provide us with the notion of substance which then, by analogy, we apply to the immobile substances[52]. This notion, naturally, does not serve to demonstrate the existence of the immobile substances, which must be proved on the basis of the existence of precise causal connections, i.e. of an ontological dependence, but serves to demonstrate their possibility, i.e. their being objects of thought for us[53].

The unity of the sciences that study the three genera of substance remains thus guaranteed by the causal, or ontological, dependence of all these genera on the primary one, as also by the analogical, hence logical, unity between them, which is ascertained starting from what is ontologically the last. Hence it can be said that these sciences are not properly distinct sciences, but "parts" of a unique science, philosophy, i.e. the science of substance, which itself is, as we know, nothing but the science of being *qua* being[54]. By means of this conception which avoids the extreme opposites of a pure equivocity of the notion of substance, implying the impossibility of philosophy, thus skepticism, and of its essential univocity, implying the deduction of all the sciences from philosophy, such as developed in the Platonic Academy and then in Neoplatonism, Aristotle manages to ensure the unity of the science of the substances, i.e. the possibility of philosophy, guaranteeing to the sensible substances the logical independence that is necessary to ground the autonomy of the particular sciences.

NOTES

[1] Cf. Aristot., *Metaph.* XII 1, 1069a33-34; 6, 1071b3-4. For convenience I mention the former under the denomination of terrestrial substances, though they occupy the whole sphere under the sky of the moon, and the latter under the denomination of supracelestial substances, though, to be exact, they, being immaterial, could not be localized spatially.

[2] J. Owens, *The Doctrine of Being in the Aristotelian Metaphysics*, Toronto, 1963[2], 279-300, 455-473; G. Patzig, *Ontologie und Theologie in der "Metaphysik" des Aristoteles*, Kant-Studien 52, 1960-61, 199-201.

[3] By "ontological priority" (*physei* or *ousiai*) I mean the possibility that some things have of existing independently of others, while the latter cannot exist without them (cf. *Metaph.* V 11, 1019a1-4); by "logical priority" (*logōi*) I mean the fact that the notion of some things is necessarily contained in the notion, or definition, of others, while the notion of these others is not contained in the definition of the former (*Metaph.* V 11, 1018b30-36). On this distinction cf. G. E. L. Owen, *Logic and Metaphysics in some earlier works of Aristotle*, in: *Aristotle and Plato in the mid-fourth century*, Göteborg 1960, 170-72.

[4] H. J. Krämer, *Zur geschichtlichen Stellung der "Metaphysik" des Aristoteles*, Kant-Studien 58, 1967, 349; H. Happ, *Hyle*, Berlin 1971, 337-342.

[5] G. Colle, Aristote, *Métaphysique*, Livre IV, Louvain-Paris 1931, 63; J. Tricot, Aristote, *La Métaphysique*, Paris 1962[2], I, 190, n.4; G. Reale, Aristotele, *La Metafisica*, Napoli 1968, I, 329.

[6] *Metaph.* X 2, 1053b22-24.

[7] Cf. *Metaph.* VII 4, 1030a17-b7, where it is shown that the essence belongs in the primary sense to the category of substance and in a derived sense to the other categories as well.

[8] This is probably what pseudo-Alexander means, when he observes that here the subject is *ousia* in general (*katholou*) (*In Metaph.* 612,31).

[9] These last two possibilities are envisaged by A. Schwegler, *Die Metaphysik des Aristoteles*, Tübingen 1847-48, IV, 192.

[10] *Metaph.* III 3, 998b22-27. In this chapter two other arguments are introduced, where it is demonstrated that there is no genus either for things of which one is prior and the other posterior (999a6-13) or for those of which one is better and the other worse (999a13-14). But it is not clear whether they also concern being and the one.

[11] *Metaph.* X 10, 1059a6-7.

[12] Cf. *Metaph.* X 3, 1054b27-28, where Aristotle asserts that things which do not have their matter in common differ not only in species but also in genus. This conclusion very much reduces the importance of the discussion which took place among the commentators concerning the exact meaning of the term *genos* at the beginning of *Metaph.* X 10 (cfr. H. Bonitz, *Aristotelis Metaphysica*, Bonn 1848-1849, II, 449; W. D. Ross, *Aristotle's Metaphysics*, Oxford 1924, II, 305).

[13] Cf. *Metaph.* XII 6, 1071b17-20.

[14] It does not seem to me that this conclusion could be invalidated by statements such as those at *Phys.* I 6, 189a14 and 189b23-24, according to which "substance is a single genus of being", because they manifestly refer to the terrestrial substances alone, or *De an.* II 1, 412a6, according to which "we say that substance is a genus of entities", because here 'genus' probably equals 'category'. As regards those passages in which Aristotle seems to consider all the sensible substances as belonging to the same genus (cf. e.g. *Metaph.* IV 3, 1005a34), it must be observed that the difference between the substances whose matter is the substrate of generation and corruption (the terrestrial substances) and the substances whose matter is the substrate of the locomotion alone (the celestial substances) is undoubtedly less important, and probably less justified within Aristotelian philosophy itself, than that between material substances (the terrestrial and celestial substances together) and immaterial substances. Aristotle himself seems to be conscious of this fact, as he (see *Metaph.* XII 1, 1069a30-b1) establishes first the distinction between the sensible and the immobile substances, and only later on, with relation to the sensible substances, introduces the distinction between the corruptible and the incorruptible substances. In the same passage, furthermore, he asserts that all sensible substances, whether corruptible or incorruptible, are the objects of physics, while the immobile substance is the object of another science (cf. C. Natali, *Cosmo e divinità. La struttura logica della teologia aristotelica*, L'Aquila 1974). On the other hand the distinction between terrestrial and celestial substances, though not entirely justified by Aristotle, is a doctrine which he inherited from the culture of his times and therefore cannot be glossed over in the context of a historical reconstruction of this thought.

[15] The closest treatment of this problem ever provided is that by A. C. Lloyd, *Genus, species and ordered series in Aristotle*, Phronesis 7, 1962, 67-90.

[16] *Metaph.* III 3, 999a6-13.

[17] It should be noticed that this argument is immediately followed by another, based on the difference between the better and the worse (999a13-14), in which Aristotle simply asserts that between these terms there is no common genus, without mentioning any sort of separation.

[18] *Eth. Nic.* I 6, 1096a17-23. In the parallel passage of *Eth. Eud.* I 8, 1218a1-10, though there is no explicit allusion to the Platonic origin of the argument, the term 'separated' (*choriston*) is used more than once.

[19] *De an.* II 3, 414b20-32.

[20] *Metaph.* V 28, 1024b4-6.

[21] Cfr. Lloyd, o.c. 72-84.

[22] *Pol.* III 1, 1275a34-b5.

[23] *Top.* V 4, 141b25-29.

[24] Concerning the equivalence between the priority according to species and the priority according to notion, cf. *Metaph.* XIII 8, 1084b9-13. In my view the priority according to species, in that it attributes the function normally explicated by the genus to the prior species, satisfies the requirements indicated by Thomas Aquinas, *In peri herm.* I, VIII, n.93, as necessary to exclude the univocity of the genus.

²⁵ *Metaph*. IV 2, 1004a2-9. According to most of the commentators this passage refers to the three types of substance admitted in *Metaph*. XII, but according to some of them the term *ousiai* is used instead in a more general sense, as indicating the different categories of being (cfr. L. Lugarini, *Aristotele e l'idea della filosofia*, Firenze 1961, 251; W. Leszl, *Philip Merlan e la metafisica aristotelica*, Riv. crit. di storia della filosofia 25, 1970, 241, n.101).

²⁶ *Metaph*. IV 2, 1005a10-11. According to most of the commentators the assertion that some entities are arranged in relation to some "one" (*pros hen*) and others in succession (*ephexes*) demonstrates that some of them are the categories and the others are the different genera of substance. But it must be kept in mind that in *Metaph*. XII 1, 1069a20-21, Aristotle admits the possibility that the categories themselves are arranged in succession, so that the passage could indicate that some categories are in relation to some "one" and the others in succession.

²⁷ Cfr. D. Prò, *La substancia primera en la filosofia de Aristoteles*, in: *Estudios de historia de la filosofia en homenaje al prof. R. Mondolfo*, I, Tucuman 1957, 294-300.

²⁸ *Metaph*. XII 7, 1072a31-32.

²⁹ *Metaph*. IV 3, 1005a33-35. The expression "primary substance" is referred to being *qua* being by Leszl, o.c. 22-23, who agrees on this point with P. Merlan, *Postskript zu einer Besprechung*, Philosophische Rundschau 7, 1959, 148-53. However it must be kept in mind that Merlan in his turn identifies being *qua* being with the immobile substance, thus reestablishing the equation primary substance = immobile substance. If, on the contrary, one refuses the reduction of being *qua* being to immobile substance, as Leszl rightly does, and understands being *qua* being as the totality of reality, it is not clear any more with reference to what it should be "primary".

³⁰ *Metaph*. VI 1, 1026a29-30. As it is well known, once the authenticity of the whole passage was questioned for reasons of content. Nowadays nobody seems to question it any more, with the exception of Leszl, *Logic and Metaphysics in Aristotle*, Padova 1970, 533-35, who, however, limits himself to proposing the deletion of the lines 31-32, which do not concern the "primary substance".

³¹ *Metaph*. XII 8, 1073a29-30; 1074b9.

³² *Metaph*. XII 8, 1073a35-36.

³³ It is sufficient to mention the passage in which Aristotle asserts that the motive causes of man are, in addition to his father, the sun and its oblique course (*Metaph*. XII 5, 1071a14-17).

³⁴ Cfr. *Metaph*. V 11, 1018b36; XIII 2, 1077b1-11.

³⁵ Cfr. *Metaph*. VII 1, 1028a31-b1; *Eth. Eud*. VII 2, 1236a15-31.

³⁶ Cfr. *Phys*. V 3, 227a1. *Ephexes*, just as the equivalent *hexes*, derives probably from the verb *echesthai* in the sense of "to follow".

³⁷ *Phys*. V 3, 226b35. On these grounds it seems to me useless to discuss whether the relationship of succession is different from the relation *pros hen* (as is maintained e.g. by Alexander, *In Metaph*. 1005a10, and G. Rodier, *Quelques remarques sur la conception aristotélicienne de la substance*, Année philosophique 1909, 1-11), or is a special case of it (as is maintained by L. Robin, *La théorie platonicienne des idées et des nombres d'après Aristote*, Paris 1908, 168 ff., n.172; G. Mainberger, *Die Seinsstufung als Methode und Metaphysik*, Freiburg Schweiz 1959, 171-179; Krämer, o.c. 338-39; Happ, o.c. 337-342). It is clear in fact that, while the relationship *pros hen* implies by itself a logical priority, the relationship of succession can either imply it or not imply it. It is probable that, when it implies it, this is of the same nature as that encountered in the case of the relation *pros hen*, with the difference that in the case of succession the many terms are not all related to the same term, but each of them is related to the immediately preceding term.

67

[38] Cf. *De gen. et corr.* II 10, 336b27-337a7; *De an.* II 4, 415a26-b7; *Metaph.* IX 8, 1050b28-29.

[39] A relationship of this sort among the three types of substance seems to be suggested by Owens, o.c. 460-466.

[40] This doctrine, which is attributed to Aristotle already by Krämer, o.c. 350, has been expounded systematically by Happ, o.c. 342-358.

[41] The first of the two characters is indicated mainly in *Cat.* 5, 2a11-14; *Metaph.* V 8, 1017b13-14; *Metaph.* VII 3, 1029a7-9; the second in *Metaph.* V 8, 1017b14-16, 21-22; *Metaph.* VII 3, 1029a9-27. They are put together in *Metaph.* V 8, 1017b23-26; *Metaph.* VII 3, 1029a27-28; *Metaph.* XII 5, 1070b36-1071a1, etc. It does not seem to me that the doctrine of the *Metaphysics* is different or more evolved than that of the *Categories*, as is maintained respectively by S. Mansion, *La première doctrine de la substance: la substance selon Aristote*, Rev. philos. de Louvain 44, 1946, 349-369, and C.-H. Chen, *Aristotle's Concept of Primary Substance in Books Z and H of the Metaphysics*, Phronesis 2, 1957, 46-59, with whom however I am in agreement in other respects; I should only say that it is better worked out, that is more complete. Cfr. also G. Reale, *La polivocità della concezione aristotelica della sostanza*, in: *Scritti in onore di C. Giacon*, Padova 1972, 17-40.

[42] *Cat.* 5, 2a14-19. I do not think that this conception of substance, which after all is the same as that which is at the basis of the distinction between substance and the other categories, has ever been rejected by Aristotle, as is maintained by R. Boehm, *Das Grundlegende und das Wesentliche*, Den Haag 1965. In this connection I find the observations made by R. Claix, *Le status ontologique du concept de "sujet" selon la Métaphysique d'Aristote*, Rev. philos. de Louvain 70, 1972, 335-359, convincing.

[43] *Metaph.* VII 3, 1029a5-7; 11, 1037a29-30; 17, 1041b7-9, 27-28. In my view, however, this is not the reason why the expression "primary substance" sometimes indicates the form (cfr. *Metaph.* VII 7, 1032b1-2; 11, 1037a5, 28-29). Even in this book, in fact, "primary" signifies something which cannot be predicated of anything further, exactly as in the *Categories*, and indicates the last or indivisible species falling under any genus, among which of course there are the last species of the genus substance (cf. 4, 1030a10-12; 6, 1031b13-14; 1032a4-5; 11, 1037b1-4).

[44] Cf. *Metaph.* VIII 1, 1042a26-31. For Aristotle, 'separated' does not mean separated from matter, i.e. immaterial, but existing in itself and not in something else (cfr. Bonitz, *Index aristotelicus*, 860a27-38; E. de Strycker, *La notion aristotélicienne de séparation dans son application aux Idées de Platon*, in: *Autour d'Aristote. Récueil offert à A. Mansion*, Louvain 1955, 119-39): in this sense separation belongs to the same extent to material and to immaterial substances; both the former and the latter, in fact, are called "separated" in *Metaph.* VI 1, 1026a13-16 (cfr. the well known correction by Schwegler).

[45] *Metaph.* IX 8, 1049b10-11. That what is mentioned is the actuality of the immobile substances is clear from what follows. The only mention of the priority of a different genus of substance is in 1050b6-8, but this is clearly a purely ontological priority.

[46] *Metaph.* XII 7, 1072a30-32.

[47] Cfr. *Metaph.* VII 10, 1035b33-1036a11; 11, 1036a26-31; 1037a21-29. The meaning of the passage 1037a33-b7 seems rather uncertain to me, since it could allude not to the coincidence between the notion with the form, but to the identity of essence with the individual, which is asserted in chs. 4-6 against the Platonic doctrine of the transcendence of the essences.

[48] The frequent comparisons made by Aristotle between divine and human thought,

divine and human happiness, divine and human life (cf. *Metaph*. XII 7; *Eth. Nic.* X 7-8; etc.), make one thing of a relationship of analogy between the immobile substance and the others.

[49] The possibility of this inversion between the ontological and the logical priority has been envisaged by L. Conti, *Il problema dell'unificazione dei generi di sostanza in Aristotele* (typewritten dissertation), Padova 1972.

[50] *An. Post.* I 2, 71b33-72a4; 3, 72b27-29; *Phys.* I 1, 184a16-18; I 3, 188b30-33; 189a4-5; *De an.* II 2, 413a11-12; *Metaph.* V 11, 1018b29-32; VII 3, 1029b3-12; *Eth. Nic.* I 2, 1095b1-2.

[51] The celestial substances constitute the transition necessary for the demonstration of the existence of the immobile substances, as demonstrated by K. Oehler, *Der Beweis für den unbewegten Beweger bei Aristoteles*, Philologus 99, 1951, 129-159.

[52] This procedure appears obvious in *Metaph*. XII 8, 1073a34-b1.

[53] This is the function which *Metaph*. VII ascribes to the study of the sensible substances (cf. 3, 1029a33-b1; 11, 1037a10-17; 17, 1041a6-9.)

[54] *Metaph*. IV 2, 1004a2-9. Obviously the "parts of philosophy" which study respectively the terrestrial and celestial substances must not be confused with the terrestrial and celestial physics understood as particular sciences. These last, in fact, though studying respectively the terrestrial and celestial substances, do not consider their causal dependence nor their logical analogy with the immobile substance. The above-mentioned "parts of philosophy" are successive moments of the same discourse, the complete exposition of which is the *Metaphysics* of Aristotle itself and its summary in *Metaph*. XII.

UN PASSAGE OBSCUR
DU DEUXIEME LIVRE
DE LA PHYSIQUE

(ch. 2, 194a27-b8)

SUZANNE MANSION

Pour répondre à la question de savoir quel est l'objet précis de la science physique, si c'est la nature considérée comme matière, comme forme ou dans ces deux sens à la fois[1], Aristote présente trois arguments tendant à montrer que c'est la dernière hypothèse qui est la bonne. Le premier de ceux-ci s'appuie sur le principe selon lequel l'art imite la nature pour conclure que, puisque la connaissance requise du technicien enveloppe non seulement la forme (qui est pour lui la fin à réaliser), mais jusqu'à un certain point aussi la matière (les moyens)[2], il doit en être de même de la science physique[3]. Le troisième argument tient en une ligne: "la matière est un relatif, car, à une forme différente, correspond une matière différente"[4]. Sa portée paraît être que, la forme exigeant une matière appropriée pour s'y incarner, la connaissance de la forme est inséparable de celle de la matière[5].

Reste le deuxième argument, qui fera l'objet de notre examen. Il couvre les lignes 194a27 à b8. Les particules qui l'introduisent, en marquent les articulations et la conclusion, ainsi que celle qui annonce l'argument suivant, en délimitent clairement l'étendue et obligent à traiter ce morceau comme un tout, malgré l'apparente absence de lien logique entre certaines de ses parties[6].

Bien que très succinctement exprimé au début, le sens général de l'argument est clair. La connaissance de la fin et celle des moyens appartiennent à une même science. Or la nature est fin, elle est «ce en vue de quoi»[7]. La conclusion non formulée se supplée aisément: la science de la nature comme fin sera aussi connaissance des moyens que cette nature emploie. Pour arriver à la proposition désirée, il est cependant nécessaire d'ajouter encore une prémisse sous-entendue, mais facilement suppléable eu égard à l'argument précédent: le couple fin-moyens correspond au couple forme-matière. Si l'on admet ce qui a été démontré au chapitre I, à savoir que la nature au sens fort est la forme[8], on comprendra que le physicien, nécessairement attentif à la forme, doive néanmoins se soucier aussi de la matière. Mais aucune des conséquences que nous venons d'énumérer n'est énoncée dans la suite du texte. Après une parenthèse destinée à éclaircir la notion de finalité des processus naturels[9], le lecteur rencontre une série de considérations sur la technique dont le lien avec ce qui précède est rien moins qu'évident. Introduites par ἐπεὶ καί, ces remarques paraissent pourtant devoir éclairer l'argument précédent. Le font elles, comment et en quelle mesure, c'est ce que nous voudrions examiner.

Le texte présente quelques difficultés de détail qu'il faut examiner avant de se poser les questions plus ardues du sens général du passage et de sa place dans le contexte de ce chapitre. Avec Ross, nous lisons δέ au lieu de δή à la ligne 194b1. En 194b4, nous supprimons ἡ ἀρχιτεκτονική, que Ross considère comme une glose se rapportant à ἡ δέ (une autre possibilité serait de placer avec Prantl les mots litigieux après ἡ δέ; joints à ὡς ποιητική, ils formeraient alors une parenthèse explicative du deuxième membre de la disjonction). Ainsi amendé, le texte est assez clair, au moins dans son sens immédiat. Nous en proposons la traduction suivante.

"Car les arts font leur matière, les uns la produisent au sens absolu, les autres la rendent facile à travailler, et nous faisons usage de tout comme si cela était là pour nous (nous sommes en effet nous-mêmes, en un sens, une fin, car "ce en vue de quoi" a deux sens: on l'a dit dans le traité *Sur la philosophie*). Or, il y a deux arts qui gouvernent la matière et qui connaissent: celui qui utilise les choses et celui qui en dirige la fabrication (littéralement: la partie de l'art de fabrication qui dirige). C'est pourquoi l'art qui utilise est, lui aussi, directeur en quelque manière, mais la différence est que l'un connaît la forme, l'autre, en tant que producteur, la matière. En effet, le pilote sait quelle doit être la forme du gouvernail et donne les directives, l'autre sait de quel bois la pièce doit être faite et par quelles opérations. Donc, dans les choses artificielles, c'est nous qui produisons la matière en vue de l'œuvre, tandis que, dans les choses naturelles, elle est donnée"[10].

Si l'on ne tient pas compte de la parenthèse des lignes 194a35-36, dont nous nous occuperons plus loin, on peut présenter comme suit le contenu de ce passage. Les techniques ne se contentent pas de se servir des matériaux fournis par la nature, elles fabriquent leur matière ou au moins l'aménagent en vue de l'œuvre à faire[11] et c'est toujours en considérant la matière comme étant en quelque sorte à la disposition de ses fins que l'homme agit ainsi. Mais il y a deux arts qui comportent à la fois un pouvoir directeur sur la matière et un savoir: celui de l'utilisateur du produit manufacturé et celui du technicien qui en dirige la fabrication.

L'utilisateur, connaissant la forme, c'est-à-dire sachant à quoi doit servir l'objet, est capable de donner des ordres à celui qui est chargé de conduire la production. La science de ce dernier concerne les matériaux à employer et les opérations à faire: il pourra donner des directives précises aux ouvriers qui exécutent le travail. Et Aristote conclut: une différence subsiste entre l'art et la nature; celle-ci se sert de matériaux donnés, tandis que l'art étend son action fabricatrice jusqu'à la nature elle-même.

On le voit, les explications d'Aristote ne concernent que les activités humaines. C'est au lecteur à faire l'application à la nature et à la science qu'on en peut avoir du modèle offert par l'art, en tenant compte de la remarque restrictive formulée par l'auteur en conclusion. Mais, pour cela, il faut d'abord, cela va de soi, bien comprendre les considérations proposées au sujet de l'art, ce qui n'est pas chose si facile.

Trois ou même quatre genres de techniques sont ici en jeu. En commençant par les plus élémentaires, disons qu'il y a d'abord toutes les techniques de production de la matière elle-même. Leur but est de fournir des matériaux à façonner. Bien qu'Aristote ne le dise pas, on conçoit facilement que les techniques de ce niveau n'aient pas ou guère de directives à recevoir des artisans plus spécialisés. Les matériaux qu'ils offrent doivent pouvoir servir à beaucoup d'usages différents. Sauf pour quelques cas particuliers, il suffit par conséquent qu'ils répondent à des normes très générales[12]. Il n'empêche que, comme les autres arts, ceux-ci sont soumis à la finalité universelle de la technique: celle de l'usage du produit par l'homme. Aristote cette fois en fait lui-même la remarque[13] et nous aurons à revenir sur ce point. Au stade qui suit immédiatement celui-ci doit se placer un genre de techniques qu'Aristote ne mentionne pas explicitement, mais auquel il fait néanmoins allusion pour en distinguer celui du troisième niveau: les arts d'exécution, de fabrication proprement dite[14]. Ce sont ceux des ouvriers du chantier naval, p.ex., qui travaillent sous la direction d'un maître d'œuvres. Bien que ces ouvriers soient en fait les réalisateurs du bateau, leur savoir-faire particulier n'intéresse pas Aristote. Ils sont en effet sous la dépendance étroite d'un chef qui dirige leur travail en connaissance de cause et auquel revient, plus qu'à ses subordonnés, le titre de constructeur de navires. Dans des cas plus simples, il serait normal d'ailleurs que la conception et l'exécution de l'œuvre à faire relèvent d'un même artisan.

Quoi qu'il en soit de ceci, c'est l'art du maître d'œuvres et, au-dessus de celui-ci, l'art de l'utilisateur du produit qui retiennent surtout l'attention d'Aristote. Ce troisième et ce quatrième niveau de la technique méritent tous deux, bien qu'à des titres différents, la qualification d'architectoniques, le premier, pour la raison évidente qu'il commande la fabrication de l'objet, le second, pour une raison moins apparente mais plus profonde : c'est l'utilisateur qui, en fin de compte, possède la raison formelle du produit, car c'est lui qui exerce l'activité en vue de laquelle celui-ci est fait. Aussi a-t-il pouvoir de commandement même sur le maître d'œuvres.

Pour arriver à cette conclusion, Aristote s'est appuyé sur un double caractère qu'il a reconnu aux arts que nous avons appelés du troisième et du quatrième niveau : un pouvoir directeur sur la matière et une connaissance[15]. Le premier ne fait pas problème. Il est clair, en effet, que tant le pilote, quand il fait usage du gouvernail, que le constructeur naval, quand il en dirige la fabrication, plient une certaine matière à leurs fins[16]. Quant au second, Aristote prend soin de faire à son propos une distinction importante. La connaissance de l'utilisateur porte sur la forme, celle du fabricant en tant que fabricant, sur la matière[17]. En effet, le pilote sait quel doit être l'*eidos* du gouvernail[18], entendons, la configuration, les qualités de résistance, de souplesse, etc., qu'il doit avoir pour remplir son office. Mais c'est au constructeur à savoir quels matériaux il faut employer et quelles opérations il faut faire pour arriver au résultat cherché[19]. Cette distinction ne signifie évidemment pas que le constructeur ignore la forme, mais simplement que sa compétence particulière concerne la matière, tandis que la connaissance qu'il a de la forme lui est seulement communiquée d'en haut par le pilote, dont c'est le savoir propre. Pour ce dernier, en revanche, rien n'indique qu'il doive avoir une connaissance des matériaux ni de la manière de les traiter. S'il la possédait, son art englberait celui du maître d'œuvres.

Les idées présentées ici par Aristote semblent n'avoir rien d'original. Leur similitude avec les vues de Platon est un fait reconnu. La dépendance de l'art de fabrication par rapport à l'art d'utilisation est affirmée à plusieurs reprises dans les Dialogues, l'exemple du pilote et du constructeur de navires se trouve dans le *Cratyle*[20]. Mais on n'a pas pris garde à une légère différence d'accent entre les deux philosophes, qui a son importance dans la question présente. Platon, au moins dans la *République* et le *Cratyle*, s'exprime comme si des deux arts subordonnés l'un à l'autre seul l'art supérieur comportait un savoir véritable : le fabricant, qui écoute les avis de celui qui sait, c'est-à-dire de l'utilisateur, n'a sur la perfection ou l'imperfection du produit qu'une "foi juste", tout entière dérivée de la science de son guide. De son savoir à lui, de ce qu'Aristote appelle la connaissance de la matière, Platon ne souffle mot[21]. Dans le *Politique*, il est vrai, la pensée est plus nuancée. Platon reconnaît à l'architecte un savoir théorique et un pouvoir de direction sur les ouvriers ;

mais c'est sans songer apparemment à subordonner la technique architecturale à un "art d'habiter les maisons", qui devrait, pour maintenir le parallélisme avec le cas précédent, fournir à la première ses normes[22]. Plus loin la similitude avec la pensée d'Aristote se fait plus étroite. Platon attribue aux techniques particulières que sont la rhétorique, l'art militaire et le droit une compétence propre, qui ne s'efface pas devant l'art royal et souverain qu'est la politique, mais qui s'y subordonne néanmoins[23]. On aurait donc ici un analogue exact des rapports affirmés par Aristote entre l'art d'utilisation et l'art de fabrication (compétences distinctes et subordination du second au premier), s'il ne manquait précisément, dans la description de ces rapports par Platon, le schème le plus caractéristique de la pensée aristotélicienne, celui qui sera d'application stricte dans le problème envisagé, nous voulons parler du couple matière-forme. Que les compétences des arts inférieurs et supérieurs puissent être appelés respectivement connaissance de la matière et connaissance de la forme, c'est ce que Platon ne dit pas, c'est ce que ses exemples du *Politique* n'évoquent en aucune façon[24].

Reprenons à présent le problème que nous nous étions posé. La longue analyse du modèle technique que nous venons de faire permet-elle de mieux comprendre la pertinence de ces considérations sur l'art quant à la question de l'objet précis de la physique? Il nous semble que oui. En premier lieu, la différence marquée pour terminer entre l'art et la nature[25] prend à sa lumière un sens précis. Si nous avons eu raison de croire que quatre niveaux distincts de techniques sont ici en question, il est clair que c'est le premier seulement qui est éliminé de la comparaison avec la nature, puisque celle-ci se sert d'une matière préexistante[26]. Restent donc les trois autres sortes de techniques, que l'on peut désormais réduire à deux en groupant sous le titre unique d'art de production les différentes techniques d'exécution et l'art de diriger et de coordonner les diverses phases de celle-ci. L'art de production et l'art d'utilisation, qui le domine, doivent donc, par leur enchaînement, nous fournir une image du fonctionnement de la nature et, puisqu'ils opèrent consciemment, nous donner en même temps le modèle cherché de la science physique. Pour comprendre comment cela est possible, il nous faut revenir en arrière à la parenthèse des lignes 194a35-36, dont nous avions réservé l'examen, et à la remarque qui la précède immédiatement. Là se trouve en effet, pensons-nous, la clé de tout le morceau, comme nous allons tenter de le montrer.

Bien que formulée à propos des techniques du premier niveau, l'idée que nous disposons de ce qui nous entoure comme si c'était là pour nous, est valable évidemment pour toute forme d'art. La parenthèse qui explique ceci renvoie probablement à un traité perdu[27], mais la distinction invoquée entre les deux sens du mot "fin" est familière aux lecteurs d'Aristote[28] : la fin, c'est la chose qu'on se propose de faire, mais c'est aussi l'être au profit duquel la chose est faite. Ce deuxième sens est toujours présent dans l'art humain, note ici Aristote. Et il est évident que la fin prise en ce sens prime et justifie l'autre : quels que soient les objectifs que nous poursuivions ou les produits que nous fabriquions, c'est toujours en dernier ressort pour nous-mêmes , pour notre profit que nous entreprenons d'atteindre ces buts[29]. Cette réflexion nous permet de rapprocher plus étroitement l'art de la nature. Il n'est plus possible, en effet, si l'on en tient compte, d'opposer l'un à l'autre en disant que le mouvement du premier va à produire des objets extérieurs, tandis que la seconde a une fin immanente[30]. Aucun produit de l'art, comme aucune production de la nature, n'a sa fin en lui-même. Ils ne se comprennent l'un et l'autre que rattachés à l'être – homme ou substance naturelle – qui en est à la fois l'origine et la fin (on peut voir là la raison dernière pour laquelle l'utilisateur domine le producteur et lui dicte ses ordres). Mais alors ce n'est pas seulement l'art d'utilisation, c'est aussi l'art de production qui peut être comparé au processus de la nature pour peu que celle-ci suscite ses propres instruments en vue de parvenir à son accomplissement. Or, c'est bien ainsi qu'Aristote se représente les choses, au moins pour ce qui concerne la nature animée. L'être vivant, selon lui, se maintient et s'épanouit dans l'existence en exerçant des fonctions qui nécessitent des organes. Ceux-ci ne lui sont pas donnés tout faits, mais sont en quelque sorte créés par lui au cours de son développement[31]. Un parallèle exact se révèle donc, dans ce cas, entre les opérations de l'art et celles de la nature. La seule différence est que l'ensemble des processus se déroulant au sein d'un seul et même être naturel peut être scindé en tâches variées et confiées à des compétences distinctes s'il s'agit de technique humaine. Mais, justement, le modèle de l'art, parce qu'il s'analyse en techniques diverses et enchaînées, éclaire le point particulier qu'Aristote veut faire comprendre. La compétence particulière du constructeur porte sur les matériaux, celle de l'utilisateur sur la forme, et les deux sont nécessaires pour l'accomplissement de l'œuvre que l'homme s'est proposé. Ainsi également dans la science de la nature, au sein de laquelle des fonctions s'exercent par l'intermédiaire d'organes, la connaissance de la forme, c'est-à-dire de la fin ou fonction, ne suffit pas : celle de la matière dans son rôle de condition nécessaire à la production de l'instrument approprié, se révèle, elle aussi, indispensable.

En dépit des apparences, l'argument que nous avons tenté d'interpréter, forme donc bien un tout cohérent. Il établit d'une manière originale et plus précise qu'on ne le croirait à première vue le rapport que la connaissance de la matière et celle de la forme doivent entretenir dans la science physique. Tout imprégné de réminiscences platoniciennes, il porte néanmoins la marque de l'esprit réaliste d'Aristote.

NOTES

[1] *Phys.*, II 2, 194a15-17.

[2] Avec Ross (Comment., p. 508), nous pensons que le μέχρι του de la ligne 194a23 porte seulement sur τὴν ὕλην et non sur τὸ εἶδος: il est évident que le technicien doit avoir connaissance de la forme à réaliser (fût-ce en recevant cette connaissance d'un autre, comme on le dira plus loin). La connaissance de la matière, en revanche, n'est exigée que pour autant qu'elle est utile à cette réalisation.

[3] 194a21-27.

[4] 194b9.

[5] Voir *De anima*, I 1, 403a29-b16, en particulier 403b2-3.

[6] Selon Hamelin (*Aristote, Physique II, traduction et commentaire*, Paris, 1907, 70), «l'unité et la marche du développement ont échappé aux commentateurs». Thémistius fait commencer un nouvel argument en 194a33; Simplicius et Philopon n'ont pas saisi davantage le lien entre la seconde partie de l'argument, qui commence là, et la première. Tout en nous accordant avec Hamelin sur l'unité et le sens général du passage (exposé pp. 71-72), nous nous éloignons de son interprétation sur un certain nombre de points plus particuliers. Notre lecture du texte, qui se rapproche davantage de celle d' A. Mansion (*Introduction à la Physique Aristotélicienne*, Louvain-Paris 1945, 199-201), ne coïncide cependant pas avec celle-ci.

[7] 194a27-29.

[8] II 1, 193b6-8.

[9] II 2, 194a29-33. Sur ce texte, voir A. Mansion, *op.cit.*, 99 avec la note 9.

[10] 194a33-b8.

[11] On peut songer p. ex., pour le premier cas, à la production d'un alliage de métaux, pour le second, au sciage du bois en planches.

[12] C'est pourquoi les exemples de production et de préparation de la matière cités par Thémistius (*In Phys.*, p. 43, 4-5) et Simplicius (*In Phys.*, p. 303, 4-7) sont à écarter comme trop particuliers et trop liés à la fabrication d'un seul produit fini.

[13] 194a34-35.

[14] 194b2: «la partie architectonique de l'art de production» s'oppose à une autre, qui ne peut être que l'art d'exécution; elle indique les matériaux à employer et les opérations à faire (194b6-7) par les détenteurs de ce dernier.

[15] 194b1. Contre Ross nous préférons garder αἱ devant γνωρίζουσαι avec la «vulgate» (mss EIJ). Les lignes suivantes montrent en effet que l'objet de la connaissance propre à chacun d'eux est différent. Celui-ci n'est donc pas exprimé par τῆς ὕλης, mais laissé dans le vague: «il y a deux arts qui commandent à la matière et qui connaissent».

[16] Peu importe que ce pouvoir sur la matière soit exercé par celui qui le possède ou par d'autres auxquels ce dernier commande (pilote-barreur; constructeur-ouvriers). L'essentiel à remarquer est que chacun des deux types d'art comporte, outre un certain savoir, un pouvoir de faire quelque chose. C'est pourquoi l'utilisateur a autorité sur le fabricant (διὸ καὶ ἡ χρωμένη ἀρχιτεκτονική πως, 194b2-3). Si l'art de la navigation n'était qu'un savoir théorique, le pilote n'aurait pas d'ordres à

donner au constructeur. Mais, parce que cet art se propose comme fin de mener le navire à bon port, celui qui le possède a le droit de formuler ses exigences au maître du chantier naval.

[17] 194b3-5.

[18] 194b5-6.

[19] 194b6-7.

[20] Voir A. Mansion, *op.cit.* 200, note 11, qui cite *Crat.*, 389c. 390b-d, *Rép.*, X 601c-602a et Ross, *op.cit.* 510, qui renvoie à *Crat.* 390d et, pour la dépendance des arts manuels par rapport à un ἀρχιτεκτών, à *Polit.* 259e.

[21] *Rép.* X, 601e7-602a2; cf. *Crat.* 390b1-d3. Aristote dit de même dans la *Politique* (III 4, 1277b28-30) que l'opinion droite suffit au subordonné, tandis que le savoir (*phronèsis*) est la vertu du chef, «car le subordonné est comme le fabricant de flûtes, le chef comme celui qui en joue». Ceci n'exclut cependant pas une compétence réelle du technicien dans la fabrication elle-même. Le *Protreptique* (fr. 4 Walzer) déjà fait état de ces «sciences» subordonnées. Les deux textes sont signalés par A. Mansion, *ibid.*

[22] *Polit.* 259e-260b.

[23] *Polit.* 303d-305e. Le respect pour la compétence du technicien, si limitée soit-elle, est du reste un trait constant et bien connu de Platon (et de Socrate). Cf. p. ex. *Apol.* 22c9-e1.

[24] Le schème usuel du *Politique* pour présenter la relation de l'art politique à ses «parents» (303e9) inférieurs est le rapport commandement-service. Voir 304b-305e.

[25] 194b7-8.

[26] Les interprètes ne comprennent en général pas notre texte dans ce sens. A. Mansion écrit (*op.cit.* 201): «en réalité il n'y a qu'un art, celui qui fait usage des choses, auquel on puisse à bon droit... assimiler 'la science physique', car tous les autres s'occupent de la production ou de l'adaptation de la matière; or dans la nature cette fonction n'a pas d'équivalent, puisque la matière est donnée». Voir dans le même sens le commentaire de Ross *ad loc.* (p.510). Les commentateurs anciens, lorsqu'ils ne passent pas la question sous silence, font à son sujet des considérations peu claires ou peu pertinentes.

[27] Le dialogue περὶ φιλοσοφίας, cf. Ross, *op.cit.* 509.

[28] Ross, *ibid.*, renvoie à *De anima*, II 4, 415b2 et 20, *Métaph.*, Λ 7, 1072b2-3. Pour une étude détaillée de la distinction en question, cf. K. Gaiser, *Das zweifache Telos bei Aristoteles*, dans: *Naturphilosophie bei Aristoteles und Theophrast* (Verh. des 4. Symp. Arist., Göteborg 1966, hrsg. von I. Düring, Heidelberg 1969, 97-113). Bien que notre interprétation de *Phys.* 194a27-b8 s'accorde sur bien des points avec celle de M. Gaiser (o.c. 106-110), on constatera que certaines différences nous séparent néanmoins de cet auteur.

[29] Nous limitons la validité de cette proposition au domaine de la technique, qui nous intéresse seul ici, pour ne pas entrer dans la question beaucoup plus délicate de la possibilité d'une fin transcendante pour notre action prise en général.

[30] Dans les êtres vivants, dit Aristote, tout est orienté vers l'âme comme vers la fin (*De an.*, II 4, 415b15-20).

[31] Epinglons deux textes parmi tous ceux auxquels on pourrait penser: «Puisque le corps est un instrument, – car de même que chacune de ses parties a une finalité, ainsi en est-il du tout, – il doit nécessairement, pour exister, posséder tels et tels caractères et être fait de tels et tels matériaux» (*De part. anim.*, I 1, 642a11-13). «La nature fait les organes pour la fonction et non la fonction pour les organes» (*Ibid.*, IV 12, 694b13-14). En prenant les choses largement, ce schéma s'applique même à la génération proprement dite: les individus nouveaux sont comme les organes du maintien de l'espèce.

MORAL BEHAVIOUR AND TIME
IN ARISTOTLE'S
NICOMACHEAN ETHICS

In the *Nicomachean Ethics* Aristotle does not formally deal with the concept of time and yet he could not avoid to have frequent recourse to it in order to explain some basic topics of his moral treatise, such as ethical knowledge, moral intuition, virtue, friendship and happiness. In Aristotle's view the formal study of time belongs to the philosophy of nature: it is treated in the fourth book of the *Physics* (chapters 10 to 14). This position is quite understandable: time is closely connected with the becoming of the sensible world, without merely coinciding with it. As a matter of fact each change is limited to its subject and takes place where the subject is located, whereas time could not be enclosed within the frontiers of a single being, since it embraces in the same way whatever exists. There is only one time: whatever happens in the universe at the same moment, is necessarily simultaneous. In Aristotle's view several times existing simultaneously make nonsense. Even in the case of a plurality of worlds there will be only one time including all of them[1].

In the opinion of Aristotle however time is not a sheer physical concept, because it always involves consciousness[2]. Time requires a subject which, thanks to the common sense – the basic sensitive faculty – is aware of the sequence, the before and after in the process of becoming; those who, according to the myth, had slept with the heroes in Sardinia, were not conscious of the time that had elapsed; when they awoke, they spontaneously connected the previous period with the moment of their awakening, as if nothing had occurred in the meantime[3].

In the framework of the *Physics*, probably under the influence of Plato, the Aristotelian concept of time is rather pessimistic. Since time is directly connected with the becoming of the sensible world, it is considered a source of instability, decline, passing away, forgetfulness and ignorance. In this context the author mainly emphasizes the ecstatic nature of time, which introduces into our world and into our existence a ceaseless change. In the *Nicomachean Ethics* the appreciation of time is obviously much more positive. How should this new appraisal be explained? Does it mean that Aristotle has already moved further away from the Platonic philosophy, which he adopted at the beginning of his career? I believe we rather have to look at the subject matter of the Ethics. There Aristotle, being concerned with human behaviour, with the progressive attainment of moral knowledge and virtue, discovered the positive value of time as an opportunity of implementing the ideal of human existence.

This explanation becomes even more obvious, if one directs one's attention to the kind of ethical treatise Aristotle has elaborated. In handling the whole range of moral questions, the Stagirite never has recourse to any transcendent being. He rejects the transcendent and everlasting moral standards introduced by Plato in his theory of Ideas, for in Aristotle's view they are quite useless, since they are unable to supply any help or guidance in everyday practical conduct[4]. He never calls on the existence of a Supreme Being, a Pure Act, in order to substantiate moral rules or ethical conduct. Man has to behave as a moral being not because of a divine commandment, but for the sake of the good itself[5]. Finally, moral behaviour is not introduced as a necessary preparation to a life of happiness after death. The question whether the human soul survives after death or not, does not play any role in Aristotle's ethical treatise[6]. Consequently moral life is really enclosed within the boundaries of human existence on earth, and so within the frontiers of an existence in time without any reference or relation to something else. In this perspective, much more importance will be attached to time. When studied as a feature of the physical world, time was held to be a sign of a deficiency and the expression of the unsteadiness of the material beings. When introduced in an ethical context, time becomes a kind of open opportunity or a neutral space in which the perfection of human existence may be achieved. Time is seen as a challenge in which the highest values of man are at stake. In this context, then, time is not primarily a principle of decline and passing away, but a constant call on steady progress and improvement.

At the beginning of his ethical treatise, Aristotle deals with the particular features which are required from a student of Political Science. In his view the young are not fit to study that kind of discipline[7], mainly for two reasons: first, because they lack the indispensable experience of life and human behaviour[8]; second, because in the conduct of their life they are too much influenced by emotions and feelings, and not sufficiently guided by reason and reflection[9]. Let us look more closely at this way of arguing in order to uncover its implications and true

79

meaning: why is experience demanded of a student of Political Science?

Primarily, because such a requirement corresponds to the theory of knowledge as it is exposed in Aristotle's *De anima*, a theory which is in agreement with the doctrine of the soul being the first entelechy or perfection of the body. Hence no human thinking is totally independent of sensible data or experience, not only at the origin of the process but also at each stage of intellectual activity[10]. According to Aristotle, then, our thinking not only derives and springs from experience, but it could never be exerted without reference to sensible data. Intellectual activity is never considered an autonomous, self-sufficient process, but is always maintained and fostered through sensible experience. Moreover, there is a more special argument why ethical knowledge has to rely on experience. Aristotle often compares moral behaviour to medicine or navigation. A doctor or a sailor always has to cope with particular situations or circumstances and each must find a solution with respect to the special context in which he happens to be[11]. Neither doctor nor sailor could have recourse to or rely on merely general rules or patterns, since each situation has a special physiognomy, not interchangeable with any other. The same applies to moral behaviour: all individuals have to display their existence in different contexts, which moreover are constantly changing from one time to another. Aristotle concludes, therefore, that "the agents themselves have to consider what is suited to the circumstances on each occasion"[12].

Nobody could tell what is morally good in all possible circumstances. In his ethical treatise Aristotle does not formulate any general commandment or moral rule; but rather he carefully analyses and describes virtues and vices as they may be observed in the daily life of fourth century Greece. To a certain extent and with a critical mind he relies on traditional moral patterns without stiffening them and making them into universal laws of conduct. In his view the only rule or law of moral behaviour is the *phronimos*, a living individual endowed with ethical intuition, a wise man who by his own experience knows how to behave in the changing context of steadily different situations[13]. If the study of ethics was only concerned with universal moral commandments, able to be applied automatically to all kinds of situations or circumstances, it should be easy, even for the young, to assimilate it. This knowledge becomes difficult when in each particular case one has to find out what is truly valuable, and with a view to that purpose, time is a good inventor or at all events coadjutor[14]. Apparently the last term is more correct than the first one, for properly speaking time does not invent anything, but, as a source of moral experience, is an indispensable coadjutor in order to discover what is valuable in a given context.

Let us come back to the second reason why the young are not fit to study Political Science. According to the Stagirite, in the conduct of their life the young are led by their feelings, so they will study the subject to no purpose or advantage, since the end of this science is not knowledge but action[15]. Does Aristotle intend to say that through the study of ethics the young could possibly get moral knowledge, but could not be educated to moral behaviour? This interpretation would be quite incompatible with Aristotle's conception of moral knowledge, since in his view ethical wisdom and moral behaviour are inseparable[16]. According to the Stoics there is only one virtue, one moral wisdom, which includes all possible aspects of ethical life. It is impossible therefore to have one moral virtue without possessing them all. Aristotle also stresses the unity of moral life without going that far. He agrees that there are several virtues clearly distinguishable from each other; and still they are all closely connected to the point that they could not be separated, provided they are possessed in a perfect degree[17]. Thus it is impossible to be courageous in a perfect way without possessing all other virtues. As to prudence or ethical intuition, it could only exist joined with moral virtue: "The Supreme Good only appears good to the good man; vice perverts the mind and causes it to hold false views about the first principles of conduct. Hence it is clear that we cannot be prudent without being good"[18]. Here again Aristotle is not talking about a set of abstract moral laws, but about a capacity of passing ethical judgments in the variety of situations in which man happens to be. Ethical intuitions could only be warranted through moral behaviour, for otherwise they would be influenced by irrational emotions and feelings and the moral agent would be prevented from grasping what is really to be done in a concrete situation.

Aristotle emphasizes the importance of moral education starting early in life, since without previous education prudence or right moral intuition would be unattainable[19]. Therefore he attaches much value to legislation in a political society. Laws aim at shaping the character of the citizens in order to enable them to pass right moral judgments[20]. Of course, prudence, as well as other virtues, supposes a kind of natural predisposition, called *deinotes*. This state of mind however is not always concerned with right actions. It may be mere astuteness. In order to achieve a firm capacity of passing right ethical judgments, the *deinotès* must be completed by moral virtue[21]. In a chronological and teleological sequence three steps may be distinguished leading to the attainment of prudence: first, a natural

81

ability of choosing appropriate means with a view to a specific goal; second, the practice of ethical actions leading to firm moral habits or virtues preventing our ethical judgments from being distorted through emotional influences; finally, the virtue of prudence, which is not only an occasional but a constant ability of fashioning right moral judgments. In the light of this explanation Aristotle quite obviously has to state that the young are not fit to study Political Science and are not yet ready to elucidate and solve ethical problems, since they lack experience, which comes only over a long space of time.

According to Aristotle, virtue is a settled disposition of the mind determining the choice of actions, ἕξις προαιρετική[22]. Instead of being a temporary or passing capacity, it is a durable or lasting ability of implementing ethical actions, a disposition which is the result of previous repeated acts belonging to the same field[23]. Let us analyse this notion against the background of the Aristotelian Ethics. In his *Politics* the Stagirite points to the fact that man is by nature a political being, able to attain the perfect development of his capacities only in a political society[24]. Two characteristics of man originate this position: first, man is gifted with speech, and so is able to converse with other people, to discourse with them on all possible topics. This means an ability of man not only to transmit some indications or messages, as irrational animals also do, but a capacity of explaining and disclosing what he is talking about[25]. On the other hand, man is endowed with moral sense, especially with the sense of justice[26]. According to the myth of Plato's *Protagoras*, man has received some special gifts springing from the gods: *aidôs* or self-respect and *dikè* or sense of justice. For that very reason he wants to live in a community and to partake with other people in a common moral feeling[27]. In Aristotle's view, man is a moral being, so that ethical progress is far from being something alien, a kind of constraint or a compulsion from outside. On the contrary it corresponds to the very nature of a human being. Speaking about prudence, we already pointed to the importance of the *deinotès*, which though morally neutral, still is a kind of natural predisposition that may be gradually developed into the virtue of prudence. The same applies to each moral and intellectual virtue. All of them require an inborn predisposition making any further improvement possible.

On the other hand, however, moral virtue is not at all the result of an automatic display. It is far more than the outcome of a mechanical process. It is rather the issue of repeated actions, freely chosen by each individual, and the consequence of constant efforts and endeavours. In

82

a word, it is the result of many choices which have been made after conscious deliberation[28]. Thus virtue may be termed a personal attainment, an individual property, belonging intimately to the core of each human being[29]. This theory of Aristotle is very suggestive and must be interpreted in the light of Socratic and Platonic philosophy. The Stagirite opposes Socratic intellectualism as well as Platonic dualism. In Aristotle's view, human action is not merely a consequence of some theoretical knowledge. In a way it is true that man always behaves in agreement with his moral intuition, provided moral judgment is held to be not merely speculative, but practical – not independent of our previous activity, but deeply influenced by it. Our moral judgments are gradually fashioned in a constant symbiosis with our ethical behaviour[30]. Consequently man is responsible not only for what he is doing, but also for what he is thinking. In other words he is responsible for his moral intuitions[31]. Aristotle also opposes Platonic dualism. Our moral behaviour is not shaped by a hidden awareness of ethical values alone, an inborn knowledge which has been awakened through the experience of the sensible world and the dialogue with other people[32]. In Aristotle's opinion, moral knowledge is a real discovery, slowly progressing both through individual experience and the accumulated experience of human society as a whole. Here again the concept of time plays an important part, because there is a progressive discovery of moral values throughout the flowing of history. Aristotle has frequent recourse to prephilosophical moral opinions, as he found them embodied in the culture of his time, in language, proverbs, sentences, myths, religion and literature[33]. He is convinced that human society as a whole, with the help of a large experience going back to the most ancient times, gradually discovers the true meaning of moral values. The growth of moral experience and insight may be noticed not only in the life of each individual, but also in the history of mankind.

Let us now come back to the concept of virtue: moral behaviour springs from settled dispositions which are the result of ethical actions, dispositions which have been gradually acquired through repeated and free initiatives or decisions. Why does Aristotle propose this interpretation of moral behaviour? Three reasons are mentioned for adopting this point of view: first, the agent must act with knowledge, on the basis of personal moral intuition. Here again one has to take into account that right moral insight is unattainable without experience, without ethical practice. As we tried to explain above, what is concerned here is not a theoretical knowledge, but a practical intuition of what is to be done in a particular situation[34]. Second, the agent must deliberately choose the act and choose it for its own sake. In Aristotle's view deliberation takes a lot of time[35]; one must consider different possibilities of behaving and make a choice in the light of his moral knowledge. An action could not get a moral qualification, unless it be the outcome of a free responsible choice, which is far from being an abstract decision. Each choice is in a way linked to all previous options and so a right choice is never unprepared, since it has been induced by a series of preceding decisions, without being mechanically determined by past ethical actions. Moreover in order to be a truly moral choice, the good or valuable must be chosen for its own sake, and not for any other reason. The good must be chosen because of its goodness. Is it possible to find any more fundamental reason why the good must be done? Not in Aristotle's opinion, for doing what is valuable because it is valuable, without any other reference, is the attitude of a truly moral person, and his behaviour does not need any further substantiation[36]. Finally, a moral act must spring from a fixed and permanent disposition of character[37]. Why does Aristotle mention this third requirement? In his view, a real assent to the good for its own sake is only possible if it originates from a permanent disposition or a habit. In other words, a casual moral act is impossible. An ethical action could not be implemented by chance, because it not only implies an external performance, but also an internal attitude. If it was just an incidental act not stemming from a permanent disposition, it would inevitably be influenced by irrational emotions, and so would not be truly moral.

According to Aristotle, there is a kind of survival of our moral actions in the sense that everybody carries with him the burden of his previous acts. When they have been performed, these acts of course belong to the past, but this does not entail that they completely disappeared. After they have been accomplished, they neither fall in a vacuum of nothingness nor are they annihilated. In a way they are still there, influencing our present behaviour. Particularly when actions of the same kind have been often repeated they originate an inclination to behave in the same way, and thus they make it easier than before to implement the same actions. As there is a continuity in time, so there is a continuity in human activity. The past is not simply lost, but is still embodied in the present. In Aristotle's view, to learn something is not to recall previous knowledge, because we learn only by doing the acts we shall have to do: "men become builders by building houses, harpers by playing on the harp. Similarly we become just by doing just acts, temperate by doing temperate acts, brave by doing brave acts"[38]. Hence moral behaviour is not an alteration, since through moral actions man becomes more truly what he really is[39]. Is time merely ecstatic? Not merely: in a way it is ecstatic since it is closely related to the becoming of the world, but on the other hand it is not ecstatic because it provides the opportunity of developing hidden capacities and of becoming more truly oneself. In Aristotle's opinion, nobility or moral beauty is long-lived[40]. Although the utility of a good action passes away for the recipient, for the benefactor the achievement is not lost. It remains and may become a disposition or source of many similar actions. The same applies to friendship, as a virtue or at least as implying virtue. For true friendship requires time and familiarity[41] and while a wish of friendship may arise quickly, friendship itself does not[42]. It needs the gradual development of growing familiarity between men who are good. Otherwise it will not be permanent.

In his investigation concerning the nature of human perfection, or moral excellence, Aristotle again could not disregard the concept of time. The highest level of human happiness is represented by the active exercise of the faculties of the soul and primarily by the activity of the most characteristic faculty of man, the intellect. Thus the most perfect intellectual activity, which coincides with philosophical inquiry and in particular with the reflection of first philosophy, makes up what Aristotle calls εὐδαιμονία or happiness[43]. This definition certainly represents a considerable progress in ancient moral philosophy, for according to the original meaning of the term, eudemony refers to some higher powerful beings (*daimones*) upon whom human happiness or misfortune depends. This etymological signification corresponds to an ancient belief, widespread in the Greek world, according to which the gods are not indifferent towards man, but frequently intervene in his life and to a large extent determine his destiny. Besides, the Greeks largely accepted that human existence is dominated by the decisions of blind fate. As is clearly shown by the subjects treated in tragedies, people, without being formally guilty, are stricken with horrible blows. Apparently Aristotle has demythologized the ancient concept of eudemony. Well-being does not depend any more upon the goodwill of higher powers but must be implemented by each individual as a personal duty. In Aristotle's view the exercise of philosophical inquiry depends only upon man's ability and dedication. On the other hand one swallow does not make Spring. It would be meaningless to call somebody happy, because he exercised the highest intellectual activity during a short period. In Aristotle's view, one has to take into account the whole lifetime[44]. A man will only deserve

85

to be called happy when during his whole life he has devoted himself to the highest philosophical research[45]. Why does Aristotle emphasize this temporal dimension of eudemony? Two reasons may be put forward: first, contemplation is the most continuous of all human actions: we can reflect more continuously than we can carry on any form of action[46]. Second, human activity in general, including contemplation, becomes more perfect by being exercised, and a brief period of contemplation could not terminate in an intellectual habit or a permanent disposition whereas a philosophical investigation exerted during a whole lifetime will lead to the most perfect display of the highest human activity. According to the *Physics*, time is mainly a principle of ignorance and forgetfulness. In the perspective of human eudemony, one could hardly deny time to be a very positive factor of progress, improvement and development.

The conclusion of this paper may be summarized in the following way:
1. The concept of time as it is exposed in the fourth book of the *Physics* ought to be completed and corrected in a more positive way when applied to ethical activity. In this perspective time is not primarily a principle of decline, ignorance, forgetfulness and passing away. It does not push man outside himself, but provides him with the opportunity of attaining his true perfection.
2. Lack of time prevents the young from being able to study political science, because lack of time entails both deficiency of experience and deficiency of practice.
3. In the framework of the Aristotelian ethics, time is an indispensable condition with a view to moral experience, ethical knowledge, the habit of virtue and the performance of the highest ideal of human perfection.
4. The value of moral behaviour does not depend on an existence beyond time, a survival of the soul after death. Moral acts ought to be implemented not to avoid divine punishment, but simply for their own sake, for their goodness without reference to anything else. The meaning of ethical conduct must be found within the frontiers of a temporal existence.
5. Moral life is not ruled by everlasting commandments or norms; it is neither governed nor directed by ideal values that belong to a transcendent world, without being subject to temporal change. All moral values are shaped within the framework of changing circumstances, closely connected with varying temporal situations.

[1] Cf. G. Verbeke, *Le statut ontologique du temps selon quelques penseurs grecs*, in: *Zetesis. Bijdragen op het gebied van de Klassieke Filologie, Filosofie, Byzantinistiek, Patrologie en Theologie*. Antwerpen-Utrecht, (s.d.), 188-205.

[2] In his *De part. an.* (I,1, 641a32 sq.) Aristotle deals formally with the question whether the study of the soul belongs entirely to physics. In fact, his treatise *De anima* is to be counted among the physical works, meaning, at any rate, that the study of the soul, generally speaking, pertains to the province of the physicist, without excluding, however, the possibility that some souls are to be put on a higher level. In the *De part. an.* Aristotle maintains that not every soul belongs totally to the domain of physics. His answer is obviously based on a criterion he explained at the beginning of the *De Anima* (I,1, 403a3 sq.): when he asked the question whether any human activity, more particularly intellectual knowledge, is quite independent of the body. In other words what is at issue is to know to what extent the activity of mind relies on sense experience. If any activity of the human mind does not depend totally on sense perception, then the soul of man transcends the level of physics.

[3] *Phys.* IV,11, 218b21-29. Cf. G. Verbeke, *art. cit.* 190-191.

[4] Cf. G. Verbeke, *La critique des Idées dans l'Éthique Eudémienne*, in: *Untersuchungen zur Eudemischen Ethik*, hrsg. P. Moraux u. D. Harlfinger. Berlin 1971, 135-156.

[5] *Eth. Nic.* VI,2, 1139b3; VI,5, 1140b7: ἔστι γὰρ αὐτὴ ἡ εὐπραξία τέλος. – *Eth. Eud.* VIII,3, 1149b13: "For God is not a ruler in the sense of issuing commands" (transl. Rackham).

[6] Cf. G. Verbeke, *L'idéal de la perfection humaine chez Aristote et l'évolution de sa noétique*, in: *Fontes Ambrosiani*, XXV, *Miscellanea G. Galbiati*, Vol. I, 1951, 79-95.

[7] *Eth. Nic.* I,3, 1095a2: διὸ τῆς πολιτικῆς οὐκ ἔστιν οἰκεῖος ἀκροατὴς ὁ νέος. – In this respect one may recall the educational scheme proposed by Plato: practical training in ruling the state starts at the age of 35, after the study of mathematics and dialectics, whereas the responsibility of governing the city may only be entrusted to people who, after they had been educated in an appropriate way, have reached at least the age of 50. Both Plato and Aristotle are convinced that the young are not endowed with *phronesis* or practical wisdom (*Eth. Nic.* VI,8, 1142a13; VI,12, 1143b11-14). They may become outstanding mathematicians, or be very fit to study geometry, but they are unable to acquire moral intuition, since this kind of knowledge deals constantly with individual cases and particular situations. In Aristotle's view, the way in which man ought to behave has not been settled once and for all: it has to be disclosed, or rather invented, day by day in the complexity of a changing world: the young are not able to disentangle intricate situations and to discover proper conduct in individual cases because experience always requires a long expanse of time (*Eth. Nic.* VI,8, 1142a15.)

[8] *Eth. Nic.* I,3, 1095a3; VI,8, 1142a15.

[9] *Eth. Nic.* I,3, 1095a4. Aristotle distinguishes two groups of young people – those who are young in age, and those who are young in character, – but this makes no difference with respect to the question under consideration. What is needed for the study of ethics is a sufficient maturity, that may be lacking even among people who are old enough to possess it. If someone lives according to his emotions and pursues whatever he likes, he misses the maturity which is required for a fruitful study of political philosophy. With regard to this latter case, the question may be asked whether a change of mind could be produced by the study of ethics. Aristotle does not envisage this possibility, since the sense of moral values always presupposes ethical behaviour (cf. J. D. Monan, *Moral*

Knowledge and its Methodology in Aristotle. Oxford, 1968, 78 sq.) That is the reason why moral education should start very early in life; when a stone has been dropped, it is no longer possible to bring it back (*Eth. Nic.* III,5, 1114a17).

10 Several passages in the *De anima* emphasize this important Aristotelian doctrine: III,7, 431b2; III,8, 432a7-9; III,8, 432a13-14. Our intelligible objects are never separated from their origin: the mind always understands them and grasps them in the data of sense experience (ἐν τοῖς φαντάσμασι νοεῖ). In the process of knowing, Aristotle does not discern two separate stages: the first being sense perception, the second intellectual abstraction. Such a theory would still imply a hidden dualism, since sensation and understanding would be separate activities performed by different powers and belonging to a different level of our psychic life. In Aristotle's view, sense perception is not a preliminary step leading to intellectual abstraction as a later stage: our knowing is at the same time sensitive and intellectual, since ideas are always comprehended within sense data. This doctrine also applies to the intuition of values: even moral values are seized only within the framework of sense experience. Trying to explain the nature of moral perfection, Aristotle starts from something familiar and visible: the body with its states of health and disease. The health of the body is parallel with ethical excellence. So the Stagirite is able to disclose the unknown, setting out from what is known to us (cf. Th. Tracy, *Physiological Theory and the Doctrine of the Mean in Plato and Aristotle*. Chicago 1969, 225).

11 *Eth. Nic.* II,2, 1104a8. Cf. I,6, 1097a8-14; *Eth. Eud.* I,8, 1218b1 sq. The same doctrine may be found at the beginning of the *Metaphysics* (I,1, 981a12sq.) where the different levels of knowledge are studied: "With a view to action experience seems in no respect inferior to art, and men of experience succeed even better than those who have theory without experience. (The reason is that experience is knowledge of individuals, art of universals, and actions and productions are all concerned with the individual...)" (transl. W. D. Ross).

12 *Eth. Nic.* II,2, 1104a8. From an Aristotelian viewpoint, the scientific level of a discipline is closely related to the nature of the object to be studied: if an object is immutable and uncomposed, the science concerned with it will attain the highest degree of accuracy; on the contrary, if the subject matter of a discipline is inserted in our world of becoming and presents a complex structure, the study of it could not reach the same degree of scientific precision. Consequently, moral philosophy could not be put on the same level as metaphysics nor even as physics, since it always has to cope with individual cases that are never exactly the same. Does it mean that the study of values or norms is useless? Certainly not, provided the norms are applied to individual cases with the help of experience. In Aristotle's view each individual pertains to a species and it has the same intelligible structure as the other members of the group; from a logical viewpoint, the individual features of a being refer to the accidental order. If we have to deal with individual cases, they will present the same essential pattern as the other cases of the same nature, although they will differ from each other in some accidental characteristics. Consequently, the knowledge of both elements, the essential structure and the individual characteristics, is necessary: this latter knowledge could only be supplied by experience, whereas the first also relies on the investigation of particular cases, leading to universal insight.

13 It is certainly noticeable that this viewpoint is already adopted in the *Protrepticus* (fr. 5, p.33 Ross): "Again, what standard, what determinant, of what is good have we, other than the man of practical wisdom? (πλὴν ὁ φρόνιμος)" The *phronimos* is a moral standard indeed not only for himself, but also for other people: because of his ethical behaviour and experience, he is endowed with moral intuition; he is able to disclose what is truly good for man in the complexity of

88

ceaselessly changing situations. For that very reason the *phronimos* is mentioned in the definition of virtue: he has to determine the mean relative to us, in which ethical virtue essentially lies, and he is able to do it in an appropriate fashion since his mind is not clouded by irrational movements or emotions (*Eth. Nic.* II,6, 1106b36-1107a2).

14 *Eth. Nic.* I,7, 1098a23: in this passage Aristotle is referring to his own investigation concerning human perfection. He is quite aware of the fact that he has sketched only a rough outline: others will have to pursue the inquiry he launched. With respect to this further development, Aristotle adds, time will be a good inventor (εὑρετής) or at least a coadjutor (συνεργός). The Stagirite is not referring here to the progress of moral intuition in an individual, but to the evolution of ethical knowledge throughout history: in his view, the development of moral philosophy keeps pace with the evolution of the arts. It is not only a performance of some privileged individuals, everybody has to contribute to the advancement of truth (I,7, 1098a25; *Eth. Eud.* I,6, 1216b30: ἔχει γὰρ ἕκαστος οἰκεῖόν τι πρὸς τὴν ἀλήθειαν). Thus the progress of moral philosophy is at least partly the work of time, since the development of time entails an increase of individual contributions to the knowledge of moral values, and also a growth of ethical experience of human society as a whole.

15 *Eth. Nic.* I,3, 1095a3-6.

16 *Eth. Nic.* VI,12, 1144a34. Cf. III,5, 1114a31 sq.; III,5, 1114b22-24.

17 J. R. Moncho, *La unidad de la vida moral según Aristóteles*. Valencia 1972, Cap. IV: La connexión general de las virtudes y su fundamento, 150-187.

18 *Eth. Nic.* VI,12, 1144a34.

19 *Eth. Nic.* II,1, 1103b23-25.

20 *Eth. Nic.* X,9, 1179b29 sq. Cf. II,1, 1103b2-6.

21 *Eth. Nic.* VI,12, 1144a23 sq. In Aristotle's view, practical wisdom is not the same as *deinotes*, but it could not exist without this natural predisposition. Is everybody gifted with this inborn capacity? It is hard to answer this question. Everybody can afford his own contribution to the advancement of truth, but, on the other hand, the Stagirite maintains that some people are slaves by nature (*Pol.* I,5, 1255a1-3). Does it mean that those who are rightly slaves are deprived of reason? Not exactly; they are gifted with reason to the extent that they are able to perceive and follow the instructions issued by others: they are unable to be their own guide (*Pol.* I,5, 1254b20 sq.). Thus everybody insofar as he is endowed with reason and participates in ethical life is able to promote moral knowledge.

22 *Eth. Nic.* II,6, 1106b36.

23 *Eth. Nic.* II,1, 1103a31-1103b1: ἃ γὰρ δεῖ μαθόντες ποιεῖν, ταῦτα ποιοῦντες μανθάνομεν.

24 *Pol.* I,2, 1253a2 sq.

25 *Pol.* I,2, 1253a9sq.

26 *Pol.* I,2, 1253a15 sq.

27 *Protagoras* 320c-322d.

28 Cf. *De anima,* III,10, 433b5 sq. Deliberation is necessary, since inevitable conflicts arise between reason and desires; this is to be connected with our sense of time: «For while mind bids us to hold back because of what is future, desire is influenced by what is just at hand: a pleasant object which is just at hand presents itself as both pleasant and good, without condition in either case, because of want of foresight into what is farther away in time" (transl. J. A. Smith). Without sense of the future, man would always stick to his present desires.

29 *Eth. Nic.* III,5, 1113b6.

30 *Eth. Nic.* VI,13, 1144b17 sq.

[31] *Eth. Nic.* III,5, 1114b3: καὶ τῆς φαντασίας ἔσται πως αὐτὸς αἴτιος. – Moral value judgements are deeply influenced by our habits, which in their turn are the outcome of previous behaviour. Thus indirectly ethical valuations are in the power of each individual.

[32] Cf. G. Verbeke, *La critique des Idées dans l'Ethique Eudémienne*, 143 sq.

[33] Cf. G. Verbeke, *Philosophie et conceptions préphilosophiques chez Aristote*, in: Rev. Philos. de Louvain 59 (1961), 405-430.

[34] In Aristotle's view a choice is made μέτα λόγου καὶ διανοίας (*Eth. Nic.* III,2, 1112a15). Quite in agreement with his doctrine of moral knowledge, the Stagirite asserts that an individual may be responsible for his own ignorance (*Eth. Nic.* III,5, 1113b30).

[35] *Eth. Nic.* VI,9, 1142b3: βουλεύονται δὲ πολὺν χρόνον.

[36] *Eth. Nic.* VI,5, 1140b7; VI,2, 1039b3.

[37] *Eth. Nic.* VI,2, 1139a33.

[38] *Eth. Nic.* II,1, 1103a30 sq.

[39] *Phys.* VII,3, 246b21. Cf. G. Verbeke, *The Aristotelian Doctrine of Qualitative Change in Physics VII, 3*, in: *Essays in Ancient Greek Philosophy*, ed. J. P. Anton and G. L. Kustas, Albany N.Y. 1971, 546-565.

[40] *Eth. Nic.* IX,7, 1068a16.

[41] *Eth. Nic.* VIII,3, 1156b25.

[42] *Eth. Nic.* VIII,3, 1156b31.

[43] *Eth. Nic.* I,7, 1098a16-18.

[44] *Eth. Nic.* I,7, 1098a18-20.

[45] *Eth. Nic.* X,7, 1177b25.

[46] *Eth. Nic.* X,7, 1177a21.

PHRONESIS UND SOPHIA
IN DER NICOMACH.
ETHIK DES ARISTOTELES

OLOF GIGON

Wir wissen heute, dass das Denken Platons schon seit dem *Laches* und *Charmides* als eine dauernde Spannung zwischen einem aporetischen sokratischen und einem entschieden systematischen Moment zu verstehen ist; der Ansatzpunkt der Systematik ist die Tradition der eleatischen Philosophie, die Platon zunächst durch Sophistik und älteste Sokratik vermittelt entgegentrat und mit der er sich später unmittelbar auseinandersetzte.

Wir wissen weiterhin, dass für das Bild des Aristoteles als eines starren Systematikers wesentlich jene Jahrhunderte verantwortlich sind, die das Organon systematisch interpretierten und das so interpretierte Organon als seine eigentliche philosophische Leistung auffassten. Wir werden heute als Charakteristikum der grossen Pragmatien gerade nicht die Systematik, sondern vielmehr das unablässige Experimentieren empfinden. Die gegebenen Probleme sucht er bald mit der einen, bald mit einer anderen Lösung zu bewältigen. Es gibt nur wenige Doktrinen, die er durch sein ganzes Oeuvre hindurch unverändert festgehalten hat (negativ etwa die Ablehnung der platonischen Ideenlehre, positiv etwa die Lehre von der Ewigkeit der Welt); und wenn die systematische Absicht vor allem an kompakten Begriffsreihen abgelesen werden kann (Musterbeispiele sind die vier Stufen des Erkennens, die fünf Elemente oder die vier Kardinaltugenden), so lässt sich zwar aus den Pragmatien eine ansehnliche Liste solcher Reihen gewinnen, doch die Untersuchung hält sich meist nur für kurze Zeit bei solchen Reihen auf, und manche der Reihen sind in sich selbst problematisch und verraten in ihrer Struktur, dass sie lediglich das Resultat eines Kompromisses sind. Von einer solchen Reihe soll hier die Rede sein.

Das sechste Buch der *Nik. Ethik* bietet in 1139b15-17 eine Liste von fünf Erkenntnisweisen, in denen ἀληθεύει ἡ ψυχή. Es sind in der Reihenfolge unseres Textes *Techne, Episteme, Phronesis, Sophia* und *Noûs*[1]. Dass diese Folge die systematische Zusammengehörigkeit der verschiedenen Weisen missachtet, zeigt sich auf den ersten Blick. Techne und

Phronesis gehören zusammen als die zwei Weisen des Umgangs mit dem veränderlichen und veränderbaren Sein, wobei die Techne das Herstellen, die Phronesis das Handeln meint. Die verbleibenden drei Weisen sind der Theoria zugeordnet; aber da taucht eine unübersehbare und absonderliche Schwierigkeit auf. Was die Episteme ist, erläutert 1139b18-36, und was der Noûs ist, teilt uns in ebenso summarischer wie umständlicher Formulierung 1140b31-1141a8 mit. Die Episteme ist das aus gegebenen Voraussetzungen zwingend folgende Wissen; der Noûs ist das Wissen der letzten Voraussetzungen selbst, deren Richtigkeit nicht zwingend gefolgert, sondern nur unmittelbar eingesehen werden kann. Es handelt sich also um zwei eindeutig unterscheidbare Erkenntnisweisen, die eine der platonischen διάνοια entsprechend, die ἐξ ὑποθέσεων arbeitet, die andere dem νοῦς, der die Anschauung des ἀνυπόθετον hat (Plat. *Rep.* 509d-511e).

Was aber leistet die Sophia? Sie ist, wie Aristoteles unbedenklich erklärt, lediglich der Oberbegriff über Episteme und Noûs (1141a1-3, expliziert durch 1141a16-20). Sie fällt also evident aus der Reihe der fünf Erkenntnisweisen heraus, da sie als einzige gegenüber den vier anderen weder einen eigentümlichen Gegenstand noch eine spezifische Erkenntnishaltung besitzt. Wir sind gezwungen zu schliessen, dass sie nicht ursprünglich der Reihe zugehört, sondern von Aristoteles aus einem besonderen Grunde angehängt worden ist.

Wir müssen demnach den gesamten fraglichen Text etwas genauer untersuchen. Ueber Episteme (1139b18-37) und Techne (1140a1-23) können wir rasch hinweggehen; wir werden nur den Hinweis auf die Exoterikoi logoi beachten (dass ich immer noch der Interpretation, die W. Jaeger nach anderen von diesem Begriff gegeben hat, den Vorzug gebe vor den unwahrscheinlich gewaltsamen Auslegungen F. Dirlmeiers oder gar W. Wielands[2], merke ich nur beiläufig an) und konstatieren, dass 1140a17-20 eine nachträgliche Einlage ist, augenscheinlich dem Komplex Tyche-Eutychia entnommen, der bei Aristoteles in weiter Streuung zu fassen ist und einmal eine intensive monographische Behandlung verdiente, die auch den Ausblick auf Theophrast und schliesslich sogar Demetrios v. Phaleron Frg. 79-81 W. nicht verschmähte.

Beim Abschnitt über die Phronesis dagegen müssen wir stutzig werden. Von der Phronesis wird sofort auf die Person des Phronimos zurückgegangen; in der Ethik des Aristoteles begegnet dieses Verfahren nicht selten, – seine prinzipielle Bedeutung ist hier nicht zu diskutieren. Der Phronimos wird durch zwei Dinge charakterisiert: erstens vermag er τὰ αὑτῷ ἀγαθὰ καὶ συμφέροντα gut zu planen, und zweitens betrifft dieses

92

Planen nicht einen begrenzten Sektor des Lebens, sondern τὸ εὖ ζῆν ὅλως.

Was den ersten Punkt betrifft, so überrascht es, wie eindeutig die Phronesis auf den persönlichen Nutzen des Phronimos selbst bezogen wird; und was den zweiten Punkt angeht, so wird der aufmerksame Leser konstatieren, dass zwei Antithesen nicht sehr übersichtlich mit einander kombiniert sind. Um es kurz zu sagen: die eine Antithese ist diejenige zwischen μέρος und ὅλον, die andere diejenige zwischen dem blossen ζῆν und dem εὖ ζῆν. Von der Sache her ist die erste Antithese die ursprünglichere. Die Phronesis hat es in der Tat, im Gegensatz zur Techne, nicht mit partikularen Aufgaben zu tun, sondern mit der Gestaltung des Lebens im ganzen (mutatis mutandis darf man *Pol.* 1254a5-8 vergleichen).

Der nachfolgende Text ist unproblematisch bis 1140b5-11. Da wird als Beispiel eines Phronimos Perikles "und seinesgleichen" genannt, und zwar, weil diese Menschen fähig sind, das "für sie selbst" und für die Menschen Gute ins Auge zu fassen; dies sind die Oikonomikoi und Politikoi. Wiederum muss es auffallen, wie sehr es zum Phronimos gehört "für sich selbst" zu sorgen. Von 1140b11 an fehlt es zwar nicht an Härten im Text, doch berühren sie unsere besondere Schwierigkeit nicht. Wir halten nur den Eindruck fest, dass das gesamte Kapitel über die Phronesis zwei verschiedene Bedeutungen dieses Begriffs im Auge hat. Zur Hauptsache wird die Phronesis im Hinblick auf ihre Aufgabe ganz allgemein beschrieben, und zwar so, dass ihre Abgrenzung von der Techne auf der einen, von der Episteme auf der andern Seite deutlich wird. Dazu kommen die zwei Stellen, die ich heraushob, und an denen nicht nur das betonte αὐτῷ bzw. αὐτοῖς bemerkenswert ist, sondern auch der Hinweis, dass die Phronesis die besondere Qualität der Oikonomikoi und Politikoi ist. Die Dinge klären sich in dem entscheidenden Abschnitt 1141a20-b8.

Es gehen voraus zehn Zeilen über die Sophia. Im allgemeinen Sprachgebrauch ist sie zunächst ἀρετὴ τέχνης, woraus Aristoteles entnimmt, dass ihrem Begriff formal ein Maximum an ἀκρίβεια eigentümlich ist. In äusserster Knappheit wird zweitens anhand eines Zitates aus dem *Margites* (es kehrt nur noch bei Clem. Alex. *Strom.* I, 25, 1 wieder, nicht aus unserer Stelle, wohl aber aus einem sehr nahe verwandten Zusammenhang) festgestellt, dass es auch einen Begriff des σοφός gebe, der nicht auf eine Qualität κατὰ μέρος ziele, sondern ὅλως gemeint sei. Dies genügt dem Verfasser, um nun zu folgern: Philosophisch muss die σοφία (1) die ἀκριβεστάτη τῶν ἐπιστημῶν sein und (2) die Totalität von Episteme und Noûs umfassen. Sie wird auf diese Weise rangmässig die Episteme der τιμιώτατα. Die reichlich unbestimmt formulierte Metapher ὥσπερ κεφαλὴν ἔχουσα mag auf irgendeine Weise mit dem platonischen Gedanken zusammenhängen, dass eben die Philosophie ihren Sitz im Kopfe des Menschen hat (*Tim.* 91E).

Danach geraten wir auf eine unerwartete und polemisch getönte Erwägung. Es wird plötzlich mit der These gerechnet, es sei (nicht die Sophia, sondern) die πολιτική oder die Phronesis (die zwei Dinge rücken also wie in 1140b7-11 eng zusammen) als die höchste Erkenntnisweise anzusehen. Diese These sei nur vertretbar, wenn man gleichzeitig behaupten wolle, der Mensch sei τὸ ἄριστον τῶν ἐν τῷ κόσμῳ. Damit kommt ein neues Element in die Debatte: Im Aufbau des Kosmos wird die Phronesis in den menschlichen Bereich verwiesen, während die Sophia einem höheren Bereich zugeordnet ist. Gewiss war eine derartige Stufung schon in 1139b22-24 vorbereitet; doch war dort der Gegensatz zwischen dem Ewigen und dem Veränderlichen ontologisch akzentuiert, während er hier kosmologisch gemeint ist. Die Sophia ist, um es pointiert zu sagen, nicht allein durch ἀκρίβεια ausgezeichnet und dadurch, dass sie die Gesamtheit der theoretischen Erkenntnis umfasst, sondern auch dadurch, dass ihr Forschungsgegenstand die höhere, göttliche, supralunare Region des Kosmos ist.

Der Gedanke wird freilich nicht weiter verfolgt. 1141a22-28 steht vielmehr 1140a25-28 nahe. Der Unterschied zwischen Sophia und Phronesis zeigt sich darin, dass der Gegenstand der einen immer und überall derselbe ist, derjenige der anderen dagegen immer wieder ein anderer; die Phronesis verfolgt ja den jeweiligen Nutzen des Phronimos selbst.

Der Abschnitt beginnt mit einer für Aristoteles ungewöhnlichen Gegenüberstellung von Mensch und Fisch, bzw. des ὑγιεινὸν καὶ ἀγαθόν hier, des λευκὸν καὶ εὐθύ dort. Wir verstehen, dass den Kategorien des Nützlichen zwei Kategorien der theoretischen Erkenntnis (das Weisse die ὄψις, das Gerade die geometrische Episteme betreffend) konfrontiert werden, werden es aber doch etwas sonderbar nennen, dass für die Wahrnehmung des Weissen und das Erkennen der geraden Linie neben dem Menschen auch der Fisch in Anspruch genommen wird; die Vermutung, dass Aristoteles mit einer Reminiszenz aus Heraklit *VS* 22B61 spielt, drängt sich auf.

Es folgt eine allgemeine Feststellung, wo das περὶ αὐτό auf 1140a26 und b9 zurückverweist. Dann kommen wir zurück zu den Tieren, die Phronimoi heissen, weil sie περὶ τὸν αὐτῶν βίον vorzusorgen vermögen. Dass an Ameisen, Bienen usw. gedacht wird, ist deutlich; nur an Fische hat Aristoteles ganz bestimmt nicht gedacht.

1141a28-33 wirkt wie eine Variante des Vorangehenden. Abermals gilt es als Phronesis, τὰ ὠφέλιμα τὰ αὐτοῖς zu bedenken, woraus folgt, dass es

94

ebenso viele Arten der Phronesis gibt wie Interessen der Lebewesen (ἀπάντων... τῶν ζῴων, in der nächsten Zeile mit arger Flüchtigkeit durch πάντων τῶν ὄντων aufgenommen). Im Gegensatz dazu gibt es nur eine einzige Sophia.

1141a33-b2 kehrt zu 1141a20-22 zurück. In nicht sehr klarer Verknüpfung mit dem unmittelbar Vorausgehenden wird zuerst gesagt, der Mensch sei zwar unter den (irdischen) Lebewesen das βέλτιστον; doch über dem Menschen stehen noch andere göttlichere Wesen. Als Beispiel werden, einmal mehr in höchst unsauberer Formulierung, genannt die φανερώτατα ἐξ ὧν ὁ κόσμος συνέστηκεν. Damit können nur die sichtbaren Götter der supralunaren Welt gemeint sein. κόσμος ist offenbar Aequivalent zu οὐρανός. Wieder sollen wir wie bei 1141a20-22 entnehmen, dass die Sophia eben diesem Bereich zugewandt ist und von ihm her ihre Dignität erhält.

1141b2-3 gibt sich als Conclusio, parallel zu 1141a18-20. Etwas hart wirkt es, dass an dieser Stelle, an der die Bindung der Sophia an den supralunaren Raum als an ihren Gegenstand herausgearbeitet ist, noch einmal die Aufteilung in Episteme und Noûs in Erinnerung gerufen wird, eine Aufteilung, die als solche der reinen Wissenschaftstheorie angehört; da sind sehr verschiedene Perspektiven zusammengeschoben.

Fragen wir, welche Argumente der Text für den Rang der Sophia geltend gemacht hat, so gewinnen wir nicht mehr als zwei. Erstens: Wenn die Phronesis eine ausschliesslich mit dem Menschen befasste Erkenntnisweise ist (was schon 1140b5 und 9 andeutete), so muss auch eine Erkenntnisweise vorhanden sein, die auf den übermenschlichen Bereich gerichtet ist. Zweitens: Während die Gehalte der Phronesis immer wieder andere sind, ist die Sophia stetsfort eine und dieselbe.

Dieser Gegensatz expliziert sich nun vollends in 1141b3-8. Die Phronesis ist wandelbar, weil sie den Nutzen für den Phronimos sucht; die Sophia ist unveränderlich, weil sie eben diesen Nutzen nicht sucht. Die σοφοί kennen nicht τὰ συμφέροντα ἑαυτοῖς. Ihr Wissen ist nutzlos, weil sie nicht nach den ἀνθρώπινα ἀγαθά streben.

Diese Feststellungen haben augenscheinlich nicht die Absicht, deskriptiv die verschiedenen Erkenntnisweisen von einander abzugrenzen. Ihr Ziel ist vielmehr, die Sophia der Phronesis so überzuordnen, wie eben der Umgang mit den göttlichen Dingen der Planung des menschlichen Lebens übergeordnet ist.

Ich glaube nicht fehlzugehen mit der Hypothese, dass Aristoteles in ein erstes Schema, das Techne, Phronesis, Episteme und Noûs aus gleichmässiger Distanz und unter wesentlich wissenschaftstheoretischem Aspekt charakterisierte, ein zweites Schema eingearbeitet hat, das thematisch auf eine Empfehlung der Sophia hinsteuert. Der Text, in dem dieses Schema vor allem zu Tage tritt, 1141a20-b2, ist, wie wir sahen, schlecht formuliert, anspruchsvoll und gleichzeitig flüchtig. Es liegt nahe, ihn als nachlässige Zusammenfassung einer viel sorgfältiger und reicher ausgebauten Diskussion zu verstehen. Er ist etwa auch (neben dem schon Gesagten) auf den Gedanken hin angelegt, dass der Mensch durch die Sophia mit übermenschlichen, göttlichen Dingen in Beziehung steht, durch die Phronesis aber mit dem Tiere verbunden ist, sofern einige Tiere geradezu φρόνιμοι genannt werden können; freilich ist von dieser Stellung des Menschen zwischen Gott und Tier in der Mitte nirgends ausdrücklich die Rede.

Der Befund gestattet indessen einen letzten Schritt zu wagen. Aristoteles hat, wie allbekannt, auch Dialoge geschrieben. Die Adressaten der Dialoge waren andere als diejenigen der uns erhaltenen Pragmatien. Aristoteles ist jedoch nicht schizophren gewesen, und wir haben keinen Grund anzunehmen, dass er seine linke Hand prinzipiell nicht wissen liess, was die rechte tat. Konkret bedeutet dies zweierlei. Einmal darf angenommen werden, dass er zwar nicht voraussetzte, die Leser der Dialoge seien auch über den Inhalt der Pragmatien (die in der Auseinandersetzung mit Spezialisten entstanden und für Spezialisten niedergeschrieben waren) informiert, dass er aber unzweifelhaft damit rechnete, dass die Spezialisten auch seine Dialoge lasen; und da in den Dialogen nur bestimmte ausgewählte Problemkreise zur Sprache kamen (man kann sie teilweise an den Titeln ablesen: zentrale philosophische Fragen, Abgrenzungen gegen andere Doktrinen, vor allem diejenigen Platons, endlich einige Probleme der praktischen Lebensführung einerseits, der allgemeinen Bildung andererseits), so ist zu erwarten, dass er eben diese Problemkreise in den Pragmatien verhältnismässig knapp abgehandelt hat. Genauer, und dies ist unser zweiter Punkt: Wo Aristoteles in den Pragmatien eben jene Dinge zu erörtern hatte, die in den Dialogen ausgebreitet waren, hat er mit aller Wahrscheinlichkeit seine eigenen Dialoge benutzt und deren Formulierungen in der Verkürzung übernommen, die ihm zweckdienlich schien. Dies hat schon Werner Jaeger im Prinzip richtig gesehen, so anfechtbar auch seine Folgerungen im einzelnen sein mögen (vgl. etwa: *Aristoteles* 1923, 68 ff.). Es ist absonderlich genug, dass die spätere Forschung auf diesem Wege nicht nur nicht weitergeschritten ist, sondern geradezu ängstlich bemüht war, sich jeden Weg, der vielleicht zu einer genaueren Vorstellung vom Inhalt der Dialoge hätte führen können, systematisch zu verbauen.

Uns dagegen scheint es nahezu selbstverständlich, dass die Pragmatien auf die Dialoge Rücksicht genommen und dort, wo es angezeigt war, deren Gesichtspunkte und Formulierungen in der geeigneten Abbreviatur rezipiert haben[3].

Ein derartiger Fall dürfte hier vorliegen. Die Gegenüberstellung von Phronesis und Sophia, dazu die Wesensbeschreibung und das Lob der Sophia stammt aus einem Dialoge. Aristoteles wollte diesen Komplex hier aufnehmen, was allerdings dazu führte, dass die homogene Reihe Techne-Phronesis-Episteme-Noûs um ein fünftes Glied erweitert wurde, das augenscheinlich anders strukturiert war als die übrigen; ausserdem drangen in die Beschreibung der Phronesis einzelne Momente ein, die dem ursprünglichen Entwurf, in welchem die Phronesis zur Hauptsache ein Gegenstück zur Techne war, fremd waren.

Nun werden in der Tat für die Distinktion von ποίησις und πρᾶξις die Exoterikoi Logoi zitiert; dies ist, wie schon bemerkt, für den Leser ein Hinweis darauf, dass er in einem Dialog genauere Informationen über den Punkt finden könne. Methodisch werden wir indessen gut daran tun, dieses Zitat von unserem Textkomplex zu trennen. Denn unserem Text liegt es gerade nicht bloss an der begrifflichen Distinktion von Phronesis und Sophia, sondern am Lob der Sophia und einer spürbaren Entwertung der Phronesis. Allgemein gesehen dürften sich als Ursprungsort eines solchen Textes zwei Dialoge anbieten.

Das erste wäre der *Protreptikos*, der zwar formal kein Dialog war, sondern ein Sendschreiben an König Themison von Zypern. Sein Thema ist unzweifelhaft eine Empfehlung der Philosophie. Ich will hier nicht auf die leidige Frage eingehen, in welchem Umfang Iamblich *Protr.* p.34, 5-61, 4 Pist. aus jenem Sendschreiben exzerpiert ist, sondern beschränke mich darauf, einen methodischen Gesichtspunkt zu nennen, der in der umfangreichen Literatur über den *Protreptikos* in der Regel viel zu wenig beachtet wird. Der aristotelische *Protreptikos* richtet sich nicht an beliebige Freunde der Philosophie oder an irgendwelche anonyme νέοι (wenn Elias *CAG* 18, 2 p.3, 17 ff. B. und David *CAG* 18, 2 p.9, 2 ff. B. dies behaupten, so beweist dies nur ihre auch sonst feststellbare Flüchtigkeit und Uninformiertheit), sondern an einen regierenden Stadtkönig; und wenn Isokrates in *Or.* 2 durchaus bedacht hat, was er seinem Adressaten, König Nikokles, sagen muss, kann und darf und was nicht, so haben wir alles Recht vorauszusetzen, dass auch Aristoteles seinen *Protreptikos* sorgfältig auf die Person seines Adressaten abgestimmt hat. Dies bedeutet unter anderem, dass er ihm zwar die Philosophie empfehlen, aber sicherlich nicht darüber belehren wird, dass der Bios politikos neben dem Bios theoretikos nichts taugt, oder gar, dass der Mensch jeglichen irdischen Ehrgeiz hinter sich lassen und nur auf die Befreiung des Geistes von der Fesselung an den Körper hoffen soll. Aristoteles hat, anders gesagt, den *Protreptikos* ganz bestimmt nicht in der Absicht geschrieben, seinen Adressaten mehr oder weniger diskret zum Verzicht auf sein politisches Amt und zum Rückzug in das stille Kämmerlein philosophischer Theoria zu veranlassen. Wenn er ihm Philosophie anempfahl, so in erster Linie darum, weil sie das πολιτεύεσθαι zu orientieren und auf die richtige Bahn zu leiten berufen sei, subsidiär gewiss auch, weil philosophische Bildung auch einem praktisch tätigen Fürsten wohl anstehe.

Damit ist schon gesagt, dass unser Lob der Sophia auf Kosten der politischen Phronesis schwerlich aus dem *Protreptikos* an Themison stammen kann. Wir werden also vielmehr an den Dialog περὶ φιλοσοφίας zu denken haben. Der Titel selbst verrät so viel, dass in ihm die Fundamentalfrage nach dem Wesen, der Leistung und der Geschichte der Philosophie verhandelt worden sein muss. Wo φιλοσοφία das Stichwort war, muss auch von σοφία die Rede gewesen sein, zunächst ganz abgesehen von dem Problem, wie Aristoteles die Relation zwischen den beiden Begriffen bestimmt hat; zu dieser merke ich nur an, dass es sehr unwahrscheinlich ist, dass er sich die aporetische Exegese des φιλοσοφεῖν, die bei Platon *Apol.* 21b ff., *Phaidr.* 278d u.a. sowie bei Herakleides Pontikos Frg. 87 Wehrli greifbar ist, zu eigen gemacht hat; dagegen spricht von allgemeinen Erwägungen abgesehen der prägnante Satz *Eth. Nik.* 1177a26-27.

Von den Sieben Weisen hat περὶ φιλοσοφίας mit Sicherheit gehandelt. Von ihrer Lebensweisheit war die Rede, und Thales dürfte da schon die Doppelfunktion gehabt haben, die dann an ihm haften blieb: Er war ebenso der weise Ratgeber in politischen Schwierigkeiten wie der Archeget einer ganz der Erforschung des Kosmos zugewandten Bios theoretikos[4].

In diesen Zusammenhang passt unser Text, zu dem wir nun zurückkehren. Er nennt ausdrücklich Anaxagoras und Thales als Vertreter einer Sophia, die unnütz ist. Wenn von beiden gesagt wird, sie hätten τὰ συμφέροντα ἑαυτοῖς nicht beachtet, so dürfen wir vermuten, dass in der ausführlicheren Fassung des Dialoges gerade dafür auch Beispiele berichtet wurden.

Wir lassen dies indessen auf sich beruhen und sehen uns in den auf unseren Text nachfolgenden Seiten des sechsten Buches der *Nik. Ethik* noch etwas um.

Von der Phronesis ist in 1141b8-1142a30 noch einmal ausführlich die Rede. Der Text verrät freilich auf den ersten Blick, dass er ziemlich heterogenes Material umfasst. Ich greife nur das wichtigste heraus. Von 1141b23 an wird das Verhältnis von Phronesis und πολιτική etwas genauer untersucht (vgl. oben 1140b10-11). Es ergibt sich fürs erste zur Hauptsache, dass die politische Phronesis zwei Stufen hat, die Gesetzgebung, die sich beim Allgemeinen aufhält, und die eigentliche Politik, die das καθ' ἕκαστον, also die Einzelnen, in die ψηφίσματα einmündenden Aktivitäten besorgt. Zu beachten ist, dass die Gesetzgebung der ἀρχιτεκτονική verglichen wird, der Politiker dagegen mit den χειροτέχναι. Dies erinnert nicht nur von weitem an *Metaph.* 981a30 ff., sondern, was in unserm Zusammenhang interessanter ist, an eine Briefstelle Ciceros *Ad fam.* 9, 2, 5. Cicero schreibt im April 46 an Varro, er stehe auch jetzt noch (es ist die Zeit der Diktatur Caesars) für den Staat zur Verfügung, wenn jemand ihn brauchen könne, *non modo ut architectos, verum etiam ut fabros ad aedificandam rem publicam.* Das griechische Wort *architectus* ist bei Cicero noch selten genug, um nicht sofort die griechische Herkunft der ganzen Wendung zu indizieren; dann aber entspricht *faber* dem griechischen χειροτέχνης. Es ist kaum zu bestreiten, dass zwischen *Nik. Eth.* 1141b24-29 und der Briefstelle Ciceros eine Beziehung besteht. Dass Cicero die *Nik. Ethik* gelesen hätte, davon kann ernstlich keine Rede sein. Beide Texte hängen von Darlegungen in einem Dialoge ab; allerdings wird man in diesem Falle, wo die Struktur der politischen Phronesis als solcher zur Debatte steht, weniger an περὶ φιλοσοφίας, als vielmehr an den aristotelischen πολιτικός zu denken geneigt sein.

Anders orientiert ist 1141b29-33, in gewissem Umfang eine Variante des vorangehenden 1141b24-29. Da wird, ohne dass diese Intention klar herauskommt, zwischen zwei Formen der Phronesis unterschieden: Phronesis als Tugend des Einzelnen und Phronesis im Bereiche des Staates; die zweite wird dreigeteilt, genauer besehen zunächst albiert in Verwaltung des Hauses (vgl. 1140b10) und Verwaltung des Staates, diese abermals (im Sinne von 1141b24-29) in Nomothetik und Politik, die Politik endlich in Staatsregierung und Rechtsprechung. Wir haben also eine Folge von drei Dichotomien, die vielleicht nicht ganz zufällig von ferne an die Dichotomien des platonischen *Politikos* erinnern. Mit 1141b33-1142a11 gelangen wir insofern wieder in die Nähe von 1141a20-b2, als entschieden abwertend von der Politik gesprochen wird. Der ominöse Begriff des Wissens zu seinem eigenen Nutzen (τὸ αὑτῷ εἰδέναι) taucht wieder auf, vgl. 1140a26, b9, 1141a25, 27, 30, b6. Seltsamerweise wird aber innerhalb dieses Begriffes distinguiert. Der φρόνιμος ist derjenige, der in der Tat τὰ περὶ αὑτὸν weiss: von ihm wird der Politiker unterschieden, der bloss πολυπράγμων ist; die Verse des Euripides belegen

99

(oberflächlich genug) die Meinung, dass nur derjenige, der ἀπραγμόνως zu leben weiss, φρόνιμος heissen darf. Ebenso holperig gehts weiter. Man hält die πολιτικοί für φρόνιμοι weil sie auch τὸ αὐτοῖς ἀγαθόν suchen sc. wie der wirkliche φρόνιμος. Aber sie suchen es offenbar auf falsche Weise, nämlich ohne Wissen von der Verwaltung des Hauses und des Staates.

Schon dieser aufs äusserste verkürzte Satz, dann der nächste leiten über zu 1142a11-20. Die Einzelheiten gehen uns hier nichts mehr an. Dass auch da der Text schwer gestört ist, lehrt der Umstand, dass in einem ersten Abschnitt (a11-16) die Empeiria für die Phronesis beansprucht wird, während die mathematischen Wissenschaften ohne Empeiria auskommen; in einem zweiten Abschnitt (a16-20) bedarf der σοφὸς ἢ φυσικός der Empeiria, während abermals die Mathematik auf sie verzichten kann. Der Leser hat den Verdacht, dass da von zwei verschiedenen Typen von Empeiria die Rede ist, erfährt aber gerade darüber nichts. Ueberdies meldet sich eine leichte Paradoxie: Derselbe νέος, von dem schon 1095a2-6 erklärt hat, es fehle ihm nicht bloss die Empeiria, sondern er lebe auch gemäss den πάθη (er ist ja im strengen Sinne noch ἄλογος), soll nach unserer Stelle einen besonders mühelosen Zugang zu den mathematischen Wissenschaften haben; wir verstehen, was Aristoteles meint (impliziert ist ein Urteil über die Mathematik, das von demjenigen des Aristippos in *Metaph.* 996a29-b1 nicht weit entfernt ist), aber vermissen dennoch eine Explikation.

Wir überspringen die nachfolgenden Ausführungen und wenden uns noch kurz zu dem schwierigen Schlussteil des Buches 1143b18-1145a11.

Vorangeht eine Conclusio, die in souveräner Vereinfachung erklärt, es seien nun das Wesen, der Gegenstand und der psychologische Aspekt von Phronesis und Sophia erörtert worden. Nun wird überraschend gefragt, wozu diese beiden Erkenntnisweisen brauchbar seien[5].

Ein erster Abschnitt ist aporetisch 1143b19-36. Die in allem einzelnen unsaubere Formulierung lässt gerade noch einen ursprünglich wohlüberlegten Aufbau erahnen. Vorausgesetzt wird, dass Nützlichkeit an ein Produzieren gebunden ist. Dann aber gilt: I. von der Sophia, dass sie überhaupt nichts produziert, also völlig nutzlos zu sein scheint, II. von der Phronesis eine der nachfolgenden drei Möglichkeiten, die am klarsten anhand des (im ganzen Kapitel besonders stark hervortretenden) Modells der Medizin und Gesundheit formuliert, werden können: a) die Phronesis ist das Wissen vom Wesen der Tugend als seelischer Gesundheit; doch das blosse Wissen macht weder gesund noch tugendhaft, b) sie ist insofern produktiv, als sie zur seelischen Gesundheit hinzuführen vermag; dann aber gilt einerseits, das derjenige, der diese Gesundheit schon besitzt,

100

ihrer nicht mehr bedarf, und andererseits, dass derjenige, der sie nicht besitzt, ihrer auch nicht bedarf, da es genügt, den Empfehlungen jener zu folgen, die die Gesundheit besitzen. Also ist sie auch in diesem Fall überflüssig und nutzlos. c) Sie vermag tatsächlich die seelische Gesundheit herzustellen; dann aber ergibt sich die Absurdität, dass die Sophia als der Inbegriff der seelischen Gesundheit sich den Anweisungen der Phronesis zu fügen hat, obschon sie, wie wir aus 1141a20-b2 wissen, an Rang der Phronesis überlegen ist. Die Beantwortung dieser Aporien ist ebenso umfangreich wie unübersichtlich und teilweise in erstaunlich schlechtem Stile gehalten[6]. Ich greife nur noch das für uns Relevante heraus.

1144a1-3 ist eine erste Antwort, die für Sophia und Phronesis gleichmässig gilt (für die Phronesis wird sie in der Rekapitulation 1145a2-4 wiederholt). Sie greift zurück auf das psychologische Schema 11139a6-17. Was dort in 1139a15-17 als Frage stehen geblieben war, wird nun mit einer Antwort erledigt. Die optimale Verfassung desjenigen Seelenteils, der dort ἐπιστημονικόν hiess, ist die Sophia und die entsprechende Verfassung des λογιστικόν ist die Phronesis. Beigegeben wird die genau besehen erstaunliche Behauptung, dass eine solche optimale Verfassung erstrebenswert sei, auch wenn sie weiter nichts leistet; sie ist also ein vollkommener Zustand, der sich nicht durch die Nützlichkeit irgendeiner Leistung zu rechtfertigen braucht. Wir lassen das Problem auf sich beruhen, wie es Aristoteles hier möglich ist, Zustand und Leistung derart von einander zu trennen.

Die nachfolgenden Antworten werden für Sophia und Phronesis gesondert gegeben mit Ausnahme der letzten, die sich auf 1143b33-35 bezieht und die gegenseitige Beziehung von Sophia und Phronesis bestimmt. Wir nehmen sie voraus, 1145a6-11: Auch wenn wir voraussetzen, dass die Phronesis die Sophia herzustellen vermag, ist sie ihr ebenso wenig übergeordnet wie etwa die Medizin der Gesundheit; die Anweisungen, die sie erteilt, gehen ja nicht an die Gesundheit bzw. die Sophia, sondern an denjenigen, der das eine oder das andere zu erlangen sucht. Schön und bedeutungsvoll und auf dem Niveau von 1141a20-b8 wird präzisiert: Die Politik erlässt zwar Verfügungen über die Art, auf die der Staatsbürger die Gottheit kultisch zu ehren hat, doch dies besagt keineswegs, dass sie der Gottheit selbst Anweisungen erteilt; und wir wissen, dass die Sophia der erkennende, philosophische Umgang mit dem Göttlichen ist.

1144a3-6 bezieht sich augenscheinlich auf die Sophia allein, obschon dies nicht klar zum Ausdruck kommt. Die Sophia, hören wir, ist durchaus produktiv, aber nicht wie die Medizin die Gesundheit, sondern so wie die

Gesundheit das Wohlbefinden produziert; in diesem besondern Sinne des ποιεῖν schafft die Sophia die Eudaimonia. Eine Unstimmigkeit, über die sich freilich der aufmerksame Leser der *Nik. Ethik* kaum verwundern wird, darf hier notiert werden. Wir hatten soeben aus 1143b33-35 und 1145 a6-11 zu entnehmen, dass die Sophia an Rang über der Phronesis steht; als Umgang mit dem Göttlichen steht sie überhaupt über allen anderen menschlichen Aktivitäten. Dann werden wir erwarten, dass sie auch für sich allein ausreicht, um die Eudaimonia des Menschen zu konstituieren. Dies tut sie jedoch an unserer Stelle nicht. Sie schafft zwar die Eudaimonia und ist zugleich nur ein μέρος τῆς ὅλης ἀρετῆς. Offensichtlich wird damit ein Vorbehalt angemeldet. Es soll ein Platz freigehalten werden für die ἠθικὴ ἀρετή. Dass auch sie Eudaimonia schaffen kann, wird später in 1178a9 ff. ausdrücklich festgestellt. Dieser, spätere Text respektiert indessen die Rangfolge (1178a9: δευτέρως), während unser Abschnitt sie zu vernachlässigen scheint. Da ist die Sophia nur ein Teil der gesamten ἀρετή scil. neben anderen Teilen. Aristoteles ist eben vom Beginn der *Nik. Ethik* an bis zu 1176a33 systematisch bedacht, den von der Sache her nicht zu bestreitenden Vorrang des Bios theoretikos vor dem Bios praktikos optisch möglichst wenig in Erscheinung treten zu lassen; Belege für diese Absicht finden sich schon in ersten Buch in beträchtlicher Anzahl.

Genau diese Absicht ist schliesslich auch darin greifbar, dass die Erledigung der Aporien für die Phronesis sehr viel umfangreicher ist als für die Sophia. Diese wurde in wenigen Zeilen abgetan; von der Phronesis allein spricht 1144a6-1145a6. Ich nenne hier nur noch das Gesamtergebnis der umständlich und schwerfällig voranschreitenden Untersuchung.

Zunächst bleibt es dabei, dass die Phronesis als solche nur eine Weise des Erkennens und nicht eine solche des Handelns ist, wie dies 1139b15-17 entspricht. Als ihre besondere Aufgabe gilt hier (etwas unerwartet), dass sie nicht das Ziel des Handelns erkennt, sondern die zur Erreichung des schon gegebenen Zieles notwendigen Mittel. Entscheidend ist schliesslich das Folgende. Wenn sie ihren festen Platz in der Ethik hat (ich formuliere modern), so deshalb, weil sie nicht nach den technisch zweckmässigsten Mitteln zur Verwirklichung eines beliebigen Zieles fragt (dies tut die δεινότης), sondern weil sie es mit den richtigen Mitteln zur Verwirklichung des einen Zieles der ethischen Vollkommenheit zu tun hat. Damit ist auch gesagt, dass die Phronesis und die ἠθικὴ ἀρετή gegenseitig an einander gebunden sind (vgl. 1144a36-b1, 1144b16-17 und zusammenfassend 1144b30-32). Die ethische Vollkommenheit ist nur erreichbar, wenn man die adäquaten Mittel einsetzt; und dies wiederum kann man nur, wenn man zuvor durch die Phronesis darüber belehrt worden ist, welches die adäquaten Mittel sind. Die Phronesis wiederum ist nur, was sie ist, wenn sie ihr Fragen nach den Mitteln nicht an beliebigen Zielen, sondern an der ἠθικὴ ἀρετή orientiert. Dies bedeutet endlich, dass die aristotelische Phronesis, wie sie hier beschrieben wird, eine Position der Mitte zwischen zwei Extremen einnimmt. Sie ist weder ein neutrales, – wir dürfen wohl sagen: wertindifferentes Wissen im Sinne von 1143b20-28, noch ein Wissen, das für sich allein schon die ethische Vollkommenheit zu konstituieren vermag, wie dies Sokrates gemeint hatte (1144b17-30), sondern ein Wissen, das die präzise Aufgabe hat, den Menschen über die Mittel zu belehren, mit denen er die ethische Vollkommenheit erlangen kann; es muss dann freilich eine andere δύναμις dazukommen, damit dieses Wissen sich in Handeln umzusetzen vermag. Ethisches Handeln setzt sich demnach immer aus zweimal zwei verschiedenen, aber kooperierenden Faktoren zusammen: hier τέλος und τὰ πρὸς τὸ τέλος, dort das Erkennen und die das Erkennen ins Handeln überführende δύναμις.

Damit mag unsere Interpretation schliessen. Der Text von *Nik. Eth.* 6, 13 ist, wie gesagt, so unübersichtlich und schlecht formuliert, dass man sich fragen wird, ob er vielleicht nur ein grober Auszug aus einem umfangreicheren und sorgfältiger redigierten Ganzen darstellt. Wenn ja, könnte es sich noch einmal um περὶ φιλοσοφίας handeln? Allgemein gesehen wäre es ja nicht ganz unwahrscheinlich, dass Aristoteles zunächst Wesen, Leistung und Geschichte der Sophia und Philosophia in der frühen Zeit verfolgte, dann auf Sokrates kam und darstellte sowohl, womit dieser eine neue Epoche in der Entwicklung der Philosophie einleitete, wie auch, in welchem entscheidenden Punkte er gerade in seinem eigensten Bereiche, der Ethik, in die Irre ging, endlich zu Platon überging, auch da Leistungen und Fehlgriffe gegen einander abwog und den Dialog abrundete mit einer Diskussion über die grundlegenden Thesen seiner eigenen Philosophie. Doch über ein solches Programm von περὶ φιλοσοφίας zu spekulieren ist vielleicht etwas zu waghalsig. Es muss genügen es als eine ferne Möglichkeit gelegentlich in Erwägung zu ziehen.

ANMERKUNGEN

1 Die nahe verwandte Reihe *An. po.* 89b7-9, die als sechste Erkenntnisweise noch die διάνοια dazugibt, vermehrt bloss die Schwierigkeiten, die allerdings weder von D. Ross im Kommentar zur *Analytik* noch von F. Dirlmeier im Kommentar zu *Nik. Eth.* 1139b15-17 bemerkt worden sind.

2 Dirlmeier im Kommentar zu *Nik. Ethik* 1096a3; Wieland Hermes 86, 1958, 323 ff.; etwas sonderbar bleibt es, wie leichthin die meisten Interpreten Cicero

Ep. Att. 4, 16, 2 beiseite zu schieben pflegen: es müsste erst einmal bewiesen werden, dass das Selbstzeugnis des Aristoteles, auf das sich Cicero beruft, nichtig ist.

3 Methodisch ist es durchaus legitim, beispielsweise bei Titeln wie Περὶ πλούτου oder Περὶ εὐγενείας die einschlägigen Stellen in den Pragmatien zu sammeln und daraufhin zu prüfen, ob sich an ihnen Indizien finden, die auf eine Benutzung der Dialoge hinweisen; ebenso legitim ist es, von der Annahme auszugehen, dass etwa der aristotelische Σοφιστής und Πολιτικός bewusst die entsprechenden platonischen Dialoge ebenso zu überspielen beabsichtigten, wie der Philoktetes des Sophokles denjenigen des Aischylos und derjenige des Euripides diejenigen seiner beiden Vorgänger.

4 Nur in aller Kürze weise ich auf *VS* 11 A 9 und 10 und 59 A 1 § 6-7 hin.

5 Zweifellos besteht zwischen 1143b18 und 1141b3-8 ein Widerspruch. Vernünftigerweise ist es kaum möglich, in dem früheren Text die Sophia gerade damit zu charakterisieren, dass sie nicht dem Interesse des σοφός nachgeht, sondern sich mit Dingen befasst, die nicht ἀνθρώπινα ἀγαθά und deshalb ἄχρηστα sind, und in dem späteren Text gewissermassen naiv und als ob der frühere Text gar nicht existierte, die Frage aufzuwerfen, wozu eigentlich die Sophia χρησίμη sei. Der Widerspruch (auf den Dirlmeier nicht eingeht) ist nicht damit wegzuschaffen, dass er in den Aristotelesexzerpten im *Protreptikos* des Iamblich ähnlich wiederkehrt: p.52, 16 ff. und 54, 10 ff. Pist. Er lässt sich auch bei Iamblich nicht rechtfertigen, sondern nur als das Resultat des Zusammenschiebens verschiedener Exzerpte erklären. An unserer Stelle wird man beachten, dass der Begriff χρήσιμος im nachfolgenden Texte überhaupt nicht mehr erscheint. Anvisiert ist in Wahrheit die Frage, was die Leistung von Sophia und Phronesis im weitesten Sinne ist (dass dabei fast unterschiedslos bald von ποιεῖν, bald von πράττειν geredet wird, ist eine andere Frage). Ich vermute, dass der Einleitungssatz 1143b18 sekundär und ohne Rücksicht auf den Inhalt dem Gesamttexte vorangesetzt worden ist.

6 Mit der Erklärung, die Gedankengänge dieses Kapitels seien ,,dialektisch" (so Dirlmeier) ist kaum etwas gewonnen. – Die Verwendung der vornehmen Metapher ὄμμα τῆς ψυχῆς in 1144a29-30 empfinde ich jedenfalls als ausgesprochen geschmacklos.

ATHENODORUS ON THE CATEGORIES AND A PUN ON ATHENODORUS

B. L. HIJMANS

Soon after the rediscovery of Aristotle's manuscripts a spate of commentaries on the *Categories* comes into being. Simplicius (*In Cat.* p.159, 31 Kalbfleisch) lists five names. He states that Achaïcus and Sotion have understood Aristotle's use of the plural τὰ πρός τι. He continues: "Having understood this they oppose the ancient commentators of the *Categories*, Boethus and Ariston and Andronicus and Eudorus and Athenodorus, who neither understood nor remarked upon it but both used the words indiscriminately and sometimes uttered the singular τὸ πρός τι though Aristotle always has the plural."[1]

There is no hard evidence to link Athenodorus' commentary on the *Categories* with Athenodorus son of Sandon, but there are some items of circumstantial evidence:

1. This is the commentary that L. Annaeus Cornutus, also a professional Stoic philosopher, chose to comment on[2].

2. From Diogenes Laërtius (VII, 68) it appears that an Athenodorus, who may well have been the son of Sandon (cf. Zeller[5], 607), dealt with questions of logic and was hence interested not only in questions of moral behaviour but also in more technical ones. Indeed he must have been a professional, something which would fit his relationship with Cicero (below p.106 n.6) very well.

3. Athenodorus of Rhodes (Quint., II 17, 15) is unknown but for his objections to the art of rhetoric.

4. Athenodorus Cordulion was dead before Andronicus' edition of Aristotle came out[3].

5. There seems to be no other Athenodorus to whom the testimonies may refer with anywhere near the same probability.

This Athenodorus, son of Sandon, nicknamed Calvus, remains a somewhat elusive figure partly since Sandon took the unfortunate decision to give his son a name that was not precisely uncommon in the Greek-speaking world, and partly because of the curious accident that he had a slightly older namesake, equally associated with the city of Tarsus, equally associated with the Stoa. Were it not for a few scant indications that require the distinction it would be highly unlikely that any would be made. We learn from Strabo (XIV 5, 14) that the persons of the two may be distinguished by their respective connections with Marcus Cato and Augustus respectively. Cato's notorious suicide of 46 B.C. fixes a *terminus ante quem* for the death of Cordulion[4]. Sandon's son, on the other hand, died in Tarsus at the age of eighty-two (Ps.-Lucian, *Macrob*. 21) after having made his name as a teacher and a close friend of Augustus (*ibidem*). There is no evidence elucidating the origin of their relationship. Bowersock[5] supposes that Octavian may have brought him to Rome in 44. He is mistaken: Cicero in a letter written in February of 50 B.C. (*Ad fam*. III 7, 5) indicates that Athenodorus, son of Sandon, was known in Rome and possibly present in that city several years before. Cicero's precision ('*Sandonis filius*') just conceivably may imply that confusion with another Athenodorus (Cordulion?) was possible[6]. Several authors indicate that Augustus' relationship with Athenodorus was reasonably close. We possess not only the famous[7] story in Cassius Dio 56, 43 according to which he burst in upon Augustus from a covered sedan-chair (such as was used by women) brandishing a sword in order to demonstrate the need for more effective safety precautions, but also the statement in Dio Chrysostom (*Or*. 33, 48, p.311, 1 v.A.) that Augustus 'revered' him.

Furthermore there are Zosimus' opinion (I 6, 2) that Augustus at the beginning of his reign listened to Athenodorus' advice and Plutarch's anecdote (*Reg. et imp. apophth*. 207C) concerning the refused resignation. The curious banality of Athenodorus' piece of advice ("when you become angry recite the alphabet before saying or doing anything") stamps the story itself as the typical vignette that is so common in the diatribe, but there is no reason to doubt either the familiarity or the fact that Augustus retains Athenodorus for another year. When at the end Athenodorus returns to Tarsus he does so with a special commission from Augustus to replace Boethus, a follower of Antony[8]. Strabo's account of his dispensation (XIV 5, 14 ff.) insists on both his competence and his wit.

If we try to determine the content of Athenodorus' commentary on the *Categories*, we run into some peculiar difficulties, chief of which is the fact that much of our information ascribes opinions on Aristotle's *Categories* to Athenodorus and Cornutus together, though we are also reliably informed that Cornutus opposed Athenodorus. The first such piece of information deals with the question of the scope of the *Categories*. Simplicius (*In Categ. Prooem*. p.18, 22 ff. Kalbfleisch) presents it as follows:

"It remains, then, to speak about the book's division into chapters. Some people, not understanding how the chapter incisions have been made at joints and how they neatly perform their function with regard to the aim of the whole and preserve a coherence with one another, think the chapter headings have been put down in too confined a space, memorandum fashion.

And, what is more, some people oppose him, rejecting the division, one group maintaining it is fruitlessly in excess of what is needed, another that it is deficient in many respects. Thus Cornutus and Athenodorus, who thinking the scope of the book regards *lexeis* (words and phrases) as such, cite many *lexeis*, some in basic some in figurative senses, in the opinion that they thereby challenge the division as not encompassing all *lexeis*. They think, too, that the division into homonyms and synonyms and paronyms is one of nouns[9] and they take the book to be a mass of logical and physical and ethical and theological theses: for (they say) the reflections on homonyms and synonyms and paronyms belong to logic as does the section on opposites, but the remarks on change belong to physics, those on virtue and vice are ethical, just as the enquiries on the ten genera are theological."

Simplicius, then, tells us that Athenodorus and Cornutus felt that the scope of the *Categories* was basically linguistic and that as such it was deficient. We may hesitate concerning the meaning of *lexis* in this passage. The Stoic definition of Diocles: φωνὴ ἐγγράμματος (*SVF* III, p.213, 5) distinguishes carefully between *lexis* (the word as a series of sounds) and *logos* (the word as a signifier). Some two and a half centuries earlier, however, Porphyry had mentioned the same objection (*In Categ. Prooem.*, p.59, 10 ff. Busse); he did not distinguish between Athenodorus and Cornutus either, but he fixes the meaning in which *lexis* is used:

"They cite as examples the questions concerning *lexeis* as *lexeis*, e.g. '*lexeis* in their basic sense', '*lexeis* in their figurative sense' and the like (for there are differences between *lexeis* in so far as they are *lexeis*), and, unable to determine to what category they belong or to solve the problem, say the division is defective, since not every significant sound is included within it."

Lexis, then, is to be understood as "words capable of carrying a meaning", and the categories are regarded as categories of such words. An example of the method indicated by Porphyry would be welcome. Such an example is indeed forthcoming: in Simplicius (*In Categ.* c. 9, p.359, 1 Kalbfleisch) we read the following statement:

Cornutus is at a loss: if the where of place and the when of time have been distinguished according to the typology of the *lexeis* and thus been placed under their individual categories (since the thesis deals with types of *lexeis*), why on earth did he not also add the following examples to that category, e.g. "from Dio" and "to Dio" and many others of the same nature; for they are equivalent to "from Athens" and "to Athens".

Unhappily we no longer possess the precise Aristotelian passage the Stoic here reacts to, but the burden is clear: there are words that fall in the same grammatical category as e.g. Ἀθήνηθεν but that are excluded from Aristotle's category. We note in passing that the remark is ascribed to Cornutus only. Simplicius curtly rejects the objection: the categories do not deal with the typology of *lexis*. Essentially he repeats Porphyry's remark. The latter had, just before the passage translated above (p.59, 10 ff. Busse), discussed the fact that many had not understood how Aristotle argues in the *Categories* about the primary application of *lexeis* to objects, whereas in the *Peri hermeneias* he deals with *lexeis* signifying types of *phonai* such as 'noun' and 'verb'. This distinction, he says, was not clear to all who wrote about the categories "for otherwise the situation would not have arisen that some held that Aristotle in this work went deeply into the *genera* of the ὄντα primarily, whereas others disagreed and rejected the division on the grounds that it passed over many things and was not all-embracing or, on the contrary, was in excess of what was necessary." Follows the passage quoted above in which it becomes clear that "Athenodorus and Cornutus" feel the division lacks essential items.

Our two main passages (Simpl. p.18, 22 K. and Porph. p.59, 10 B) are apparently contradictory with Simplicius' statement elsewhere (p.62, 24 K, cf. below p.112) that Athenodorus denounced the division into "so large a number". We may have to resort to some rather desperate guess-work in order to resolve the problem.

It seems there are two main possibilities to be considered:
1. Both Athenodorus and Cornutus used in themselves contradictory objections in a hypothetically phrased attack on the *Categories*.
2. Athenodorus and Cornutus disagree with one another, but their objections have become fused in the tradition, e.g. because Athenodorus was known only through the medium of Cornutus' reaction.

In favour of the first hypothesis may be quoted the phrasing of Simplicius' statement (p.187, 24 ff., see the translation below) concerning the objections to Aristotle's treatment of πρός τι, which contains both the phrases ὡς καὶ αὐτῷ δοκεῖ τῷ Ἀριστοτέλει and ὡς Ἀθηνόδωρος οἴεται πρός τι εἶναι κατὰ ᾿Αριστοτέλη. They could conceivably be interpreted to indicate an element of Aristotle quoted against himself and one of Aristotle interpreted for that purpose. But when we then see that Athenodorus' interpretation of πρός τι looks precisely as if it were the Stoic category πρός τί πως ἔχον it seems much more likely that we have to do with a reaction starting directly from his own position, and that contradictions have to be accounted for by the differences between Athenodorus and Cornutus. We are actually aware of a number of those differences and on the face of it, therefore, the second possibility is to be taken rather more seriously.

There are three pieces of evidence and once again Simplicius is our source. Not only does he tell us (p.62, 24 K.) that Athenodorus' and Coınutus' respective books differed in scope, but that the latter actually opposed the first. Athenodorus confined himself to an examination of the 'division into so large a number', whereas Cornutus 'opposed almost all' of Aristotle's treatise. Second, Simplicius contrasts Athenodorus' interpretation of πρός τι with that of Cornutus, in the following passage (p.187, 24-34):

> "Others say that the distinction of such reciprocity is inept. For 'wing' and 'rudder' and 'head' are unsuitably quoted for reciprocation. For they do not belong entirely to the 'relative', since each one of them is part of a 'substance' and (itself) a 'substance'. No substance, however, belongs to the 'relative', also in Aristotle's own opinion. Whether, then, as Athenodorus thinks, 'relative' according to Aristotle is that for which the name begs that with relation to which it is uttered (for if one hears 'slave' one looks for the slave's owner), or as Cornutus maintains, relative are those things whose condition coincides with (or: has an inherent reference to) something else, though not the condition of combination, such as in the case of possessors and possessed, but the condition of essence, when it has in its very being the allusion to the other thing, – in no way is 'rudder' or 'wing' relative."

It is clear from this passage that both Athenodorus and Cornutus give definitions of πρός τι that are entirely based on their own Stoic notions. As a matter of fact the passage is not without its importance for the Stoic doctrine of categories, since it confirms the fixed order of the Stoic foursome (substance, quality, disposition, relative disposition) in the statement that "no substance belongs to the relative". This is to be taken in the sense that one may study an object and be forced to admit that nothing can be predicated of it but its existence, but if one studies the object 'mother' one has to admit the existence of at least one child (relative disposition), the fact that she had given birth (disposition), that she is a woman (quality) and that she exists. (Cf. Simpl. *In Categ.* c. 7, p.165, 36 πρός τι δέ πως ἔχοντα οἷον δεξιόν, πατέρα καὶ τὰ τοιαῦτα).

Cornutus' definition of the πρός τι seems to be meant as an improvement, rather than an attack, on Athenodorus' phrasing. For where Athenodorus had fairly simply dealt with an example, Cornutus seems to try his best to weave into his definition a careful distinction between the third and fourth Stoic categories. He first speaks of the σχέσις which at once refers to something else (such as 'mother' automatically refers to 'child'), then carefully excludes mere possession (e.g. 'having legs'). Indeed we hear that 'the Stoics' refer ἔχειν and hence presumably also mere possession to their own category πως ἔχειν(Simpl. *In Categ.*, p.373, 7 K, *SVF* II, p.132, 12). And, just in case we had not yet understood, he adds that the σχέσις is πρὸς ὑπόστασιν meaning, no doubt, that motherhood in its essence presupposes at least one child, whereas neither 'rudder' necessarily presupposes a ship nor 'wing' a bird in the same sense.

There is a third piece of evidence: when Simplicius discusses (p.128, 7 K) a series of objections to Aristotle's treatment of the category *quantity* and its bipartition into number and size he adds: "They also object to the fact that the division is one into two; for one ought to add, after number and size, a third kind: heaviness or weight. Archytas made the addition and afterwards Athenodorus and Ptolemy the Mathematician." On the other hand Simplicius tells us on the next page (p.129, 1-2) that Cornutus as well as Porphyry regard weight as a *quality*. The two statements may not be simply opposed to one another since they are imbedded in two different layers of polemic. In his answer to the first Simplicius compares heaviness (βαρύτης) with density and thickness and argues for a designation as ποιόν. Weight (ῥοπή) on the other hand is, in itself, a quantity since it exhibits the mark of quantity, viz. the equal-unequal. Simplicius then refers to Iamblichus' discussion of the question and the latter's reaction to the second statement: weight is not heaviness or lightness but the measure of heaviness and lightness. Iamblichus' beautiful, though not very helpful, phrase closes the section: "In themselves things heavy and light could proceed endlessly as they have no limit of themselves, but since the power deriving from the measures of weight has provided order and limit, in so far have things heavy and light been placed in an orderly arrangement."

Apparently Athenodorus discussed Aristotle's categories by themselves. We must not conclude from his reference to weight that he himself admitted a category 'quantity': we have no evidence for such a conclusion, nor is it very likely. This is no more than a hint that he felt that questions of weight were closely related to questions of extension (cf. Sext. Emp., *Adv. Math.* X, 7, *SVF* II, p.162, 14 ff.). Cornutus, on the other hand, may have pointed out that in a properly Stoic sense weight, like all quantitative judgements, is to be listed under *quality*, but the context of his remark is lacking, as is that of Athenodorus'. Certainly we must not construe it as directed immediately against his predecessor.

So far our attemps to determine a usable distinction between Athenodorus and Cornutus have not been crowned with more than scanty results. We have

a. a hint that Cornutus was particularly interested in the technical linguistic aspect of the problems concerning categories and

b. a hint that Athenodorus, who confined his attention to the categories as such, discussed them one by one; and we may now add

c. an indication that Athenodorus wished to reduce their number.

On the other hand there seems to be no possibility to determine which one of the two was responsible for the remark that Aristotle's *Categories* consists of "a mass of logical and physical and ethical and theological theses" (above p.107). The contradiction mentioned above p.108, however, may have to be resolved by the hypothesis that it was mostly Cornutus who found he could not include all types of linguistic phenomena under Aristotle's categories, whereas it was mostly Athenodorus who felt that, as aspects of being, there were altogether too many of them. But it is unlikely that we shall ever know precisely in what respects Cornutus opposed Athenodorus.

In the passage translated below (p.62, 24 ff. K.) it is clear that Simplicius is dealing with an attack on the *Categories* that falls precisely within the confines of Athenodorus' book as indicated by himself. It seems likely therefore that the italicised phrases contain at least an attempt to include chiefly Athenodorus' objections. It is true that Cornutus and others also are mentioned, but their work is said to have had a much wider scope whereas Simplicius here is interested in the division as such, and may therefore have preferred to turn to Athenodorus. If the passage indeed reacts to Athenodorus it is to be noted that the latter offers serious argument on major Aristotelian points rather than restricting himself to a mere substitution of the Stoic items for those of Aristotle:

"Many others argued against it (sc. the division into ten) merely denouncing the division into so large a number. *Thus Athenodorus in his treatise Against Aristotle's Book Entitled the Categories, which examines only the division into so large a number*[10]. And Cornutus in the treatise he entitled *Against Athenodorus and Aristotle*, as well as Lucius and Nicostratus and their circle, opposed almost all of it, including the division. We must now take the opposing arguments, after arranging them into three well-defined groups. For some people object that the division exceeds what is required, others object that it falls short of what is needed, and there is a third group who feel certain items have been introduced instead of others; there are also those who combine objections of different kinds, some arguing both 'lack' and 'redundancy', others in addition also 'exchange of genera'. With each group some difficulties must be mentioned and the solutions for them, through which it will be possible to learn the type of the objection, so as not to drag on and on by giving the solutions for all.

Those, now, who object on the ground of redundancy say *that he was wrong in opposing 'being-affected'* [11] *to 'doing', for one genus common to both should have been defined: 'moving'.* Against those it must be said that the agent, in so far as it acts, is not in motion, but causes motion being itself unmoved. But some of the agents in the sensible world are accidentally in motion when those two principles, of 'doing' and of 'being-affected', occur together. *But with respect to 'doing' and 'being-affected' the problem should perhaps have been raised why they are not listed under the category of 'relative'. For the agent is active in the passive and the passive suffers the agent.* Indeed in that context they must be listed under 'relative' but in so far as activity and passivity have a different nature they produce different genera; for also in the case of other items under 'relative', e.g. 'father' and 'son', they are themselves-as-subsisting-by-themselves listed under 'substance', but according to their condition under 'relative'. *But how is 'being-in-a-position' not 'being-affected', and how is 'having' not 'doing'?* Surely 'being-in-a-position' is no more passivity than activity. For 'being-in-a-position' is 'to sit', 'to stand'. And in the category it is taken not with respect to its activity or passivity, but with respect to its placement in something else. Thus also 'having' is not taken with respect to its activity, and no less 'being armed' or 'being shod' is not 'being-affected', but respects the state of dress." [12]

Thus Athenodorus Calvus remains, at least in matters logical, a slippery figure. He certainly does in Plutarch's anecdote (*Reg. et Imp. Apophth.,* 207B):

"In Sicily Augustus appointed Arius as his procurator in Theodorus' stead; and when someone handed him a tablet with the inscription 'Theodorus the Tarsian is bald or a thief; how does it look to you?' Caesar wrote underneath: 'It does'."

Cichorius[13] has plausibly emended the text to refer to Athenodorus Calvus rather than the otherwise unknown Theodorus. Philippson[14] perceiving more difficulties in the text, accepted Cichorius' emendation but in addition crossed out the words ἢ κλέπτης and changed φαλακρός to φαλακρῶν.

Neither author has suggested the possibility that the witticism is to be sought in the double meanings of the word φαλακρός (bald) and κλέπτης (thief), both of which have their applications in the general field of logic, a field with which, as we saw, Athenodorus was not unacquainted. The *phalakros* is a variant of the *sorites* (Does one grain make a heap? No. Do two grains make a heap? No. And so on, until the answer is Yes, and the interlocutor is compelled to admit that n grains did not, but $n + 1$ grains do make a heap and that therefore 1 grain makes a heap). We possess no detailed statement of the *phalakros*, but it may well have asked at what point in plucking a man's head we may start calling him bald[15]. Thus the pun of our anecdote seems to lie in the fact that Athenodorus is at once referred to as a baldhead – in Cicero he is called Calvus[16] – and as an insoluble problem. Or are we to imagine that he was in the habit of setting insoluble problems? Since, however, the *sorites* was also in the Stoa referred to as ἡσυχάζων λόγος i.e. a problem consisting of a series of questions during which the wise man, at a certain point, suspends his judgment[17], it is just possible that the pun is a triple one: Athenodorus is bald, he sets insoluble problems (or is one himself), he rests.

The *kleptes* is not found in Stoic context and there is no evidence that Stoics discussed the problem specifically. Since, however, both Aristotle and his commentators mention it, there seems to be every reason why at least Athenodorus should be acquainted with it. The problem was stated in two different ways. Aristotle implies (*SE* 180b15 ff.) by his reaction that it ran somewhat as follows: 'A thief is an evil; if one catches a thief one catches an evil; to catch a thief, therefore, is evil.' The Ps.-Alexander commentary, however, tells us that the argument was phrased as follows: 'Does anyone want his own *kakon*? No. But to steal is *kakon*? Yes. Does the thief want to steal? Yes. In that case he wants his own *kakon*'[18]. No doubt the Aristotelian version is the more attractive, but whichever was the current version, it may not be too fanciful to suggest that in Athenodorus' circle the word *kleptes* came to signify a man who causes himself to come to grief... much in the manner related in Plutarch's apophtheg-

113

ma 7: Athenodorus requests permission to return to Tarsus, but during the interview he gives Augustus a piece of advice which causes the latter to retain his court-philosopher for another year. The unknown, then, who in *Apophth.* 5, hands Augustus the tablet, plays a punning joke on Athenodorus, and in his answer the Emperor shows that he is quick-witted enough to appreciate the pun.

NOTES

1 The absence of Cornutus seems to indicate that Simplicius intends to confine the list to the first generation.
2 On Cornutus see R. Reppe, *De L. Annaeo Cornuto*, Diss. Leipzig 1906. The fragments concerning the *Categories* are discussed p.18 ff. The author makes no real attempt to distinguish between Cornutus and Athenodorus.
3 For form and date of that edition see now I. Düring, *RE*, Suppl. XI, 196 ff.
4 Plut., *Cato Minor* 10, 1 calls him ἤδη γηραιὸν ὄντα, indicating that he was well over fifty in ca. 70 B.C.
5 G. W. Bowersock, *Augustus and the Greek World*, Oxford 1965, 32.
6 Cf. Tyrrell and Purser vol. 3, 171-172. They indicate that Athenodorus returned to Tarsus in 33 B.C., but do not present any evidence. From the manner in which Cicero refers to A. in this passage one might even suspect that Athenodorus was fashionable in Rome just then. Cicero's request for the Posidonius epitome (*Ad Att.*, XVI 11, 4) some years later argues an established familiarity.
7 The story is repeated with the addition of several lurid details by Zonaras, *Ann.* X, 38B-D; Georgius Cedrenus, *Hist. Comp.*, 172A-C, adds his mite and Const. Manasses, *Comp.chron.* 1871 ff., puts it all in verse.
8 Cf. Bowersock, *op.cit.* 48. Strabo XIV 5, 14 concerning Boethus: ἐπῆρε δ'αὐτὸν καὶ 'Αντώνιος, and after some information concerning Boethus' corruption: διακρουσάμενος δ'οὖν θεραπείαις τισὶ τὴν ὀργήν, οὐδὲν ἧττον διετέλεσεν ἄγων καὶ φέρων τὴν πόλιν μέχρι τῆς καταστροφῆς τοῦ 'Αντωνίου. When Athenodorus arrives he finds Boethus still there and does not try to remove him until a little later. Obviously Tyrrell and Purser are wrong in taking 33 as the date of Athenodorus' arrival (cf. above note 6).
9 To point out that this is not so is a task of the commentators to this day. Cf. e.g. J. L. Ackrill (1963, 71) on 1a1. We note that this mistaken opinion suggests that Athenodorus and Cornutus approached the *Categories* from their own, Stoic, terminological point of view.
10 The phrase is redundant: one might think of a gloss.
11 The names of the categories have been translated according to Ackrill's suggestion.
12 Cf. *Cat.* 2a2, the examples of 'having'.
13 *Römische Studien* 280.
14 *RE*, Suppl. V, 49 ff.
15 The *phalakros* in a list of similar problems invented by Euboulides, cf. Diog. Laërt. II 108. Horace, *Ep.* II 1, 45 apparently refers to both *phalakros* and *sorites*. Cf. Cic., *Acad.* II, 49; 92.
16 *Ad Att.*, XVI 11, 4.
17 Cic. *Acad.* II, 93, also Sext. Emp. *Adv. math.*, VII, 146; *SVF* II, p.91 ff.
18 Cf. also *Paraphrasis in Soph. El.* p.59, 7 Hayduck.

LOGOS-RELIGION?
ODER NOUS-THEOLOGIE?

DIE HAUPTSÄCHLICHEN ASPEKTE DES
KAISERZEITLICHEN PLATONISMUS

HEINRICH DÖRRIE

1. *A la recherche des étapes précises entre Platon et le Néoplatonisme*

Durch ihren Aufsatz[1], der diesen Titel trägt, hat die verehrte Jubilarin
vor nunmehr zwanzig Jahren einen bedeutsamen Beitrag zu einem bisher
ungelösten[2] Problem gegeben. Fast scheint es, als sei das damals Gesagte
in der Flut des seither Geschriebenen untergegangen. Nun aber bietet
dieser zu Frau de Vogel's Ehren erscheinende Band den erwünschten
Rahmen, die einst von ihr geäußerten Gedanken aufzugreifen und – wenn
es möglich ist – weiter zu fördern.

Der antike Platonismus macht es dem modernen Forscher schwer, zu
eindeutiger und klar umrissener Darstellung der vielschichtigen Problematik, die er in sich birgt, zu gelangen. Vor allem hat sich bisher die
folgende Diskrepanz als unauflösbar erwiesen:

Einerseits sind alle Platoniker auf Platon bezogen; alle sind darum
bemüht, die von Platon ausgesprochene, vielleicht gar offenbarte Wahrheit nachzuvollziehen, um sie den Schülern weiter zu geben. Das jeweils
erreichte Ergebnis steht indes in schroffem Widerspruch zu dieser Absicht. Der ungemeine Abstand, der (jeweils in anderer Weise) Plutarch,
Plotin, Porphyrios von Platon trennt, kann weder übersehen noch gar in
Abrede gestellt werden.

Andererseits aber, sobald sich die Untersuchung dem Detail zu-
wendet, muß den späteren Platonikern Punkt um Punkt zugestanden
werden, daß sie bestimmte Gedanken Platons in vollauf adaequatem
Verständnis nachvollzogen haben. Frau de Vogel hat im eben zit. Aufsatz
zu den zahlreichen dort behandelten Einzel-Problemen[3] mit vollem Recht
festgestellt, daß nicht nur Ansätze zu den bezeichneten Theoremen bei
Platon vorliegen, sondern daß die späteren Platoniker durchweg Lehr-
stücke wieder geben, die Platon unmißverständlich formuliert hatte.

Die bisher ungelöste Paradoxie besteht in diesem Mißverhältnis:
Obwohl Platon in vielen Einzelheiten zutreffend abgebildet wird, ent-
fernen sich alle Platoniker, wenn man auf das Ganze sieht, sehr weit von
Platon. Dabei erfolgt dieses Sich-Entfernen von Platon keineswegs

geradlinig; sondern es entsteht der verwirrende Eindruck, daß immer neue Schritte in immer andere Richtungen unternommen werden, wobei man sich, trotz der offenkundigen Absicht, sich Platon zu nähern, immer weiter vom Ziel entfernt[4].

Dieses Paradoxon mit den ihm anhaftenden Schwierigkeiten hat eine durchaus erwartbare Wirkung ausgeübt und übt sie noch aus: Die wissenschaftliche Literatur der letzten 70 Jahre ist überreich an meist wohl fundierten einzelnen Beiträgen. Denn im Detail ist der Platonismus durchaus schlüssig; es ist reizvoll und meist sehr ertragreich, die Entfaltung einzelner Motive nachzuzeichnen. Zur Synthese aber ist keiner vorgestoßen...

Angesichts dieser wenig befriedigenden Lage in der Erforschung des Platonismus soll nun versucht werden, einige Grundlinien für eine Synthese zu zeichnen. Daß das ein Wagnis ist, ist mir wohl bewußt – denn damit muß ein Vor-Verständnis an den Platonismus heran- und in ihn hineingetragen werden – ein Vorverständnis, das sich – wenn überhaupt – erst an seinem Ergebnis bestätigt wird. Es wird heutzutage so viel – ja viel zu viel – von methodischen Vor-Überlegungen gesprochen; von solchen ist das, was nun vorgetragen werden soll, weithin frei. Vielmehr soll (auch das eine *vox modernissima*) "ein Modell angeboten" werden, in welchem sich die Bausteine, die ja reichlich bereitliegen, möglichst bruchlos, ja harmonisch zusammenfügen.

2. *Platonismus als* διαδοχή

Die Unsicherheit liegt im Ausgangspunkt. Von welcher Art und von welcher Intensität waren die auf Platon zurückreichenden Überlieferungen zu Beginn des 1. Jahrh. vor Christus – also in den Zeiten des Poseidonios, des Antiochos von Askalon, des jungen Cicero? Hier liegt recht eigentlich das X in der nun anzustellenden Rechnung.

Auf jeden Fall ist zu jener Zeit die Entscheidung gefallen – und das gewiß erst nach eingehender Erörterung – daß es geboten sei, auf Platons *Schriften* zurückzugreifen und aus ihnen den Inhalt einer Lehr-Überlieferung zu begründen. Das war aus mehreren Gründen durchaus nicht selbstverständlich:

Die ältere Akademie, vor allem Xenokrates, hatte zum Gegenstande der *Diadochè* vor allem das gemacht, was die Schüler von Platon im Unterricht, also *hörend*, erfahren hatten. Von hier aus ist es gewiß gerechtfertigt, die „ungeschriebene Lehre Platons" aufzusuchen; schwer vorstellbar ist freilich, daß diese der Sache nach von dem abwich, was hinter den Formulierungen der Dialoge steht. Auf jeden Fall aber ist, was Platon sagen wollte, ἐκ πολλῆς συνουσίας ganz anders zum Leuchten gekommen als in schriftlicher Fixierung – einer Fixierung, der Platon das Unsagbare, das *Arrheton*, weder anvertrauen konnte noch wollte. Aus den Dialogen ist deutlich abzulesen, wie Platon die sprachliche Form dessen, was er sagen wollte, immer wieder neu wendete; oft genug weist das Ringen um den sprachlichen Ausdruck darauf hin, daß weitere Aspekte des jeweils untersuchten Problems – wie Facetten eines Kristalls – in den Gesichtskreis treten. Xenokrates mußte versuchen, das vielfältig Gesagte und sicher oft vielfältig in der *Theōria* Geschaute in ein übersehbares und vor allem tradierbares System zu verdichten – also gleichsam den Kristall in einer Ebene abzubilden. Es ist sicher lehrreich, wenn festgestellt werden kann, welche Ebene den Schülern der „ungeschriebenen Lehre" als die hauptsächliche, als die eigentliche Ebene erschien. Aber es wäre vermessen, Platon abzusprechen, daß er seine *Theōria* auch auf anderen Ebenen vollzogen habe. Kurz, die Suche nach der „ungeschriebenen Lehre" führt nicht auf den ganzen Platon, sondern sie führt auf den von Xenokrates gesehenen Platon. Aristoteles muß ein anderes, damit kaum vereinbares Platon-Bild gehabt haben.

Diese vor allem von Xenokrates zu einem System ausgestaltete *Diadochè* wurde von Arkesilaos verlassen. Während der nun folgenden 'skeptischen' Periode der Akademie wurde Platon als Kronzeuge für das Axiom der Skepsis in Anspruch genommen: Wie schon Sokrates, so habe Platon kein Dogma formuliert, weil er von der Unzuverlässigkeit positiver Dogmatik überzeugt gewesen sei. Ohnehin war – weit über den Kreis der Skeptiker hinaus – die Ansicht verbreitet, daß Dialoge keine Dogmata erhalten[5], also nicht dazu benutzt werden dürfen, ja können, um festzustellen, welche Dogmata ein Philosoph vertrat[6].

Hieraus erklärt sich, warum Antiochos von Askalon einen so seltsamen Weg einschlug, als es darum ging, eine dogmatisch fundierte *Diadochè* neu zu begründen: Er zog es vor, aus dem, was (angeblich) die ersten Stoiker, vor allem Zenon, der Alten Akademie entnommen hatten, das zurückzugewinnen, was die *veteres* lehrten; dafür nahm er Aristoteles und Theophrast – aber nicht die schriftliche Hinterlassenschaft Platons in Anspruch. Kurz, des Antiochos Versuch, die Lehre der Alten wiederzugewinnen, war nicht auf Platon bezogen; so kann er nicht wohl als 'Platoniker' bezeichnet werden, und an der Wiederbegründung des Platonismus hat er nur geringen, vielleicht keinen Anteil[7].

Ein fast übersehener Satz Augustins[8] läßt noch erkennen, daß es einmal zu einer Art Sezession gekommen ist: Die *recentiores* – so Augustin – wollen weder Akademiker noch Peripatetiker genannt werden, sondern Platoniker. In der Tat ist die Bezeichnung πλατωνικοί = *platonici* für Anhänger Platons[9] erst seit dem 2. Jahrh. n. Chr. nachzuweisen.

3. *Umfang und Inhalt der* διαδοχή

Stand noch für Antiochos und seinen Kreis das von der Skepsis geprägte Urteil fest, Platons Schriften dürften weder für eine Dogmatik noch für eine Doxographie ausgewertet werden, so galt doch dieses Urteil außerhalb der Akademie bereits um 80 v. Chr. nicht mehr. Denn außerhalb der Akademie unternahm man es, gestützt auf den Wortlaut Platons, zu dem zurückzufinden, was Platon lehrte. Dabei scheinen die Bedürfnisse der Doxographie eine durchaus stimulierende Rolle gespielt zu haben. Nun suchte man durch eigenes Lesen – vor allem des Timaios – zu Informationen zu gelangen, welche die Akademie nicht geben konnte oder wollte.

Bei dieser Arbeit des Wiedergewinnens ging man behutsam vor; noch immer hatte man Rücksicht auf eine Kritik zu nehmen, die diesem Vorhaben mit Argwohn gegenüberstand. Darum vertraute man sich nicht irgendwelchen 'ungeschützten' Wendungen Platons an, sondern man hielt sorgsam Umschau, welche Teile aus Platons schriftlichem Erbe tradierbare δόγματα zu bieten schienen. Dazu boten sich vor allem an:
1. Erstens und vor allem die Rede des Timaios, der die Entstehung, ja Erschaffung der Welt darstellt, und zwar besonders *Tim.* 27C-48C, d.h. vom Beginn der Rede bis zu der Stelle, da Timaios sagt, er werde nun noch mehr als bisher genötigt sein, δι' εἰκότων zu sprechen[10].
2. Nicht selten stützt ein Wort Platons das andere. Dem Nachweis des Eudoros, daß Platon an vier Stellen in vierfach verschiedener Diktion eine τέλος-Lehre[11] verkünde, kam sachlich[12] wie methodisch[13] eine ganz außerordentliche Bedeutung zu. Denn von solchen Beobachtungen aus ließ sich das skeptische Mißtrauen ebenso wie der epikureische Vorwurf entkräften, daß Platon lediglich Inkohärentes sage[14].
3. Neben solche Belege, wo Platon aus sich selbst gestützt wird, treten andere, durch welche eine Bestätigung durch Aristoteles gewonnen wird.

Ein weiterer, über das Bisherige hinaus führender Schritt bestand darin, daß man sich Platon in zwei Richtungen anvertraute, wo gerade keine Verifizierung möglich war:
4a. Man machte sich (wieder) die Verhältnisgleichung zu eigen, die Platon im *Staat* 6; 509D ff. vorträgt (sog. Linien-Gleichnis) und die er *Tim.* 29C stark raffend wiederholt: Sein : Werden = Wahrheit : Mut-

maßung. Da konnte man scheinbar keinen Fehler machen; man übernahm ja nur die mathematische Form dieser Gleichung, ohne Platon auf den Inhalt der in ihr verglichenen Begriffe festzulegen[15].

4b. Zugleich gingen große Stücke aus der metaphorischen Sprache Platons in die Fachsprache der Platoniker ein – so die Wendung vom Auge der Seele[16], vom Gefängnis[17], in dem wir uns befinden, – dies sogleich kombiniert mit dem Höhlengleichnis, die Wendung vom Felde der Wahrheit[18] und im Kontrast dazu vom Felde der Ungleichheit[19] – hier ist nicht der Ort, diese überreiche Metaphorik auszubreiten. Nur das damit verbundene Paradox ist eine Bemerkung wert: Eine Metapher verliert nun einmal ihren heuristischen Wert, sobald sie tralatizisch wird; sie wird dann entweder zum Versatzstück oder zum Rätselwort[20]. Danach gelingt es nur selten und nur Könnern, Verhärtetes wieder aufzuweichen oder gar mit vertieftem Sinn zu erfüllen[21].

Anfangs wählte man derlei Zitate, Halbzitate oder Reminiszenzen, um der unerwünschten dogmatischen Festlegung zu entgehen. Nachmals sollte sich diese aus Platon entlehnte Bildersprache so fest einprägen, daß sie zur eigentlichen Basis des platonischen Dogmatismus wurde.

4. *Die eigentliche Konstante im Platonismus*

Auf verschiedenen Wegen und mit verschiedenen Mitteln ist von etwa 70 v. Chr. bis 40 n. Chr. festgelegt worden, an welchen Stellen und mit welchen Ausdrücken Platon sich so äußert, daß seine δόγματα ergreifbar und begreifbar werden. Als Anhalt – freilich als sehr grober Anhalt – darf etwa das angesehen werden, was Philon von Alexandreia an platonischem Gut besitzt, sei es, daß er es zitiert, sei es, daß er Platons Metaphern weiter bildet.

Der so umrissene, stets verfügbare Schatz an Zitaten und Metaphern ist Bezugspunkt, ja Substanz des künftigen Platonismus. Nicht der ganze Platon, sondern eine so zu Stande gekommene, weil als aussagekräftig angesehene Auswahl aus Platon liegt von da an allem Platonismus zu Grunde; auf sie gründen sich alle Versuche, zu einer Systematik der platonischen Philosophie zu gelangen. Wohl ist die Zahl der als legitim angesehenen Bezugsstellen hernach noch langsam gewachsen; wohl gelingt ab und an ein 'Schriftbeweis' aus Platon; aber derlei bleibt Ausnahme. Denn wer vom Wortlaut her das ihm bisher ungenügend scheinende Verständnis Platons berichtigen möchte, hat zunächst und vor allem den Nachweis zu führen, daß er sich mit dem, was rezipiert ist, mit der διαδοχή also, im Einklang befindet. Denn was etwa über das bisher Gewußte hinauszuführen beansprucht, ist in hohem Maße verdächtig. Jene Stelle[22], an der Plotin einen solchen Verdacht von sich weist, muß als der locus classicus für das 'Schriftverständnis' im Platonismus bezeichnet werden.

Nicht Antiochos von Askalon, nicht Poseidonios von Apamea, nicht ein Wieder-Aufleben alt-akademischer Traditionen haben die Erneuerung des Platonismus bewirkt; gewiß haben sie, mit anderen Faktoren, früher oder später auf den sich fort entwickelnden Platonismus eingewirkt; sie haben wichtige Modifikationen in ihn hineingetragen. Sondern am Anfang stand die Frage: „Was hat Platon gelehrt?" genauer: „Welche δόγματα Platons sind zweifelsfrei belegt?" Zur Antwort auf diese Frage gelangte man, indem man vor allem solche Aussprüche Platons aufsuchte, die sich gegenseitig stützen. Das mit solcher Tendenz wiedergewonnene Erbe stellt die eigentliche Konstante des Platonismus dar.

5. Genügt es, Platons Erbe wortwörtlich zu verstehen?

Denen, die aus Platons Schriften den Schatz des Gültigen sammelten, scheint sich die Frage, wie das derart Gesammelte auszulegen ist, garnicht gestellt zu haben. Wenn das Prinzip zutrifft, das man entdeckt zu haben glaubte, nämlich daß Platon sich selbst erklärt, indem er auf anderen Orts Gesagtes interpretierend zurückkommt – dann allerdings ist neben solcher Kommentierung durch den Meister selbst jedes eigene Bemühen nutzlos, ja geradezu vermessen.

Vor allem wurde in schroffem Widerspruch zur alt-akademischen Tradition der Timaios Platons im wörtlichen Sinne verstanden: Der Schöpfer, den man sich als persönlich wirkende Gottheit zu denken hat, hat zu bestimmter Zeit die Welt geschaffen[23]; daß Platon, im Unterschied zu Aristoteles, dieser Ansicht gewesen sei, hat Cicero als gesichertes Wissen angesehen[24].

Vor allem setzt die sog. Drei-Prinzipien-Lehre, aus der im Timaios vorgetragenen Kosmogonie abgeleitet, ein derart wörtliches Verständnis voraus; die präpositionale Verschlüsselung bildet geradezu Platons Wortlaut nach[25].

Das sog. Linien-Gleichnis, das im Staat 6, 509D ff. vorgetragen wird, vollzieht Ps.-Archytas[26] im Wortsinn und nur im Wortsinn nach; dieser Autor vermag nur den erkenntnistheoretischen Aspekt dieser Analogie zu sehen, und er wendet sie nur auf den einzelnen Menschen und seine Erkenntnisfähigkeit an. Daß die von Platon aufgestellte Analogie-Formel weit über den menschlichen Bereich, nämlich auf einen transzendierenden Noûs weist, ist dem Ps. Archytas völlig entgangen[27], wogegen Albinos[28] die Tragweite dieses Theorems gesehen und gewürdigt hat.

Diese naivisch anmutende Phase, da man über den Wortsinn nicht hinauszugehen wagte, ist bald verlassen worden. Schon Philon führt Klage darüber, daß spitzfindige[29] Erklärer den Wortsinn des Schöpfungsberichtes im Timaios in sein Gegenteil verdrehten.

Nur ein Platoniker hat noch im 2. Jahrh. den nun bereits archaisch anmutenden Standpunkt weiter vertreten, Platon habe alles eindeutig und vordergründig, also nicht etwa in Rätseln[30], ausgesprochen. Das war die Ansicht des Attikos[31], der dem Aristoteles und den Aristotelikern wieder und wieder den, wie er meint, eindeutigen und unmißverständlichen Wortlaut Platons entgegenhält.

6. *Spricht Platon in Rätseln?*

Auf die Dauer ließ sich nicht verkennen, daß viele Worte Platons über den vordergründigen Sinn hinausweisen: Das gilt von allen Metaphern, es gilt besonders von den Mythen. Zudem mußte die Überzeugung vom eindeutigen, durch keine Verschlüsselung verhüllten, wörtlichen Sinne gerade dann erschüttert werden, wenn man die verschiedenen Formulierungen desselben Dogmas verglich; dann fällt nicht nur die Übereinstimmung im Grundsätzlichen, sondern ebenso die Abweichung im Einzelnen auf.

Ebensowenig ließen sich die vielfachen Warnungen Platons überhören, daß sich die Wahrheit nicht durch vordergründige Aussage, und daß sie sich nicht für alle verständlich mitteilen läßt. Man sah sich also alsbald vor die Frage gestellt, wie von dem nun einmal anerkannten und als verbindlich angesehenen Besitz aus Platon der richtige Gebrauch zu machen sei.

Die erst vor kurzer Zeit gewonnene und erhärtete These, dass Platon δόγματα mitteilt, genügte mithin nicht; es war mindestens zu fragen ποσαχῶς δογματίζει Πλάτων; So wurde die Frage von Gaios[32] und von Albinos formuliert; die Antwort darauf wird an Hand von *Tim.* 29B gewonnen[33]. Das δογματίζειν Platons vollzieht sich auf zwei Ebenen ἢ ἐπιστημονικῶς ἢ εἰκοτολογικῶς. Je nach dem, welchem Gebiet sich die λόγοι, d.h. die philosophischen Untersuchungen, zuwenden, haben sie verschiedenen Wahrheitsgehalt[34]; diese συγγένεια mit dem Eigentlichen drückt sich somit in den λόγοι aus, die von ihm handeln[35].

Indes darf das, was als Lehr-Entscheidung des Gaios und des Albinos hierzu bezeugt ist, nur als eine partiell gültige[36] Lösung des Problems angesehen werden. Im Ganzen genommen ist in dieser Zeit auf Platon übertragen worden, was für die Exegese Homers schon lange galt: Der Dichter und der Philosoph, hierin dem delphischen Gotte ähnlich, ja von ihm inspiriert, sprechen das Wesentliche und das Eigentliche in Rätseln aus. Wer da meint, das vordergründig Gesagte enthalte die ganze Wahrheit, täuscht sich[37].

So ist alle Platon-Auslegung – mehr noch als die Auslegung Homers – von der Tendenz beherrscht, es gelte ein halb verborgenes Wissen aufzufinden, das sich dem erschließt, der Platons αἰνίγματα richtig löst. Als Kriterium für die Richtigkeit der Lösung gilt nach einhelliger Meinung dieses: Diejenige Erklärung, die am nächsten an die πρώτη φιλοσοφία heranführt, hat die größte Wahrscheinlichkeit für sich, richtig zu sein. Wohl können mehrere Erklärungen angeboten werden – es ist sogar die Regel, daß man einem Leser deren mehreren vorträgt[38]; er wird aufgefordert, die richtige Wahl zu treffen. Zugleich aber wird kein Zweifel daran gelassen, welche (unter mehreren möglichen Erklärungen) den Vorzug verdient.

Von Anfang an zeigt der Platonismus unverkennbar starke religiöse Züge. Das oft extrem rationalistisch anmutende Bemühen, in der oben S. 118 geschilderten Weise aus Platons Schriftenmasse das im dogmatischen Sinne Gültige zu extrahieren, verdeckt oft genug diesen Grundzug: Entweder war dieser stets vorhanden, oder er gelangte nach einer kurzen rein rationalen Phase im Platonismus zu tiefgreifender Wirksamkeit.

Es würde zu weit führen, diese an Hand weiterer Zeugnisse darzustellen. Im gegenwärtigen Zusammenhang kommt es darauf an, daß festgestellt wird, in wie hohem Grade die Auslegung Platons – also die Nutzung des platonischen Erbes – von dieser Tendenz zum Religiösen bestimmt ist: Die Rätsel, die Platon dem Leser aufgibt, seine αἰνίγματα also, fordern eine Lösung in dem Sinne, daß ihnen entweder religiöse Offenbarung oder theologische Erkenntnis zu entnehmen ist. Mit dieser Antithese (religiöse Offenbarung/theologische Erkenntnis) wird auf die Alternative vorgegriffen, die unten weiter ausgeführt werden soll.

Schon jene erste, nahezu anonym bleibende Generation von Platonikern, die man fast Platon-Philologen nennen dürfte (vgl. oben S. 118), hat eine bemerkenswerte Hellhörigkeit bewiesen, was die seltenen, fast stets vorsichtig verhüllten Äußerungen Platons zur πρώτη φιλοσοφία anlangt. Mit unbestreitbarem Geschick hat man die an das ἄρρητον rührenden Worte Platons wieder zum Tragen gebracht.

Von da an kulminierte die Aufgabe, den aus Platon geborgenen Schatz an Weisheit recht zu gebrauchen, darin, seine πρώτη φιλοσοφία nachzuzeichnen. Das geschah nicht nur aus Freude an metaphysischer Spekulation. Vielmehr ist der von Platon mehrfach ausgesprochene Lehrsatz, daß es allein durch λογισμὸς καὶ διάνοια gelingen kann, sich dem Höchsten erkennend zu nähern, stets gehört und beachtet worden. Philosophische Bemühung um die Erkenntnis von Noûs und Logos ist Gottesdienst[39]; sie trägt dazu bei, das Ziel zu erreichen, das als ὁμοίωσις θεῷ κατὰ τὸ δυνατόν[40] definiert ist.

Wenn zuvor (oben S. 122) gesagt wurde, daß der Platonismus tief religiös fundiert ist, so ist das zum Teil aus der eben gegebenen Begründung abzuleiten: Gesicherte Erkenntnis vom Göttlichen zu gewinnen, heißt zugleich, die σωτηρία der erkennenden Seele, d.h. ihre Erhaltung[41] über das gegenwärtige Leben hinaus zu sichern. Bald schien es jedem Zweifel entrückt zu sein, daß alle αἰνίγματα Platons um diesen zentralen Lehrsatz kreisen[42].

7. *Zwei unterschiedliche Haltungen gegenuber dem platonischen Erbe*

Nun sind zwei voneinander stark verschiedene Haltungen abzugrenzen – Haltungen, mit denen man Gebrauch von diesem Erbe machte. Allerdings hat sich wohl kein Platoniker kompromißlos auf die eine oder die andere Seite gestellt. Das Bild, das der Platonismus bis hin zu Plotin bietet, ist ja eben darum so bunt, weil alle möglichen vermittelnden Positionen bezogen wurden. So geht es im Folgenden darum, zwei Extreme herauszuarbeiten. Wer eine dieser beiden Linien unbeirrt und ohne Einschränkungen verfolgt hätte, hätte ein gut Teil des als platonisch Bezeugten opfern müssen. Was platonisch ist, liegt zwischen den beiden Linien, von denen nun die Rede sein soll. Alle Platoniker, mochten sie der einen, mochten sie der anderen Haltung zuneigen, haben sich bemüht, möglichst viel vom vorgegebenen Erbe zu bewahren; sie alle möchten zu einer Integration (*sit venia verbo*) gelangen.

Um möglichst klar darzustellen, was mit den beiden Haltungen = *habitus* = ἕξεις gemeint ist, sollen zunächst zwei kurze Charakteristiken gegeben werden:

a. Die eine Haltung ist dadurch gekennzeichnet, daß *Analogie* ihre hauptsächliche Methode ist. Hier steigt man vom durch Erfahrung gewonnen Befund *per analogiam* zu höheren Wissem auf. Dabei verzichtet man nicht auf Anschaulichkeit. Die alten Weisen, unter ihnen besonders Platon, waren, ebenso wie die Natur selbst, hervorragende Didaktiker; sie haben den Menschen nur solche Rätsel aufgegeben, die diese ihrer Natur nach lösen können. Hierin, und in vielem anderen, äußert sich die Vorsehung, die als Fürsorglichkeit Gottes verstanden wird. Dieser Gott ist der Welt *zu*gewandt[43], denn er ist ständig in der Welt, zum Guten wirkend aktiv. Diesem Gott kann man sich über viele Zwischenstufen nähern; umgekehrt entfaltet er sich über viele Zwischenstufen in diese Welt hinein. Die Vorstellung von mehreren oder vielen, zu einander im Verhältnis der Analogie stehenden Stufen ist analogen Vorstellungen der Gnosis verwandt. Im Übrigen kommt hier auf Schärfe theologischer Unterscheidungen wenig, auf Frömmigkeit und auf Religiosität sehr viel an.

Da Gott sich dieser Welt durch den Logos, ja als Logos mitteilt, ist es für den, der diesen *habitus* einnimmt, subjektiv wie objektiv gleich wichtig, den Logos, wo immer er sich halbverborgen manifestiert, aufzufinden; objektiv, weil jede Auffindung des Göttlichen dazu dient, das Göttliche zu verkünden; subjektiv, weil der Finder nur kraft eines ihm innewohnenden Logos den in Natur-und-Geistes-Welt verborgenen Logos zu entschlüsseln vermag. Jeder Erkenntnisvorgang ist Gewinn für den, der ihn vollzieht.

Darum wird diese Haltung in enzyklopädischer Breite, ja in universaler Betrachtung aller Wissensgebiete und aller in diesen zu Tage liegenden Wunder und Geheimnisse eingeübt. Wer diese Haltung einnimmt, tendiert nicht so sehr dahin, sogleich – geschweige denn überstürzt – den steilen Anstieg zur πρώτη φιλοσοφία zu wagen; da er es vermeidet, in Gebiete vorzudringen, in welchen die Anschaulichkeit verloren gehen könnte, hält er sich mit Vorzug da auf, wo sich ihm sein Gott – der Logos – in überreicher Variation erschließt. Ist seine Methode die der Analogie, so ist sein Ergebnis nahezu pantheistisch: Der Logos ist überall gegenwärtig.

Die Gruppe derer, die diese Haltung einnahmen, muß recht eigentlich als die der Logos-Sucher (und-Finder) bezeichnet werden. Vieles von dem, was von den Vertretern der entgegengesetzten Haltung gegen die φιλόλογοι geäußert wurde[44], trifft diese Vertreter einer Logos-Religion, die in allem, was in Natur, Geschichte, Kultus und Bildung kontinuierlich ist, die Manifestation des göttlichen Logos erblickten. Aus der enzyklopädischen Beherrschung des gesamten damaligen Bildungserbes wurde ein ganzes Arsenal von Argumenten gewonnen, die gegen diejenigen zu richten waren, die da behaupteten, eine historisch fixierte Herabkunft[45] des Logos in der Person Christi habe alle früheren Manifestationen des Logos entwertet und aufgehoben.

Platoniker, die diese Haltung einnahmen, lassen oft genug erkennen, daß unter ihnen der Einfluß des Poseidonios von Apamea nachwirkt;

124

besonders die Forderung, daß es gelte, in allem den Logos erkennend zu verwirklichen, geht auf ihn zurück. Zugleich wurden Strömungen, die von der Gnosis ausgingen, von diesen Platonikern leichter rezipiert als von ihren Gegnern: Der Logos teilt sich denen, die ihn suchen, durch viele Medien und über viele Zwischenstufen mit. Zwar ist es für einen Platoniker undenkbar, daß der Logos sich auf diesem Wege zum Bösen pervertiert; aber der Gedanke der stufenweisen Herabkunft und der stufenweise sich vollziehenden Rück- und Heimkehr findet in dieser Gruppe von Platonikern lebendigen Widerhall.

Vor allem führt der so skizzierte *habitus* nicht – oder kaum – zu reflektierter Theologie. Es dominiert die Vorstellung vom gütigen Weltschöpfer, so wie ihn Platons *Timaios* zeichnet. Insbesondere wird dieser Schöpfer und Lenker der Welt als eine Gottheit gedacht, die ihrer Schöpfung in Fürsorge zugewandt ist. Diese Fürsorge wird nicht nur in dem sichtbar, was er den Menschen an materiellen *beneficia* geschenkt hat (Wechsel der Jahreszeiten, günstiges Klima, Fruchtbarkeit der Äcker). Sondern das wichtigste Geschenk, das dieser Gott der Menschheit gemacht hat, besteht darin, daß er sich *per analogiam* von den Menschen finden läßt. Die *theologia naturalis*, durch die er sich für die, die ihn zu erkennen vermögen, offenbart, ist die sublimste Gabe[46] dieses Gottes, der durchaus Züge des Apollon von Delphi trägt. Es war folgerichtig, daß Plutarchs Theologie apollinische Theologie war. Der Mensch ist diesem Gotte verwandt – συγγενής[47]. Dank dieser Verwandtschaft kann er im Logos – auch dem Logos, den er in sich hat – Gott erkennen. Darum hat die delphische Forderung γνῶθι σαυτόν für diese Platoniker den Wert einer alles klärenden Offenbarung.

b. Die entgegengesetzte Haltung tut sich in folgenden Merkmalen kund:

Hier geht man vom erkenntnistheoretischen Dualismus Platons aus. So wie das Sein radikal verschieden ist vom Werden, so sind ἐπιστήμη und δόξα von einander substantiell verschieden. Im einen wie im anderen Bereich kann weder Übergang noch Vermittlung stattfinden. Mithin kann die *via analogiae* nicht als Brücke dienen; es ist falsch, Vorstellungsbehelfe, die aus diesseitiger Erfahrung gewonnen sind, für die Erkenntnis des ganz Anderen auswerten zu wollen. Ihm kann man sich nur nähern, wenn man alles Diesseitige negiert, wenn man von allem Diesseitigen, bis hin zur Aussage, abstrahiert. So bevorzugt man die Methode *per abstractionem* = καθ᾽ ἀφαίρεσιν.

Das schließt den Verzicht auf Anschaulichkeit ein. Wer so denkt, verzichtet zugleich auf Platons Mythen; zugleich ist er geneigt, sich bei dem Schüler Platons Rat zu holen, der es sich versagte, auf Anschaulichkeit zu rekurrieren: Aristoteles.

Hier gilt nicht so sehr die Berufung darauf, daß man uraltes Wissen vor sich hat; der Zeugniswert der Alten Weisen ist gering. Viel mehr kommt darauf an, daß die vorzutragenden Beweisgänge logisch schlüssig sind. Darum macht man sich hier nicht nur Physik und Metaphysik des Aristoteles, sondern besonders die Logik zu eigen.

Man geht eine logisch determinierte, von Anschaulichkeit freie *via negationis*. Von solchem Ansatz her ist es unzulässig, sich ein nur intermittierend tätiges höchstes Prinzip vorzustellen: Dieses kann nicht etwa einer Welt, in die es wieder und wieder eingreifen muß, zugewandt sein. Sondern hier wird das höchste Wesen von aller Verantwortung für diese Welt entlastet; es nimmt sie garnicht zur Kenntnis, denn es muß als Noûs von höchster Subtilität vorgestellt werden, d.h. als reines Denken, das stets sich selbst denkt[48].

Auch hier werden Seins-Stufen (man dürfte, mit Blick auf Albinos[49] auch sagen: Aktions-Stufen) unterhalb des höchsten Prinzips vermutet. Das Vorbild-Abbild-Schema wird nahezu ignoriert; statt dessen wird unterstrichen, dass die jeweils untere Stufe der jeweils höheren im Grunde inkommensurabel ist.

Darum kann der Aufstieg zum Höchsten nicht etwa auf der bequemen *via analogiae* stattfinden, sondern er vollzieht sich in paradoxalen Sprüngen, die über eigentlich garnicht überwindbare Zerklüftungen hinwegführen.

Von da erklärt sich, wieso die Anhänger dieser Haltung eher der Mystik zuneigen als diejenigen, die sich auf der *via analogiae* bewegen. Unklar ist freilich, ob Vorgänger Plotins das Erlebnis der mystischen Einung hatten, und ob sie darüber sprachen. Nur soviel steht fest, daß die *via abstractionis* in eine solche Spannung, ja Gespanntheit führen kann, daß der menschliche Verstand, ohnehin dem Diesseits verhaftet, nicht zur Lösung führen kann; diese muß von dem paradoxalen Erlebnis der *unio mystica* erwartet werden.

Mit der Vorstellung von den (fast) unüberwindbaren Seins-Stufen dürfte es zusammenhängen, daß diese Haltung nicht mit der Gnosis vereinbar war; auf diese Gruppe von Platonikern scheint die Gnosis nicht anziehend oder gar stimulierend, sondern abstoßend gewirkt zu haben.

Der Aufstieg zum Höchsten und zum Eigentlichen erfordert die ganze Kraft des Philosophierenden; auf dieses Ziel ist alle Intensität zu richten. So sieht man es als unnützen Umweg an, den Logos in seinen unübersehbar vielen Manifestationen aufzuspüren und zu beschreiben. Nicht

auf das Viele kommt es an, sondern auf das Eine. Dieser Satz hat wahrscheinlich als eine Werte bezeichnende Leit-Linie gegolten – lange bevor er als ein zentrales ontologisches Axiom verstanden wurde.

Bald gelangen die Vertreter dieser Haltung dazu, einen geradezu schroffen Monismus auszuprägen. Daß der Logos überall anwesend ist, interessiert kaum, – gilt es doch zum Ursprung, zur ἀρχή dieses Logos aufzusteigen. Hier hat eine sorgsam formulierte, durchaus *in abstracto* konstruierte negative Theologie ihre Wurzel, – eine vorzugsweise spekulative Theologie, in welcher sich oft ein geradezu scholastisches Denken äußert.

In nachstehender Zusammenfassung wird die antithetische Spannung im Platonismus mit Absicht überspitzt beschrieben:

Da steht auf der einen Seite eine Logos-Religion, auf der anderen Seite eine Noûs-Theologie. Die zuerst genannte Haltung ist auf einen als allgegenwärtig vorgestellten Logos gerichtet; ihre Vertreter stehen dem spätstoischen Pantheismus nahe. Hier vor allem wirken die Konzeptionen des Poseidonios nach.

Dagegen läßt ein Platonismus, der sich vor allem als Noûs-Theologie versteht, die Einwirkung aristotelischer Logik und aristotelischer Metaphysik erkennen; er ist nicht darauf gerichtet, die Verwirklichung des Göttlichen in dieser Welt zu erkennen, statt dessen sucht er mit rationalen, ja z.T. mit überrationalen Mitteln zur Erkenntnis des höchsten Wesens jenseits allen Seins zu gelangen.

Der von der Logos-Suche inspirierte Platonismus sucht den Gegenstand seines Forschens (und seiner religiösen Verehrung) *in* der Vielfältigkeit dieser Welt auf; die auf den Noûs gerichtete Spekulation strebt aus der Immanenz hinaus in den Bereich des Transzendenten. Die Logos-Religion weist auf unendlich viele Manifestationen des Göttlichen in dieser Welt hin; die Noûs-Theologie beschränkt sich auf einen Gegenstand, den Urgrund aller nachgeordneten Manifestationen = ὑποστάσεις.

Der Platonismus als Logos-Religion ist bereit, jeden Stoff zu ergreifen, sich mit jedem Phänomen auseinanderzusetzen; er ist bereit, aus Bräuchen, besonders kultischen Bräuchen ferner Völker, aber auch aus den Meinungen anderer Philosophen das mit Anerkennung hervorzuheben, worin sich ein Funke des Logos kundtut; so könnte man ihn fast tolerant nennen – jedenfalls im Unterschied zum Platonismus als Noûs-Theologie: Dort wird kein Irrtum verziehen; es wird mit Schärfe polemisiert; nicht Zugehöriges – ἀλλότρια – wird rigorös abgewiesen.

8. Wesensbestimmung und Aufgabe der Philosophie

Auf beiden Seiten ist man davon überzeugt, das eigene geistige Bemühen sei Philosophie. Wahrscheinlich läßt die skizzierte Antithese sich am ehesten lösen, wenn man sie darauf zurückführt, daß den beiden Haltungen ein weithin verschiedenes Verständnis zu Grunde liegt, was denn Philosophie sei, und wie sie auszuüben sei.

Freilich vermag ich nur zwei Äußerungen nachzuweisen, durch welche Vertreter der Noûs-Theologie es einem Gegner bescheinigen, daß sie ihn entweder nicht als Philosophen oder nicht als Platoniker anerkennen können:

Plotin deklassierte den Longinos, Vertreter eines enzyklopädischen Platonismus, zum bloßen Philologen[50]; und Syrian forderte von Plutarch und seinen Anhängern, sie müßten ihre Irrtümer in der Ideen-Lehre ablegen, wenn sie denn Platoniker bleiben wollten[51]. In beiden Fällen werden die Gegner darum so hart abqualifiziert, weil sie es unterlassen haben, ihr Forschen (so Longin) oder die Gegenstände des Forschens (hier: die Ideen) mit der gebotenen Zielstrebigkeit auf den Noûs als *causa generalis*[52] hin zu ordnen. Ein solcher Mangel an geradliniger Methodik begründet den Zweifel, ob der Kritisierte Philosoph oder Platoniker sei. Zugleich muß an die zweifellos strenge Eingangsprüfung erinnert werden, durch die Tauros[53] sich Gewißheit verschaffte, ob einer die διάθεσις, also die Eignung zum Philosophen habe.

Der Tadel, den Plotin und Syrian aussprachen, enthält die Feststellung, daß da ein von Natur Ungeeigneter sich ein Urteil über Philosophisches anmaße; sein Urteil muß unverbindlich bleiben, weil der so Urteilende entweder nicht die Kompetenz dazu hat, oder weil er außerhalb der διαδοχή steht.

Nun sind Stimmen wie diese im Ganzen selten. Aber sie weisen eindeutig auf die folgende, bisher verborgene Diskrepanz hin: Nach der einen Ansicht legitimiert der Logos einen jeden, der eine Manifestation des Logos auffindet, diese zu verkünden; aufnehmen und verstehen können seine Botschaft ohnehin nur die, denen der Logos in gleicher Weise nahe ist: Allein der Logos befähigt zum Verstehen und zum Verkünden.

Gegenthese: Eine Legitimation zu philosophischem Urteil hat nur der, der folgende Voraussetzungen erfüllt: 1) Er muß die notwendige διάθεσις mitbringen; diese muß er in einem früheren Leben derart erworben haben, daß die unbestechlich gerechte πρόνοια ihm in diesem Leben die inneren und die äußeren Voraussetzungen gewährt, dank dener er philosophieren kann. 2) So vorbereitet, muß er sich, was sein Philosophieren anlangt, im

Rahmen der διαδοχή bewegen; d.h. das, was die παλαιοί σοφοί, vor allem Platon, lehrten, bleibt verbindlich. Dabei besteht ein innerer Zusammenhang: Wer 2) verletzt, beweist damit, daß er 1) nicht erfüllt.

Diese Haltung tendiert dahin, daß der Platonismus sich zu schulgerechtem, ja zunftgerechtem Philosophieren einengt; Anregungen von außen werden abgewiesen. Kein Wunder, daß man Platonikern dieses Schlages bald einen *immanissimus tyfus*[54], einen unerträglichen Dünkel, nachsagte. Das ist nach dem Ausgeführten ebenso verständlich wie das andere, ebenso oft wiederholte Pauschalurteil über den Platonismus und über Platoniker: *subtilitas*[55]. In beidem drückt sich aus, daß an die Philosophie und an die Philosophierenden so erhebliche Anforderungen gerichtet wurden, daß viele diese Hürde nicht zu nehmen vermochten.

Die Vertreter des entgegengesetzten Aspektes waren durchaus nicht in solchem Sinne selektiv. Im Gegenteil, wenn man für viele Phänomene drei oder vier Erklärungen bereit hielt (vgl. oben S. 122), so nicht etwa aus Unsicherheit. Sondern gerade denen, die zu höherem Verständnis nicht fähig sind, soll eine befriedigende, ihrer Auffassungskraft angemessene Antwort geboten werden[56]. Der riesige Bau des vom Logos erfüllten Wissens ist in allen seinen Ebenen stimmig – eben weil diese Ebenen zu einander im Analogie-Verhältnis stehen.

Kurz, in der Frage, was Philosophie ist und wie sie gehandhabt werden soll, treten die beiden Aspekte, die hier skizziert werden, zu polarer Gegensätzlichkeit auseinander: Hier wird Philosophie als Logos-Suche möglichst jedem zugänglich gemacht; Abkürzungen und Vereinfachungen, ja sogar Vulgarisierungen werden in Kauf genommen, ja manchmal gar gepflegt. Davon unterscheidet sich ein schulebildender und darum meist schulgerechter Platonismus, der sich mit unverhohlener Schroffheit von den ἀμαθεῖς absondert, ja abkapselt.

Beide Aspekte sind in Platon angelegt. Es wäre müßig, ein Urteil zu wagen, welchem Aspekt Platon selbst zugeneigt hätte. Platon wäre sicher den Extremen entgegen getreten, zu denen jeder der beiden Aspekte verleiten kann – im Übrigen können sich beide Richtungen darauf berufen, daß sie bei Platon Angelegtes 'richtig' wieder geben. In hundert, vielleicht in tausend Einzelheiten trifft das zu. Nur ist keiner der Nachfahren in der Lage gewesen, die in Platon angelegte antithetische Spannung jemals nachzuvollziehen. Was Platon zu umgreifen vermochte, schließt sich bei seinen Nachfahren gegenseitig aus.

10. *Schematisierende Zusammenfassung*

Gewiß ist wenig damit getan, die beiden sich abzeichnenden Haltungen durch die nunmehr naheliegenden Schlagworte zu kennzeichnen. Trotzdem soll, um das bisher Gesagte zusammenzufassen, die Gegensätzlichkeit der sichtbar werdenden Tendenzen schematisch aufgezeichnet werden:

Hier wiegt vor:	Dort wiegt vor:
exoterische Haltung	esoterische Haltung
Öffnung zum Publikum	Ausschluß nicht Vorgebildeter
Didaktische Rücksichtnahme	*immanissimus tyfus*
Anschaulichkeit	Verzicht auf Anschaulichkeit
Analogie	Abstraktion
Einflüsse der Stoa	Einflüsse des Aristoteles
Nähe zur Gnosis	Opposition zur Gnosis
Religiosität	Theologie

Die eigentliche Verehrung gilt

dem immanenten Logos	dem transzendenten Noûs

Zu Gott führt

via analogiae	*via negationis*

Gott ist der Welt

zugewandt	abgewandt
Er teilt sich der Welt mit durch	Gott ist nur auf sich selbst bezogen;
Emanation[57], d.h. durch seinen	die Emanations-Vorstellung wird
Logos.	abgelehnt.

Gewiß ist es zulässig, die bekannteren Platoniker vom 2. Jahrh. n. Chr.[58] an vorzugsweise einer der beiden Gruppen zuzuordnen. Dann würde etwa dieses Bild entstehen:

Plutarch von Chaironeia	Gaios
Kelsos von Alexandreia	Albinos
Cassius Longinos	Plotin

Sicher hat Porphyrios bewußt den Ausgleich, ja die Addition beider Seiten angestrebt, wobei er die Antithese in eine Stufung umwandelte.

11. *Vom Nutzen und Nachteil einer solchen Schematik*

Es wäre ganz falsch, wenn die soeben vorgetragene Grob-Einteilung so angewendet würde, daß man durch sie die vielschichtige Problematik des

Platonismus simplifizierend verkürzte. Sie soll vielmehr dazu beitragen, daß diese Problematik besser, d.h. mit mehr begründeter Differenzierung, verständlich wird.

Sicher wäre es ebenso falsch, einzelne Platoniker in das obige Schema zu pressen – dieses Schema würde sich alsbald als ein Prokrustes-Bett erweisen. Eher dürfte man die philosophische Leistung aller Platoniker als einen Mittelweg beschreiben, der zwischen den skizzierten Extremen hindurchführt; es ist unverkennbar, daß alle (vom 2. Jahrh. n. Chr. an) den Ort gesucht haben, von dem aus ein harmonischer Ausgleich zwischen den in obiger Schematik bezeichneten Gegensätzen gefunden werden kann. Vielleicht läßt sich etwas für die Kennzeichnung einzelner Platoniker gewinnen, wenn man es unternimmt (soweit die erhaltenen Bezeugungen es gestatten), die philosophische Position von diesen Koordinaten her zu bestimmen.

Bisher wurden widersprüchliche Ansichten darüber geäussert, in welchem Verhältnis der Platonismus zur Gnosis steht; ein erster, nachmals stark modifizierter Ansatz[59] ließ den Platonismus als vorwiegend gnostisch geprägt erscheinen. Wahrscheinlich muß die Lösung in folgender Richtung gesucht werden: Sicher hat die Gnosis Einfluß auf den Platonismus ausgeübt[60]; aber ebenso sicher haben sich starke Kräfte im Platonismus dagegen gewendet, daß bestimmte, für die Gnosis konstitutive Ansichten im Platonismus Platz griffen[61]. Anziehende und abstoßende Kräfte scheinen sich die Waage gehalten zu haben. Auch hier wird es notwendig sein, jeweils im Einzelnen abzuwägen, welche Stellung einzelne Platoniker zwischen diesen Fronten einnahmen.

Platonismus kann nicht nur als Philosophie im modernen Sinne definiert werden; nur selten haben sich Platoniker auf dem Niveau Plotins bewegt, und schon dessen Zeitgenossen liessen deutlich erkennen, wie ungewohnt ihnen das war.

In der Tat erschließt sich der Platonismus nicht nur dem philosophischen Mit- oder Nachvollzug. Ebenso legitim ist es, den Weg der Motiv-Forschung zu beschreiten; dabei müssen als 'Motive' die einzelnen Bausteine angesehen werden, die man (vgl. oben S. 119) zwar in großer Zahl, aber zugleich in zielstrebiger Auswahl vor allem aus Platons Schriften zusammentrug (nur ganz weniges entstammt anderen Werken).

Geht man diesen Weg, dann erweist sich die oben vorgetragene Einteilung als ein oft hilfreiches Ordnungsprinzip. So sehr die einzelnen Platoniker im Ganze zu vermitteln suchen, so radikal sind sie oft in ihrer Auswertung einzelner Motive = Reminiszenzen aus Platon. Die seltsame, bisher kaum zu überwindende Diskrepanz (vgl. oben S. 123) ist zum Teil in dieser Haltung der meisten Platoniker begründet, in der Behandlung der Einzelheiten sich in einer Einseitigkeit, die bis zur Absurdität gehen kann, festzulegen – so sehr man auch im Ganzen zu toleranter Ausgeglichenheit neigt.

Die Aufgabe, den Platonismus von der Fülle des in ihm verarbeiteten Details aus aufzuarbeiten, ist in vielen *specimina* geleistet. Wenn es nun darum geht, von der Fülle des Details zur Synthese zu gelangen (vgl. oben S. 116), dann leistet die oben versuchte Beobachtung der zwei einander entgegenwirkenden Tendenzen recht viel Hilfe, um das Detail zu ordnen; ein großer Teil davon wird besser verständlich, wenn man es zu den beiden Koordinaten, von denen hier gehandelt wurde, in Beziehung setzt.

Plotin sah (vgl. oben S. 128) im Philologen den (eigentlich ganz unnützen) Widerpart zum Philosophen, der allein nach dem Eigentlichen fragt. Im Platonismus ist die Geschichte seiner Konventionen und seiner Motive so eng mit dem eigentlich Philosophischen verknüpft, ja vermengt, daß beide Forschungsrichtungen dazu aufgerufen sind, möglichst *passibus aequis* an die Problematik des Platonismus heranzutreten. So darf es der Philologe wohl wagen, diese Überlegungen in einen Band einzufügen, der einer Philosophin als Ehrengeschenk gewidmet ist: Auf keinem anderen Felde hat sich das Miteinander von Philosophie und Philologie in so reichem Maße bewährt wie auf diesem.

ANMERKUNGEN

[1] C. J. de Vogel: *A la recherche des étapes précises entre Platon et le Néoplatonisme,* Mnem. 1954, 111-122; eine knappe Zusammenfassung ist mitgeteilt in den *Actes du Congrès G. Budé* 1954, 193 ff.

[2] Ph. Merlan: *From Platonism to Neoplatonism,* [1]1953, [2]1960, geht ausdrücklich von der Kluft – „the gap" – aus, die den Neuplatonismus von Platon trennt. Bei der Aufzählung der trennenden Merkmale nennt er nahezu alle Themen, zu denen Frau de Vogel a.O. Stellung nimmt; vgl. die folg. Anmerkung.

[3] Die wichtigsten unter ihnen sind: Die These von der hierarchischen Stufung des Seienden; der Noûs als der Ort der Ideen; die Seele als Ort, ja als Inbegriff von Geometrie, Arithmetik und Harmonie.

[4] Dieser Mißstand ist von einigen damaligen Platonikern erkannt worden. Man suchte ihn zu beheben, indem man nach der allein zulässigen Methode Ausschau hielt, wie Platon erklärt werden muß: Wo sind seine Worte κυρίως, wo sind sie μεταληπτικῶς oder τροπικῶς zu verstehen? Vgl. dazu Gaios und Albinos bei Proklos *In Tim.* I 340, 24; vgl. A. Eon, *La notion Plotinienne d'exégèse*; Revue Internat. de Philosophie 24, 1970, 252-289. Nachmals wies Porphyrios alles Mißverstehen, alle Polemik und allen Streit der sprachlichen Ebene, also dem philologischen Bereich zu, die er als eine *regio dissimilitudinis* ansah. Jenseits des Diskursiven, im Bereich des dem Noûs zugewandten Verstehens entfallen alle Gegensätze: Alle Philosophen meinen die gleiche Wahrheit.

132

[5] Hier lag das Motiv für Cicero, sich über Philosophisches möglichst in Dialogen auszusprechen; Dialoge boten die Möglichkeit, den betr. Gegenstand in Rede und Gegenrede zu erörtern.

[6] Bis zur Wieder-Auffindung der aristotelischen Lehrschriften war die Lage der Bezeugung für Platon und Aristoteles gleich: Es lagen nur Dialoge vor. Dieses Gleichgewicht verschob sich vom Jahre 86 an, dem Datum der Wieder-Auffindung. Wahrscheinlich hatte das auch Rückwirkungen darauf, wie man den dogmatischen Gehalt der Dialoge Platons einschätzte.

[7] Ich weiß es wohl (und ich bedaure es), daß ich mich im Widerspruch befinde zu W. Theiler, der bes. im Kap. 1 seiner *Vorbereitung des Neuplatonismus* eben Antiochos als das Bindeglied vermutet hat.

[8] *Civ. Dei* 8, 12 (Ende).

[9] Die ältesten Belege dürften sein: Sextos Emp., *Adv. math.* 7, 143; Attikos bei Eusebios, *Praep. ev.* 15, 7, 2; 804d Viguier; Lukian, *Hermotimos* 16; Tertullian, *Praescr.* 7. – Plutarch verwendet das Wort nie; Gellius, *Noct. Att.* 15, 2, 1 spricht von einem nichtswürdigen Menschen – *homo nihili* – der es sich anmaßte, ein *philosophus Platonicus* genannt zu werden.

[10] Aus dieser Stelle ist offenbar in Verbindung mit *Tim.* 29B gefolgert worden, alles Voraufgehende sei δογματικῶς oder ἐπιστημονικῶς zu verstehen; vgl. B. Witte: *Der εἰκὼς λόγος in Platos Timaios. Beitrag zur Wissenschaftsmethode und Erkenntnistheorie des späten Plato*; Arch. Gesch. Phil. 46, 1964, 1-16.

[11] Auch das muß mit den Erfordernissen der Doxographie in Verbindung gestanden haben: Der grundlegenden und mit Sorgfalt ausgearbeiteten τέλος-Lehre der Stoiker mußte etwas Analoges in Platons ἀρέσκοντα entsprechen.

[12] Denn das hieß: Alle Bereiche der Theorie und der Praxis sind auf das Göttliche bezogen und haben in ihm ihre Spitze. Zuvor war der Platonismus fast einseitig auf die Grundfrage der Kosmologie bezogen.

[13] Gewiß ist schon vorher ab und an auf *Theait.* 176AB verwiesen oder angespielt worden. Aber der vierfache Nachweis, den Eudoros antritt, hat bewirkt, daß die aus *Theait.* 176AB abgeleitete τέλος – Formel zum konstitutiven Lehrstück wurde – das ist der entscheidende Punkt, in welchem H. J. Krämers Bemerkung: *Platonismus und hellenistische Philosophie* 1971, 174, Anm. 284 richtig zu stellen ist.

[14] Cicero, *Nat. deor.* 1, 30 mit den von A. St. Pease z. St. gesammelten Belegen.

[15] Fast unbeachtet blieb bisher, daß in der Schrift des Ps. Archytas περὶ νοῦ καὶ αἰσθάσιος eben diese Stelle für Archytas, d.h. für altpythagoreische διαδοχή in Anspruch genommen wird. Das steht in engster Entsprechung zur Schrift des Timaios Lokros. Auch im Sprachlichen liegt die gleiche Retro-Version in die pythagoreische Diktion vor. Der Text ist derzeit am bequemsten zugänglich bei H. Thesleff: *The Pythagorean Texts* etc., Abo 1965, 36-39. Zu Th.s Vermutung, hier liege ein authentischer Text des Archytas vor, durchschlagend W. Burkert: Gnomon 1962, 768. – Zentrale Bedeutung hat das sog. Liniengleichnis für Albinos, *Did.* 7; S. 162, 12 ff. Hermann und bes. Kēlsos 7, 42.

[16] Ausgangspunkt: Platon, *Staat* 7, 533 D.

[17] Vgl. *Phaidon* 62B; vgl. P. Boyancé: *Note sur la* φρουρά *Platonicienne*, RPh 89, 1963, 7-11.

[18] Vgl. *Phaidros* 248B. Plutarch stellt *De defectu oraculorum* 21 und 22 bes. 422b einen pythagoreischen Versuch dar, die Wendung vom Feld der Wahrheit zu überbieten; dieser in der Tat dreiste Versuch wird dann a.O. 23, 422d durch ein gelehrtes Zitat entlarvt und zurückgewiesen.

[19] Auf diesem Felde hat P. Courcelle mit ungewöhnlichem Erfolg gejagt: 1) *Tradition néoplatonicienne et traditions chrétiennes de la région de dissemblance*;

Arch. d'hist. doctr. et litt. du Moyen Âge 24, 1957, 5-33; 2) *Témoins nouveaux de la région de dissemblance*; Bibl. de l'école de chartes 118, 1960, 1-36; 3) *Complément au répertoire des textes relatifs à la région de dissemblance*, Augustinus 13, 1968, 135-140; 4) *Treize textes nouveaux sur la région de dissemblance*; RevEt-August., 16, 1970, 271-281. – Die Bezugsstelle ist Platon, *Politikos* 273D.

[20] Das ist gut abzulesen aus der Art und Weise, wie Apuleius, *Apol.* 64 mit Platons Wort vom „König", 2. *Brief* 312E, regelrecht Verstecken spielt.

[21] Vgl. m. Aufsatz: *„Der König". Ein platonisches Schlüsselwort, von Plotin mit neuem Sinn erfüllt*, Rev. Int. Phil. 24, 1970, 217-235.

[22] So besonders *Enn.* VI 2 [43] 1, 5; dort rechnet sich Plotin mit zu denen, die den Versuch machen τὰ δοκοῦντα ἡμῖν... εἰς τὴν Πλάτωνος ἀνάγειν δόξαν.

[23] Die epikureische Kritik, von der Cicero, *Nat. deor.* 1, 18 ff. berichtet, gefiel sich darin, die Tätigkeit des Schöpfers so konkret wie möglich, und das heißt, so trivial wie möglich darzustellen, um die Vorstellung vom sinnvoll wirkenden Schöpfer ad absurdum zu führen. Damit ist also nicht etwa alt-epikureische Kritik wiederholt worden, denn diese hätte sich gegen Xenokrates' oder Krantors Auffassung von der Zeitlosigkeit der Welt richten müssen; es wäre gegenstandslos gewesen, gegen den in persona wirkenden Demiurgos zu polemisieren. Sondern Cicero gibt zeitgenössischer Kritik Raum – einer Kritik, die sich mit gleicher Schroffheit gegen stoische wie gegen platonische (nicht akademische) Kosmologie richtet. Das heißt: Nicht Epikur, sondern Philodem ist Urheber der *Nat. deor.* 1, 18-32 vorgetragenen Argumentation. Daß die dort zu Grunde liegende Doxographie, die zum Beweis der *inconstantia philosophorum* dient, aus Philodem περὶ εὐσεβείας abgeleitet ist, hat H. Diels: *Doxographi Graeci* 529-550 bewiesen.

[24] Cicero, *Tusc.* 1, 70 *possumusne dubitare quin is praesit aliquis vel effector – si haec nata sunt, ut Platoni videtur – vel – si semper fuerunt ut Aristoteli placet – moderator tanti operis et muneris?*

[25] Der Form nach – nämlich durch die präpositionale Verschlüsselung – lehnt sich diese Prinzipien-Reihe (die Theiler'sche Reihe) an eine viel ältere Art religiöser Rede an, nach welcher alle Richtungen, die sich durch Präpositionen ausdrücken lassen, auf Gott weisen. In der Sache differiert die Theiler'sche Reihe davon fundamental; denn hier weisen die drei Präpositionen ὑφ' οὖ, ἐξ οὖ, πρὸς ὅ auf drei verschiedene ἀρχαί, die einander bedingen. Vgl. m. Aufsatz: *Präpositionen und Metaphysik. Wechselwirkung zweier Prinzipienreihen*, Mus-Helvet. 26, 1969, 217-228.

[26] Vgl. oben S. 118. Sicher muß Ps. Archytas in engen Zusammenhang mit Ps. Timaios von Lokroi gerückt werden; die Tendenz beider Schriften, Texte Platons als altpythagoreisch auszugeben, ist die gleiche.

[27] Hier liegt ein Unterschied zum Ps. Timaios von Lokroi; denn dieser bezeichnet den Kosmos als der Zeit nach nicht entstanden; vgl. den Kommentar von M. Baltes, 1972, 23(e) und 48.

[28] Albinos, *Did.* 10, S. 165, 17 ff. Das dort Gesagte ist vorbereitet ebda 4, S. 155, 34-156, 10. Stärker noch wertet Kelsos, bei Origenes *c.C.* 7, 42 die Analogie-Formel des Linien-Gleichnisses für den Nachweis des transzendenten Noûs aus. Mithin dürfte eine Spät-Datierung des Ps.-Archytas (etwa: nach 150 n. Chr.) schwerlich in Frage kommen.

[29] *De aet. mundi* 14; mit herbem Tadel werden diese Erklärer als σοφιζόμενοι getadelt.

[30] So Attikos bei Euseb, *Praep. ev.* 15, 6, 3 σαφεῖ καὶ τρανῷ τῷ στόματι und gleich darauf, ebda. 15, 6, 4 μὴ δι' αἰνιγμάτων.

[31] Im *Chronikon* von Eusebios/Hieronymus wird die ἀκμή des Attikos in das Jahr 176 gesetzt; er war also jünger als Tauros und Albinos und gehörte der Generation des Kelsos an.

134

[32] Zentrale Stelle: Proklos *In Plat. Tim.* 29B; I 340, 23 ff. Die Bedeutung des dort Gesagten wurde zuerst erkannt von K. Praechter: *Zum Platoniker Gaios*, Hermes 51, 1916, 510-529 = *KlSchr*. 81-100.

[33] Was Tim. 29B gesagt wird, wird 48CD wieder aufgenommen – ein Zusammenhang, der in der Antike fast immer beachtet wurde, vgl. oben S. 118.

[34] Um das völlig klar zu machen, wiederholt Platon hier die bereits mehrfach zit. Analogie-Formel in folgender, verkürzter Formulierung: ὅτιπερ πρὸς γένεσιν οὐσία, τοῦτο πρὸς πίστιν ἀλήθεια.

[35] Gaios und Albinos gewinnen also zunächst eine Querverbindung zu dem rhetorischen Terminus δι' εἰκότων. Das ist vergröbernde Vereinfachung. Die Ambivalenz bei Platon besteht nicht allein darin, daß er εἰκότα im Sinne der Rhetorik verwendet; freilich ist richtig erkannt, daß der *Timaios* auf weite Strecken ein εἰκὼς λόγος ist. Im Übrigen darf, was Gaios und Albinos lehrten, nur auf den *Timaios*, und im strengen Sinne nur auf 29B und 48CD angewendet werden.

[36] Eine universale Anwendung dessen, was Gaios und Albinos zu *Tim.* 29B vortrugen, ist aus folgendem Grunde ausgeschlossen: Gewöhnlich spricht Platon ja gerade über das, was dem erkennenden Noûs unmittelbar zugänglich sein müßte, in Gleichnissen und in Einkleidungen. Menschliche Sprache ist dem δοξαστόν zugeordnet; sie ist gerade dann als Vehikel unzureichend, wenn der Noûs und die Ideen Gegenstand der Aussage sein müßten.

[37] Hier muß an die große Zahl delphischer Kultlegenden erinnert werden, die immer wieder in diese Lehre einmünden: Wer einen Spruch des Gottes vordergründig, leichtsinnig oder egoistisch auslegt, verschuldet damit seinen Untergang. Ob der Spruch des Gottes Hilfe bringt oder Strafe, ist im ἦθος des Fragenden begründet. Auch darum galt: γνῶθι σαυτόν.

[38] So immer wieder Plutarch; besonders eindrucksvoll etwa in *De facie in orbe lunae* oder in *De genio Socratis*.

[39] Dies ein Wesenszug, der den kaiserzeitlichen Platonismus ebenso auszeichnet wie die zeitgenössische Stoa; vgl. Seneca, *Ep*. 95, 47 *deum colit qui novit*; ähnlich Klemens Al., *Strom*. 7, 47, 3; dazu W. Theiler, *Vorbereitung des Neuplatonismus* 105 ff.

[40] Vgl. Platon, *Theait*. 176BC und oben S. 118 mit A.13

[41] Wohl ist die Seele unsterblich; aber die stets gerechte πρόνοια kann ihr im nächsten Leben eine Existenz zuweisen, die es ihr unmöglich macht zu philosophieren. So muß σωτηρία verstanden werden als: Erhaltung der Fähigkeit zu philosophieren.

[42] Eben weil Philosophieren und Seelsorge (zu verstehen als Fürsorge für die Seele) synonym sind, darum muß erwartet werden, daß Platons Rätselworte hierauf zielen. Seine αἰνίγματα sind dann heilbringende λόγια, die ebenso erklärt, ja entschlüsselt werden müssen wie die Orakel des Apollon. Hiermit ist die Motivation angedeutet, aus der heraus im 3. Jahrh. weitere λόγια – die chaldäischen und die des Priesters Iulianos – neben die aus Platon zu gewinnende Offenbarung gestellt wurden.

[43] Ein wichtiges Beispiel bietet Plutarch, *Def. or*. 30, 426d; dort wird ausdrücklich abgelehnt, daß der höchste Gott – der wahre Zeus – nur sich selbst denkt: οὐδὲ ἑαυτὸν ἄλλο δὲ οὐδέν – ὡς ᾠήθησαν ἔνιοι – νοῶν....

[44] Vgl. unten S. 128.

[45] Vgl. hierzu die pointierte Richtigstellung durch Kelsos bei Origenes *c.C.* 7, 45.

[46] Das wird im *Tim*. 47A ausgesprochen; der Gedanke wird von Cicero, *Tusc*. 1, 64 aufgegriffen und neu gewendet; seither ist das eines der oft wiederholten, für den Platonismus kennzeichnenden Motive.

[47] Vgl. Ed. des Places, *Syngeneia. La parenté de l'homme avec Dieu d'Homère à la Patristique*, Et. et Comm. 51, 1964. Verständlicherweise wird der συγγένεια-Gedanke ergänzt und bereichert durch die aus dem *Theait.* 176AB abgeleitete

Forderung ὁμοίωσις θεῷ κατὰ τὸ δυνατόν. Vgl. H. Merki, Ὁμοίωσις θεῷ. *Von der platonischen Angleichung an Gott zur Gottähnlichkeit bei Gregor von Nyssa*, diss. phil. Freiburg/Schweiz 1951.

48 Der *locus classicus* für alles dieses ist Aristoteles, *Met.* Λ 9; diese Stelle, die von der Aktualität und von der Aktivität des höchsten Noûs handelt, ist von Philon bis Plotin als das wichtigste θεολογούμενον immer wieder nachvollzogen worden.

49 *Did.* 10, S. 164, 17 ff.

50 Porphyrios, *Vita Plot.* 14, 19. Plotin tat den berühmten Ausspruch, als zwei Werke Longins, zuletzt eine Schrift Φίλαρχαῖος, vorgelesen worden waren. Wahrscheinlich wurde in dieser die Gültigkeit des Alten Logos an Hand vieler antiquarischer Beispiele belegt.

51 Syrian, *In Arist. Met.* M 4, S. 106, 13 ... ἔστε ἂν ἐθέλωσιν εἶναι Πλατωνικοί.

52 In der Forderung, daß es allein darum gehe, sich auf das Entscheidende zu konzentrieren, waren diese Platoniker mit den Stoikern einig: voll Ironie tadelt Seneca, *Ep.* 65, 11 ff. die unkonzentrierte Vielfältigkeit der platonischen Lehre von den *causae*; er fordert, die *causa prima et generalis* müsse aufgesucht werden. Eng damit verknüpft ist der Tadel, daß die Philosophie ihre Aufgabe, zum Wesentlichen zu führen, nicht mehr erfüllt, *Ep.* 108, 23 *quae philosophia fuit, facta philologia est*, denn es geht nicht mehr darum, daß der *animus*, sondern daß das *ingenium* kultiviert wird – ein Tadel übrigens, den Tauros an seine Hörer richtete, – so Gellius *Noctes Att.* 1, 9, 10 und 17, 20, 6 – sobald er bemerkte, daß einer aus unangemessener Motivation Philosophie trieb. Endlich muß an Arrian/Epiktet, *Diss.* 2, 19, 6 – *Encheir.* 49 erinnert werden; dort grenzt Epiktet seine Werte setzende Philosophie deutlich vom wertfreien (und darum wertlosen) Wissen der γραμματικοί ab.

53 Vgl. vor allem Gellius, *Noctes Att.* 1, 9, 8 ff., dazu m. Aufsatz: *L. Kalbenos Tauros. Das Persönlichkeitsbild eines platonischen Philosophen um die Mitte des 2. Jahrh. n. Chr.*, Kairos NF 15, 1973 (in honorem E. von Ivanka) 24-25.

54 So Augustin, *Conf.* 7, 9 Anf. über einen Platoniker; generell urteilt Lukian, *Hermotimos* 16 Ende.

55 Seneca, *Ep.* 58, 20; Tertullian, *De an.* 6, 1 und 29, 4.

56 Was hier gemeint ist, verdeutlicht der oft mißverstandene Vers des Terentianus Maurus

pro captu lectoris habent sua fata libelli.

Das eigentliche Schicksal eines Buches ist, richtig verstanden zu werden. Das aber hängt von der Auffassungskraft der Leser ab.

57 Vgl. m. Aufsatz: *Emanation. Ein unphilosophisches Wort im spätantiken Denken*; *Parusia*, Festschr. f. Joh. Hirschberger 1965, 119-141.

58 Von der Tendenz, die frühere Platoniker, wie etwa Eudoros oder Thrasyllos vertraten, ist im Detail zu wenig erkennbar. Zugleich darf man vermuten, daß die oben schematisch dargestellte Differenzierung noch garnicht eingetreten war. Diese wurde ja erst sinnvoll, als die Phase des wörtlichen Platon-Verständnisses überwunden war.

59 Vgl. H. Jonas, *Gnosis und spätantiker Geist* I ¹1934, ²1954, bes. in dem einführenden Kapitel. Der (bisher nicht erschienene) Schlußteil II 2 soll die Darstellung der Gnosis im Platonismus enthalten.

60 Auf christlicher Seite war man der Ansicht, daß alle Gnosis auf Platon zurückgehe – so Tertullian, *De an.* 23, 5 *doleo bona fide Platonem omnium haereticorum condimentarium factum*; ähnlich *Praescr.* 7 über Valentinus: *Platonicus fuerat.*

61 Wahrscheinlich darf als beispielhaft gelten, wie sich Plotin mit der Gnosis auseinandersetzte. Daß es viele Berührungspunkte gab, ist unverkennbar: Schließlich aber erweisen mindestens zwei Grund-Thesen der Gnosis sich als unannehmbar: Daß die Welt von Grund auf – also auch ihrer Idee nach – schlecht sein solle, und daß es eine sehr große Zahl von Stufen des Auf- und Absteigens gebe.

136

PLOTIN, PLUTARCH UND DIE PLATONISIERENDE INTERPRETATION VON HERAKLIT UND EMPEDOKLES

WALTER BURKERT

„Plotin las sichtlich den Heraklit selber, und genau"; so urteilte Richard Harder[1] über die Passage, an der Plotin originale, anderweitig nicht bezeugte Heraklitworte anführt. Geoffrey S. Kirk[2] freilich hatte bereits auf die deutlichen Anklänge an theophrastische Doxographie in Plotins einleitenden Formulierungen hingewiesen und auf ein doxographisches Werk als Zwischenquelle geschlossen. Evangelos Roussos[3] wiederum, der den ganzen Plotintext auf Heraklitspuren hin sorgfältig durchgearbeitet hat, wandte ein, daß Plotin sehr wohl in doxographischen Zusammenhang Früchte eigener Lektüre einordnen konnte. Doch geht es nicht um Heraklit allein. Plotin stellt ihm Empedokles an die Seite, wobei gerade Harder konstatierte: „es ist klar, daß auch Plotin einen bereits gedeuteten Empedokles vorfand"[4]; beide, Heraklit und Empedokles, sind indes nur Vorspann, vorläufige Zeugen für die Frage nach dem 'Abstieg der Seele in die Leibeswelt': beide haben davon gesprochen, in Formulierungen, die weiterklingen und zu denken geben, doch selbst erst nach Deutung verlangen. „So bleibt denn der göttliche Platon" (4, 8, 1, 23), unter dessen Führung die Abhandlung ihren Verlauf nimmt.

Die Zusammenschau von Heraklit, Empedokles, Platon unter der Fragestellung nach dem Abstieg der Seele ist nun keineswegs Plotin allein eigentümlich. Wenn Hierokles im Kommentar zum 54. Vers des *Carmen aureum*[5] die 'amphibische' Natur des Menschen zwischen Überwelt und Diesseits zu fassen sucht, geht er aus von einem Heraklitwort über Tod und Leben (B 62), zitiert anschließend Empedoklesverse (B 115, 13-14), die auch Plotin anklingen ließ, in genauerer, metrischer Form und läßt, nach weiteren Empedoklesversen (B 121, 2-4), seine Ausführungen gleich Plotin in eine Anthologie von Platonpassagen münden, die sich allerdings mit den von Plotin angeführten nur berühren, kaum überschneiden[6]. Das Thema ist das gleiche, 'Absteigen' und 'Aufsteigen' der Seele, und hier wie dort wird auf die Beziehung des Empedokles zum Pythagoreismus ausdrücklich hingewiesen.

Hierokles hat seine Zitate nicht von Plotin, hat sie bei ihrer Knappheit

137

aber auch kaum eigens nachgeschlagen. Der Gedanke an eine gemeinsame Quelle drängt sich auf. Daß und wie Hierokles vorplotinisches Gut benützen konnte, hat Willy Theiler[7] gezeigt: zu denken ist an *scholai*, Vorlesungsnotizen, die sich im alexandrinischen Schulbetrieb fortpflanzten, auch gelegentlich vervielfältigt und so 'veröffentlicht' werden konnten.

In der Tat läßt sich die Dreiheit Heraklit, Empedokles, Platon im Themenbereich des Seelenabstiegs vor Plotin im alexandrinischen Platonismus fassen: Clemens sucht im dritten Buch seiner *Stromateis* Markion nachzuweisen, daß er seinen Haß gegen die Welt und ihren Schöpfer nicht aus christlicher Lehre, sondern aus griechischer Philosophie (3, 12, 1; 21, 2) genommen hat, genauer von "Platon und den Pythagoreern" (12, 1) bzw. in erster Linie eben von Platon (21). Für diese Philosophen sei alles Werden böse, zwar nicht an sich, doch für die Seele, „die das Wahre geschaut hat. Denn sie lassen die Seele, die göttlich ist, hierher herabsteigen in diese Welt, wie in ein Zuchthaus..." (13, 2). Eine bunte Zitatenreihe soll dies belegen. Sie beginnt mit Heraklit (B 20), der „das Werden schmäht", und Empedokles (B 118; 125; 124), der „mit ihm zusammengeht" (14, 1-2). Es folgen (14, 3-16, 2) die Sibylle, Homer, Theognis, Euripides, Herodot, nochmals Homer; schließlich kommt, weitaus am ausführlichsten, Platon zu Wort (16, 3-20, 3), unterbrochen durch Zitate aus Philolaos[8], Pindar und dem Römerbrief.

Mannigfache Fäden hat Clemens mit spielerischer Gelehrsamkeit zu seinen *Teppichen* verknüpft; der Hauptstrang ist hier aber leicht auszumachen: Sibylle, Homer, Theognis, Euripides, Herodot, Pindar und der Apostel Paulus sind auch für Clemens keine griechischen Philosophen, deren Lehre darzustellen er doch angekündigt hat. Als eigentlich philosophische Autoritäten für den Abstieg der Seele in die böse Welt bleiben dann eben Heraklit, Empedokles, Platon und der diesem verdächtig nahestehende Pythagoreer. Diese Reihe trägt den Gedankengang des Abschnitts. Thema, Zeugen und Abfolge entsprechen damit dem Befund bei Plotin und Hierokles. Wiederum freilich überschneiden sich die Zitate nur zum Teil: das *Kratylos*- und eines der *Phaidros*-Zitate steht auch bei Plotin[9], einen Empedoklesvers, den Hierokles anklingen läßt, zitiert Clemens vollständig und genau[10]. Das Heraklitzitat des Clemens (B 20) ist in der Bezeugung so einzigartig wie das des Plotin (B 84). Es ist jedoch, wie seit langem erkannt, durch ein Glossem unterbrochen: der Wunsch nach dem 'Tod' der leiblichen Existenz sei 'vielmehr' ein Verlangen nach 'Ausruhen'[11]. Eben dieses 'Ausruhen' aber ist das Kennwort jenes durch Plotin erhaltenen Heraklitzitates. Clemens hat offensichtlich

138

Heraklit mit Heraklit interpoliert. Dies konnte am leichtesten geschehen, wenn in Clemens' Vorlage beide Zitate nebeneinander standen: die Hypothese einer Quellengemeinschaft von Plotin und Hierokles findet damit ihre Bestätigung. Die gemeinsame Tendenz, der gemeinsame Aufbau, die sich berührenden und ergänzenden Zitate gehen zurück auf die Arbeit eines alexandrinischen Platonikers vor Clemens. Formulierungen von Heraklit und Empedokles waren hier als wirkungsvolle Einleitung für die platonisch-pythagoreische Lehre vom Niedergang der Seele in die Körperwelt zusammengestellt. Dieser Tradition verdankt Plotin – dies beweist die 'Interpolation' des Clemens – auch jenen von ihm allein weiter überlieferten Ausspruch Heraklits; er wird ihn nicht nachgeschlagen haben.

Ein Jahrhundert weiter zurück führt Plutarch, der bereits das gleiche Dreierschema kennt und sich zu eigen macht. In dem frühen Dialog *Über die Klugheit der Tiere*[12] läßt Plutarch den eigenen Vater Autobulos auf den 'Weg' hinweisen, „den unter Führung Platons mein Sohn zeigt" (964d); dies also ist Plutarchs eigene Philosophie: „daß nicht frei von Unrecht der Mensch ist, der so mit den Tieren umspringt, ist nach der Auffassung von Empedokles und Heraklit wahr; sie jammern und schelten ja oft über die Natur, die 'Notwendigkeit' und 'Krieg' sei, nichts Ungemischtes, nichts Reines enthalte, sondern auf dem Weg mannigfachen und verdienten Leidens[13] zum Ziel komme; sagen sie doch, daß selbst das Werden aus Unrecht geschieht, indem dem Sterblichen das Unsterbliche sich verbindet, und daß das Gezeugte widernatürlich sich nährt von den abgerissenen Gliedern des Erzeugers". Für Plutarch freilich sind solche Formulierungen „untemperiert und bitter bis zum Überdruß"; „harmonischer Zuspruch", dem man folgen kann, stammt von Pythagoras, der die Unschuld der Urzeit wieder entdeckt hat und lehrt, wie man von Tieren, ohne sie zu töten, Nutzen ziehen kann.

Gleichsam als Siegel ist von Anfang an der Name Platon über den Abschnitt gesetzt: zur pythagoreisch-platonischen Lehre bekennt sich Plutarch. Das Thema der Schrift stellt die Tier-Problematik in den Vordergrund; doch in der Formulierung, wie „dem Sterblichen das Unsterbliche sich verbindet", klingt auch hier das Motiv vom Abstieg der Seele an. Als Zeugen sind Empedokles und Heraklit vorangestellt. Sie „schelten über die Natur" – sie „schmähen das Werden", schreibt Clemens. – Die Zitate freilich sind von Plutarch auf Anspielungen reduziert, wobei die beiden Vorsokratiker fast zur Ununterscheidbarkeit verschmelzen. Man erfaßt Stichwörter: Heraklits 'Krieg' (B 53), Empedokles' 'Ananke' (B 115, 1); vom Umschlag des Unsterblichen ins Sterbliche haben beide gesprochen[14]; der Schlußpassus scheint auf die Zertrümmerung des Sphairos bei Empedokles zu zielen[15], ohne daß Assoziationen mit der kannibalischen Opfermahlzeit der *Katharmoi*, vielleicht auch mit dem Rätsel vom Feuer, das seine eigenen Eltern frißt[16], ausgeschlossen wären.

Bedeutender ist der Zusammenhang in einer der spätesten Schriften Plutarchs, *Über Isis und Osiris* 48 (370d): Plutarch hat im Osiris-Typhon-Mythos die – für die Philosophie noch durchaus neuartige[17] – Lehre gefunden, daß nicht ein einziges, gutes Prinzip die Welt erklären kann: eine Gegenkraft, ein böses Prinzip stehe ihm entgegen. Persisches und Chaldäisches, griechischer Kult und griechischer Mythos müssen Bestätigung bringen. „Und betrachte die Philosophen, wie sie mit diesen übereinstimmen. Denn Heraklit nennt geradezu 'Krieg' als 'Vater und König und Herr von allem' (B 53)... Empedokles aber nennt das Gutes wirkende Prinzip Philotes und Philia, oft auch 'scheu blickende Harmonia' (B 122, 2), das schlechtere Prinzip aber 'verhängnisvollen Hader' (B 17, 19) und 'blutigen Streit' (B 122, 2)..." Die dualistische Lehre der Pythagoreer[18] schließt sich an, und nach einem Seitenblick auf Anaxagoras und Aristoteles folgt, ausführlich und abschließend, Platon. Wiederum bilden Heraklit und Empedokles die Einleitung zur Philosophie überhaupt, die sich in Pythagoreismus-Platonismus erfüllt. Sie eint der Blick auf das Böse in der Welt.

Nun steht im Falle Plutarchs fest, daß er sowohl Heraklit wie auch Empedokles im Originaltext und genau gelesen hat; hat er doch, nach dem Zeugnis des Lamprias-Katalogs, über beide eigene Werke verfaßt, „Über die Frage: was lehrte Heraklit" (Nr. 205) und „Zu Empedokles, 10 Bücher" (Nr. 43)[19]. So sind denn auch durch Plutarchs erhaltene Schriften eine Fülle von Heraklit- und Empedokleszitaten auf uns gekommen, vom wörtlichen Exzerpt bis zur fein verarbeiteten Anspielung[20]. Mit welch wacher Einfühlung er dem Wortlaut des Empedokles nachgegangen ist, läßt die beiläufige Bemerkung in den *Tischgesprächen* ermessen, Empedokles pflege „keineswegs des schönen Stils wegen mit den prunkvollsten Epitheta wie mit blumigen Farben die Sachverhalte auszuschmücken, vielmehr sei mit jedem Beiwort ein bestimmtes Wesen, eine bestimmte Wirkungsweise klar bezeichnet" (683e). Aus dem Spezialwerk ist ein einziges Zitat in der *Refutatio* des Hippolytos erhalten (5, 20, 5 = Fr. 24 Sandbach); Plutarch hat demnach Empedokles auch mit entlegenen Kulten – hier den Mysterien von Phlya – konfrontiert. Weiter führt die Vermutung von Hermann Diels[21], daß das spätere, gehaltvolle Empedokleskapitel des Hippolytos (7, 29-31) mit seinen erlesenen Originalzitaten gleichfalls auf das Werk Plutarchs zurückgeht.

Hippolytos hat im 1. Buch seiner *Refutatio* Pythagoras, Empedokles und Heraklit in dieser Reihenfolge hintereinander behandelt und dabei durch Querverweise, ja durch Konfusion der Lehren miteinander verbunden[22]; daß er hier schon von dem Dreierschema mit beeinflußt ist, läßt sich vermuten. Jedenfalls sind es eben diese drei, Pythagoras, Empedokles, Heraklit, deren Lehren er in späteren Abschnitten seines Werks ausführlich heranzieht, nicht ohne auf die frühere Behandlung jedesmal zu verweisen[23]; dabei hat er weitere, reichhaltigere Quellen herangezogen, für Heraklit vielleicht sogar sein originales Buch, während der Pythagorasabschnitt eine heterogene Kompilation darstellt[24].

Inwieweit der Empedoklesabschnitt auf Plutarch weist, ist nicht einfach auszumachen. Was Hippolytos seinem Beweisziel zuliebe – daß nämlich Markions Dualismus von Empedokles 'gestohlen' sei – zurechtgebogen hat, wäre zunächst abzutrennen. So ist die 'dritte', 'geistige' Kraft, die Hippolytos gegen Ende seiner Darstellung unversehens bei Empedokles entdeckt und erst mit B 110, dann mit B 131 belegt, auf Markion bzw. seinen Schüler Prepon hin zurechtgemacht[25]. Sodann ist von vornherein unwahrscheinlich, daß Hippolytos für diesen Abschnitt ein zehnbändiges Spezialwerk durchgearbeitet hat. Sein ausdrückliches Zitat (5, 20, 5) ist entlarvend: die sehr spezielle Angabe über Phlya stehe „in den 10 Büchern gegen Empedokles" – statt, beispielshalber, 'im 4. Buch' –; so schreibt, wer die einzelnen Volumina nicht in der Hand gehabt hat. Zudem ist ein Stück des Empedoklesabschnitts bereits in das Pythagoraskapitel aufgenommen[26], teils im gleichen Wortlaut, teils um weniges ausführlicher; so fassen wir in doppelter Brechung die Vorlage, die nicht direkt Plutarch heißen kann. An beiden Stellen wird der Neikos 'Demiurg' genannt, was Plutarch nicht sagen konnte; im Pythagoraskapitel ist der Gegensatz von 'wahrnehmbarer' und 'intelligibler Welt' entwickelt, im Empedokleskapitel erscheint dann auf einmal der Kosmos der Philia als 'intelligible Welt'[27]; eine solche Auffassung bestimmt zwar dann bei den Neuplatonikern bis hin zu Simplikios das Empedokles-Verständnis, sie paßt aber weder in der Terminologie noch in der Intention zu Plutarch, dem doch das Werden des Kosmos in der Zeit so wichtig war.

Andererseits stimmt der grundsätzliche Dualismus, den Hippolytos bei Empedokles findet, durchaus zu Plutarchs philosophischer Position, ja die Charakterisierung der Wirkungsweise von Neikos und Philia hat mit der Beschreibung von 'Andersheit' und 'Selbigkeit' in Plutarchs *Timaios*-Kommentar[28] bemerkenswerte Ähnlichkeit. Kernpunkt der Empedokles-deutung bei Hippolytos ist die strenge Parallelisierung von Weltwerden und Seelenschicksal, *Naturgedicht* und *Katharmoi* des Empedokles. Eben dies aber ist für den Umgang mit Empedokles im erhaltenen Plutarch bezeichnend. So verteilen sich gerade an den beiden behandelten Stellen die Zitate und Anspielungen fast gleichmäßig auf beide Werke; an beide läßt das Wort vom 'Sterblichen' und 'Unsterblichen' denken (Anm. 14), ebenso das grelle Bild von den 'abgerissenen' Gliedern. Mit eben diesem Wort, 'abreißen', wird im Hippolytosabschnitt wiederholt das Wirken des Neikos beschrieben, sei es daß er die Welt aus dem Sphairos schafft, sei es daß er die Seele in die Körperlichkeit herabzwingt. So dürfte in der Tat, wenn auch indirekt vermittelt, plutarchisches Gut der Behandlung des Hippolytos zugrundeliegen.

Wir fassen in Plutarch einen philosophierenden Autor, der Heraklit, Empedokles und Platon im Original kannte, der den Blick aufs Seelenschicksal mit einer dualistischen Weltsicht verband. Trotzdem ist nicht er die 'Quelle', der Ausgangspunkt des alexandrinischen Dreierschemas Heraklit-Empedokles-Platon. Setzt er dieses doch seinerseits schon in einer frühen Schrift voraus; und zudem fühlt er sich persönlich von Empedokles ebenso angesprochen wie abgestoßen: seine 'Handgreiflichkeit', seine 'untemperierte' Direktheit[29] ist ihm zuwider. So wird ihn umgekehrt das bereits vorgegebene Schema bestimmt haben, unter den Vorsokratikern gerade Heraklit und Empedokles eingehendem Studium zu unterziehen. Sein philosophischer Lehrer, Ammonios, stammte ja seinerseits aus Alexandreia[30].

Daß man Heraklit und Empedokles zu den Vorläufern platonisch-pythagoreischer Seelenlehre macht, dies kann nun aber auch nicht wesentlich älter sein als die Generation von Plutarchs philosophischen Lehrern. Gewiß waren Heraklit und Empedokles seit Platon (*Soph.* 242d) und Aristoteles oft als kontrastierendes Paar erschienen; doch nicht an den Abstieg der Seele ließen diese Namen denken. In der von Theophrast fundierten Auffassung galt Heraklit zunächst als 'Physiker'[31], und der Ruhm des Empedokles beruhte auf seinem Naturgedicht, zumal der populären Elementenlehre. Demgegenüber scheinen die *Katharmoi* mit ihrem Seelenmythos geradezu von einer Mauer des Schweigens umgeben. Platon, der doch aus erkenntnistheoretischer Argumentation einen neuen Zugang zur Seelenwanderungslehre fand, nennt in diesem Zusammenhang nie Empedokles, obgleich er ihn imitiert[32]. Aristoteles, der sich mit dem 'Physiker' Empedokles auf Schritt und Tritt auseinandersetzt, zitiert die *Katharmoi* einzig in Rhetorik und Poetik, als Topos, als Stilfigur[33]. Theophrast hat für die Doxographie einzig das Naturgedicht herangezogen, selbst unter den Rubriken 'Seele' und 'Daimon'[34]; in der Schrift *Über Frömmigkeit* freilich sind die *Katharmoi* zitiert für die kultur-geschichtliche These vom ursprünglichen, unblutigen Menschenleben[35], und die Frage nach Tiertötung und Gerechtigkeit wird dann weiterhin unter Rückgriff auf Empedokles abgehandelt[36]. Der Historiker Timaios hat die *Katharmoi* historisch ausgewertet, für Pythagoras, für Em-pedokles selbst[37]. Aber was die Späteren fasziniert: die Welt eine Höhle, der Leib ein Gewand, der Orakelspruch der Notwendigkeit, Fall des Daimon und schließliche Vergottung – dies bleibt, soweit wir sehen, ohne Echo in der hellenistischen Welt. Den Kritikern blieb es vorbehalten, den Epikureern, über die 'langlebigen Daimones' zu spotten[38]. Einige grell-dunkle Bilder aus den *Katharmoi* allerdings scheinen populär geworden zu sein: das Diesseits in Hadesfarben gemalt; das Weinen des neu-geborenen Kindes, das in diese Welt eintritt[39]. Im übrigen blieb das Gedicht den Grammatikern überlassen[40].

Noch für Philon ist Empedokles 'Physiker'[41]; mit Seelenabstieg und -aufstieg wird er nie verbunden; Heraklit wird, selbst wo er von 'Seelen' spricht, ins Kosmologische uminterpretiert[42]. Ein pessimistischer Vers der *Katharmoi* klingt in der Schrift *Von der Vorsehung* beiläufig an[43]. Dabei ist für den Platoniker die Unvollkommenheit der Welt nicht Widerlegung, sondern Bestätigung göttlicher Ordnung; das Niedere lässt sich vom Höheren ergänzen und tragen. Die Chance ist gegeben, die Gesamtschau der empedokleischen 'Reinigungen' nachzuvollziehen und auch das heraklitische 'Hinauf und Hinab' in den umfassenderen Rahmen zu stellen. Noch vor Plutarch ist die Chance genutzt, sind Heraklit und Empedokles als Vorankündigung platonisch-pythagoreischer Seelen-lehre neu entdeckt worden. Für Plutarch sind die *Katharmoi* des Empedo-kles der „Anfang seiner Philosophie" (*De exil.* 607c), während die helle-nistische Ausgabe das Naturgedicht vorangestellt hatte[44]. Plutarch hat sich auch energisch bemüht, die hellenistische Natur-Allegorese der Mythen durch eine metaphysische, platonische Allegorese zu ersetzen. Die Umwertung der Vorsokratiker entspricht diesem Wandel genau.

Nicht zufällig trifft die neue Sicht zusammen mit dem Aufbruch der Gnosis in eben dieser Epoche. Die gnostischen Mythen scheinen in wesent-lichen Punkten vorweggenommen im Gedicht des Empedokles[45]; in gnostischen und hermetischen Schriften wird denn auch Empedokles zitiert und benützt[46]. Doch was so zu neuer Wirkung kommt, war Jahr-hunderte lang ignoriert worden; Entstehung und Wirkung fallen aus-einander – was auch fürs Problem der Orphik zu bedenken ist –. Die Rezeptionsgeschichte hat ihre eigene Dynamik, bedingt vom Verständnishorizont der Epoche; man kann, jenseits der Ideengeschichte, nach sozialpsychologischen Faktoren fragen, die die Veränderungen bedingen, etwa einer 'Grossstadt-Neurose', die auch in der Gnosis sich dokumentiert[47]. Im Rückgriff auf alte, klassische Texte sucht dann das Neue sich seiner selbst zu versichern und erweckt diese damit zu unvorhergesehenem Leben, schafft weiterwirkende Tradition. Philologen wie Plutarch studieren und kommentieren die Texte, während ein Philosoph wie Plotin die Anregung aufnimmt und in der Bewegung des eigenen Denkens aufgehen lässt.

ANMERKUNGEN

[1] *Plotins Schriften* I (1956), 444 zu Plot. 4, 8 [6] 1, 11-17, Heraklit B 84 = Fr. 56 Marcovich (*Heraclitus*, Editio maior, Merida 1967). Plotin zitiert daneben B 60 und läßt B 101 anklingen, das in der vorangehenden Schrift 5, 9 [5] 5, 31 zitiert ist; er greift B 84 interpretierend auf 4, 8, 4, 11 (eine Stelle, auf die weder Marcovich noch Roussos verweisen) und 4, 8, 5, 5.

[2] Heraclitus, *The Cosmic Fragments* (1954), 250-4.

[3] Ο ΗΡΑΚΛΕΙΤΟΣ ΣΤΙΣ ΕΝΝΕΑΔΕΣ ΤΟΥ ΠΛΩΤΙΝΟΥ (Athen 1968), 17-27, bes. 21 f.

[4] a.O. 445 zu 4, 8, 1, 17-20, Empedokles B 115; Plotin läßt dann 4, 8, 1, 34 kurz Empedokles B 120 anklingen, das Porphyrios genauer zitiert: „er folgt offenbar derselben Quelle wie Plotin", Harder ib.; J. Mansfeld hat zur Platonisierenden Heraklitauffassung des Numenios (u. Anm. 20) und Plotin die entsprechende Parmenidesdeutung des Simplikios gestellt, Mnemosyne 20 (1967) 8; 17; *Die Offenbarung des Parmenides und die menschliche Welt* (1964) 168-74.

[5] F. W. A. Mullach, *Fragmenta Philosophorum Graecorum* I (1883), 470 f.; ἀμφίβιος Hierokles p.471b14 Mullach, Plot. 4, 8, 4, 32.

[6] Plotin zitiert Plat. *Phd.* 67d, *Krat.* 400c, *Phd.* 62b, *Resp.* 514a, 515c, 517b, *Phdr.* 246c, 247d, 249ab, *Tim.* 34b, 29a, 30b, 39e; Hierokles *Phdr.* 248c, *Tim.* 42c, *Tht.* 176a.

[7] *Forschungen zum Neuplatonismus* (1966), 37 f.

[8] B 14, vgl. W. Burkert, *Lore and science in ancient Pythagoreanism* (1972) 248.

[9] *Krat.* 400c, *Phd.* 62b (*phroura*), vgl. Anm. 6; dazu bringt Clemens *Phd.* 66b, 65cd, 114bc; *Polit.* 273bc und *Resp.* 328d, 329c sind speziell gegen Markion herbeigeholt (3, 18, 4-5), *Phd.* 69c erscheint im Gefolge von Pindar Fr. 137a (3, 17, 3).

[10] B 118, 1, vgl. G. Zuntz, *Persephone* (1971), 200.

[11] μᾶλλον δὲ ἀναπαύεσθαι, vgl. Marcovich 522. K. Reinhardt, Hermes 77 (1942), 4 = *Vermächtnis der Antike* (1960) 44 f. meinte, Clemens habe in christlichem Sinn interpoliert; doch gibt das Thema vom 'Abstieg der Seele' keinen Anlaß, der ewigen Ruhe in Gott zu gedenken; also ist das 'Ausruhen' wie bei Plotin (Anm. 1) vom Abstieg zu verstehen, vgl. *Strom.* 5, 105, 2, wo ebenso Heraklit und Platon für den Seelenabstieg zusammengestellt sind. O. Gigon, *Untersuchungen zu Heraklit* (1935) 121 f. sprach von einer „alten gelehrten Notiz" aus B 84; doch μᾶλλον δὲ ist gerade für Clemens charakteristisch, Marcovich a.O.

[12] Zur Datierung K. Ziegler, *RE* XXI 709.

[13] Den überlieferten Text verteidigt J. Bollack, *Empédocle* I (1965) 157, III (1969) 148 gegen die Herausgeber und J. de Romilly REG 79 (1966) 788.

[14] Heraklit B 62 (von Hierokles a.O. zitiert), Empedokles B 125 und B 35, 14.

[15] Vgl. Bollack III 148 zu Fr. 103.

144

16 Plut. *Q. conv.* 730e (dazu M. L. West CQ 11 [1961] 143).

17 Vgl. E. Zeller, *Die Philosophie der Griechen* III 2 (1902;) 186-9, der Plutarch zwischen Neupythagoreer und Numenios stellt. Ein protognostisches System in *De Iside* 54: A. Torhoudt, *Een onbekend gnostisch systeem in Plutarchus' De Iside et Osiride* (Louvain 1942), vgl. J. G. Griffiths, *Plutarch's De Iside et Osiride* (1970) 49; 504. Zur Datierung der Schrift Ziegler 716; Griffiths 17.

18 Entwickelt nach Arist. *Met.* 986a22, vgl. Burkert a.O. 51 f.

19 Zur genauen Titelform vgl. Sandbach zu Fr. 24, 10.

20 So läßt das Bild vom Seelensturz in *De sera num. vind.* 566a Heraklit B 77, B 36, B 15 anklingen (vgl. Numenios T 46 Leemans = Fr. 30 des Places bei Porph. *Antr.* 10).

21 SBBerlin 1898, 399 = *Kleine Schriften zur antiken Philosophie* (1969) 130; mit Fragezeichen in *Poetarum philosophorum Fragmenta* und in den *Fragmenten der Vorsokratiker* zu Empedokles A 33. Vgl. Bollack a.O. III 174, 3; 147.

22 Vgl. H. Diels, *Doxographi Graeci* (1879) 145, der eine Diadochai-Quelle, letztlich Herakleides Lembos erschließt. Die Ekpyrosis mutet auch Clem. *Strom.* 5, 103, 6 dem Empedokles, neben Heraklit und Stoikern, zu.

23 6, 21 p.149, 5; 7, 29 p.210, 13; 9, 8 p.241, 11 Wendlandt.

24 6, 23 baut auf doxographischer Grundlage, vgl. Aët. 1, 3, 8; 6, 24 verwendet Pseudopythagorica, vgl. Th. Szlezák, *Pseudo-Archytas über die Kategorien* (1972) 89 f. und auch Archytas p.36-9 Thesleff; es folgt ein Empedokles-Stück, u. Anm. 26, dann nach vermischten Notizen ein Abschnitt über pythagoreische Symbola (vgl. Burkert a.O. 166 f.), schließlich ein astrologisches Stück.

25 7, 30, 25; 7, 31, 2-4. Erstaunlich, doch bezeichnend fürs begrenzte Wissen des Hippolytos ist, daß Empedokles B 134 nicht erscheint. Weitere Zusätze des Hippolytos verraten sich durch Termini wie κτίσις p.211, 14-20; p. 214,28.

26 6, 25, 1-4 ∼ 7, 29, 10-12.

27 6, 24, 1; 3; 7, 29, 71; 31, 3. Das Reich der Philia als intelligible Welt dann bei Plot. 6, 7, 14, 18 f.; Syrian *Met.* p.11, 28-36; 43, 6-28; 187, 19-27; Askl. *Met.* p.197, 17; Simplikios übernimmt und modifiziert diese Interpretation, *Cael.* p.140, 25-30; *Phys.* p.31, 18-34, 10, vgl. *Cael.* p.294, 10-13; *Phys.* p.160, 22-25; 1123, 26-1124, 3; 1186, 30-35.

28 *Procr.* 1025c: διιστάναι καὶ ἀλλοιοῦν καὶ πολλὰ ποιεῖν − συνάγειν καὶ συνιστάναι δι' ὁμοιότητος, vgl. Hippol. *Ref.* 7, 29, p.212, 3 τὸ νεῖκος… ἀποσπᾶ καὶ ποιεῖ πολλά… ἡ φιλία προσάγει καὶ προστίθησι καὶ προσοικειοῖ τῷ παντί. Die Begriffe μετακόσμησις, μετακοσμεῖν erscheinen bei Hippolytos nur hier (p.213, 12; 23), sie sind bei Plutarch geläufig und werden gerade mit Empedokles verbunden, Plut. Fr. 200, 11; 21 Sandbach.

29 *Def. or.* 418e, vgl. oben *Soll. an.* 964e.

30 Zeller III 2, 177, 1; Ziegler 651-3.

31 Vgl. die Zusammenstellung der Zeugnisse zu B 60 = Fr. 33 Marcovich bei Marcovich 165-170.

32 Diels hat Plat. *Phdr.* 248b als 'Anklang' zu Empedokles gestellt (31 C).

33 *Rhet.* 1373b6 (B 135); *Poet.* 1457b13 (B 138; 143).

34 Aët. 4, 5, 8 bringt in der Seelenlehre von Empedokles nur die Bindung des Denkens ans Blut (aus B 105); Aët. 1, 8 erwähnt unter dem Stichwort 'Daimones' Empedokles nicht. Diog. Laert. 8, 77 hat einen Satz über Seelenwanderung (mit B 117). Für Hippol. Ref. 1, 3 dagegen ist die Dämonen- und Seelenlehre Hauptinhalt der empedokleischen Lehre.

35 B 128 bei Porph. abst. 2, 20 f., vgl. J. Bernays, *Theophrastos Schrift über die Frömmigkeit* (1866) 95 f.; Zuntz a.O. 206, 3. Eine Spezialschrift des Theophrast über Empedokles nennt der Katalog Diog. Laert. 5, 43.

36 B 135-136 bei Sextus *Math.* 9, 126 f. und Cic. *Rep.* 3, 19 (Poseidonios?).

37 B 129 – *FGrHist* 566 F 14; B 112, 4-5 – *FGrHist* 566 F 2.
38 Plut. *Def. or.* 420cd. Hermarchos schrieb 22 Briefe über Empedokles, Diog. Laërt. 10, 25. Die Kritik des Kolotes, Plut. *Adv. Col.* 1111f-1113e, gilt dem Naturgedicht, wie die der Stoiker, Plut. *Fac.* 921e-922c.
39 B 118 bei Sextus *M*. 11, 96 = *Epicurea* 398 Usener als Beleg natürlicher Unlustreaktion; als Argument pessimistischer Weltsicht, ohne Wortanklang an Empedokles, erscheint das Weinen des Neugeborenen [Plat.] *Ax.* 366d, Lucr. 5, 226. Zum Diesseits-Hades J. Carcopino, *La Basilique Pythagoricienne de la Porte Majeure* (1926) 271-4, F. Cumont, *Lux perpetua* (1949) 200, 204-6. Zuntz 199 f. bestreitet, nach Wilamowitz, daß Empedokles mit Hadesmetaphern das Diesseits meinte; die antike Rezeption ist von dieser Deutung jedenfalls bestimmt.
40 Vgl. B 142 (Zuntz 228), B 115, 6 (M. L. West CR 12 [1962] 220), Herodian bei M. L. West Maia 20 (1968) 199.
41 Empedokles ist im erhaltenen Philon-Corpus nie mit Namen genannt. Anspielungen verzeichnet der Index von Cohn-Wendlandt.
42 B 36 = Fr. 66 Marcovich bei Philon *Aet. mundi* 111.
43 B 121, 3 bei Eus. *Praep. ev.* 8, 14, 23.
44 Lobon bei Diog. Laërt. 8, 77; Zuntz 237-9.
45 Wenn Gnosis definiert wird als „Vorstellung von der Gegenwart eines göttlichen 'Funkens' im Menschen... welcher aus der göttlichen Welt hervorgegangen und in diese Welt des Schicksals, der Geburt und des Todes gefallen ist, und der durch das göttliche Gegenstück seiner selbst wiedererweckt werden muß, um endgültig wiederhergestellt zu sein" (C. Colpe, in: *Christentum und Gnosis* [1969] 130), so fehlt davon bei Empedokles – wie bei Plotin – nur eben jenes göttliche Gegenbild, der Erlöser.
46 B 109 bei Simon Magus, Hippol. *Ref.* 6, 11; B 119 beim Naassener, Hippol. *Ref.* 5, 7, 30; die Seelenlehre in der 'Kore Kosmou', Zuntz 232-4.
47 Vgl. H. Dörrie, *Divers aspects de la cosmologie de 70 av. J. C. à 20 ap. J.C.*, Revue de Théologie et de Philosophie 1972, 400-12, bes. 410 f.

METAPHYSICAL AND PERSONAL RELIGION IN PLOTINUS

THEO GERARD SINNIGE

One of Plotinus' characteristic methods in metaphysics consists in explaining what a thing is by stating the hypostatic level on which it is found. The higher this level is, the more Being it has. This method is the natural consequence of the architecture of Plotinus' system. Reality proceeds from a central source by a process of emanation. In the process an infinite number of beings come into existence, displaying an endless variety but losing the supreme unity of their first origin. As a counterpart to this descent from original unity and perfection, a movement of return is found in the universe. All beings endeavour to return to their origin, that is they endeavour to achieve a higher degree of unity and being. Their urge to strive back may be weaker or stronger between the various beings, dependent on the measure in which they possess a conscious intelligence. As a teleological process this urge is found on every level of being. It permeates the universe as a desire for contemplation, as Plotinus explains in his treatise *On Nature and Contemplation* (*Enn.* III, 8 [30]). In the human soul it determines man's fundamental impulse: to set out on the journey which is to lead him through the life of Soul and Noûs to his first origin, the ineffable One (Enn. VI, 9 [8]).

The description of this journey of the Soul is given by Plotinus in a fixed set of images, predominantly that of the circle and its centre. In the first treatise of the fifth *Ennead* Plotinus says:

"Both the Noûs and the Deity, which is the cause and origin of Noûs, are found within us, just as the centre stands on its own but has in itself each of the points of the circumference." (V 1 [10] 11, 6-12).

And in the last treatise of the last *Ennead*, placed there by Porphyrius probably because its descriptions form a kind of coping-stone to the whole metaphysical architecture of the *Enneads*, we find the soul's inward journey explained by means of the same symbol:

"The soul's natural movement is circular and therefore not directed to something outside it, but around a centre" (VI 9 [8] 8, 3-4).

"Because the soul is from there, it (the ἐκεῖ) is both its origin and its aim (τέλος), because its Good is there, and when it arrives there, then soul becomes what it was itself" (ibd. 9, 21-22).

"When it has come to form part of that first principle, then it has arrived at unity, uniting as it were its own centre with that (universal) centre" (ibd. 10, 16-17 cf. ibd. 8, 19-20).

In these and many parallel passages the human soul is described as living somewhere at the circumference of a circle, at a remote distance from the real source of its life. The way to return for the soul is from the circumference to the centre. This centre is at the same time the soul's centre and the centre of all things in a metaphysical sense. The soul must unite its own centre to the universal centre of being (ibd. 8, 19-20).

It will be observed that the image as a whole implies a direction for the soul's journey which is opposite to the direction of the journey in Plato's *Phaedrus*. Plotinus uses an image in which the soul is directed to the inner life in things and in itself. The metaphor is essentially metaphysical. Though it is given with the aid of a mathematical description, it should be divested of even the last bonds with the material world. On the circumference of the circle there are many points, separated from each other and each having an individuality of its own. The soul should give up this separate individuality and seek for the centre, where, *via* the various radii, the various points coincide in the one central point which is their origin. In Plato's image (*Phaedr.* 247A-248C) the soul goes in the opposite direction in order to find the world of divine beings on the outskirts of this universe. The soul needs the wings of righteousness to take its outward course to what is 'on high' (248A), that is, to the vision of Being. If a soul is not strong enough to keep pace with the blessed gods who easily maintain themselves for ever in the 'meadows of truth' (248B), this soul is bound to lose its wings and fall back on to the earth. The whole description is introduced by Plato as a hymn to the 'regions above the heavens' (247C).

Though it is obvious that Plato is speaking in symbolic language, the images he uses clearly imply a spatial conception. The realm of truth, where the gods are living, is outside the boundaries of the universe. The immortal souls who are to take part in the vision must take their stand on the spine of heaven, where they are carried about by the revolution of the spheres. The idea that the realm of the gods is to be found outside the outermost spheres was taken over by Aristotle. In his early work *De caelo* he argues that in our sublunar world every material thing is either carried downward or upward when it is left to itself, whereas the outermost heaven has a circular and therefore perfect movement. He wants this to be understood as an empirical argument, intended as a foundation for a more scientific method in physics, but, despite his intention to give a reasoned and empirical account, at more than one point the scientific argument gives way to theological convictions. Probably Aristotle tried to demythologize his master's symbolic language, without however abandoning the conviction that the abode of the gods is to be found at the outermost boundary of the universe.

When we come to Plotinus the image has been reversed and, at the same time, immaterialized. It is no longer this visible universe which sets the stage, even symbolically, for the ascent of the soul to the divine world. The soul must find its centre within itself and unite its own centre with the one centre of all being. To explain this, Plotinus makes use of the symbol of the circle and its centre. The symbol is no longer based on a cosmological picture but has a mathematical setting, as well as a metaphysical meaning. We may ask if it was Plotinus who first used it in this sense.

Probably Bréhier was the first to make an attempt at a systematic presentation of Plotinus' sources. He did so in his introductions to the several treatises in his edition of the Enneads. The index at the end of the sixth volume gives a tentative survey of the influences registered. There are several entries s.v. Alexander of Aphrodisias. For our purpose the most important of these are the passages from Alexander's *De anima*, commented upon by Bréhier in his *Notice* to *Enn.* IV 7. Two of these have been taken up by Mahnke (*Sphäre und Allmittelpunkt* 225, note 2), followed by P. Henry (*Sources de Plotin* 429-444).

The use of the image seems to have been introduced by Alexander in the context of a commentary upon Aristotle's theory of sense-perception. Aristotle had pointed out that the impressions received by the different senses can be compared with one another by the perceiving subject. Therefore, he argued (*De an.* III 2, 426b12), it was necessary to postulate a centre where the different impressions come together in one point. This centre will have different functions, though it is one in itself. Aristotle explains this by taking as an example a geometric point which divides a line into two parts. The one point is at the same time the end of one half and the beginning of the other half (427a10, cf. *Phys.* 263a23). When commenting on this passage, Alexander replaces Aristotle's elementary mathematics by a much more profound symbol. He says that the *sensus communis* (τὴν κοινὴν αἴσθησιν) is the point in which the impressions received by the different senses come together just as the radii join each other in the centre of the circle. For that reason the centre is at the same time one and many, because it is one in itself, but it is also the point where the many radii end[1].

We may observe that Alexander does not use the symbol of circle and centre in a cosmological nor in a metaphysical sense. This is confirmed by another passage (*Quaestiones* p. 40,8-23 Bruns), where Alexander explains the striving after metaphysical perfection by means of the Aristotelean and Platonic world-picture, as we know it from the *De caelo* and the *Phaedrus*. He says that the body of this universe, a divine body acting under the impulse of Soul, is urged forward on its circling course by the desire to be like the eternal and unmoved Mover. In the work of Alexander the use of the image of circle and centre is obviously restricted to the explanation of the functioning of the centre of perception or *sensus communis*. When explaining the soul's return to the contemplation of eternal being, he uses the world-picture of a spherical cosmology with divine life on the outmost boundaries.

Plotinus must have drawn rather extensively on Alexander of Aphrodisias, as Bréhier's indexes make clear. He uses the image of the circle and its centre in the same sense as Alexander did, e.g. in *Enn.* IV 7 [2] 6, 11-14, where we read: "This must be as it were a centre, where the radii coming from the circumference meet each other, bringing to their terminal point the perceptions which have come from everywhere." In the whole of the *Enneads*, however, this psychological use of the metaphor is only incidental. Plotinus has made the symbol of the circle and its centre into the fundamental image of his metaphysical theory. Not only is it found in numerous passages where he is explaining the fundamentals of his theory of hypostases, but it must even have formed a regular starting-point for his oral teaching, as we can see from *Enn.* VI 5 [23], 5, 1-3:

> "When the argument has to give an idea of how multiplicity comes into existence, I often draw many lines coming from one centre, in order to give a clear explanation."

Among the many passages where Plotinus makes use of the symbol, there are a few where the image is extensively analysed and detailed. One of these is *Enn.* VI 8 [39] 18, 7-25:

> "A circle is as it were in touch with its centre, and we must say that it takes its force and receives its form from that centre. The radii come together in that one point and have their ending in the centre in such a way that it is the goal to which they were brought back as well as the origin from which they sprang.
> ...Thus we must envisage Noûs and Being as having sprung from

150

the One and, as it were, having flown from and developed out of it, and being dependent on its Noûs-like nature. They point to that Noûs which, being in the One, if we may say so, is not yet Noûs, because it is One. In our example the centre *is* not the radii or the circumference, but the father of radii and circumference[2], producing the radii and the circumference as a reproduction of itself. They are born from its power without being separated." (cf. VI 5 [23], 4, 20-24 and 5.)

A similar passage is IV 4 [28] 16, 21-28:

"If we place the Good at the centre, then we may give Noûs its place in an unmoved circle and Soul in a circle which is moving. The movement of Soul is caused by its desire, for, whereas Noûs is in direct possession of the Good, Soul must strive after what is transcendent. Now the spherical universe has within it the Soul, which is driven on by desire and which, according to its nature, strives after the Good. As a body, the universe can only strive after what is outside itself, and this means that it must embrace itself and make a movement around itself. This explains why it moves in a circle."

The second half of this last passage shows a transition from metaphysics to the description of cosmic movement, and a parallel transition from the symbol of the circle, having the Good at the centre, to the Platonic and Aristotelean world-picture. In the physical cosmos the soul is within the universe and strives for a good which is outside it. The same description is found in *Enn.* II 2 [14] and *Enn.* IV 3 [27], 17, 1-2. The striving after a good which is outside the outermost heaven reminds one of Ar. *De caelo* I 9, 279a8-28 and *Met.* XII, 1072b2-15. In the same vein is *Enn.* IV 3 [14], 17. Here the highest heaven is said to be what is best within the visible universe. For that reason it borders upon the lowest region of the intelligible universe, from where Soul descends into this world. The architecture of the universe is modelled here on Plato's and Aristotle's descriptions, and accordingly has the earth at its centre and eternity on the outside. It seems that this world-picture is used by Plotinus with a certain preference in places where he describes the descent of Soul into this world (cf. III, 2 [47], 3, 30-34). In the whole of the *Enneads*, however, the reversed and metaphysical image is dominant. It represents Plotinus' fundamental world-view in which divinity is at the centre of all things. The metaphor of circle and centre was adapted to this purpose by Plotinus himself.

In some places the mathematical metaphor is accompanied by that of the central light as source of emanation. In *Enn.* I, 7 [54], 1, 21-28 we find the circle and its centre, and next to it the central light of the sun. This may remind us of Plato's symbol of the sun in *Rep.* 508E-509B, but the difference is that, as far as Plato's text goes, the sun is in his simile not a centre of emanation for hypostases of Being. In other places the related metaphor of the central light stands by itself, e.g. IV, 3 [27], 17, 12-20. The central light is described as a source standing unmoved and transcendent. Around the source is circling the Noûs as an 'emanated radiance' (περίλαμψις). The same description and the same terms are found in V, 1 [10], 6, 28-30; V 3 [49], 12, 40-44; VI, 4 [22], 7, 23-36.

When replacing the image of a universe which is enveloped by an outermost sphere of divine life by that of a metaphysical universe having its One origin at its centre, Plotinus did more than introduce a new metaphor. In comparison with Aristotle's theology, a shift in accent has been produced. Aristotle's piety had an extravert character and was directed to the contemplation of the cosmic perfections and their first moving Cause[3]. In Plotinus, theology has moved from a cosmological to a metaphysical basis. He knows the step which leads us from the contemplation of the starry spheres above us to the question who sets these spheres moving. This is the path along which Aristotle's theology moved in the *De Caelo*. Plotinus mentions it in his treatise *On Contemplation* (III, 8 [30], 11, 33-39) but only to add that, having contemplated the beauties of the sky and asked for their maker, we must next ask who it was who brought the intelligible world into existence. At the same time it is no more the Mover of the Spheres who is the object of our search, but the first Source of Being. In order to find this source we must concentrate on the One centre of being, the ever-present origin from which all things flow. This brings us to our last point.

The metaphysical method, which Plotinus made the cornerstone of his theology, is in the *Enneads* accompanied by a pervasive stress on our personally taking part in the divine life of the highest hypostases. This element comes to the fore at every point where Plotinus explains our way of finding the One. He insists that it cannot be found by arguments, but only by being conscious of its presence, just as well in ourselves as in the universe. The point has been worked out best so far by Bréhier (*La philosophie de Plotin* 107-133), who considers it a proof for oriental influence. Schwyzer (*RE* 21, 1, 580) has a curious criticism of Bréhier's argument. He first recognizes that the identification of man's most inner self with the absolute One is practically without antecedent in Greek thought. Then he goes on to argue that Plotinus cannot have come to know Indian philosophy, because Gordian's expedition failed and Plotinus did not reach India. This is very much a simplification on Schwyzer's part. The presence of Indian yogi's in the Greek world has been attested for centuries before Plotinus, and the trade-routes converging in Alexandria cannot have failed to bring a considerable number of Indian travellers to this centre of the Greek and Eastern world. Moreover, why did Plotinus take part in Gordian's expedition, if he hadn't yet had some knowledge of Indian thought and knew what it was about? Though direct textual evidence may be lacking, it is probable rather than not, that in Alexandria information was available about some Indian systems of thought.

The identity of our own inner centre with the first and one centre of all being is fundamental in the Upanishads. The formula of this theory is that the centre of our personal being, called 'vital breath' or Atman, is united with and identical to the centre and origin of all being, called Brahman. We can find this divine centre only by looking for it within ourselves. This reminds us strikingly of the point which again and again is stressed by Plotinus: "Noûs and the origin of Noûs are found within ourselves", "When our soul arrives at its Good, then it becomes what it was itself", "The soul must unite its own centre with the universal centre" (see the passages quoted above, p.147). The accents laid by Plotinus are at times rather characteristic. In V, 1 [10], 11, 13-15 he says:

"This is the point of our being where we touch him, are together with him and are dependent on him."

In VI, 8 [39], 18, 1-8 he says:

"When you go seeking, do not seek for anything outside him, but try to find in him everything that comes after him. ... He is in the depth of all things. What is outside him is touching him, as if in touch with him by circling round, and completely dependent on him. It is as if a circle were in touch with its own centre."

In VI, 9 [9], 11, 38-41 we find:

"When our soul goes the other direction [i.e. to Noûs and the One] it will come not to something alien, but to itself. And to be in itself only and not even in the realm of being, that is being in him [the One]."

The distinction made here between "in itself" and "in the realm of being" is significant. The soul must transcend even the level of being in order to find its own self and to be in its centre.

In the course of this study we have followed the history of a metaphor. One of the developments in this history was the reversal of a world-picture which was used as a symbol. It may be interesting by way of

153

corollary to mention that the opposition of the two world-pictures was noticed by Dante in his *Paradiso*. In canto 38, 41-80, Beatrice points to the fiery centre of divine life and explains: "On that point the heavens and the whole of nature are dependent", thereby quoting Aristotle (*Met.* 1072b14 and *Cael.* 279a29). The symbol she uses is, however, the Plotinian one of circle and centre. She goes on: "The circle which is nearest to that point moves with such a great intensity because it is driven by such a powerful love." Dante then remarks that in the visible world the revolutions of the spheres are on the contrary more accelerated as they are more remote from the centre, which would mean that the architecture of the visible world follows a pattern opposite to the archetype of the heavenly world. Thus the poet points out the opposition between what we have called the cosmological and the metaphysical world-picture. Beatrice gives a solution to the problem by explaining that in a material world every greater degree of goodness requires a greater extension in space to manifest itself in. For that reason the sphere which has the highest degree of love must be the widest of all, that is, must be the outermost sphere, 'loving most and knowing most and carrying with it the whole of the universe'. By this explanation the Aristotelean world-view is saved. It has a touch of artificiality, but also a touch of originality, because in the process the concepts of greater and smaller in the sense of more and less perfect are divested of their spatial connotations. It would be interesting to know if Dante's solution had been prepared by medieval philosophy.

NOTES

[1] Alexander gives this explanation in the two places discussed by Mahnke and P. Henry: *De anima* ed. Bruns (= Suppl. Ar. II,1), Berolini 1887, p. 63, 8-13, and *Quaestiones* ed. Bruns (= *Suppl. Ar.* II,2), Berolini 1892, p. 96, 14-18.

[2] An allusion to Plato *Ep.* II, 312 DE. If the epistle should be authentic, the metaphysical use of the symbol would seem to go back to Plato, because the author of the epistle speaks of a drawing of a sphere to be made on a wax-tablet.

[3] See the author's *Cosmic Religion in Aristotle*, Greek, Roman and Byzantine Studies XIV (1973), 15-34.

SPECIAL LITERATURE

PHIL. MERLAN, *Plotinus Enneads* 2,2, Tr. Proc. Am. Phil. Ass., 74, 1943, 179-191.

R. FERWERDA, *La signification des images et des métaphores dans la pensée de Plotin*, Groningen 1965, 24-36.

EM. BRÉHIER, *La philosophie de Plotin*, Paris, ³1961, 107-133.

P. HENRY, *Une comparaison chez Aristote, Alexandre et Plotin*, Entretiens sur l'Antiquité Classique, 5. Vandoeuvres-Genève, 1957, 429-449.

DIETRICH MAHNKE, *Unendliche Sphäre und Allmittelpunkt*, Halle 1937, Nachdruck Stuttgart-Bad Cannstatt 1966, 215-230.

G. POULET, *Le symbole du cercle infini dans la littérature et la philosophie*, Rev. métaph. mor. 1959, 257-275.

BEAUTY AND THE
DISCOVERY OF DIVINITY
IN THE THOUGHT OF PLOTINUS

A. H. ARMSTRONG

Plotinus would probably have been much surprised to discover that he had an 'aesthetic' – or even that, for moderns, 'aesthetic' is a distinguishable and respectable part of philosophy. He thought much about the beauty of art and nature, and an intense feeling for beauty is apparent in his thought at every level. But for him the apprehension of beauties in the world of sense was a beginning of the journey to the interior during which the soul discovers its own divinity and the source from which it comes, and the perception of the deeper beauties which make the beauties of sense is part of that journey: you can no more separate aesthetic from religion in Plotinus than you can separate religion from philosophy. In this paper, therefore, I propose to explore his thought about beauty entirely in the context of the soul's discovery of divinity, in the hope that this may enable us to understand both better.

The first stage in the soul's journey to the interior is its discovery of its unity with all Soul, and, in the totality of Soul, with the great soul which made the world of sense. If we consider his thought about the beauties of this world of sense in the context of this discovery, we shall at once become aware of the intricacies of the relationship between the Second and the Third Hypostasis and the outer world of space and time which both make, and may arrive at some interesting discoveries about the relationship of the human artist to his work. It is always the belief of Plotinus that we too can "walk on high and direct the whole cosmos", as Plato says of Soul[1]. We can share the ideal relationship to body which belongs to the Soul of the All and the great divine souls of sun, moon, stars and earth. This is a relationship of free detached creativity, in which soul gives everything to body and takes nothing from body, and is present to the material world without experiencing the hindrance or disturbance which a self-isolating fuss about the needs of our particular bodies brings with it. In the great meditation by which we are to realise our unity with universal soul, which occupies the second chapter of the treatise *On The Three Primary Hypostases*[2] the beauty of the world of sense is certainly present to Plotinus' mind. It is a real cosmos, an ordered beauty, which soul brings into being: and the beauty is shown in a very Plotinian way to be a beauty due to life and light. The life-giving function of soul is stressed throughout the chapter, and the symbolic 'entry' of soul into body is expressed in one of Plotinus' finest light images: "As the rays of the sun shedding light on a dark cloud, make it shine and give it a golden look, so soul entering the body of the universe gives life, gives immortality and wakes what lies inert."[3] But there is no indication in this passage or anywhere else in the *Enneads* that universal soul takes delight in the beauty which it creates, or is even aware of it. There is nothing in Plotinus which corresponds to "God saw that it was very good" in the *Book of Genesis*. Creation is always for him the spontaneous reflex of contemplation. The beauty of this world springs indeed from delight, but it is delight in that inner, intelligible beauty which the beauties here below only image imperfectly. This of course lies above Soul in the Second Hypostasis, Intellect, in which divine Soul lives and from which it derives its power. And what is true of divine creativity seems also to be true of the human creation of beauty. The artist can create beauty, even sometimes a greater beauty than that of nature, but only because he contemplates the intelligible realities from which the beauties of nature derive: and the beauty which he manages to put into his works of art, though it is truly a beauty of living form, is always less than the beauty which remains in his contemplative soul[4]. Plotinus seems to leave little more room for human than for divine joy in the act of creation, and none at all for what we should be inclined to take into account in considering great works of art, for the degree to which the artist might discover in the course of his work insights and capacities of which he had not been previously conscious and even be stimulated to surpass himself by the difficulties and newly discovered possibilities of the medium in which he was working. The artist in Plotinus can never discover anything, it would seem, in his work, which is not present in a higher degree in the "art within him", and the material medium in which he works can only hinder his expression of the beauty of living form and not stimulate him to genuinely new achievement[5]. The beauties of art, like the beauties of nature, can serve as effective reminders to others of the intelligible beauty which they image, but it does not appear that the artist who has truly attained to the contemplation from which all beauty proceeds can be helped by his work any more than he should enjoy it. But here there are some important qualifications to be made. First of all, however philosophic Plotinus may make the contemplative creation of the artist sound, he is not likely to have put the artist on the level of the true philosopher. Anyone who actually tries to produce a sensible image of intelligible beauty, instead of being content to contemplate it in interior silence, would seem to fall into the class of 'weak' contemplatives whom he discusses so interestingly in the treatise *On Contemplation.* "Men too, when their power of contemplation weakens, make action a shadow of contemplation and reasoning. Because contemplation is not enough for them, since their souls are weak and they are not able to grasp the vision sufficiently, and therefore are not filled with it, but still long to see it, they are carried into action, so as to see what they cannot see with their intellect. When they make something, then, it is because they want to see their object themselves, and also because they want others to be aware of it and contemplate it as well as possible"[6]. Those in this inferior class, whether artists themselves or those who enjoy their works, might certainly gain greater awareness of intelligible beauty through contemplation of the sense-images with which they were concerned: and they would, of course, be by far the greater part of the human race. For Plotinus, as for all ancient philosophers, those capable of philosophy were only a tiny minority of mankind. He might well have thought that the concern for the external obviously shown in this paper made it clear that its author was not one of that minority. And we may, perhaps, even go a little further. There is much in the *Enneads* to suggest (and nothing in the *Life* to contradict the suggestion) that Plotinus himself was helped rather than hindered in his contemplation by having to produce his ideas in teaching, discussion and writing, from the time when he took part in the seminars of Ammonius onwards. And we may surmise that the distinctively artistic or poetic part of his philosophical production, his unsurpassed choice and verbal expression of sensuous images to express the living power and beauty of the intelligible, may greatly have enhanced his awareness of intelligible beauty. At any rate, there is nothing in the *Enneads* to exclude the supposition that there were always times when he, like the rest of mankind, stood much in need of "images of beauty to remind them"[7].

There is another line of thought in the *Enneads* which may lead us to conclude that, even in the unlikely event of the artist being a perfect philosophic contemplative he might in the process of artistic production acquire a greater awareness *on the conscious level* of the intelligible reality which he contemplated. This is the remarkable doctrine about consciousness which is clearly stated in three places in the *Enneads*[8]. Consciousness for Plotinus must be sharply distinguished from the noetic activity in which the higher part of our soul, which does not "come down" but always remains on the level of Intellect, is according to him continually engaged. We can only be conscious of this higher activity of thought when it penetrates to those lower regions of our soul which are intimately connected with the body, and its adequate reception and imaging there depends to a great extent on our bodily condition. In the great treatise *On Difficulties About the Soul* when he is discussing how we remember our acts of intellection, which we can only do if they in some way enter the image-making power[9] he suggests "Perhaps the reception into the image-making power would be of the verbal expression which accompanies the act of intelligence"[10]. This theory would enable Plotinus to explain how the artist, on the lower and less important level of ordinary consciousness, could gain greater awareness of the realities which his intellect contemplates in the process of artistic creation through the formation of images, verbal, musical or visual, which would be a necessary part of that process. (We can see from the well-known chapter of the treatise *On Intelligible Beauty* in praise of hieroglyphics[11] that Plotinus thought that non-verbal, non-discursive symbols were better adapted than verbal ones to express intelligible forms). But this discovery of the intelligible realities in their images on the conscious level would be for Plotinus a matter of small importance for the philosophic artist, and nothing like it would be possible in the case of divine creation. Divine creation must be the spontaneous, unplanned, reflex of inward contemplation which cannot increase the self-knowledge or the joy in intelligible beauty which is in that originative contemplation: and human creation should approximate to this as closely as possible.

It is clear from what has been said that soul in creating beauty is always acting as a mediator between the two worlds of Intellect and sense. Soul never seems to be thought of as having a distinct world of its own, with a beauty distinct from and intermediate between that of the intelligible and that of the perceptible, though of course it contains *logoi* which are intermediate between the intelligible forms and those in nature and body[12]. Its world is either the world of Intellect in which at its highest it lives and contemplates, or the world of sense which it brings into being and fills with life and beauty but to which it should not, and in its higher forms does not, direct its contemplative attention. In our 'aesthetic' consideration of the soul's journey to the interior (or our 'spiritual' consideration of Plotinus' aesthetic) it is therefore to the beauty of the world of Intellect which we must now turn. It is by considering his descriptions of intellectual beauty[13] that we can best understand what beauty meant

158

to him both in the inner and the outer worlds. For the two beauties are not for him opposed or contrasted, though the first is immeasurably superior to the second. He is not inclined to make the sort of contrast which we so easily slip into when we distinguish intellectual and sensuous beauty, a contrast between a beauty of abstract pattern contemplated with a rather cool enjoyment and a warm, mobile, concrete beauty which excites our feelings. (It is a contrast, by the way, which cannot be applied to the masterpieces of what is at once the most abstract and intellectual and the most sensuous and passionate of arts, the music of J. S. Bach, for instance, or the last quartets of Beethoven. Modern European music at its greatest can illustrate Plotinus' accounts of intelligible beauty in a way of which he never dreamed). We can in fact best understand what kind of beauty moved and excited Plotinus in our world of the senses by studying the imaginative language in which he describes the beauty of the world of Intellect, which holds together all the beauties dispersed and separated here below in a more perfect unity and a greater glory of mutual translucence. This imaginative language has been carefully studied by Schwyzer and Ferwerda[14] and need not be discussed in detail here. But the general impression which it makes suggests that the kind of beauty which delighted Plotinus here below (perhaps at times rather more than he would have wished) was vigorous and vital, with the bloom and radiance of abounding life upon it, and full of the wild profusion of change and variety which goes with abundant life. As I have remarked elsewhere[15], nothing is more remarkable in Plotinus' accounts of intelligible beauty than the way in which he insists, at some risk to logical coherence, on introducing values which to our way of thinking are inextricably bound up with change and process into his eternal world. This of course brings the two worlds very close together. The world of Intellect is really an 'inner' rather than an 'other' world.

But we can only fully appreciate the importance of life in both the aesthetic and the religion of Plotinus when we understand that the life which glorifies his intelligible world (and in which that world has its origin) comes from beyond it. The awareness that life has a certain ontological priority to form and comes from a source beyond the reach of the supreme self-forming and self-structuring Intellect[16] is an important part of the general awareness that what we are really looking for, the ultimate object and origin of our love, lies "over the horizon" of thought, which impels us at the last to leave even intelligible beauty behind and seek union with the Good beyond intellect and being. This sense of the priority of life and the transcendence of its source affects the whole of the thought of Plotinus about beauty, and seems to be responsible for some of its most interesting features. It may well be behind his rejection of the commonplace Stoic definition of beauty as "good proportion with pleasant colour" in the treatise *On Beauty*[17], and his preference for the simple statement that beauty is due to the presence of form. His arguments here are not altogether convincing, as Anton has pointed out[18]. His contention that beauty can be present in something absolutely simple, unrelated to anything else, is as it stands somewhat problematical. His insistence that the simple parts of a beautiful composite whole must themselves be beautiful is contradicted in the much later treatise *On Providence*[19], and Plotinus' second thoughts here seem to be more in accordance with the aesthetic facts. And it is difficult to see how form in a composite thing of beauty can manifest itself otherwise than in a harmony of proportions and colour: the 'proportion' definition and the 'form' definition of beauty seem on strictly Platonic principles to complement rather than to contradict each other. But if the implicit contrast is not simply between 'proportion' and 'form' but between proportion and colour considered abstractly as the conformity of a lifeless thing to certain aesthetic rules, and the living presence of a power in which the life coming from the Good structures itself into creative form, this first chapter of the treatise *On Beauty* makes a good deal more sense: and the 'dynamic' way in which form has just been described is in perfect accordance with the normal thought of Plotinus about the intelligible world and its contents.

Form, then, we may suggest, as the cause of true beauty in the sensible world, is always *living* form. But if we turn our attention to intelligible beauty, and consider it in relation to its source, we shall discover that Plotinus finds it possible, once at least, to consider the beauty of form in abstraction from the living light which plays upon it from the Good. This he does in a famous and much discussed chapter from the treatise *How the Multitude of Forms came into Being, and on the Good*[20]. Here we are told that intelligible beauty is 'inert' by itself[21] and cannot move or attract the soul until the light, warmth, colour, life, or grace (all these words are used in the chapter) which comes directly from the Good, descends upon it. Only then can it arouse the *erōs*, the passionate love, which is the proper response to beauty for any Platonist. There is an interesting inconsistency of language in this chapter. In the first part, where he is dealing directly with intelligible beauty, it is that beauty itself which he declares unattractive and uninteresting without what comes upon it from the Good. Something, that is, can be beautiful without moving or exciting us. The conception of unattractive or uninteresting beauty with which Plotinus seems to be operating here has considerable practical aesthetic usefulness. It enables us to give a balanced account of works of classicist or academic art to which we cannot altogether deny beauty, in some sense of the word, but to which we must, if we are honest with ourselves, deny any interest or attractiveness. But in the analogy from the beauties of the sense-world which concludes the chapter, Plotinus goes back to a more Platonic way of speaking in which beauty *is* that transcendent radiance of life which is "the lovable"[22], and statues are more beautiful in so far as they are "more lifelike"[23], and an uglier living man more beautiful than a statue of a beautiful man. The cause of beauty and giver and goal of *erōs*, the Good, is still placed beyond beauty, but beauty is identified with *living* form[24], and the conception of a dead or inert beauty is no longer being used.

To appreciate fully the significance of what is said in this chapter we need to compare it with another famous passage which at first sight seems to contradict it. This is the description of the conflict which can arise in our souls between the attractions of the Good and of Beauty in the treatise *That the Intelligibles are not Outside the Intellect and on the Good*[25]. The beauty here in question is, unmistakably from the context, in-tellectual beauty, not the beauty of the sense-world. The perpetual presence of the Good, we are told here, and the unbroken attraction which it exercises on us, lies deep below the level of consciousness: the Good is always there, always drawing us to itself "even when we are asleep": when we do see it, we are not surprised, and do not have to make an act of recollection to know what it is. The awareness of beauty on the other hand is a conscious (and therefore on Plotinian principles more superficial) awareness, which provokes shock and astonishment and the pain of passionate love. And this disturbing awareness of beauty may lead to one of two undesirable consequences. Some people set themselves up as rivals to beauty, and compete with it for its proper place in the second rank of the universal hierarchy, "next to the King": and it is also pos-sible for the ignorant to be distracted by beauty and drawn away by it from the Good "as a lover draws a child away from the father". In one passage, then, beauty derives all its power to excite and attract us from the Good, and it is only when we are aware of the "light from the Good" shining upon it that our passionate love is stirred. In the other, beauty seems to have an ambiguous, disputable, spiritually dangerous, erotic attraction of its own. There would be nothing surprising about this, of course, if it was said of the beauty of the sense-world[26], but its application to the beauty of Intellect is rather startling. The two passages can, I think, be reconciled, once we realise clearly that Plotinus must, in both of them, be talking about varying attitudes of our selves to intelligible beauty rather than giving variant objective accounts of that beauty itself and its relation to the Good. Intellect in all the glory of its beauty must always stand next to the Good and be our way to the Good, and receive its glory eternally and unchangingly from the Good. But we, it seems, (though this is perhaps not altogether consistent with what is said elsewhere about our higher selves) can adopt various deviant and unsatisfactory attitudes to beauty, and it is these which seem to be described, with fine psychological insight, in the two chapters under discussion[27]. We can consider beauty abstractly, by itself, apart from its relationship to the Good: and if we do so we can either find it quite unexciting and uninteresting or much too exciting in the wrong way. We can be bored by it or carried away from the Good by it in a sort of erotic-aesthetic hallucination: further, since either boredom or intoxication can easily end in hostility, either of these deviant states may lead to a further deviation in which we quarrel with beauty and deny it its true place next after the Good: which means, perhaps, that we may adopt a thoroughly anti-aesthetic and anti-metaphysical religious attitude. This, at least, seems to be a Plotinian way of bringing the teachings of these two great chapters into harmony. If we escape these deviations, and always see beauty in the worlds of sense and intellect in its true nature and place, the sensible as the best possible image of the intelligible and the intelligible as the rich and complex radiance of the One; and always look beyond beauty when we contemplate it to the source of its radiance, travelling ever onwards till we reach the spring of living light; then the *erōs* which beauty properly excites in us will be the true *erōs* which comes from and will lead us back to the Good.

There is nothing more truly Hellenic in the philosophy of Plotinus than the way in which aesthetic and religious values, in spite of all his awareness of possibilities of conflict between them in our spiritual lives, are held firmly together in his thought about beauty. We may well be able to learn something from him here in our own age, in which an unnecessary and monstrous civil war between the defenders of different values has gravely weakened our civilisation and reduced its capacity to resist the destructive domination of those whose only values are money and power. If we can re-Hellenize rather then de-Hellenize our thought in this respect, so that the love of beauty and the love of metaphysical truth are seen as parts of the love of God, the prospects for both religion and civilisation will be better.

162

NOTES

1 *Phaedrus* 246C 1-2. *Enn.* IV 8 [6], 2, 20-21; IV,3 [27], 7, 17; V, 8 [31], 7, 34.

2 V, 1 [10], 2.

3 l.c. lines 20-23.

4 V, 8 [31], 1.

5 l.c. lines 18-26. My account of this passage owes much to a former pupil of mine at Dalhousie University, Mrs. N. Hare.

6 III, 8 [30], 4, 31-39 my own translation from *Plotinus* III (Loeb Classical Library): cp. ch. 7, 18-22, on 'creativity' in general, and see my note in the Loeb edition on ch. 6, pp. 372-373.

7 I, 8 [51], 15, 28.

8 IV, 8 [6], 8: IV, 3 [27], 30: I, 4 [46], 9-10. See my article *Aspects of the Thought of Plotinus at Variance with Classical Intellectualism* in Journal of Hellenic Studies XCIII (1973), 13-22.

9 φανταστικόν.

10 τοῦ λόγου τοῦ τῷ νοήματι παρακολουθοῦντος IV, 3, [27], 30, 7.

11 V, 8 [31], 6.

12 IV, 3 [27], 10-11.

13 Especially the two great "visionary" passages V, 8 [31], 3-4 and VI, 7 [38], 12-13.

14 H. R. Schwyzer, *Plotinos*, RE 21, 1. (1951), 526-7; R. Ferwerda, *La signification des métaphores dans la pensée de Plotin*, Groningen 1965.

15 *Eternity, Life and Movement in Plotinus' accounts of* Νοῦς, in: *Le Néoplatonisme*, Paris 1971, 67-76.

16 III, 8 [30], 9, 29-30.

17 I, 6 [1], 1: cp. Cicero, *Tusc.* IV, 31.

18 John P. Anton, *Plotinus' Refutation of Beauty as Symmetry*, Journ. Aesth. and Art. Crit. XXIII, 1964, 233-237.

19 III, 2 [47], 17, 64-74.

20 VI, 7 [38], 22.

21 ἀργόν τε γὰρ τὸ κάλλος αὐτοῦ line 11.

22 τὸ ἐράσμιον line 26.

23 ζωτικώτερα line 30.

24 cp. chapter 32.

25 V, 5 [32], 12.

26 cp. I, 6 [1], 8 and the remarkable description of the "enchantments" of this world in IV, 4 [28], 43.

27 In V 5, 12,20-4 we are told (i) that everyone does not recognize beauty (ii) that people think it belongs to itself, not to them (iii) that they find it sufficient to seem to be beautiful, even if they are not really. And in the some chapter, line 35, there is a phrase (συμμιγῆ τῷ ἀλγύνοντι τὴν ἡδονήν) which suggests the "mixed" pleasures of *Philebus* 46A ff. All this suggests that these deviant attitudes may only be possible at that stage of inadequate awareness of intelligible beauty in which we still see it as external and other than ourselves (cp. VI, 7 [38] 15, 30-32). For it is only that which is external to ourselves which, when present at the conscious level, can remain unrecognised, or appear to have nothing to do with us, or be acquired in seeming only, or satisfy a painful need.

ON PLOTINUS IV, 7 [2], 8[3]

MODESTUS VAN STRAATEN O.S.A.

In this chapter of his treatise on the immortality of the soul Plotinus is engaged in a controversy with the Stoics, who held that the human (and animal) embryo is organized by a merely vegetative force and only at birth starts to be ruled by a soul, i.e. by a sensitive and appetitive power[1]. It seems to be worth while to analyse Plotinus' train of thought and, especially, to inquire into the question, whether he understood fully and rendered precisely the Stoic tenet concerning the origin of the human soul.

To broach the subject, let us first give a translation of the passage concerned[2]:

"The theory, too, that the same breath which was previously a vegetative force, develops into a soul when entering the cold and being hardened by it, because in the cold it becomes finer, – which is absurd in itself; for, many living beings arise in warmth and have a
5 soul which has not been cooled down – means anyhow that the vegetative force exists before the soul, which comes into being only by external circumstances. Thus, they make the inferior come first and, before that, another still lower force, which they call 'coherence'; in the last place, then, the mind obviously springs from the soul.
10 If, however, Mind is first of all beings, Soul should be placed immediately after it, then the vegetative principle (should follow); in general, that which is posterior, always must be placed on a lower level, in correspondence with its nature. If, then, in their opinion, God is also later in respect to the mind, and engendered and endowed
15 with intellection acquired from without, it could be that there might be neither soul, nor mind, nor God. If anything could exist potentially without anything existing in actuality previously, namely Mind, it would all the same not come into actuality. For, what will be there to lead it (into actuality), if, besides itself, nothing else
20 exists before? And even if it would itself lead itself (to actuality), which is absurd, it will do so looking on something which doesn't

164

exist potentially, but actually. And indeed, even if that which is
potential were able to remain always the same, it would tend of
itself to actuality, and actuality will be of a higher degree than the
25 potential, because it is the object of its desire. Thus, the higher is the
earlier and it has a nature different from body and exists always in
actuality; consequently, Mind as well as Soul is earlier than Nature.
Therefore, Soul is not on a level with breath nor with body. That
soul is not to be named body, however, has been said by others
30 differently, but what precedes will be sufficient too."

Remarks on the translation of the text[3]

5-6. We render (with Henry-Schwyzer, Harder, Cilento and, perhaps,
Bréhier) προτέραν φύσιν ψυχῆς εἶναι as 'that the vegetative force exists
before the soul', explaining ψυχῆς as a *genitivus comparationis* to be
linked with προτέραν. Bouillet and MacKenna, on the contrary, explain
ψυχῆς as a *genitivus possessivus* to be joined with φύσιν and translate
respectively: 'la première nature de l'âme' and 'soul has an earlier form'.
Both, however, fail to appreciate the specifically Stoic meaning of φύσις
as a lower level of manifestation of the Λόγος, namely as a vegetative,
non-sensitive-appetitive force. Cf. *SVF* II, 714, 715 *et al.* Since the very
argument of the passage is concerned with the change of the φύσις into a
soul, it seems to be unquestionable that φύσις cannot have the meaning
of essence, nature (of the soul) here.

6. With Kirchhoff, Bréhier, Cilento and Harder we read γιγνομένης,
the proposal 'γιγνομένην scil. ψυχὴν praedicativum' (made by Henry-
Schwyzer in order to save the reading of the manuscripts) being, in my
opinion, grammatically rather improbable.*

9. In Stoic texts ἕξις frequently means the universal breath (πνεῦμα)
as far as it holds together non-living beings as stones, wood, bones etc.
Cf. *SVF* II, 458, 714, 716 and 1013. Therefore, we prefer the translation
'coherence' (though not given by Liddle-Scott), in which the *dynamic*
aspect of the Stoic concept seems to be sufficiently expressed. This
aspect, in our opinion, is ignored in the translations proposed by Bréhier
('disposition'), Cilento ('stato') and Harder ('Zuständlichkeit'). Bouillet
('habitude') and MacKenna ('Habitude') understand the term in its
Aristotelian sense and are, therefore, wrong. There cannot be any doubt
that the word must here have its Stoic sense.

11. In my opinion, the phrase κατὰ τὸν νοῦν ὕστερος means: 'later in
respect to the mind', i.e. as compared with the mind lower in the pre-

sumed Stoic scale of beings. For it seems to be clear that Plotinus here has in view the possibility (εἰ) that the Stoics, making the mind spring from the soul, could go further and could let God derive from the mind. In that case, indeed, God would be engendered from the mind, would have acquired intellection from the mind, i.e. from without, and there would be, according to the Stoics, *three* beings after the vegetative principle: soul, mind and God. Therefore, in this passage God and mind cannot be identical, and for this reason the translation given by Cilento ('rispetto allo Spirito è posteriore') is the most correct one. As to the translations proposed by Bouillet ('par cela même qu'il possède l'intelligence, est postérieur') and Bréhier ('en tant qu'intelligence, est postérieur'), it must be observed that they assume an identification of the mind and God. God, indeed, is later (than the soul), because he is or has intellection, intellection being later than the soul. If, however, God has intellection ἐπακτόν, as coming from without (i.e. from the mind), as is said in the following line, he cannot be identified with the mind, but must be later than the mind. This identification of God and mind, it is true, is not found in the translations given by MacKenna ('if they treat God as they do the Intellectual principle, as later') and Harder ('entsprechend dem Geist, später') but, in my view, they do not express clearly enough Plotinus' (incorrect) supposition that the Stoic God is later than the mind.

13-14. As to the text, it may be observed that only Henry-Schwyzer and Cilento retain the tradition of the manuscripts and read εἰ τὸ δυνάμει, μὴ ὄντος πρότερον τοῦ ἐνεργείᾳ καὶ νοῦ, γένοιτο, whereas Bréhier, Harder and MacKenna accepted the conjecture made by Kirchhoff and read οὐκ ἂν γένοιτο. Bouillet ('car jamais ce qui est en puissance ne peut passer à l'état d'acte, s'il...') seems to have adopted the suppression of καὶ νοῦ first proposed by Creuzer (Plotinus, *Opera omnia*, Oxford 1835).

The text, indeed, is difficult and many proposals concerning its exact meaning have been made. After all, however, I do not see any reason to deviate from the unanimous tradition of the manuscripts. For what exactly does Plotinus intend to say here? The kernel of his argument, undoubtedly, is that, for an only potentially existing being, it is absolutely impossible to come into actuality without the causality of an actually existing being. It seems to me that Plotinus, in order to emphasize the absolute character of this impossibility, adds (or rather prefixes), in a hypothetic sense, the thesis that this also holds in the case that there could exist a being-in-potentiality without there existing previously a being-in-actuality. Within this context the addition καὶ νοῦ is rather superfluous. It should, however, be kept in mind that in Plotinus' mode of thought *all* actual being is necessarily connected with the Mind, for the Mind is the first and highest level of being and most actually existing. It is, therefore, not unthinkable that Plotinus, broaching the concept of τὸ ἐνεργείᾳ, spontaneously thought of the νοῦς; in his thought it was, indeed, *impossible* that there could exist any actual being without the Mind existing. The meaning of the sentence could be then: 'without something-in-actuality existing before, *and especially* (or: namely) the Mind'. Perhaps Cilento, bracketing *lo Spirito* ('che non è superfluo', o.c. 567) in his translation, is right, making in this way καὶ νοῦ to express the totality of all actual being.

18-20. In my translation I follow the text of Henry-Schwyzer, but (with Bréhier and Harder) insert a comma after ἕξει (instead of after ἑαυτό)*. In my thought, the passage, then, really makes sense within the context and there seems to be no reason to consider it (with Bréhier) as a gloss. For Plotinus' trend of thinking apparently is as follows: having declared (13-16) that no potential being is able to come into actual existence without the causality of another actually existing being, he moots (16-17) the (immediately rejected – ὅπερ ἄτοπον) supposition that a potential being could itself bring itself into actuality and declares that, even in this case, actuality plays a part in the process, *viz.* the intended (actual) end, which the potential being strives after. Finally, Plotinus presumes a third possibility (18-20): even if the potential being would have the possibility to remain always identical and the same (εἴπερ ἕξει τὸ ἀεὶ μένειν τὸ αὐτό), i.e. to remain invariably in its potential condition, still, Plotinus says, an actuality would be involved, because every potential being is, by definition and as being potential, potential to some actuality; it tends of its own nature (i.e. by being potential) to an actuality (καθ' ἑαυτὸ εἰς ἐνέργειαν ἄξει) and this actuality is, even in the case that it is never reached, of a higher level than the potential being, because it is the end which every potential being naturally aims at.

In this interpretation of the text the active form ἄξει (19) has to be understood as an *intransitive* form, i.e. in the sense of *to go* or *to tend*. In my opinion, this is possible; Cf. Plato, *Nom.* 701e (ἐπὶ δὲ τὸ ἄκρον ἀγαγόντων ἑκατέρων) and *Ev. Marc.* 1, 38 (ἄγωμεν ἀλλαχοῦ). Perhaps, it is possible (with Harder, o.c. 399) to supply αὐτὸ (from line 16-17 αὐτὸ ἄξει) and to understand ἄξει (αὐτὸ) as ἄξεται. However that may be, the most probable translation of the passage seems to be: 'if that which is potential, would be able to remain always the same, it would tend of itself to actuality!'

167

As to the translations proposed by several authors, it may be observed that not one of them is, in my opinion, satisfactory. In fact, Bouillet ('si l'on admet que ce qui est en puissance puisse toujours demeurer identique, *il passera de lui-même à l'état d'acte*'), Harder ('wenn das Potentiale die Eigenschaft haben soll immer das Nämliche zu bleiben, dann *kann es sich nach seinem eigenen Vorbild in die Aktualität über-führen*') and MacKenna ('we may conceive a potentiality which remains eternal self-identity and *of itself imparts actuality*') forget, as far as I can see, that in the immediately preceding lines Plotinus emphatically declared that neither can a potential being come to actuality without the causality of an actually existing being, nor bring itself to actuality. Moreover, they didn't see that everlasting self-identity of a potentially existing being necessarily means an invariably everlasting potentiality. Cilento ('se un essere potenziale ha la proprietà di perseverare sempre nella sua identità, di per se stesso, *esso potrebbe addurre all'atto un altro essere*') seems to understand ἄξει in a transitive sense (without supplying αὐτό) and to supply an object ('altro essere'); in doing so he saves, it is true, the self-identity of the potential being, but, on the other hand, he makes the potentiality of a potential being into the cause of the actuality of an actual being, which seems to be even more impossible than a potential being leading itself to actuality.

Plotinus' argumentation

Plotinus' starting-point clearly is a Stoic doctrine which can be roughly summarized as follows: at the root of the totality of being there is an active and rational principle, conceived of as a tension (τόνος) or a breath (πνεῦμα), manifesting itself gradually, i.e. in anorganic matter as coherence (ἕξις), in plants as 'nature' (φύσις), in animals as soul (ψυχή) and in the full-grown man (from about 14 years) also as thinking power (λόγος). Applied to Stoic anthropology, this doctrine led to the theory that the human (and animal) embryo, living only as a vegetative being, was ruled by φύσις, i.e. by the πνεῦμα manifesting itself or working as φύσις, the organizing principle of plants. At birth, however, because the child begins to function as a sensitive-appetitive being, it must, consequently, be ruled by a sensitive-appetitive principle, a ψυχή.

The Stoics, indeed, taught that the πνεῦμα at birth *changed* from φύσις into ψυχή (*SVF* II, 806). In this respect Plotinus is right. He is also right in saying that this change was represented by the Stoics as a refrigeration, as a cooling-down or a hardening of the πνεῦμα (ibd.). It must, however, be kept in mind that this representation (handed down to us in texts from a rather late period) is probably an ontological wording of a more functional way of thinking. Plotinus himself speaks of *the same* breath which develops into a soul. In fact, the Stoics taught that *the same* breath which was hitherto operating or functioning as a vegetative power, henceforth functions as a soul, i.e. as a sensitive-appetitive force.

In the following lines Plotinus seems to push *ad extremum* this Stoic doctrine concerning the origin of the human soul. For he suggests (alluding to the Stoic tenet that λόγος, thinking power, is obtained by man only at the age of about 14 years) that the Stoics let the thinking power (Plotinus speaks of νοῦς instead of the Stoic λόγος) spring from the soul in broadly the same way as the soul springs from the φύσις. The Stoics, however, never taught that the soul of the child (originating at birth) was changed into λόγος at the age of 14 years, but only that the λόγος at that age came to full development (*SVF* I, (Zeno) 149; II, 764 and III (Diog.) 17). The soul of the human child is from the very beginning a *human* soul, but one of the functions of the human soul starts to be exercised only at about 14 years, when general concepts are derived from the *data* of the senses (ibd.).

Nor are there indications that the Stoics taught that the organizing principle of anorganic material things, ἕξις, or (to speak with Galen) πνεῦμα ἑκτικόν (*SVF* II, 716) ever changed into a φύσις. And the supposition of Plotinus (lines 11-12) that the Stoics may have derived their God from the inferior and may have taught that their God is engendered and receives his intellection from without, is in flat contradiction with the most fundamental dogma of the Stoics, viz. that at the root of all reality there is an *eternal rational* principle referred to also by the name of God (*SVF* I (Zeno) 85, 87; II, 300, 301, 306, 310 *et al.*) and surviving even the ἐκπύρωσις at the end of each cosmical period (Diog. Laërt. VII, 138).

All this makes it clear that Plotinus wrongly saddled the Stoics with an ontological scale, in which the lower would be the first. His argumentation against them, starting from the Aristotelian proposition that potential being is posterior to actual being (cf. *De anima*, 415a19; *Metaph.* 1050b3; 1072a9. *Eth. Nic.* 1170a17), however penetrating it may be, is, therefore, not to the point. Graeser (o.c. 29-30) rightly reproaches Plotinus for not even taking into account the fact that the πῦρ τεχνικόν, which survives the process of ἐκπύρωσις, is actually the first principle from which the regeneration of the *cosmos* begins. Perhaps, it could be added that Plotinus also failed to be fully alive to the functional way of thinking of the Stoics.

NOTES

[1] Andreas Graeser, *Plotinus and the Stoics*, Leiden 1972, inserts this passage in his collection of Stoic material found in Plotinus p. 44-45. Plotinus' discussion of the Stoic tenet further on in this chapter is shortly dealt with by Graeser, 29.

[2] The text used is that of Henry-Schwyzer (ed. maior, Paris-Bruxelles 1959, II, 204-206) with a few exceptions, which will be specified and defended severally in the remarks following the translation. – The numbers in the margin correspond to the lines of the *Greek* text.

[3] The well-known editions, commentaries and translations will be referred to by author's name only. *Viz.*:

Bouillet	= M. N. Bouillet, *Les Ennéades de Plotin*. Traduction française, notes et éclaircissements, Paris 1857-1861. (Unveränderter Nachdruck Frankfurt 1968).
Bréhier	= E. Bréhier, *Plotin, Ennéades*. Texte, traduction française, notices, Paris 1924-1938.
Cilento	= V. Cilento, *Plotino, Enneadi*. Versione italiana e commentario critico, Bari 1947-1949.
Harder	= Richard Harder, *Plotins Schriften*, Band I, Hamburg 1956.
Henry-Schwyzer	= P. Henry - E. R. Schwyzer, *Plotini Opera*, Paris, Bruxelles 1951-1973.
Kirchhoff	= A. Kirchhoff, *Plotini Opera*, Leipzig 1856.
MacKenna	= S. MacKenna - B. S. Page, *Plotinus. The Enneads*, London ³1962.
Volkmann	= R. Volkmann, *Enneades*, Leipzig 1883-1884.

* After I had made this article ready for the press (july 1973), I found that Henry-Schwyzer assumed in their *Addenda ad Tomum Primum et Alterum*, 396 (*Plotini Opera* III, Paris, Bruxelles, Leiden 1973) both the reading γιγνομένης in line 6 and the comma after ἕξει in line 18 instead of after ἑαυτό in line 19.

PROKLOS UND ALEXANDER
VON APHRODISIAS
UEBER EIN PROBLEM DER LEHRE
VON DER VORSEHUNG

F. P. HAGER

Proklos exponiert in der zweiten Quaestio seiner kleinen Schrift *De decem dubitationibus circa providentiam* folgendes Grundproblem bezüglich des Verhältnisses zwischen göttlicher Vorsehung und der Welt des Vergänglichen: Ist anzunehmen, dass die göttliche Vorsehung auch das Kontingente und Zufällige erkennt oder nicht? Proklos selbst bejaht diese Frage, ist sich aber bewusst, dass schon in der philosophiegeschichtlichen Tradition vor ihm das Verhältnis von göttlicher Vorsehung und Kontingentem als schwerwiegendes Problem erkannt worden ist[1].

Insbesondere erwähnt Proklos zwei entgegengesetzte Lehrmeinungen über die Frage, ob die göttliche Vorsehung das Kontingente erkennt. Die einen haben, so meint er, von der Existenz der Vorsehung überzeugt und von dieser Existenz zutiefst beeindruckt, das Zufällige geradezu aus dem Bereich des Seienden verbannt, die andern aber haben, da sie sich ausserstande sahen, irgend etwas gegen die offensichtliche Existenz des Kontingenten zu sagen, geleugnet, dass die Vorsehung bis zum Zufälligen vordringen könne[2].

Im Opusculum *De providentia* kommt Proklos noch einmal auf dieselbe Frage zurück und beleuchtet, indem er ebenfalls die zwei entgegengesetzten Ansichten einander gegenüberstellt, noch einen weiteren Aspekt dieses Problems, wobei diesmal offensichtlich die beiden Lehrmeinungen in umgekehrter Reihenfolge erwähnt werden: Die einen, sagt Proklos hier, behaupten, es sei nicht wahr, dass Gott schlechthin alles auf eine exakte und bestimmte Weise erkenne, sondern vielmehr bleibe seine Erkenntnis unbestimmt in dem, was selbst unbestimmt ist; dies behaupten sie, um die Realität des Kontingenten zu retten. Die andern aber weisen Gott bestimmte (exakte) Erkenntnis (von schlechthin allem) zu und ziehen daraus die Konsequenz, dass alles Werdende durch vollständige Notwendigkeit bestimmt sei. Dies sind, wie Proklos selbst ausdrücklich betont, die respektiven Lehrmeinungen der Peripatetiker und der Stoiker[3].

Isaak Sebastokrator, in dessen Abhandlung *Zehn Aporien über die*

171

Vorsehung H. Boese Grundlagen für die Rekonstruktion des griechischen Textes des ersten der *Tria Opuscula* des Proklos gefunden hat, verbindet in seinem Text die beiden Behauptungen, welche Proklos in *De decem dubitationibus circa providentiam* und in *De providentia* über die Peripatetiker, bzw. die Stoiker aufstellt: Die einen, so führt er aus, behaupten, die Vorsehung könne nicht bis zum Kontingenten vordringen und erkenne nicht absolut alles auf bestimmte Weise, sondern bleibe bezüglich des unbestimmten Werdenden selber unbestimmt, womit sie die Evidenz der Existenz des Kontingenten achten und bewahren wollen, die andern aber, so meint er weiter, lehrten von der Vorsehung, dass sie zu allem vordringe und über eine bestimmte Erkenntnis von allem verfüge, was unweigerlich bei ihnen zur Konsequenz führe, dass sie das Wesen des Kontingenten aus dem Sein verbannen und alles Werdende als durch Notwendigkeit bestimmt annehmen müssten[4].

Für einen künftigen Kommentator der beiden Opuscula des Proklos über die Vorsehung dürfte es nun nicht uninteressant sein, zu wissen, wer wohl der Peripatetiker ist, welcher an den genannten Stellen als Vertreter einer bestimmten Lehre von der Vorsehung gemeint ist. Am besten bietet sich hier als Vergleichsmöglichkeit Alexander von Aphrodisias an, welcher in einer bekannten Abhandlung *Ueber das Schicksal* (Περὶ εἱμαρμένης) sich mit dem Fatalismus der Stoiker auseinandergesetzt hat, sich in einer verloren gegangenen Schrift Περὶ προνοίας sowie an verschiedenen Stellen seiner kleineren Schriften (Ἀπορίαι καὶ λύσεις, *De anima libri Mantissa*) über seine eigene, an Aristoteles orientierte Lehre von der Vorsehung geäussert, und seit Plotin auf die Geschichte des Neuplatonismus bedeutenden Einfluss genommen hat[5]. Während die Zurückführung der Lehre von der Omnipotenz der Vorsehung, auf welche sich Proklos in seinen beiden Werken bezieht, auf stoische Quellen kaum Schwierigkeiten bereitet[6], muss man sich fragen, ob wirklich Alexander als der prominenteste Repraesentant der peripatetischen Lehre von der Vorsehung sowohl gelehrt hat, dass die Vorsehung nicht bis in den Bereich des Kontingenten, Zufälligen hineinreiche, als auch, dass die Erkenntnis der Vorsehung unbestimmt bezüglich der Wirklichkeit des nicht näher bestimmten Kontingenten sei.

Ein besonderes prinzipielles und nicht nur historisches Interesse erhält eine Analyse der Frage, wie Alexander von Aphrodisias das Verhältnis von Vorsehung und der Wirklichkeit des Zufälligen, Kontingenten und Werdenden sieht, auch dadurch, dass dabei ethische Probleme der Vereinbarkeit der menschlichen Selbstbestimmung und moralischen Verantwortlichkeit mit der göttlichen Vorsehung sowie der Fragwürdigkeit eines beschränkten göttlichen Vorherwissens zur Sprache kommen werden. Dies wird um so bedeutungsvoller sein, je mehr Proklos selbst der Ansicht ist, durch seine eigene Lösung der Frage, ob und wenn ja auf welche Weise die göttliche Vorsehung auch das Kontingente erkenne und bestimme, sowohl die Einseitigkeiten der peripatetischen und der stoischen Lösung beseitigt, als auch ihre positiven Momente bewahrt zu haben[7]. Es versteht sich, dass Proklos mit seiner Lösung der getreue Interpret Platons selbst zu sein glaubt. Aus prinzipiellen Gründen werden wir zum Schluss die Lösung des Proklos selbst skizzieren.

Wenn wir nun zunächst auf die für unser Thema wichtigsten Punkte der Lehre Alexanders über die Vorsehung zu sprechen kommen, so können wir dabei von den Untersuchungen und Forschungsergebnissen ausgehen, die Paul Moraux in zwei verschiedenen Werken über die Vorsehungslehre der Peripatetiker und insbesondere des Alexander von Aphrodisias veröffentlicht hat[8].

Dabei fällt zunächst auf, dass Alexander natürlich, indem er auch in seiner Vorsehungslehre von den Gegebenheiten der Kosmologie und philosophischen Theologie seines Meisters Aristoteles sich leiten lässt, den Bereich der Vorsehung sowohl nach oben wie nach unten hin einzuschränken gezwungen ist: Aristoteles selbst ist in seinen Ausführungen über das Denken des ersten unbewegten Bewegers und über den Denkgegenstand dieses göttlichen Geistes ja ganz eindeutig: Der göttliche Geist und absolut erste Beweger denkt rein nur sich selber und nichts, was weniger vollkommen wäre als er, da sein Denken keinerlei Potentialität enthält und er durch keinerlei Unvollkommenheit des Denkgegenstandes in der Ewigkeit, Identität mit sich selbst und Beständigkeit seines geistigen Lebens gestört sein kann (*Metaphysik* Λ, 7 und 9). Eine Vorsehung, welche zudem noch die gesamte übrige Welt bis ins Kleinste und Einzelne hinein denkend regelt, kann also Aristoteles selbst seinem höchsten Prinzip unter keinen Umständen zugeschrieben haben[9].

Dem entsprechend hat auch Alexander von Aphrodisias gewisse Bedenken, der höchsten Gottheit als der obersten Ursache von allem eine Vorsehung für die gesamte übrige Welt zuzuschreiben[10]. An einer bestimmten Stelle (*Probleme und Lösungen* II, 19) äussert er sich sogar eindeutig dahingehend, dass der ewig sich auf eine kontinuierliche Weise im Kreis bewegende Fixsternhimmel die Tätigkeit einer göttlichen Vorsehung gar nicht nötig hat, der erste unbewegte Beweger sich also zumindest auf ihn nicht als Vorsehung auswirkt[11]. Im Allgemeinen kann man sagen, dass nach Alexander von Aphrodisias die Aktivität der Vorsehung von den (beseelten) Gestirnen auf die Welt unter dem Monde ausgeht, ja dass bei ihm Vorsehung die bewegende Auswirkung der Gestirnssphären auf die irdische Welt ist[12]. Man sieht also, dass bei Alexander eine Synthese stattgefunden hat zwischen dem ursprünglich aristotelischen Ausgangspunkt, welcher eine göttliche Vorsehung für die Welt kaum zulässt, und dem durch die Stoa mitbeeinflussten Zeitgeist, welcher offenbar von einer dieses Namens würdigen Philosophie erwartete, dass sie aufzeigte, wie zumindest im Prinzip die irdischen Verhältnisse nach göttlicher Anordnung geregelt und gelenkt sind. Dass Alexander selbst in seiner Lehre über die Vorsehung stoisierende Züge aufweist, zeigt der Umstand, dass die von den Gestirnen ausgehende und sich auf den Bereich des irdischen Werdens auswirkende Kraft der Vorsehung bei ihm auch etwa Schicksal (εἱμαρμένη) genannt wird[13]. Natürlich glaubte Alexander selbst, die echte Lehre des Aristoteles wiederzugeben.

Viel wichtiger für unser Thema aber ist nun die Frage, inwiefern sich die bei Alexander zweifellos als wirksam angenommene göttliche Vorsehung auf den Bereich des irdischen Entstehens und Vergehens auswirkt, d.h. was genau genommen es ist, das sie in der Welt unter dem Monde verursacht. Noch wesentlicher wird sein, festzustellen, worauf sich nach Alexander die göttliche Vorsehung gerade nicht beziehen kann! Kurz zusammengefasst, lässt sich darüber folgendes aussagen: Die Vorsehung sorgt vor allem dafür, dass im irdischen Entstehen und Vergehen eine gewisse Kontinuität des Lebens erhalten bleibt, indem sie der Materie auf den verschiedenen Stufen des Lebens das Formprinzip aufprägt und so die die Elemente konstituierenden Formen oder die Formen der verschiedenen Arten von Lebewesen verleiht[14]. Die Art und Weise also, wie nach dem Vorbild des Aristoteles die Gestirnssphären und die Gestirne selbst sich auf den Bereich unter dem Monde als den Bereich des Entstehens und Vergehens bewegend auswirken, wird hier von Alexander als Vorsehung interpretiert.

Aber diese peripatetische Vorsehung unterscheidet sich nun nach Alexander vom stoischen Schicksal ganz wesentlich dadurch, dass sie eben nicht die absolute Ursache von schlechthin allem ist, was im irdischen Bereich vorgeht und existiert: In *Aporien* I, 4 polemisiert Alexander gegen die Aufhebung des bloss Möglichen und des Kontingenten, Zufälligen durch die Lehre von der Omnipotenz der Vorsehung bei den Stoikern[15] und vor allem dann auch in seiner Schrift *Ueber das Schicksal* versucht er gegenüber dem Fatalismus der Stoiker jene Bereiche der irdischen und menschlichen Wirklichkeit auszugrenzen, welche gerade nicht durch ein göttliches Vorherwissen auf absolut notwendige Weise bestimmt sind.

Besonders aufschlussreich sind für uns die Ausführungen Alexanders in *De fato*: Hier wird vor allem der Zufall, das Ungefähr, das Kontingente einerseits und der Bereich der freien Selbstgestaltung des Menschen, der Bereich der spezifisch menschlichen Aktivität andererseits der Einwirkung der Vorsehung als ihr nicht unterworfen gegenüber gestellt und die Stoiker werden dafür getadelt, dass sie durch ihre Lehre von der Allmacht der Vorsehung, welche sich auch im irdischen Bereich bis ins Kleinste und Einzelne hinein auswirkt, sowohl das Kontingente und den Zufall als auch die menschliche Selbständigkeit im handwerklich-künstlerischen Gestalten und in der sittlichen Entscheidung aufheben, während doch die Wirklichkeit von all dem sich nach peripatetischer Voraussetzung als durchaus evident erweist[16].

Ein weiterer Bereich der Wirklichkeit wird nun nach Alexander von der göttlichen Vorsehung gerade nicht so erfasst, dass er durch sie auf absolut notwendige Weise vorausbestimmt würde, nämlich der des Individuellen! Wir besitzen dafür zwei Arten von Belegstellen bei Alexander: Einerseits betont Alexander an verschiedenen Stellen, dass die Vorsehung als von den Gestirnen ausgehende Kraft hauptsächlich die Ewigkeit der Art (ἡ κατ' εἶδος ἀιδιότης) und der entsprechenden Wesensform im Bereich des Entstehenden und Vergehenden garantiert[17], ob es sich bei den von der Vorsehung betreuten Wesen nun um Pflanzen, Tiere oder Menschen handelt[18], oder gar um die Seinsweise der vier Elemente[19]. Andererseits sagt Alexander in einem bei Averroës überlieferten Fragment seines *Metaphysikkommentars* ausdrücklich, dass die Stoiker Unrecht haben, anzunehmen, die Vorsehung wache auch über alle Individuen! Zwei Gründe sprechen nach Alexander dagegen, dass die Vorsehung sich auch mit den Individuen befasst: Einerseits ist Vorsehung Wissen und dieses bezieht sich nur auf das Allgemeine, andererseits ist es unerklärlich, warum zufällige Unglücksfälle dem einzelnen Menschen zustossen, während doch die Vorsehung sich um ihn kümmert[20].

Das bringt uns aber nun zur Frage zurück, welche uns eigentlich beschäftigt: Bezieht sich Proklos auf Alexander von Aphrodisias und seine Lehre von der Vorsehung, wenn er sagt, die Peripatetiker lehrten, dass die Vorsehung nicht bis ans Kontingente heranreiche (also das Kontingente als solches nicht regle) und dass sie das Unbestimmte nur auf unbestimmte Weise erkenne (wörtlich: im Unbestimmten selbst unbestimmt bleibe), wobei das Hauptbestreben der Peripatetiker dabei sei, das Kontingente, d.h. seine evidente Wirklichkeit zu retten (und nicht wie die Stoiker zu leugnen)? Dass Proklos Alexander von Aphrodisias kannte, steht ausser Zweifel, zitiert er doch gerade an einer wichtigen Stelle seines *Timaios*-

kommentars dessen Auffassung über das Schicksal[21]. Es bleibt zunächst abzuklären, ob beide Teile dessen, was Proklos über die Vorsehungslehre der Peripatetiker an den von uns zitierten Stellen behauptet, den Gegebenheiten bei Alexander entsprechen.

Da ist zunächst einmal die (nicht direkt mit dem Namen einer Schule verbundene) Behauptung des Proklos in den *Zehn Aporien über die Vorsehung*, dass nach der Meinung der einen die Vorsehung nicht bis zur (im Übrigen unbestreitbaren) Wirklichkeit des Kontingenten vorzudringen vermöge (während die andern aus der Allmacht der Vorsehung auf die Nichtexistenz des Kontingenten schlössen)[22]. Durch diese Bemerkung wird die Lehre des Alexander über das Verhältnis der Vorsehung zum Kontingenten ganz genau bezeichnet. Alles, was Alexander zu diesem Thema sagt, stimmt mit der Bemerkung des Proklos überein. Wenn Alexander die göttliche Vorsehung nur bis hin zur Verursachung der Kontinuität der spezifischen Formen sich erstrecken lässt, wenn er den Bereich des Individuellen und der moralischen und handwerklich-künstlerischen Selbständigkeit des Menschen der Allgewalt der göttlichen Vorsehung entzieht, und schliesslich vor allem, wenn er betont, dass die Vorsehung noch Raum für das bloss Mögliche und Zufällige übriglässt[23], dann entspricht dies genau der Darstellung, welche Proklos von der peripatetischen Ansicht über das Verhältnis von Providenz und Kontingenz gibt. In diesem Zusammenhang fällt auf, dass auch der Begriff des Kontingenten, Zufälligen als dessen, was sowohl geschehen, wie auch nicht geschehen kann, bei Proklos[24], schon bei Alexander vorgebildet ist[25], wobei Alexander natürlich schon auf Bestimmungen des Aristoteles selber sich stützt.

Wie verhält es sich aber nun mit der andern Behauptung, die Proklos im Werk *Ueber die Vorsehung* aufstellt, wonach die Peripatetiker der Ansicht seien, Gott kenne nicht alles auf bestimmte Weise, sondern die Erkenntnis der göttlichen Vorsehung bleibe unbestimmt in Bezug auf das, was selber unbestimmt sei, d.h. offenbar das Kontingente, Zufällige und bloss Mögliche?[26] Gibt auch diese Behauptung des Proklos die Lehre Alexanders vom Verhältnis zwischen der Vorsehung und dem Kontingenten wieder?

Ja, wenn man diese Behauptung dahingehend versteht, dass die göttliche Vorsehung über jenen Teil der Wirklichkeit, welcher kontingent, offen zum Sein und zum Nichtsein bleibt, keine näheren Bestimmungen enthält. Proklos meint offenbar auch gar nicht, dass die göttliche Vorsehung bei den Peripatetikern etwas Wirkliches zwar erkenne, aber nur auf unbestimmte und ungenaue Weise, denn er betont, Peripatetiker und

Stoiker stimmten darin überein, dass die Vorsehung als vorsehende das, was vorhergesehen wird, erkennen muss, dass sie es aber als erkennende nicht – auf Grund der ungewissen Natur des Möglichen – auch in ungewisser Weise erkennen darf[27]. Wenn man dies beachtet und voraussetzt, gemeint sei nur, dass die peripatetische Vorsehung keine näheren Bestimmungen über die Regelung des Kontingenten enthalte, so kann man tatsächlich eine Stelle bei Alexander finden, welche darauf hinweist, dass nach ihm aus der Wirksamkeit der göttlichen Vorsehung nicht die absolute Notwendigkeit alles Kontingenten (auch der kontingenten Ereignisse in der Zukunft) folgt, und dass die göttliche Vorsehung bezüglich des Unbestimmten (= Kontingenten) in diesem Sinne unbestimmt bleibe: Im 30. Kapitel von *De fato* geht das Bestreben Alexanders dahin, zu zeigen, dass aus der Tatsache der göttlichen Vorsehung nicht, wie die Stoiker meinen, die Notwendigkeit aller Ereignisse (auch der kontingenten und zukünftigen) folge, sondern dass die Götter, wenn sie mit ihrer Vorsehung kontingente Ereignisse vorauswissen, sie als kontingent und nicht als notwendig voraussehen[28].

Nachdem sich nun so gezeigt hat, dass sich bei Alexander von Aphrodisias durchaus Stellen finden, welche den Berichten des Proklos über die Lehre der Peripatetiker vom Verhältnis zwischen der göttlichen Vorsehung und der Wirklichkeit des Kontingenten entsprechen (und zwar ziemlich genau, wie wir festgestellt haben), müsste nur noch festgestellt werden, ob es nicht andere Peripatetiker gibt, welche ebensogut von Proklos als typische Vertreter der peripatetischen Lehre von der Vorsehung gemeint sein könnten. Dies kann hier nicht mehr unsere Hauptaufgabe sein. Lediglich anhangsweise möge noch erwähnt werden, dass schon beim Peripatetiker Kritolaos eine Einschränkung des Tätigkeitsbereiches der Vorsehung auf die ewige Welt der Gestirne stattgefunden hat, während die Vorsehung sich um die Welt des Entstehens und Vergehens unter dem Monde nicht mehr kümmert[29], und dass der peripatetische Autor des Werkes *De mundo* (περὶ κόσμου) ebenfalls der Ansicht ist, die göttliche Vorsehung, welche hier offenbar vom höchsten Gott, dem ersten Beweger, ausgeht, befasse sich so intensiv wie nur möglich mit jenen Regionen der Welt, welche ihr am nächsten sind, nämlich der ewigen Welt der Gestirne, und werde umso schwächer und uninteressierter, je weiter der jeweilige Bereich der Wirklichkeit vom höchsten Gott entfernt sei, was natürlich vor allem auf die Welt des Werdens unter dem Monde zutrifft[30].

Aber wenn auch bei diesen beiden Autoren sich schon die spätere Tendenz, das Kontingente dem Erkenntnis- und Wirkungsbereich der

Vorsehung zu entziehen, ankündigt (natürlich beide Male mit der Begründung, die göttliche Vorsehung sei zu vornehm, sich mit Niederem zu befassen), so findet sich bei ihnen doch noch nicht jene ausgearbeitete Theorie über das Verhältnis zwischen der Vorsehung und dem Kontingenten wie bei Alexander (vor allem der Autor von *Ueber die Welt* schwankt zwischen der peripatetischen Einschränkung der Vorsehung auf die Welt über dem Monde und der stoischen Lehre von der Vorsehung als alldurchdringender Kraft). Proklos aber bezieht sich bereits auf eine sehr sorgfältig durchgearbeitete peripatetische Lehre über das Verhältnis der Vorsehung zum Kontingenten.

Die eigene Lehre des Proklos über das Verhältnis von Vorsehung und Kontingentem will sich nun allerdings wesenhaft sowohl von der peripatetischen als auch von der stoischen Konzeption unterscheiden, wenn sie auch für sich in Anspruch nimmt, die positiven Momente beider in gewissem Sinne entgegengesetzter Standpunkte in sich aufgenommen zu haben[31]. Die Lösung, die Proklos für das Problem hat, ist die, dass er selber in Interpretation der Ansichten Platons annimmt, die Vorsehung erkenne zwar alles und jedes Seiende, bestimme es in seinem Sein und erkenne so auch das Kontingente (insofern unterscheidet er sich von den Peripatetikern und insbesondere Alexander, die das Kontingente dem Erkenntnisbereich der Vorsehung entziehen), dadurch werde aber das Kontingente als solches und vor allem als Realität nicht aufgehoben (insofern unterscheidet er sich von den Stoikern, die aus der Allmacht der Vorsehung die Nichtexistenz des Kontigenten folgern); die Vorsehung erkennt nun aber das Kontingente und Zufällige (insbesondere auch kontingente Ereignisse in der Zukunft) nicht in der Art, wie das Kontingente, Mögliche und Zufällige selber ist, also nicht auf unbestimmte, zufällige, sondern auf bestimmte, notwendige Weise, denn die Erkenntnis, welche die Vorsehung von allem übrigen Seienden und so auch vom Kontingenten hat, erhält hinsichtlich ihres Wesens ihre Bestimmung nicht von den Erkenntnisgegenständen, sondern vom erkennenden göttlichen Subjekt der Vorsehung selber, und dieses (handle es sich nun um das höchste Prinzip des Proklos, das Eine-Gute, selbst oder um die göttlichen Henaden) erkennt naturgemäss das nicht Notwendige auf notwendige Weise, das Veränderliche auf unveränderliche Weise, ebenso wie es das Teilbare unteilbar und das Zeitliche unzeitlich erkennt[32]. Durch diese Kennzeichnung des Verhältnisses zwischen göttlicher Vorsehung und Kontingentem glaubt Proklos sowohl die Allmacht der Vorsehung (im Sinne der gereinigten und verbesserten Konzeption der Stoiker) als auch die Wirklichkeit des Kontingenten (im Sinne der Peripatetiker) bewahrt zu haben[33].

178

Zweierlei muss allerdings hier noch abschliessend festgehalten werden: Einmal darf bei einem allfälligen Vergleich zwischen der Vorsehungslehre des Proklos und derjenigen des Alexander von Aphrodisias nicht vergessen werden, dass das Subjekt der göttlichen Vorsehung in beiden Fällen auch nicht dasselbe ist (ebenso wenig wie der Geltungsbereich der Vorsehung derselbe ist): Bei Alexander geht die Vorsehung kaum vom sich selber denkenden göttlichen Geist als dem höchsten Prinzip des Aristoteles aus, sondern eher nur vom Fixsternhimmel (welcher als beseelt gedacht wird) und den einzelnen Gestirngöttern[34]. Bei Proklos dagegen wird die Vorsehung unmittelbar aus der einen allerhaltenden Kraft des Einen-Guten als des absolut höchsten Urwesens abgeleitet[35] und primär den selbst über die göttliche Intellektualität im Sinne Plotins noch erhabenen Gottheiten der Henaden zugewiesen[36]: Dementsprechend muss natürlich auch das Wesen der Vorsehung als Tätigkeit bei Proklos[37] ein anderes sein als bei Alexander.

Schliesslich ist in grundsätzlicher Hinsicht noch wichtig, dass wohl auch Proklos nicht, wie er meint, das Problem der Wirklichkeit des Kontingenten und der menschlichen Freiheit gegenüber der Allmacht der Vorsehung endgültig gelöst und mit dieser in Übereinstimmung gebracht hat: Wohl ist sein Einwand berechtigt, dass eine göttliche Vorsehung, welche nicht alles weniger Vollkommene als sie selber bis ins Kleinste und Einzelne hinein erkennt, um der Vollkommenheit und Unbegrenztheit des göttlichen Erkennens willen etwas Widersinniges hat[38]. Wohl ist seine Lösung einleuchtend, dass die Begriffe der freien Selbstständigkeit und der moralischen Freiheit der Entscheidung einerseits sowie der Kontingenz, des Zufalls, des Möglichen in der Zukunft andererseits nur im menschlichen und irdischen Bereich sinnvoll sind, während in Wirklichkeit und von Anfang an doch alles durch die Vorsehung bis ins Kleinste und Einzelne hinein geregelt ist (nur für den Menschen gibt es den Zufall)[39]. Die eigentlichen Schwierigkeiten aber beginnen für Proklos dort, wo er, ganz offensichtlich unter aristotelisch peripatetischem Einfluss, das Kontingente nicht nur als blossen Schein und Namen, sondern als ein auch für die göttliche Vorsehung Wirkliches behandelt und dann doch erklären muss, dass dieses unbestimmte Kontingente von der allwissenden Vorsehung auf bestimmte Weise erkannt und beherrscht wird[40]. Muss Proklos nicht dort, wo er in konsequenter Anlehnung an Platons Vorsehungslehre im X. Buch der *Nomoi* die Allmacht der göttlichen Vorsehung radikal zu Ende denkt, der stoischen Vorsehungslehre sehr nahe kommen?

ANMERKUNGEN

¹ *Procli Diadochi tria opuscula*, ed. H. Boese (Quellen und Studien zur Geschichte der Philosophie, Bd. I), Berlin 1960, *De decem dubitationibus circa providentiam*, Quaestio II, § 6, S. 10, Z. 1-3, S. 11, Z. 1-2.

² Op.cit., S. 10, Z. 3-7: *Propter hanc enim hii quidem providentiam esse concedentes contingentis naturam ab entibus exciderunt, alii autem ad evidentiam subsistentie contingentis nullatenus contradicere habentes providentiam usque ad hec pertingere abnegarunt.* Vgl. dazu S. 11, Z. 3-5.

³ *Procli... tria opuscula*, ed. H. Boese, *De providentia et fato et eo quod in nobis*, zitiert als *De providentia*, Cap. XVI, § 63, S. 169, Z. 1-4: »'Αλλ' οἱ μὲν ψεῦδος εἶναι ἔφασαν τὸν θεὸν ὡρισμένως εἰδέναι πᾶν, ἀλλ' ἀορισταίνειν καὶ αὐτὸν ἐν τοῖς ἀορίστως γινομένοις, ἵνα φυλάξωσι τὸ ἐνδεχόμενον· οἱ δὲ τὴν ὡρισμένην γνῶσιν ἀποδόντες τῷ θεῷ τὴν ἀνάγκην ἐπὶ πάντων τῶν γινομένων παρεδέξαντο. Vgl. op.cit., S. 168, Z. 1-5, bes. Z. 4-5: *Peripateticorum et Stoicorum heresum sunt hec dogmata.*

⁴ Isaak Sebastokrator: *Zehn Aporien über die Vorsehung*, hrsg. von Johannes Dornseiff, Meisenheim am Glan 1966, II, S. 16, Z. 11-20.

⁵ Vgl. darüber insbesondere Paul Moraux: *La doctrine de la providence dans l'Ecole d'Aristote*, in: *D'Aristote à Bessarion. Trois exposés sur l'histoire et la transmission de l'aristotélisme grec*, Québec 1970, 58 ff.

⁶ H. Boese verweist op.cit., S. 10, Anm. zu 6, 4 seqq. mit Recht auf *SVF* II, 963. Zur Lehre der Stoiker über das Fatum vgl. *SVF* II, 912 ff., über die Vorsehung *SVF* II, 1106 ff.

⁷ *Procli... tria opuscula*, ed. H. Boese, *De dec. dub.*, II, § 6, S. 12, Z. 7 ff. (= S. 13, Z. 8 ff.); *De providentia* XVI, § 63, S. 168, Z. 5 ff. (= S. 169, Z. 6 ff.); Isaak Sebastokrator: *Zehn Aporien über die Vorsehung*, ed. Dornseiff, II, S. 16, Z. 20 – S. 17, Z. 11.

⁸ Vgl. Anm. 5 dieses Aufsatzes und dazu noch den II. Anhang (Appendice II) des bekannten Werks *Alexandre d'Aphrodise Exégète de la Noétique d'Aristote*, Paris-Liège 1942, 195-202 (La théorie alexandriste de la providence), ebenfalls von P. Moraux.

⁹ Vgl. für eine Diskussion dieses Problems, welche zu einem etwas anderen Ergebnis kommt, W. D. Ross in *Aristotle's Metaphysics*, Oxford 1958, Vol. I, Introduction, Aristotle's Theology, CXLIX ff. P. Moraux hat sich zum Problem geäussert in *Alexandre d'Aphrodise...*, 195 ff. und *D'Aristote à Bessarion*, 58 ff. Moraux betont eher, dass Aristoteles gar keine genaue Theorie der göttlichen Vorsehung ausgearbeitet hat.

¹⁰ Alexander: *Apor.* I, 25: S. 40, Z. 10 – S. 41, Z. 19 ed. Bruns, vgl. besonders 41, 4-10.

¹¹ Alexander: *Apor.* II, 19, S. 63, Z. 18-28 Bruns.

¹² Alexander: *Apor.* II, 3. S. 48, Z. 19-22 Bruns und *Kommentar zu den Meteorologica des Aristoteles*, S. 6, Z. 5-6, ed. M. Hayduck, Berlin 1899.

¹³ Alexander: *De fato*, S. 169, Z. 23-28 Bruns, vgl. *De fato* 169, 18-19 Bruns und *De an. Mant.* 185, 11 Bruns.

¹⁴ Alexander: *Apor.* II, 3; *Kommentar zu den Meteorologica des Aristoteles*, S. 7, Z. 9-14 Hayduck, *De an. Mant.* 172, 17 ff.

¹⁵ Wenn die Vorsehung allmächtig ist, wie soll man dann begreifen können, dass es moralisch Böses gibt, d.h. dass es Menschen gibt, die gerade im Gegensatz zur von der Vorsehung eingesetzten guten Ordnung handeln? Alexander, *Aporien* I, 4: 10, 32 – 11, 3 Bruns.

¹⁶ Ueber den Zufall (αὐτόματον, τύχη) und das Kontingente (ἐνδεχόμενον) siehe Alexander: *De fato*, cap. VIII, bzw. cap. IX; besonders die Definition des Kontingenten in Kapitel 9 und die Behauptung, dass es in der Konzeption von der Allmacht der Vorsehung und der Notwendigkeit aller Ereignisse auch im

irdischen Bereich bei den Stoikern nichtexistent sein muss, ist für den Zusammenhang mit Proklos wichtig (vgl. auch *De an. Mant.* S. 185, Z. 3 ff. Bruns). Für die menschliche Freiheit im Bereich des Handwerklich-Künstlerischen und des Moralischen, welche durch den Fatalismus der Stoiker nach Alexander ebenfalls zerstört wird, siehe *De fato*, cap. XI-XV, besonders aber S. 169, Z. 6-18 und S. 178, Z. 8 – S. 186, Z. 12 Bruns (vgl. *De an. Mant.* S. 181, Z. 31 – S. 182, Z. 4 Bruns).

[17] Alexander: *Aporien* I, 25: S. 40, Z. 30 – S. 41, Z. 4 Bruns, besonders S. 41, Z. 3; S. 41, Z. 15-19, besonders S. 41, Z. 18; *Apor.* II, 19: S. 63, Z. 22 ff., besonders S. 63, Z. 24 Bruns; *In Aristotelis Meteorologica*, S. 6, Z. 11-17 Hayduck.

[18] Alexander: *Apor.* II, 3: S. 48, Z. 18-22 Bruns.

[19] Alexander: *Apor.* II, 3: S. 49, Z. 28 ff. Bruns.

[20] Alexander zur Metaphysik des Aristoteles, Fr. 36; in: J. Freudenthal: *Die durch Averroës erhaltenen Fragmente Alexanders zur Metaphysik des Aristoteles untersucht und übersetzt* (in: Abhandlungen der Berl. Akad. der Wiss., 1884, Nr. 1, S. 112-113).

[21] Proklos: *In Platonis Timaeum Commentaria*, ed. E. Diehl, Leipzig 1906, Nachdruck, Amsterdam 1965, Vol. III, S. 272, Z. 7-8 und Anm. zu Z. 8.

[22] Vgl. unsere Anmerkungen 1 und 2.

[23] Alexander: *Aporien* I, 4 und *De fato*, Kapitel VIII und IX.

[24] Proklos: *De decem dubitationibus circa providentiam*, ed. Boese, quaestio III, § 14, Z. 17-21.

[25] Alexander: *De fato*, cap. IX, S. 174, Z. 30 – S. 175, Z. 5 Bruns. Vgl. schon Aristoteles: *Anal. pr.* A, 13: 32a18, *De gen. an.* B, 1: 731b25; Δ, 4: 770b13; Δ, 8: 777a20; vgl. *Eth. Nic.* E, 10: 1134b31 und Z, 2: 1139a8, 14.

[26] Vgl. unsere Anmerkung Nr. 3.

[27] Proklos: *De decem dubitationibus circa providentiam*, ed. Boese, quaestio II, § 6, Z. 7-10 für die lat. Uebersetzung von G. de Moerbeka, § 6, Z. 8-10 (auf S. 13 Boese) für den griechischen Text.

[28] Alexander: *De fato*, cap. XXX, bes. S. 201, Z. 15 ff. Bruns.

[29] Vgl. Kritolaos von Phaselis (2. Jh. vor Chr.) in: F. Wehrli: *Die Schule des Aristoteles*, 10, 1959, pp. 45-74, bes. p. 52, fr. 15.

[30] Pseudo-Aristoteles: *De mundo*, cap. VI, besonders 397b27 ff.

[31] *Procli... tria opuscula*, ed. Boese, *De decem dubitationibus...*, qu. II, § 6, Z. 7 ff., *De providentia...*, cap. XVI, § 63, Z. 6 ff. (Vgl. unsere Anm. 7).

[32] *Procli... tria opuscula*, ed. Boese, *De decem dubitationibus...*, qu. II, § 8 (vorbereitet durch den erkenntnistheoretischen Exkurs in § 7); *De providentia...*, cap. XVI, §§ 62-66 (insbesondere auch über die Erkenntnis der contingentia futura durch die Vorsehung); *Elementatio theologica*, ed. E. R. Dodds, 2. Aufl. Oxford 1963, prop. 124, besonders S. 110, Z. 10-13 und Z. 20-23; vgl. auch noch *In Platonis Parmenidem commentarius*, ed. V. Cousin, Paris 1864, Nachdr. Hildesheim 1961, col. 957, Z. 18 ff. und *Theologia Platonica*, Buch I, Kap. 15 und 16.

[33] Das Objekt der Vorsehung, das Kontingente, wird dadurch, dass sie es auf bestimmte Weise erkennt, nicht selber notwendig, sondern bleibt in sich selbst unbestimmt: *Procli... tria opuscula*, ed. Boese, *De dec. dub....*, qu. II, § 8, Z. 9-16.

[34] Das ist erschliessbar aus verschiedenen Stellen bei Alexander, besonders deutlich aus *Aporien* II, 19: S. 63, Z. 18-28: II, 3, bes. S. 48, Z. 19 ff. Bruns; *In Arist. Meteorologica* S. 6, Z. 5-6, S. 7, Z. 9-14 Hayduck und *De Fato*, cap. V, S. 169, Z. 23-28 Bruns.

[35] *Procli... tria opuscula*, ed. Boese, *De dec. dub.*, qu. I, § 4, besonders Z. 1-5.

[36] *Procli Elementatio Theologica*, ed. Dodds, propp. 120-124, besonders prop. 120, S. 106, Z. 5-7.

37 Vgl. dafür besonders Proclus: *De dec. dub.*, qu. I, § 5, Z. 1 ff. Boese.
38 Besonders deutlich in Proclus: *De dec. dub.*, qu. I und *Theol. Plat.* I, 15, vgl. bes. S. 73, Z. 6 ff. Saffrey-Westerink.
39 Proclus: *De dec. dub.* qu. II, § 8, Z. 17-18 (auf S. 14 Boese): *indeterminatione quidem futura, sed non ente* = Z. 15 (auf S. 15 Boese): τῆς μὲν ἀοριστίας ἐσομένης, ἀλλ' οὐκ οὔσης.
40 Proclus: a.a.O., S. 14, Z. 18 – S. 16, Z. 23 = S. 15, Z. 16 – S. 17, Z. 21 Boese.
41 Vgl. Anm. 38 dieses Aufsatzes und Platon: *Nomoi* X, 899d-905d.

TWO QUESTIONS OF GREEK
GEOMETRICAL TERMINOLOGY*

MARIA TIMPANARO-CARDINI

1. *Euclid's Definition of a Straight Line*

It has been observed several times that Euclid's ὅροι are not real 'definitions', since those terms are the primary elements of mathematical thinking; and, as they are primary, i.e. anterior to whatever process of the mind, no 'genus' exists of which they may be considered a 'species'. G. Vacca rightly noted that Euclid's ὅροι are to be considered as illustrations or explanations similar to the ones nowadays given in dictionaries rather than as mathematical definitions[1]. And J. H. Lambert declared that Euclid's definitions "are like the suggestions from a clockmaker or another craftsman to his apprentice, when he shows him his implements, and tells him the name of each"[2]. Consequently, each term simply *contains itself*; and the term ὅρος (evidently deriving from the ancient Pythagorean space-conception of mathematical entities) properly expresses the limit occupied by that particular entity in the reality of space. (Cfr. Euclid, *Elem.* I def. 13: ὅρος is that which is the limit of something).

Yet, what is said above does not refer to all of Euclid's terms, and the fourth term, which will be examined in the present article, seems to fit in with the Aristotelian rule of *genus proximum* and *differentia specifica*; it is the definition of a straight line, of which Euclid says that it is "a line whose particular property is that it is placed ἐξ ἴσου τοῖς ἐφ' ἑαυτῆς σημείοις". How this position is to be understood is still a point of discussion; and, since the definition of a straight line was already much discussed by the ancient scholars, let us see first at which stage of this concept's development Euclid's definition should be placed.

The oldest attempt to specify the straight line is to be found in the Pythagoreans and in Heraclitus, who oppose it to the curved line: εὐθύ - καμπύλον is one of the ten couples of ἀρχαί in the Pythagorean table of opposites[3], and Heraclitus' ὁδός is εὐθεῖα and σκολιή (fgt. 59 Diels). Chronologically, Plato's, Euclid's and Archimedes' definitions are the next stage, as is also visible from their wording. Apart from these, how-

183

ever, also other definitions current among geometers of those times have been preserved, *viz.*, by Hero Alexandrinus[4] and later by Proclus[5]; evidently, people then were keenly interested in problems of this sort.

In those definitions, as has been observed by Mugler[6], three different orders of conceptions are evident: the first, by observing the craftsmanship of masons, carpenters and architects, takes as its starting-point the sensorial experience of a taut wire: the plumbline, already mentioned in Homer *Od.* 5, 245; 17, 341. The second starts from the observation of a lightbeam, whose straightness seems proved by the fact that any of its intermediate points can act as a screen to the ones at each limit; cf. Plato's definition (*Parm.* 137 E), clearly suggested by the phenomenon of eclipse, which had already been scientifically explained at that time. The third order of ideas refers to the geodetical criterion of a straight line's measure. It is Archimedes' first postulate in *De sphaera et cylindro*: "a straight line is the shortest of all the lines having the same limits".

To which of these three conceptions does Euclid's definition appear to be closest? In his comment Proclus (p.110, 12 ff.) sees in it an anticipation of Archimedes' definition; he explains, in fact, that according to Euclid's formula, a straight line lies ἐξ ἴσου with its own points, and hence is the shortest of all the lines having the same limits; if a shorter one were possible, it would not lie ἐξ ἴσου with regard to its own points. By those points the 'terminals', i.e. the limits are to be understood, and not all or some of the points lying on the line itself, as many scholars have imagined[7]: this is implied by the immediately preceding Euclidean definition, *viz.* the third, which has it that "the limits (πέρατα) of a straight line are points (σημεῖα)"; and so no doubt seems to be possible as to the fact that the points on which the position of a straight line depends are πέρατα = σημεῖα. Archimedes will solve this ambiguity by calling them just πέρατα; and then the only meaning which can possibly be attributed to Euclid's definition is: "a straight line is the line lying on a level with its limits". Indeed, this is the explanation offered by Proclus shortly before (p.109, 10 ff.), when he said that "lying ἐξ ἴσου with its own points" means that "as much as one point is distant from the other, so long is the straight line ending in those points"; and finally, concluding his discussion of the definition of a straight line, he says, with reference to the doctrine of a point generating a line by flowing: "a straight line is a simple line having its shortest advancement from one end to the other" (p.110, 24-26).

That Proclus followed a more ancient tradition, according to which the 'points' of a straight line are its own limits, results also from Heron who, whatever his date, is still close enough to the geometrical tradition upheld by Euclid. Not only in Heron's fourth definition nearly all the definitions concerning a straight line are found which are later accepted by Proclus, but in def. 1: *on the point*, it is clearly stated that a point is not part of a line, but just the beginning of a line; and in def. 2: *on the line*, it is said that a line is closed and limited by points: not constituted by points, but generated by the flowing of a point according to the principle of continuity. The argument about the constitution of a straight line and about the existence or non-existence of indivisible lines is in evidence here[8]; it was certainly well known to Euclid.

Furthermore, a simple commonsense observation seems to be pertinent here: do not both the curved and the mixed line themselves lie on all their own points?

2. Power = Square[9]

If we compare Euclid's propositions 1 and 46 (*Elem.* I), in the perfect correspondence of what is given – a finished straight line – and what is the subject of research – the construction of a figure: an equilateral triangle in the former case and a square in the latter – we notice a striking difference; in proposition 1 it is required to construct (συστή-σασθαι) an equilateral triangle on (ἐπί) the given straight line, while in proposition 46 it is required to delineate (ἀναγράψαι) a square starting from (ἀπό) the given line. It is not a fortuitous difference: when squares are to be generated (e.g. I, propp. 47, 48, X def. 4), Euclid will use the expression ἀπό... ἀναγράψαι, in any other case ἐπί... συστήσασθαι, both for figures other than squares and for lines drawn from a given line. (In I, 21, the two moments are clearly distinguished: *from* (ἀπό) what the two lines, going to meet to form a triangle, take their origin, and *on* (ἐπί) what they are drawn[10]).

Evidently, two different ideas are at the origin of the two propositions. Proclus throws some light on this circumstance, when he explains (*In Eucl.* p.423, 21) that the figure of a triangle, as if compressed on more than one side, requires a real "putting together" (the impression is given almost of something material, processed and moulded into the shape of a triangle); the figure of a square, on the other hand, is framed starting from one side only and requires only that the figure be 'delineated' or drawn. Proclus adds that to "put together" an equilateral triangle two lines must be drawn from an outside point, connecting that point with the limits of the given straight line, and the position of the outside point

185

must be found out by means of a circle, while for a square it is enough to multiply the given straight line by itself.

The arithmo-geometrical aspect of the square is, of course, in evidence here; however, this is not all: the situation as outlined may also provide us with a possibility to understand the original meaning of the term δύναμις. Geometrically, in fact, a square is formed by a procedure like the one concerning arithmetical squares for which the given straight line, namely the side, or the given number, placing itself on itself a number of times equal to its own units, projects on the plane an area enclosed by four sides equal to the line given. This area has a peculiar property, and Proclus (*In Eucl.* p.398, 13-15) points out this property when he deals with the relation existing between perimeters, angles and areas of two parallelograms respectively: he observes that, if perimeters are equal, the larger area belongs to the parallelogram having right angles and equal sides, namely the square; and he adds "For the rightness of the angles and the equality of the sides are the all-important factors (τὸ πᾶν δύναται) affecting the increase of the areas" (trans. Morrow). It follows that "the square is the largest and the rhomboid is the smallest of all isoperimeters" (Proclus *l.c.*). Hence, in my opinion, it is possible to infer that, owing to the common genesis of geometrical entities – line, surface, solid – the surface unity could be the square, generated by its own side and representing the side's power, its absolute value, on the plane, not subject to any variation of angles or heights, as is the case in other figures.

If we admit that Proclus' explanation testifies to an older geometrical tradition (δύναμις in the meaning of square seems to have been used by Hippocrates of Chios, who achieved the quadrature of lunules) one could explain the term within a strictly geometrical field, without having recourse to outside hypotheses. After all, as is well known, geometry was the practice of land-surveyors and land-accountants before rising to the dignity of an abstract science. Accordingly, the idea of a relation between perimeters, angles, sides and surface of the quadrilaterals which these perimeters etc. included may have been discovered little by little, since intelligent persons must have had the occasion to observe that of two areas that having a greater perimeter may be the smaller, and vice versa. As a matter of fact, Proclus tells us that in the distribution of land among co-proprietors it sometimes happened that certain sly persons managed to obtain surfaces of greater perimeter for themselves; but soon after, seeing that the areas left to the others, though having smaller perimeters, were larger than their own, they offered to exchange the lands, so even getting the renown of honest and unselfish people.

Hence, experience showed that among quadrilateral enclosures, the ones having right angles and equal sides, with perimeters equal to others, enclosed the largest area, i.e. the greatest power of extension on the plane; and the square of side 1 was adopted as the unit of measure for this power. Hence the practice of *squaring* any surface in order to measure its real value, and the theory of the areas' application. The error of modern translations of the term δύναμις, rightly noticed by Szabó, consists in translating *potenza* (Italian), *Potenz* (German), *potence* (French), *power* (English) and not square, which, in the modern usage, corresponds to the *second power*, "because Greek Mathematicians did not know the concept of a 'power'" (*o.c.* 44). Even if this is true, as it actually is, yet there is no reason why we should ignore the real meaning of δύναμις, since Greek mathematics distinguished the two concepts of δύναμις and τετράγωνον. My opinion is that we should continue translating δύναμις with *power*, but the exact meaning of the Greek term should be clearly defined in a footnote.

NOTES

* Translated from the Italian by dr. Lia Griselli (Pisa).

[1] "Gli ὅροι euclidei, invece di definizioni matematiche, sono piuttosto chiarimenti o spiegazioni analoghe a quelle che si danno oggi nei dizionari". Euclide, *Il primo libro degli Elementi* a cura di G. Vacca, Firenze 1916, p.2 nota.

[2] "...Das ist gleichsam eine *Nomenclatur*. Er" (i.e. Euclid) "thut dabei weiter nichts, als was z.B. ein Uhrmacher oder anderer Künstler thut, wenn er anfängt, seinem Lehrjungen die Namen seiner Werkzeuge bekannt zu machen"; cit. in M. Simon, *Euclid und die sechs planimetrischen Bücher*, Leipzig 1921, 25.

[3] Arist., *Metaph.* 986a25.

[4] Hero Alexandrinus, *Opera quae supersunt omnia*, ed. Heiberg, Lipsiae, 1912 vol. 4, 16 ff. Concerning the vexed question of Heron's date, cf. Th. Heath, *A History of Greek Mathematics*, Oxford 1921, vol. II, 298 ff.

[5] Procli Diadochi *In primum Euclidis Elementorum librum commentarii*, ex rec. G. Friedlein, Lipsiae 1873.

[6] See C. Mugler, *Sur l'histoire de quelques définitions de la géometrie grecque et les rapports entre la géometrie et l'optique*, in: Antiquité classique 26, 1957, 331-345.

[7] See U. Amaldi, *Sui concetti di retta e di piano*, in: *Questioni riguardanti le matematiche elementari* raccolte e coordinate da F. Enriques, Bologna ³1924, I, 39 ff. Heiberg's Latin translation (*punctis in ea sitis*) is dubious, and perhaps the incertain interpretation proceeds from taking the preposition ἐπί in the current meaning of *on*, *upon*, while Euclid uses it here according to the older geometrical notations expressed by ἐπί and letters, indicating proximity, closeness to etc., as in the formulas τὸ ἐφ' ᾧ B, ἡ ἐφ' ἧ Γ Δ and so forth; cf. Hippocrates of Chios, in: *Pitagorici, testimonianze e frammenti*, a cura di M. Timpanaro-Cardini, Firenze 1962, II, 45; and other examples in Liddell-Scott s.v. ἐπί B I 1 K. The same observation is valid for Euclid's def. 7, de plana superficie.

[8] See Ps.-Aristotle, *De lineis insecabilibus*, Trad. comm. M. Timpanaro-Cardini, Milano 1970.

⁹ On this subject see Árpád Szabó, *Anfänge der griechischen Mathematik*, München-Wien 1969, 43 ff. and *passim*. See also J. Mansfeld, in: *Zetesis*, Festschr. E. de Strycker, Antwerpen-Utrecht 1973, 111-114.

¹⁰ Neither Heiberg's Latin translation of Euclides nor Morrow's English translation of Proclus (the latest to appear, Princeton 1970) pays attention to this difference, though Morrow mentions it. P. VerEecke's French translation, (of Proclus), instead, emphasizes it, but doesn't suggest any explanation for it.

REMARQUES SUR
DION CHRYSOSTOME ET LE
NOUVEAU TESTAMENT

ROBERT JOLY

Le projet d'un *Corpus Hellenisticum Novi Testamenti* est déjà ancien et il a rencontré sur son chemin beaucoup de traverses et de fatalités[1]. On peut croire que, désormais solidement ancré à Utrecht[2] et à Claremont, Californie, d'une part, pour le domaine païen, et à Halle[3], d'autre part, pour le domaine juif, il va pouvoir progresser méthodiquement. Personne ne peut douter de l'intérêt capital d'une telle entreprise, ni non plus de son ampleur.

Une nouvelle collection, *Studia ad Corpus Hellenisticum Novi Testamenti* accueille en 1972, comme deuxième volume[4], le *Dio Chrysostom and the New Testament* de G. Mussies[5]. Après une brève préface sur Dion et des index, qui sont la clé d'un tel travail, s'égrènent sur deux cents pages des textes parallèles de Dion, rattachés au(x) verset(s) correspondant(s) des œuvres du Nouveau Testament, présentées dans l'ordre canonique.

G. Mussies nous offre là un splendide instrument de travail, où l'auteur s'efface volontairement, tel un ordinateur dans la coulisse. Ce genre de travail exige, on le devine bien, une érudition, une patience, une mémoire et une abnégation dignes de la plus vive reconnaissance. Je ne pense que le plus grand bien de ce volume. Les notes qui suivent proviennent essentiellement de sa fréquentation. Je ne sais si elles auront quelque utilité pour le projet lui-même, mais j'espère qu'elles ne seront pas trop indignes de l'éminente historienne de la philosophie antique que nous fêtons ici et à qui j'ai plaisir à dire mon admiration et ma gratitude.

Le but ultime étant une appréciation correcte des rapports entre paganisme et christianisme naissant, la recherche des passages parallèles est évidemment l'outil privilégié. Il faut cependant être bien conscient qu'elle ne peut tout donner. Il y a des problèmes qui, par nature, échapperaient très facilement à une telle enquête, même si elle est menée, comme dans le cas qui nous occupe, avec une acribie admirable[6].

Je prends un exemple que je crois assez typique. La prédominance d'ἀγαπάω sur φιλέω dans la littérature païenne hellénistique est un fait dont chacun peut saisir la portée, puisque cette prédominance avait paru une originalité de la littérature juive et chrétienne d'expression grecque et qu'on y voyait la marque, dans le domaine du vocabulaire, de l'originalité de l'ἀγάπη chrétienne[7]. Il se fait que c'est précisément la lecture de Dion Chrysostome qui m'a alerté en tout premier lieu. G. Mussies cite pas mal de textes où se rencontre soit ἀγαπάω, soit φιλέω[8], mais on se rendrait difficilement compte à utiliser son recueil – on me l'accordera – que Dion utilise deux fois plus ἀγαπάω que φιλέω pour traduire l'idée générale d'aimer[9].

A côté de monographies consacrées à tel ou tel auteur, il ne serait pas inutile d'en consacrer à certains termes ou groupes de termes[10] pour l'ensemble du domaine hellénistique.

Et, en dépassant l'aspect purement linguistique, il me paraît nécessaire d'étudier de la même façon certains thèmes particuliers.

On pourrait croire que les monographies consacrées aux auteurs fourniront un jour le matériel nécessaire, qu'il suffira de regrouper autrement. Mais, outre que nous serions ainsi reportés à un avenir assez lointain, il est des auteurs très éloignés du Nouveau Testament ou connus trop fragmentairement, il est des œuvres trops restreintes pour se plier naturellement au système des passages parallèles, mais qui pourtant peuvent contenir un passage précieux à tel ou tel point de vue[11].

D'autre part, la prospection par thème peut exiger de remonter plus haut que l'époque hellénistique.

Mais surtout, si nous voulons enfin mieux cerner, sans de trop longs délais, *l'essence du christianisme*, il nous faut consacrer des études à quelques concepts païens qui correspondent à des notions chrétiennes essentielles. Rien ne nous assure, en effet, que ce qu'on trouve dans les articles du *Kittel*, dans le *RAC* ou ailleurs, soit exhaustif.

Je pense, par exemple, à χάρις. On ne saurait lire des auteurs comme Dion ou Aelius Aristide sans remarquer l'extrême fréquence de ce terme et du verbe χαρίζομαι, parfois dans des contextes religieux. Ἐλπίς aussi mériterait une enquête. Ce serait d'abord la constitution du dossier le plus complet possible des textes intéressants, car cela n'a pas été fait et est indispensable si l'on veut dépasser les connaissances actuelles.

Je pense aussi à πίστις. Dans ce dernier cas, on ne dispose même pas d'une bonne étude pour les premiers siècles chrétiens[12]. Le dossier païen que l'on pourrait rassembler réservera probablement des surprises[13]. Mon assistant, M. Patrice Dartevelle, entreprend une thèse sur πίστις dans la philosophie et la religion grecques.

Je pense enfin à la charité païenne. En dépit de quelques ouvrages

190

remarquables, une étude approfondie nous manque cruellement, à commencer par un recueil de textes. Le Centre Interdisciplinaire d'Etudes Philosophiques de l'Université de Mons a accepté que je me charge de ce programme de recherche, mais, comme il ne peut aider que fort modestement, la tâche sera certainement très longue et toute collaboration serait la bienvenue, si limitée soit-elle[14].

Il faudra relire les textes, même quand on est en droit d'espérer que tel ouvrage devrait contenir, pour tel auteur, les références exhaustives. C'est ainsi que l'étude de A. Bonhoeffer, *Epiktet und das Neue Testament*[15], ne mentionne pas le passage d'Epictète qui est certainement le plus 'chrétien' de toute la littérature païenne, *Entretiens*, III, 22, 54-55: «c'est, en effet, un sort bien plaisant qui est tressé pour le Cynique: il doit être battu comme un âne et ainsi battu, il doit aimer ceux qui le battent, comme s'il était le père ou le frère de tous»[16].

Il se fait qu'il y a peu de temps, j'avais dépouillé Dion Chrysostome de ce point de vue. Tout l'essentiel se retrouve évidemment chez G. Mussies. Je crois cependant pouvoir proposer quelques petites additions.

Il arrive que G. Mussies coupe un passage de Dion en indiquant par un *etc.* que le développement continue. Un dossier sur la charité païenne devrait citer plusieurs textes *in extenso*.

C'est ainsi qu'en III, 39, cité partiellement o.c. 174, la suite du paragraphe traduit mieux encore la sollicitude du Roi pour ses sujets: «Il partage avec eux son bonheur, il ne sépare pas son intérêt du leur; c'est avant tout lorsqu'il voit ses sujets heureux qu'il connaît la joie et qu'il pense avoir le plus grand bonheur».

O.c. 128, on peut lire le second terme de la comparaison de XII, 61, mais le premier est fort précieux pour la note affective qu'il exprime à propos des rapports entre les hommes et les dieux: «Précisément comme des tout petits, séparés de leur père ou de leur mère, sont remplis de désir et frustrés, et souvent, dans leurs rêves, tendent leurs bras vers leurs parents absents, de même...».

Parmi les textes seulement mentionnés, o.c. 228, sur l'hospitalité, je citerais surtout VII, 58: «Me voyant encore mal en point au sortir de cette épreuve, il me couvrit d'une tunique qu'il prit à sa fille, laquelle se mit un haillon autour du corps. Quand nous arrivâmes au village, je la lui rendis. De sorte que c'est surtout grâce à cet homme que nous fûmes sauvés, après les dieux».

Le passage VII, 57, où se trouve une formule toute comparable à celle de Matth. XXV, 35 (*donner à manger et à boire*) est cité o.c. 84, mais un développement antérieur, au ch. 52, est tout à fait parallèle et vaut la peine d'être traduit ici: «Puisse-t-on, ô Zeus, ne jamais profiter ni gagner un tel gain du malheur des hommes! Quant à moi, on ne m'a jamais aidé, mais souvent j'ai eu pitié de naufragés survenus, je les ai accueillis dans ma hutte, je leur ai donné à manger et à boire, et pour le reste, je les ai secourus comme je pouvais et les ai accompagnés jusqu'aux terres habitées. Mais qui pourrait témoigner de ces choses en ma faveur? Je n'ai même pas fait cela pour obtenir un témoignage ou de la reconnaissance (χάριτος): je ne savais même pas d'où ils étaient. (Je ne voudrais pas) que personne d'entre vous tombe dans un tel malheur...»

De rares passages, absents du livre de G. Mussies, ont peut-être de l'intérêt au point de vue particulier qui nous retient ici.

III, 60: il vaut beaucoup mieux (pour le Roi) agir avec justice et vertu, aimé des hommes et aimé des dieux (ἀγαπώμενον δὲ ὑπὸ θεῶν)...

Dans le même *Discours*, tout un développement (73-77) est consacré aux bienfaits que nous prodigue le dieu Soleil. Il s'agit certes d'une providence générale, d'ordre astronomique et météorologique, mais il s'y trouve, ch. 74, cette formule: «Il ne se fatigue jamais de nous accorder ces grâces»[17].

En IV, 65, Diogène exhorte Alexandre à faire confiance à la bienfaisance et à la justice, non aux armes. L'expression est digne d'être remarquée: εὐεργεσίᾳ πιστεύειν.

Dans l'*Euboïque* encore, le chasseur qui a si bien secouru les naufragés sera récompensé «afin que ce soit un encouragement pour les autres d'être justes et de s'aider mutuellement», ἐπαρκεῖν ἀλλήλοις[18].

En XLIV, 7, enfin, Dion écrit qu'il serait choquant de devoir constater que les hommes sont plus injustes que les abeilles. Le développement exalte la vertu de ces insectes tant admirés par les Grecs, et projette sur la ruche tout un idéal moral. L'important pour notre propos est ceci: le détail le plus en relief est que les abeilles (d'une même ruche) s'aiment entre elles énormément, οὕτως δὲ ἄγαν αὐτάς φασι φιλεῖν ἀλλήλας...[19]

Le *Discours VII*, *Euboïque*, est sans doute le plus intéressant, malgré la richesse des discours sur la Royauté, pour qui s'attacherait à l'histoire de la charité.

Il contient notamment, aux chapitres 81-83, un développement qui montre le pauvre plus empressé qeu le riche à secourir, à aider. La phrase essentielle, ch. 82, est donnée par G. Mussies[20], mais tout le passage entrerait, lui aussi, dans le dossier de la charité païenne.

La conviction de Dion Chrysostome est à prendre au sérieux; on la retrouve d'ailleurs sous diverses formes dans les évangiles.

Le cas d'Epictète pourrait servir de confirmation: c'est un esclave, un pauvre et c'est chez lui que la charité païenne trouve son expression la plus forte. Les premiers chrétiens étaient en majorité, c'est bien connu, de petites gens. N'y a-t-il pas là toute une perspective pour une sociologie de la charité?

NOTES

[1] Sur ce sujet, on peut lire G. Delling, *Zum Corpus Hellenisticum Novi Testamenti*, in: Zeitschrift für die neutestamentliche Wissenschaft, 54, 1963, 1-15 et W. C. Van Unnik, *Corpus Hellenisticum Novi Testamenti*, in: Journal of Biblical Literature, 83, 1964, 17-33, qui donnent la bibliographie antérieure.

[2] Grâce au professeur W. C. van Unnik et ses collaborateurs du Theologisch Instituut van de Rijksuniversiteit te Utrecht.

[3] Grâce au professeur G. Delling de l'Institut für spätantike Religionsgeschichte, Martin Luther-Universität, Halle.

[4] Le premier est de G. Petzke, *Die Traditionen über Apollonius von Tyana und das Neue Testament*, Leyde, 1970.

[5] Leyde, 1972, 257 pp.

[6] Le *Plutarch und das NT, ein Beitrag zum Corpus Hellenisticum Novi Testamenti*, de H. Almquist, Uppsala, 1946, n'est malheureusement pas aussi complet.

[7] Cf. mon étude *Le vocabulaire chrétien de l'amour est-il original?* Φιλεῖν et ἀγαπᾶν *dans le grec antique*, Bruxelles, 1968, (Collection de l'Institut d'Histoire du Christianisme de l'Université Libre de Bruxelles).

[8] On devine aux brèves remarques des pages 58 et 117 que G. Mussies n'a pas eu connaissance de l'étude citée à la note précédente.

[9] La liste que j'ai donnée, *op.cit.* 22, n.72 serait à compléter comme suit:
Pour ἀγαπάω-aimer, ajouter XXXIV, 47; pour le sens restrictif, ajouter XXX, 12 et LXXVII, 4;
Pour φιλέω-aimer, ajouter XXXIII, 23 et LXXVII-VIII, 7; corriger *bis* en *ter* pour LXXIV, 5.
Voici aussi la liste des emplois de στέργω, qui sert aussi de substitut à φιλέω: VII, 140; XII, 42; XLIII, 1; XLVII, 6; L, 1 et 6; LI, 6; LXI, 4 (bis); 7 et 9.

[10] Voyez la remarque de M. van Unnik sur l'imitation de Dieu, *op.cit.* 28.

[11] Dans *A Classical Parallel to I Peter, II, 14 and 20*, in: New Testament Studies, 1955-56, M. van Unnik note que le passage parallèle de Diodore de Sicile, XV, I, 1, lui est arrivé par hasard et il ajoute: »But it clearly shows that a systematic investigation of classical authors on a wide scale may yield good and unsuspected results«, 201-202.

[12] L'étude de W. H. Paine Hatch, *The Idea of Faith in Christian Literature from the Death of Saint Paul to the Close of the Second Century*, Strasbourg, 1925, est rapide et superficielle; la grosse thèse de R. Aubert, *Le problème de l'acte de foi*, Louvain, 1945, ne consacre que peu de pages aux premiers siècles.

[13] Cf. R. Joly, *Christianisme et Philosophie. Etudes sur Justin et les Apologistes grecs du deuxième siècle*, Bruxelles 1973, 117-118.

[14] Je pense en particulier aux collègues qui s'occupent spécialement de tel texte et pour qui le relevé éventuel de passages intéressant la charité païenne ne serait pas une surcharge considérable; et à ceux qui en découvrent par hasard au cours

d'une lecture et qui voudraient bien m'adresser une fiche à l'Université de Mons, 17, Place Warocqué, 7000 Mons, Belgique.

[15] Giessen, 1909 (1964[2]); les auteurs qui se sont occupés de la même question depuis lors n'ont pas cité davantage ce texte extrêmement frappant; cf. *Christianisme et Philosophie* 225, n.122.

[16] Traduction A. Jagu, édition des Belles Lettres, tome III, 1936, 78.

[17] Καὶ ταῦτα οὐδέποτε κάμνει χαριζόμενος.

[18] *Discours VII*, 61.

[19] Je signale encore en IX, 8 une critique, par Diogène, des grands de ce monde (ce qui est, à vrai dire, assez banal) et en LXVIII, 5, un passage comparable au «cherchez et vous trouverez»: ἐλπὶς γὰρ ζητοῦντα καὶ παιδευόμενον ἐξευρεῖν τὸ δέον. — Il ne s'agissait ici que d'enrichir quelque peu un dossier. Tout commentaire des passages parallèles serait prématuré: il faut d'abord dépouiller un nombre suffisant d'auteurs. On risque beaucoup, en effet, à tirer des conclusions de rapprochements trop isolés. Comparant Dion Chrysostome, I, 67 sqq. à Matthieu 7, 13 sq., M. van Unnik constate (*Corpus Hellenisticum...* 27) que, pour Dion, la voie de la royauté est large et celle de la tyrannie étroite, alors que pour Jésus, la voie de la vertu est étroite et celle du vice, large, et il affirme qu'il y a là une différence décisive pour l'attitude à l'égard de la vie. Mais il se fait que, depuis Hésiode, ce thème des deux voies est très familier à l'hellénisme et que les voies de la vertu et du vice y sont régulièrement caractérisées comme chez Matthieu (cf. mon *Tableau de Cébes et la philosophie religieuse*, Bruxelles, 1963, 40-41). Par contre, Hermas serait du côté de Dion, et pour des raisons sans doute analogues (cf. mon édition du *Pasteur*, Paris, 1968[2], 170-171).

[20] o.c. 117, comme parallèle à *II Cor.*, VIII 2.

194

CHRISTLICHES UND NEOPLATONISCHES IM DENKEN AUGUSTINS

CORNELIA W. WOLFSKEEL

In *De immortalitate animae*, einer der frühen Schriften Augustins, finden wir Kapitel VIII, 14, Absatz 4[1], eine bemerkenswerte Aussage, welche vom Neuplatonismus her schwer erklärlich ist. Augustin sagt ausdrücklich: *Nam de gignente non absurde dicitur, hoc eum esse, quod est illud quod ab eo gignitur.* Das heisst, dass im algemeinen ohne Ausnahme der Erzeuger nur das erzeugt, was ihm ähnlich ist. Es ist bestimmt nicht ohne Bedeutung, dass Augustin hier über den Erzeuger (*eum*) – und nicht im allgemeinen über eine erzeugende Instanz – spricht. Hinsichtlich des Gottesbegriffs des jungen Augustin bedeutet dies, dass s.E. Gott, der Vater, der den Sohn erzeugt, seinem Erzeugnis, d.h. dem Sohne, ähnlich ist. Eine solche Annahme ist völlig in Übereinstimmung mit andren über dieses Thema handelnden Stellen, wo der Sohn Gottes, der ewige Logos, Gott dem Vater gleichgesetzt wird[2]. Von der Gedankenwelt des orthodoxen Christentums nach dem Konzil von Nizäa aus gesehen, ist die Gleichsetzung von Vater und Sohn allerdings nichts Neues. Eine auffallende Tatsache aber ist, dass uns in einem Neuplatonischen Kontext wie Kap. 14 von *De imm. an.* eine Äusserung begegnet, welche zwar im Rahmen des christlichen Denkens ganz verständlich ist, jedoch gar nicht der Gedankenwelt von einem der Augustin um diese Zeit bekannten Neuplatoniker entspricht. Wäre letzteres der Fall, so wäre bei Plotin die Seele dem Geist (νοῦς) ähnlich und dieser dem Einen, denn so wie die Seele ein Erzeugnis des Geistes ist, so ist der Geist vom Einen erzeugt worden. Auch in der Hypostasenlehre von Porphyrios, wie uns diese in der Schrift *De regressu animae* oder an einer beliebigen andren Stelle begegnet, fehlt die Auffassung, dass der Erzeuger und sein Erzeugnis einander ähnlich seien. Es ist zum Beispiel keinesweges so, dass die Weltseele, die von dem Geist des Vaters erzeugt worden ist, diesem auch ähnlich ist. Es ist eine nicht zu leugnende Tatsache, dass der bei Augustin begegnende Gedanke über *gignens* und *genitum* nicht den Neuplatonikern entnommen sein kann. Vom christlichen Denken aus ist dieser Gedanke aber, wie oben gezeigt, verständlich. Auch wenn es sich nicht mit Sicherheit beweisen

195

lässt, ist er schon deshalb, weil keine andere Erklärung für eine solche Äusserung in einem sonst vom Platonismus und Neuplatonismus geprägten Zusammenhang gegeben werden kann, höchstwahrscheinlich auf den Einfluss des Christentums zurückzuführen[3].

Die Auffassung des Verhältnisses von *gignens* und *genitum* in Kap. VIII, 14 hat bestimmte Folgen für das Verhältnis zwischen Gott (das heisst „dem Logos" = „den Ideen") und den vernunftbegabten Seelen[4]. Wie im Neuplatonismus, befinden diese sich in der Rangordnung des Seins unter den Ideen oder dem göttlichen Geist. Man darf aber nicht sagen, dass die Seelen aus dem göttlichen Geist hervorgegangen sind, wie sich dies die Neuplatoniker dachten; mit andren Worten, sie sind keine γεννήματα, keine *genita*, sondern *facta* des göttlichen Logos. Diese Tatsache schliesst die Ewigkeit und wesentliche Unwandelbarkeit der Seele[5] nicht aus. Im Gegenteil, die von Gott geschaffene Seele ist ihrem Ursprung nach ewig[6].

In der 388 entstandenen Schrift *De quantitate animae* XXXIV, 77 (P.L. t. 30, 1077)[7] lesen wir, dass die Seele von Gott, dem Logos, geschaffen ist. Die Seele wird an dieser Stelle ausdrücklich *creatura* genannt. Wo es sich um eine der frühen Schriften Augustins handelt, darf man aber daraus nicht die Schlussfolgerung ziehen, dass er schon in 388 die Ewigkeit der Seele verneint hat. In derselben Schrift nimmt Augustin auch die Präexistenz und den ewigen Ursprung[8] der Seele an. Noch in der 393 entstandenen Schrift *De genesi ad litteram, liber imperfectus* IV, 17 (P.L. t.34, 225) spricht er über die Weltseele als eine *creatura vitalis*, ohne deren Ewigkeit zu verneinen. Dieser schöpferische Geist Gottes, von welchem in *Genesis* I, 2 die Rede ist, ist als solcher zwar ewig und unwandelbar, aber nicht wie der Logos und der Heilige Geist zugleich *consubstantialis* und *coaeternus* mit Gott, dem Vater. Dass auch eine geschaffene Substanz[9] wie die Weltseele ewig sein kann, lässt sich erklären aus der Tatsache, dass er in seinen frühen Schriften (sogar noch in 393) den Schöpfungsvorgang in *Gen.* I, 2 in einer bestimmten Weise deutet. Die Schöpfung der Welt fand statt *in principio Verbi*, das heisst in Gott, dem Vater, selber, der *principium sine principio* ist, während der Logos *principium cum alio principio* ist. Bei einer solchen Erklärung des Ausdrucks *in principio* darf man ein ewiges Verhältnis zwischen Gott, dem Schöpfer, und Seiner Schöpfung im Denken Augustins annehmen. Gott, von dem alle Dinge *in principio* des ewigen Wortes geschaffen worden sind, hat auch die Zeit zusammen mit Himmel und Erde, d.h. zusammen mit der Materie, geschaffen. In diesem Sinne sollten wir die folgende Stelle in *De gen. ad litt. lib. imp.* III, 8 (P.L. t.34, 223) verstehen: *Sed quoque modo hoc se habeat* (*res enim secretissima est, et humanis coniecturis impenetrabilis*), *illud certe accipiendum est in fide, etiamsi modum nostrae cogitationis excedit creaturam habere initium, tempusque ipsum creaturam esse, ac per hoc ipsum habere initium nec coaeternum esse Creatori*... Die zur Schöpfung Gottes gehörige Zeit hat aber auch ihren Anfang und Grund im *principio* des ewigen Logos. Deshalb dürfen wir ohne weiteres sagen, dass für Augustin damals, in seinen frühen Schriften, die Zeit, wie auch die ganze Schöpfung, ein ewiges Verhältnis zum Logos hätte[10]. Gäbe es nicht ein solches Verhältnis, so wäre eine geschaffene, unwandelbare und ewige Weltseele[11], wie sie Augustin in dieser Schrift annimmt, unerklärlich. Bei dieser nicht temporellen Interpretation[12] des oben anlässlich *De Gen. ad litt.* III, 6-8 erwähnten Schöpfungsvorgangs dürfen wir annehmen, dass im Denken Augustins auch ein Geschöpf ewig sein könnte. In einer solchen Gedankenwelt war der vom Neuplatonismus herkommende Glaube an eine ewige Seele nichts ausserordentliches. Dieser Gedanke war auf jeden Fall nicht in direktem Widerspruch mit der (wie wir wohl annehmen müssen) dem biblischen Denken entnommenen Vorstellung der von Gott geschaffenen Seele. Noch im dritten Buch von *De lib. arb.*, Kap. 59, lesen wir folgendes:

Harum autem quattuor de anima sententiarum, utrum de propagine veniant, aut in singulis quibusque nascentibus novae fiant, an in corpora nascentium iam alicubi existentes vel mittantur divinitus, vel sua sponte labantur, nullam temere affirmare oportebit aut enim nondum ista quaestio a divinorum Librorum catholicis tractatoribus pro merito suae obscuritatis et perplexitatis evoluta atque illustrata est, aut si iam factum est, nondum in manus nostras huiuscemodi litterae pervenerunt.

An dieser Stelle zeigt Augustin eine zögernde Haltung in Bezug auf die Präexistenz und den ewigen Ursprung der Seele. Er schliesst aber die Möglichkeit, die Seele sei wirklich ihrer Herkunft nach ewig, nicht aus. Diese Stelle lässt sogar Raum für eine Neuplatonische Interpretation der Position der Seele, wie wir diese in den sehr frühen Schriften wie *De immortalitate* und *De quantitate animae* fanden[13]. In den *Bekenntnissen*, im 11. Buch, Kap. 16 und 31, begegnet uns implizit wieder die Vorstellung der Ewigkeit der Seele. Die Seele ist dort die Instanz, mit welcher wir die Zeit messen, und steht deshalb nach Augustin über der Zeit[14], die von ihm der *praesens aeternitas* Gottes gegenübergestellt wird. Wenn Augustin von der *praesens aeternitas* Gottes spricht, kann man seine Auffassung dieses Begriffes wegen einer gewissen Ähnlichkeit vom Neuplatonismus her verstehen. Man vergleiche z.B. Plotins Definition des Begriffs 'aioon' in *Enn.* III 7 [5], 24:

„Will man also hiernach die Ewigkeit bezeichnen als ein Leben, welches in der Unendlichkeit steht, indem es die Ganzheit des Lebens ist und nichts von sich aufzehrt, es kennt ja kein Vergangensein und kein Bevorstehen (sonst wäre es nicht mehr Ganzheit); so wäre man damit ihrer Definition schon nahe gekommen; denn der Zusatz *indem es die Ganzheit des Lebens ist und nichts von sich aufzehrt* ist lediglich eine Erläuterung der Definition *Leben, welches in der Unendlichkeit steht*". Wie nach Plotin die Ewigkeit zum intelligibelen Sein des 'Noûs' gehört, so gehört im Denken Augustins die *praesens aeternitas* zum Sein Gottes, der selber das Sein im höchsten Sinne ist. Wenn wir Plotins Definition der Zeit in *Enn.* III, 7, Kap. 11 in Betracht nehmen ist es jedoch klar, dass diese weit von den Ansichten Augustins entfernt ist. Nach Plotin ist die Zeit „das Leben der in ihrer Bewegung von einer zur andren Lebensform übergehenden Seele". Augustin aber stellt, wie wir oben gesehen haben, die Seele über die Zeit.

Erst viel später, in der 419 abgefassten *Epistula 166 ad Hieronymum*, verneint Augustin in expliziter Weise die ewige Herkunft der Seele. Dort heisst es im 14. Kapitel des 5. Paragraphen, es sei gar nicht notwendig, dass die Seele, weil sie unsterblich ist, auch unbedingt ewig sein müsse[15]. Er polemisiert gerade gegen diejenigen, welche der Meinung sind, die Seele sei wegen ihrer Unsterblichkeit vor allen Zeiten (*ante omnia tempora*) geschaffen, d.h. wenn wir die obengenannte Stelle in *De gen. ad litt. c. Man.*[16] in Betracht nehmen dürfen, die Seele sei in derselben Weise ewig wie Gott der Schöpfer ewig ist.

Im dritten Kapitel der oben erwähnten *Ep.* 166 sagt Augustin ausdrücklich, die Seele des Menschen könne wegen ihrer Wandelbarkeit, deren sie als Geschöpf (*creatura*)[17] teilhaftig ist, auf keinen Fall *pars Dei* sein und deshalb könne sie auch ihrer Herkunft nach nicht ewig sein[18]. Bei jeder Geburt eines neuen Menschen gibt Gott nach Augustin (in diesem Brief) diesem Menschen eine Seele. Ob diese Seele entweder innerhalb der Zeit ganz neu geschaffen wird oder ob es sich um eine Seele handelt, die in irgendeiner Weise von der Seele Adams abstammt, ist eine Frage, welche von Augustin niemals gelöst worden ist. Von den vier in *De lib. arb.* III, Kap. 59 genannten Möglichkeiten der Herkunft der Seele[19] sind aber die zwei letztere mit der Verneinung der Ewigkeit der Seele widerrufen. Weil s.E. in der heiligen Schrift die Lehre der Erbsünde gelehrt wird, hatte er aber mehr die Geneigtheit anzunehmen, dass die menschlichen Seelen ihre Herkunft auf die Seele Adams zurückführen könnten[20]. Sicherheit über diese Frage hatte er aber nie. Noch in dem aus 429 datierenden *Opus imperfectum contra Julianum* II, 178 sagt er *confiteor me nescire*.

Obwohl Augustin aus theologischen Gründen in *Ep.* 166 die Ewigkeit der Seele widerrufen hat, hat er aus denselben Gründen immer an ihre Unsterblichkeit festgehalten[21]. Eine Beweisführung dafür aber fehlt. Nur die Autorität der biblischen Schriftsteller ist der Grund seines Glaubens an die Unsterblichkeit der Seele. Aus dem obigen ergibt sich, dass die Lehre Augustins über die menschliche Seele sich im Laufe der Zeit geändert hat. Schon in *De natura boni* X, 10 finden wir eine Stelle, die implizite zeigt, dass in 399 die Art der Seele ihm nicht so klar war, wie er vorher (z.B. *De imm.*) behauptet hatte. Dort lesen wir, dass alles was *de Deo* ist, Gott ähnlich und unverderblich ist. Aus dem Zusammenhang ergibt sich, dass diese Aussage sich nur auf das Wort Gottes (der Heilige Geist wird an dieser Stelle nicht genannt) bezieht, denn alle *naturae*, welche nicht *de Deo* sind, sind erstens von Gott (*a Deo*) geschaffen worden, zweitens vergänglich, und drittens, weil sie von Gott *ex nihilo* geschaffen worden sind, nicht unwandelbar[22]. Aus dieser Stelle ergibt sich, dass nach Augustin die rationalen Seelen[23], die nicht *de Deo* sein können, als *facta* oder *creaturae* Gottes[24] ihrer Herkunft nach nicht unverwandelbar und ewig seien, sondern im Gegenteil verderblich, weil sie wie alle *naturae ex nihilo* geschaffen seien[25]. In der Verneinung der Ewigkeit der rationalen Seele zeigt sich der Unterschied mit der von uns S. 196 erwähnten Lehre. Nach den von ihm z.B. in *De imm. an.* gegebenen Ansichten kann eine Seele, obwohl sie *factum Dei* ist, trotzdem unwandelbar und ewig sein, m.a.W. sie ist als Seele unwandelbar und ewig, denn ihre Unwandelbarkeit setzt ihre ewige Herkunft und Ewigkeit voraus. In *De nat. bon.* X, 10 fehlt eine solche Auffassung, die die Ewigkeit der Seele voraussetzt. Die Seele, die auch in *De nat. bon.* Prinzip des Lebens in den Körpern ist[26], ist als solches jedem Körper überlegen. Sie ist nach Augustin in der Rangordnung des Seins ein grösseres Gut als der Körper, den er übrigens auch wie jede Kreatur Gottes als ein Gut betrachtet. Sogar wenn die Seele gewissermassen verdorben ist, ist sie immer noch ein grösseres Gut als irgendein nicht verdorbener Körper[27].

In dieser Rangordnung des Seins „Gott - Seelen - Körper" zeigt sich auch in dieser späteren Schrift, obschon in anderer Weise als in *De imm. an.*[28], der Einfluss des Neuplatonismus. Übrigens hat Gott nach Augustin die rationalen Seelen so geschaffen[29], dass sie selber wählen können, ob sie sich verderben lassen wollen oder nicht: *Creaturis autem praestantissimis, hoc est rationabilibus spiritibus, hoc praestitit Deus ut si nolint, corrumpi non possint, id est si oboedientiam conservaverint sub Domino Deo suo ac sic incorruptibili pulchritudini eius adhaeserint...*

Mit dieser Aussage hat er die Möglichkeit der Unsterblichkeit der vernunftbegabten Seelen aufrecht erhalten. Zweiffellos hat Augustin auch in *De nat. bon.* an die Unsterblichkeit der Seele geglaubt[30]. Er hat sie auf jeden Fall auf Grund der heiligen Schrift angenommen. Er sagt zwar, dass in eigentlichem Sinne nur Gott als *vera aeternitas* die Unsterblichkeit besitze (...*Deus, cuius ipsius immortalitas ipsa est vera aeternitas*[31]), aber nimmt auf der andren Seite auch implizit die Unsterblichkeit der Seele an.

Es ist bemerkenswert, dass Augustin, der noch in den *Bekenntnissen*, wie oben (Seite 197) gezeigt wurde, die Ewigkeit der Seele, welche deren wesentliche Unwandelbarkeit voraussetzt, aufrecht erhalten hat, in einer früheren Schrift wie *De nat. bon.* die Unwandelbarkeit und Ewigkeit der Seele verneint hat. Wir möchten aber darauf hinweisen, dass Augustin, der in 415 in expliziter Weise die ewige Herkunft der Seele abgelehnt hat, auch schon vorher[32] eine zögernde Haltung deren Stellung gegenüber angenommen hat. Natürlich stehen die Aussagen über die Seele in *De div. quaest.* 83, 19 und in *De nat. bon.* nicht im Einklang mit der Auffassung in den *Bekenntnissen*[33], dass die Seele der Zeit übergeordnet und deshalb unverwandelbar und ewig sei. Auf der anderen Seite kann man sich anlässlich dieser Stelle in den *Bekenntnissen* auch fragen, wie Augutin sich diese Tatsache, dass die Seele der Zeit übergeordnet sei, vorgestellt hat. Auf die Seele kann doch seiner Meinung nach nicht der Begriff der *praesens aeternitas*[34] bezogen werden. Auf der anderen Seite kann die Seele nach seinen Ansichten auch nicht als etwas in der Zeit Bestehendes gedacht werden. Ch. Boyer[35] sagt hinsichtlich der Position der Seele in den *Bekenntnissen* folgendes:,,Ils (les idées) supposent la permanence et l'identité de l'âme, mais ils impliquent aussi l'imperfection de son être, ainsi étant incapable de se posséder tout à la fois." Boyer interpretiert hier die Seele bei Augustin gewissermassen in neuplatonischer Weise[36]. Wenn wir aber in Betracht nehmen, dass gerade wegen dieser Unvollkommenheit die Seele nach Plotin nicht der Zeit übergeordnet ist[37], muss man sich fragen, weshalb Augustin andrer Meinung ist als Plotin. Die Erklärung dafür muss man wohl suchen in dem von dem von Plotin verschiedenen Zeitbegriff, den Augustin voraussetzt und der uns implizite schon in *De imm. an.* begegnet[38].

ANMERKUNGEN

[1] *Oeuvres de Saint Augustin*, in: *Bibliothèque Augustinienne*, 1e Série, *Opuscules*, V, *Dialogues Philosophiques*, II, *Dieu et l'âme*, 196.

[2] Vergleiche z.B. *De beata vita* I, 34: *Quae est autem dicenda Sapientia, nisi quae Dei Sapientia est? Accepimus autem auctoritate divina, Dei Filium nihil esse aliud quam Dei Sapientiam: et est Dei Filius profecto Deus.*

³ Ein Hinweis in diese Richtung ist auch (s. oben, S. 195) das männliche *eum* in Bezug auf den *gignens*, den man, wie *ab eo* zeigt, persönlich deuten soll.

⁴ Die menschlichen Seelen und die Weltseele.

⁵ Vergl. Kap. XIV, 23 und auch *De quant. an.* XXXIV, 77 (P.L. t. 30, 1077).

⁶ Ist etwas, was *nicht* geschaffen (*factum*) oder entstanden (*ortum*) ist, ¦notwendigerweise ewig (vergl. Kap. VIII, 14, 2. Absatz), dasjenige, was geschaffen ist, ist nicht notwendigerweise nicht ewig. Wir möchten in diesem Zusammenhang darauf hinweisen, dass Augustin an einer andren Stelle in *De imm.* (VIII, 13) in Bezug auf die Seele sagt, dass Gott sie *ex se afficit*. Offenbar spricht er an dieser Stelle mehr im Sinne des Neuplatonismus als im Sinne des Christentums.
Auf der andren Seite muss man gestehen, dass der Ausdruck *ex eo* vonAugustin auch in bezug auf die von Gott geschaffenen sichtbaren Dinge gewendet wird. Vergleiche *De lib. arb.* II, 28, Kap. 47, Abs. 2: *Satis mihi persuasum esse fateor et quemadmodum manifestum fiat, quantum in hac vita atque inter tales, quales nos sumus, potest Deum esse et ex Deo esse omnia bona quandoquidem omnia, quae sunt, sive quae intelligunt et vivunt et sunt, sive quae tantum vivunt et sunt, ex Deo sunt.* S. in diesem Zusammenhang auch *De lib. arb.* III, 13, Kap. 36, zweiter Absatz: *Omnis igitur substantia (= natura) aut Deus, aut ex Deo est, quia omne bonum aut Deus, aut ex Deo est.*

⁷ *Quemadmodum fatendum est animam humanam non esse quod Deus est, ita praesumendum nihil inter omnia, quae creavit, esse Deo propinquius. Ideoque divine et singulariter in Ecclesia traditur (Rom. I, 25): "nullam creaturam colendam esse animae" (libentius enim loquor his verbis quibus mihi haec insinuata sunt), sed ipsum tantummodo rerum, quae sunt, omnium Creatorem...*"

⁸ Courcelle hat mit Recht in *Les Lettres Grecques en Occident de Macrobe à Cassiodore* (Paris ²1948) = *Late Latin Writers*, Cambridge Mass. 1969, 179-180 hinsichtlich der Stelle *De quantitate animae* 20, 34, P.L. 32, 1055 darauf hingewiesen, dass die Seele ihrer Herkunft nach ewig ist. Es handelt sich hier um eine der sogenannten "*reditus*-Stellen" Augustins, wo er über die Rückkehr der Seele zu Gott spricht.

⁹ Siehe auch *De gen. ad litt. lib. imp.* III, 8 (P.L. t. 34, 223) und *De gen. ad litt. contra Manichaeos* I, 2, 4 (P.L. t. 34, 175): *Non enim coaevum Deo mundum istum dicimus, quia non eius aeternitatis est Deus. Mundum quippe fecit Deus, et sic cum ipsa creatura quam Deus fecit, tempora esse coeperunt; et ideo dicuntur tempora aeterna. Non tamen sic sunt aeterna tempora quomodo aeternus est Deus, quia Deus est ante tempora, qui fabricator est temporum.*

¹⁰ Später hat Augustin, wie wir noch darlegen werden, seine Ansichten in dieser Hinsicht geändert.

¹¹ Wir möchten darauf hinweisen, dass die Weltseele in dieser Schrift als die bearbeitende Instanz der von Gott in der kausalen Ordnung früher geschaffenen Materie betrachtet wird. Augustin weicht mit dieser Auffassung von seinen früheren Ansichten über die Position der Weltseele ab. In *De imm.*, Kap. 24 vertritt er noch die Meinung, die Seele sei die notwendige vermittelnde Instanz zwischen Gott und den Körpern, die auch eines finsteren, der Neuplatonischen 'hulè' vergleichbaren Elements teilhaftig seien.

¹² Dass man die Schöpfungslehre in den frühen *Genesis-Kommentaren* Augustins nicht temporell verstehen muss, ergibt sich auch aus dem 44. und 45. Kapitel des zweiten Buches der Schrift *De lib. arb.* S. für eine ausführliche Besprechung dieser Stelle Gilson, *Introduction à l'étude de Saint Augustin*, Paris ²1943, 253.

¹³ Siehe oben, S. 197. Wohl spricht Augustin in *De lib. arb.* II, 12, 34 von der Wandelbarkeit der Seele, aus dem Zusammenhang ergibt sich aber, dass es sich hier nicht um eine wesentliche Wandelbarkeit der Seele handelt, sondern nur um die Möglichkeit einer nicht wesentlichen Veränderung.

¹⁴ Sogar noch im 11. Buch der *Bekenntnisse* begegnet uns, wie Odilo Lechner in

Idee und Zeit in der Metaphysik Augustins, München 1964, 127 ff. dargelegt hat, die Auffassung, dass der Anfang der Zeit als Ursprung der Zeit zeitfrei zu denken sei, als immerwährendes Wort, das alles zugleich spreche. Wir möchten in diesem Zusammenhang auf *De diversis quaestionibus* 8, 72 hinweisen, wo Augustin in seiner Erklärung der biblischen Stelle *Titus* I, 2, wo von *aeterna tempora* die Rede ist, diesen Ausdruck des Apostels folgenderweise erklärt. Der Apostel Paulus hätte eigentlich gemeint, dass Gott *ante omnia tempora* den Menschen das ewige Leben versprochen habe: *Aeterna autem maluit dicere quam omnia, fortassis ideo, quia tempus non coepit ex tempore. An tempora aeterna aevum significavit, inter quod et tempus, hoc distat, quod illud stabile est, tempus autem mutabile?*
In *De div. quaest.* 83, 19 scheint der Terminus *aeternus* nur auf das unverwandelbare Sein Gottes bezogen zu werden: *Quod incommutabile est, aeternum est: semper enim eiusdem modi est. Quod autem commutabile est, tempori obnoxium est. Non enim semper eiusdem modi est, et ideo aeternum non recte dicitur.* Die Seele kann so ihrer eigenen Art entsprechend nicht *aeterna* genannt werden, denn in demjenigen, das *ewig* ist, kann nicht, wie im Falle der Seele, von Vorübergehen und Zukunft die Rede sein. Augustin sagt übrigens an der selben Stelle implizite, dass auch wohl die Seele ewig genannt wird, denn die folgenden Worte sind doch wohl hinsichtlich der Seele gesagt: *Vocatur autem aeternum interdum etiam quod immortale est.* Siehe weiter auch Anm. 30.

[15] *Id etiam, quod aiunt omne quod in tempore coepit esse, immortale esse non posse, quia omnia orta occidunt et aucta senescunt, ut eo modo credi cogant animum humanum ideo esse inmortalem, quod ante omnia tempora sit creatus, non movet fidem nostram; ut enim alia taceam, coepit esse in tempore immortalitas carnis Christi, quae tamen iam non moritur et mors ei ultra non dominabitur.* Siehe in diesem Zusammenhang auch die frühe Stelle in *De div. quaest.* 83, 19, die wir oben Anm. 14 besprochen.

[16] Siehe Anm. 19.

[17] Implizite wird hier gesagt, dass ein Geschöpf als solches nicht ewig sein kann. Hier wird also eine andere Meinung hinsichtlich dem Geschaffenen vertreten als vorher. In *Civ. Dei* XII, 15 (P.L. t. 41, 363) lesen wir: *Non tamen dubito nihil omnino creaturae Creatori esse coaeternum*... Und weiter: *...Ubi enim nulla creatura est, cuius mutabilibus motibus tempora peragantur, tempora omnino esse non possent, ac per hoc et si (angeli) semper fuerunt, creati sunt; nec si semper fuerunt, ideo Creatori coaeterni sunt... Quapropter, si Deus semper dominus fuit, semper habuit creaturam suo dominatui servientem; verumtamen non de ipso genitam, sed ab ipso de nihilo factam nec ei coaeternam. Erat quippe ante illam, quamvis nullo tempore sine illa, non eam spatio transcurrente, sed manente perpetuitate praecedens.* Hieraus ergibt sich (siehe auch Gilson, *Introduction ... Augustin*, 247), dass das Geschaffene überhaupt nicht ewig sein kann.

[18] Auch im 12. Buch der Schrift *De Tritinate*, Kap. 24, hat Augustin die vorher in den Frühschriften (siehe Anm. 6 und 7) von ihm vertretene Lehre der Präexistenz und Ewigkeit der Seele widerrufen: *Si recordatio haec esset rerum antea cognitarum, non utique omnes vel paene omnes, cum illo modo interrogarentur, hoc possent. Non enim omnes in priore vita geometrae fuerunt, cum tam rari sunt in genere humano, ut vix possit aliquis inveniri: sed potius credendum est mentis intellectualis ita conditam esse naturam, ut rebus intelligibilibus naturali ordine, disponente Conditore, subiuncta sic ista videat in quadam luce sui generis incorporea, quemadmodum oculus carnis videt quae in hac corporea luce circumadiacent, cuius lucis capax eique congruens est creatus.* Siehe in diesem Zusammenhang auch Ep. 164, Kap. 24.

[19] Siehe S. 196.

[20] *Ep.* 166, 7. Kap. Auch im 3. Kap. heisst es, die Seele könne wegen ihrer Veränderlichkeit nicht ewig sein.

202

[21] Vergl. *Ep.* 166, 3. Kap., wo Augustin auf *I. Tim.* 6, 16 hinweist.

[22] *Omnes igitur naturae corruptibiles nec omnino naturae essent nisi a Deo essent, nec corruptibiles essent si de illo essent, quia hoc quod ipse est, essent. Ideo ergo quocumque modo, quacumque specie, quocumque ordine sunt, quia Deus est, a quo factae sunt, ideo autem non incommutabiles sunt, quia nihilo est, unde factae sunt.*

[23] Aus dem unmittelbar vorhergehenden Kontext darf man schliessen, dass es sich besonders um die rationalen, menschlichen Seelen handelt. S. *De nat. bon.* VII, 7.

[24] Vergleiche auch *De nat. bon.* VII, 7, wo Augustin in Bezug auf die rationalen Seelen der Menschen sagt, dass sie *facta* und *creaturae* Gottes sind.

[25] Auch auf Grund von *De nat. bon.* VIII, 8 muss man schliessen, dass Augustin die Schöpfung der Seelen *ex nihilo* angenommen hat: *Caetera vero quae sunt facta de nihilo, quae utique inferiora sunt quam spiritus rationalis, nec beata possunt esse nec misera.* Weil es sich im vorhergehenden Kapitel um die rationalen Seelen handelte, sind die Worte *caetera* hier von grösster Bedeutung.

[26] Vergl. *De nat. bon.* III, 3. ...*Omnis ergo natura bona est.*

[27] Vergl. Anm. 6 und 7.

[28] Vergl. Kap. 23 ff.

[29] S. *De nat. bon.* VII, 7.

[30] Vergleiche Kap. XL, 39: *Sicut ergo dicitur homo bonus, non tamen sicut Deus de quo dictum est: "nemo bonus nisi unus Deus"* (*Marc.* X, 18). *Et sicut dicitur anima immortalis, non tamen sicut Deus de quo dictum est: "qui solus habet immortalitatem"* (*I Tim.* VI. 16). Siehe auch Anm. 14 in diesem Zusammenhang.

[31] *De nat. bon.* XL, 39: *Illa est autem vera aeternitas, quae vera immortalitas, hoc est illa summa incommutabilitas quam solus Deus habet, qui mutari omnino non potest.*

[32] In der oben (Anm. 14) erwähnten Stelle *De div. quaest.* 83, 19 begegnet deutlich diese zögernde Haltung.

[33] Siehe ob. S. 197, *Conf.* XI, Kap. 16 und 31.

[34] Siehe ob. S. 198.

[35] *Eternité et création dans les derniers livres des Confessions*, in: Giornale Metafisica 9 (1954), 444.

[36] Vergleiche z.B. Plotin, *Enn.* IV, 4.

[37] Siehe oben, S. 198.

[38] Vergleiche *De imm. an.*, wo III, 4 der Wandel und die damit zusammenhängende Bewegung der individuellen Körper ihn zu der Annahme einer unwandelbaren und ewigen Seele als *agens* der Bewegung und Ursache des Wandels in diesen Körpern veranlässt und er zugleich (Kap. III, 3) alle Bewegung und allen Wandel der Körper als ein Geschehen in der Zeit betrachtet.

QUAESTIO DE IDEIS

SOME NOTES ON AN IMPORTANT CHAPTER OF PLATONISM

L. M. DE RIJK

The opponents of Platonism as well as its adherents have to agree that there is a lot of truth in Whitehead's famous statement that the safest general characterization of the European philosophical tradition is that it consists of a series of footnotes to Plato[1].

I think one of the everlasting items of that tradition is what has been termed since St. Augustine the *quaestio de Ideis*. Indeed, the status (either ontic or merely mental) of the Ideas has fascinated many philosophers, especially the Christian, who could not dispense with a statement concerning the relationship of the eternal and immutable Ideas to God. In this short contribution to the dedicatory volume for our academic teacher C. J. de Vogel, I shall confine myself to roughly sketch the development of the problem of that relationship from Plato's days down to some fourteenth century Franciscan thinkers.

1 – *Plato*

In his later years Plato conceived Intelligible Being as an ordered whole, as even an organic unity (ζῷον, a thinking living being, as is read in *Timaeus* 37C)[2]. His First Principle, however, the Idea of the Good, was placed beyond the intelligible Realm of Being, of which it was the ultimate cause. On the other hand, according to the explicit testimony of his own pupils, Plato (presumably in his later years) identified the supreme Idea of the Good, which transcends all being (ἐπέκεινα τῆς οὐσίας, *Rep.* 509B) with the One[3]. So the question of whether Plato himself located the Intelligible World *in God* (speaking with St. Augustine: *in mente divina*) might seem to be quite a legitimate one. However, it is nothing but verbiage, I am afraid. To show this one cannot do better than try to give an answer to the question.

R. M. Jones (Class. Philol. 21 (1926), 317 ff.) argues that as early as in Xenocrates' days our question was answered in the affirmative. As a matter of fact, there existed a doxographical tradition in the first century

B.C. according to which the Platonic exemplary Ideas were explained as the eternal and immutable thoughts of the Divine Mind[4]. This much seems to be certain that beside its original meaning of *'shape'* the word ἰδέα had already obtained the subjective meaning of *thought* at a rather early date[5].

However, as has been seen by W. J. Verdenius[6], Plato seems to be of the opposite view in *Symposium* 211A-B, where Socrates explicitly affirms that the (Idea of the) Beautiful is not something existing somewhere in another substance, such as an animal or the earth or the sky or any other thing, but *existing* ever in singularity of form *independently by itself*.

One could possibly be inclined to fall back on the usual procedure of pointing to a doctrinal development in Plato's thinking, in order to explain away this apparent contradiction. However, in my view every attempt to show that, for Plato, Intelligible Being was located in God's Mind must be considered an abortive one *a priori*, because of Plato's concept of God being rather ambiguous from the modern point of view; and once this concept is understood in its ambiguity, our question lacks its specific interest, if not all good sense. Let me explain.

The Platonic *God* can certainly be conceived as the whole Intelligible hierarchic Order (τὰ νοητά, in contra-distinction to the sensible domain: τὰ αἰσθητά), which contains both Intelligible Being and the Good (the One), the latter existing beyond Being. So Plato's *God* turns out to be the (rather vague, indeed) embodiment (German: *Inbegriff*) of all which is entitled to have the epitheton *divine* (θεῖος): the Demiurge, the Realm of Intelligible Ideas, the World Soul, even the purified human soul, and – *par excellence*, no doubt – the Good (the One). Therefore, what exactly can be meant by the question: "did Plato locate the Ideas in God's Mind?" The first thing to investigate is what is meant by the *'Mind'* of God. Such a question seems to be senseless, unless the term *'God'* be taken for a *personal God* who is the Highest Principle itself, at the top of Intelligible Being, not beyond it. An explicit location of the Platonic Ideas in the Divine Mind seems to be possible only if the essential opposition which, for Plato, exists between Intelligible *Being* and the One *beyond Being* has been dropped. In other words: once the Ideas are located in the Divine Mind (whatever that may mean to Plato), *either* the Highest Principle (the One), which is definitely considered by Plato to be *beyond* Being, would be made Highest *Being*, instead of transcending all being, *or* Plato's God would not be the Highest Principle and be located beneath the One. I think both implications would be quite unacceptable to Plato.

The former, indeed, conflicts with Plato's explicit statement in the *Republic* (509B) that the Highest Principle is beyond all being. As to the latter implication, it must be borne in mind that, unlike the modern view, the ancient Greeks thought it quite normal to speak of '*God*' and '*the Divine*' on different levels, to the extent that calling the One '*God*' did not *eo ipso* prevent one from calling also Intelligible Being *God*[7]. However, locating God and the Divine exclusively beneath the One, apart from being rather awkward, would definitely be contrary to Plato's fundamental doctrine on this point.

Therefore, I am of the opinion that the *quaestio de Ideis* when asked from the personalistic point of view is quite irrelevant as far as Plato's own doctrine is concerned[8], and that it is senseless to ask the question in connection with as vague a concept of God as was Plato's[9].

2 – Philo the Jew

Since they believed in a *personal* God Jews and Christians were bound to consider the question of where the exemplary Ideas, which were the source of the created world, were to be located a vital one.

According to Philo the Jew (c.20 B.C.-c.A.D. 50) God first created the Intelligible World, as a perfect and godlike pattern for the creation of the material world (*De opif. mundi* 4, 16). The Intelligible World was located in the Divine Mind and was nothing but the Logos itself engaged in the act of creation (*ibid.*, 6, 24). For that matter, the phrase *Divine Mind* is somewhat ambiguous; Philo's θεοῦ λόγον is better translated as *God's Mind*, i.e. the Mind of the personal God-Creator, who is compared by Philo to an architect. However, Philo's representation of the God-Creator still remains rather confused. This should not surprise us, however, since after Reitzenstein's study[10] we are quite aware of Philo's syncretistic view of the Logos (containing Stoic, Egyptian and Jewish elements). As I believe the decisive moment is that for Philo the Intelligible World is not completely identical with God's Mind, but just the first phase of creation. This view seems to stress the secondary and instrumental status of the Intelligible World. He has apparently been somewhat overzealous in his efforts to reconcile the Hellenistic *Timaeus* cosmogony (esp. that of Posidonius) with *Genesis*. It is a striking fact, indeed, that Philo uses the term '*Logos*' in at least two different senses: (1) the Divine Mind as the infinite variety of Ideas and (2) the limited κόσμος τῶν ἰδέων (the Intelligible World), which was conceived by God 'afterwards', be it before time came in and, consequently, created from all eternity. As a matter of fact, this Intelligible World is put by Philo *outside* God's Mind (*De opif. mundi* 7, 29). Thus Philo has saddled Jewish-Christian thinking with the confused representation of the Ideas both in and outside God's Mind.

3 – *Plotinus*

With Plotinus (A.D. 205-270) matters are quite different. First, his emanation differs substantially from biblical creation. Besides, unlike Philo's, his Highest Principle *transcends* Being, and, accordingly, is not Highest Being. The Noûs is the Highest *Being* (τὰ νοητά or Intelligible Being); it is completely identical with its thinking (taken as an act) and its thought (taken as its object). Grammatically speaking: Intelligible Being is not the direct object of the activity of the Noûs (thinking), but rather its intrinsic object, such as the dream in *dreaming a dream*[11]. To use a Scotistic formula: there is a formal distinction between the Noûs and Intelligible Being, not a real one nor a *distinctio rationis*, whereas there is a real one between Intelligible Being and the Highest Principle (the One).

Thus, as compared with Philo's position, the founder of Neoplatonism, which was to influence Mediaeval thought so heavily, restored the strict distinction of *Highest Principle* and *Intelligible Being* on the one hand, and stressed the complete identity between the latter and Divine Mind (Noûs) on the other. So Philonian and Plotinian thinking formed an ambiguous starting-point for Christian speculation on the relation between God and the Ideas.

4 – *St. Augustine*

No doubt, St. Augustine (A.D. 354-431) was not the first Christian thinker to be nourished with Platonism, but he has the first explicit discussion of the relation between God and the Ideas. For St. Augustine Christianity and Platonism were congenial; he is of the opinion that they differ only terminologically, not really[12].

However, as a Christian thinker, St. Augustine had to change the Platonic view of the relation between God and the Ideas in quite a substantial way. While identifying the Highest Principle = Highest *Being* = the personal God-Creator he bridges the notional gap between *Highest Principle* and *Logos*; from now on Intelligible Being will be in God's Mind (*in mente divina*)[13]. The Plotinian ontological distance

207

between the Highest Principle and Being is reduced to an epistemological one: God is no longer beyond being but beyond human knowledge.

It must be admitted that in distinguishing *Verbum* or *Filius Dei* as *sapientia genita* from the *creatura spiritualis* or *intelligibilis* as *sapientia facta*, St. Augustine seems to return to the Philonian creation-in-stages-theory and even to something like Plotinus' hypostases (*De Genesi ad litt.* I 2, 4; I 4, 9; II 6, 12-13; V 12, 28). However, St. Augustine's short monograph *Quaestio de Ideis* does not contain any syncretism or complexity. In this work he takes the Ideas for the principal forms of things, forms which are *non formatae* themselves and therefore (*per hoc*) are eternally present in the Divine Mind (*in divina intelligentia*). Notice that the phrase *non formatae* is rather ambiguous; as distinguished from being eternal *formari* apparently refers to the creation of the sensible world, not to that of the *creatura intelligibilis* (*sapientia facta*, i.e. Intelligible World); the latter is the world of *rationes creandi* (*singula igitur propriis sunt creata rationibus*); these *rationes* are identical with God's Mind (*ipsa mens Creatoris*).

Roughly speaking, the whole question of the relationship between God and the Ideas seems to be settled now. However, a new problem arose, viz. whether or not God's immutability was affected by creation. St. Augustine seems to have felt the difficulty himself when addressing the Lord in his *Retractationes* XII, 19: "it is difficult to see, Lord, how without changing Itself Thy Eternity creates changeable things"[14].

5 – *The Middle Ages*

Thomas Aquinas (1225-74) and many of his contemporaries put the Ideas in God's Mind to the effect that they are really identical with the Divine Nature in so far as the latter is imitable by creation (*sub ratione imitabilitatis, In I Sent.*, dist. 36). In this view the Ideas *are* the Divine Nature as known by God in their imitability by creation.

With Henry of Ghent (d. 1293) a substantial change of view-point came in: he stresses that, apart from their identity with Divine Nature, the Ideas are something in their own right, viz. *objective* contents of God's knowledge. This objectivity constitutes them as *possibilia* or *rerum essentiae*, i.e. the natures of things to be created (*rerum essentiae in divina cognitione existentes*). They do no longer refer only retrospectively to the Divine Nature, but as *possibilia* they point ahead to things to be created (*Quodl.* IX 2, 65ᵛ-66ʳ; *Summa* 68, 1265-67). Henry left it an open question whether this view of the Ideas was Plato's own (*Quodl.* IX 2, 66ʳ), but from *Timaeus* 51B-52A (in Calcidius' translation) he gathers the suggestion that Plato, too, viewed them as being in Divine Thought, i.e. as objective contents of Divine Thinking. Henry seems to be aware of his innovation in explaining the status of the Ideas; he tries (*ibid.*) to find support with authorities such as St. Augustine, and, with more justification, with the Arabs[15].

As to the ontological status of the Ideas, they were considered *essentiae absolutae*, in contradistinction to the *essentiae universales* (= the logical *universalia*) and the *essentiae singulares* in the things created. Their own *modus essendi* is *esse essentiae* or *esse quidditativum*; this mode, however, is not a third one beside the well known modes *extra animam* and *in anima*, but subordinated under the *modus* of the *esse in anima*. As a matter of fact, the latter is subdivided into the mode of being in the Divine Mind as in its *subject*, and that of being the *objective* content of the act of cognition[16].

Duns Scotus (1266-1308) has substantially the same view of the Ideas. Suffice it to point to the Subtle Doctor's famous statement that the idea of *stone* is nothing but the stone as grasped by the intellect (*idea lapidis non est nisi lapis intellectus*)[17]. According to Scotus, the *modus essendi* of the Ideas is that of an *esse diminutum*, to be distinguished formally from the Divine Nature[18]. There are as many Ideas as there are formal objects of God's knowledge. Notice that this view is part of Scotus' general epistemology, including human thinking as well.

With Petrus Thomae (d. 1334), presumably one of the most faithful adherents of Duns Scotus', the Idea is the own *ratio* or quality of each creature, and an objective image in the infinite Mirror of the Divine Nature, from which it is clearly distinct. For that matter, its being is quite real, although in a diminished form. It is not in God as in its subject, but follows God's real being *consecutive* to the extent that its *intentional* being follows from God's Entity[19].

The most remarkable thinker on this score is Thomas of Wylton (14th cent.)[20]. According to him the Ideas have not only objective real being, but also a kind of subjective being in God (*aliquod esse in se formaliter in actu*). They do not follow from God's knowledge nor from his Nature, and are not formed at all (St. Augustine's *formatae non sunt*; see above, p.208). Thus the Divine Ideas are emphatically different from Divine Nature. For that matter, the author is convinced that his opinion is not a favourite one among his contemporaries (*op. cit.*, f 34ᵛ).

James of Ascoli O.F.M. (c. 1320) takes the Ideas to be only *intentionaliter*. Their mode of being is, accordingly, a midway between that of a

209

mere *ens rationis* and that of an *ens reale*[21]. His doctrine agrees with that of Duns Scotus, who says that the *esse representatum* is something between *esse reale* and *esse rationis* (*Oxon.* I d.36, *q.un.* = X, 577).

6 – *The Ideas (and universal concepts) as 'obiective tantum existentia'*

An interesting question was – and still is[22] – of what nature this *esse representatum* or *intentionale* is. According to James of Ascoli and the other adherents of the *esse obiectivum* it is a mode of being to be distinguished well from mental operation itself. As is known, Ockham (c. 1280-1349) originally held that the universal concept is something different from the act of thinking it (*intellectio*) and that it has no reality (*esse subiectivum*), but only logical being *qua* object of the act of thinking (*esse obiectivum*). As a *mere* object of thought, taken quite apart from the mental operation, it has no kind of reality and is just a *fictum*. This theory, which is also found with Peter Aureoli, seems to originate in James of Ascoli's[23]. Later on Ockham identified the universal concept with the very act of abstractive cognition, apparently in order to avoid every danger of Platonism.

One may ask whether or not Ockham was right in having this motive. We have to realize, first, that like almost every Mediaeval thinker James of Ascoli explicitly rejected the Platonic doctrine of the Forms[24]; so the adherents of the *esse obiectivum* theory did not take it as a concession to Platonism. I think they were quite right.

It should be noticed that the adherents of the *esse obiectivum* theory always speak of the *esse obiectivum* (or: *obiective*) *solum* (*tantum*) of the Ideas (c.q. the universal concepts), i.e. as their mode of being when they are taken just as *contents* of thinking, quite apart from the act of thinking itself[25]. Whenever they are taken together with their subject engaged in thinking, the concepts are considered not only *obiective* but also *subiective*, i.e. together with their subject as their foundation.

So it may be quite clear that, when distinguishing *esse obiectivum* from *esse subiectivum*, these Mediaeval thinkers did nothing but distinguish between two ways of approaching the same mental thing (*ens rationis*); one can take thinking as a mental act including its object, or as just (*solum, tantum*) its objective content, taken as its intrinsic object[26] quite apart from its subject (c.q. act of thinking). I think we can best compare this *esse obiectivum* with Frege's objective contents of thought[27]. It would seem an obvious step, indeed, to hypostatize these objective contents and so to join the Platonists, but, unlike Popper, Ockham

210

failed to see how to avoid such a step successfully. I have to admit, however, that although the Mediaeval adherents of the *esse obiectivum* theory did reject Platonism explicitly, they did not show as clearly as Popper the fundamental differences between their *esse obiectivum* and the Platonic Ideas. For that matter, Popper's Third World is much more densely populated than the Mediaevals' domain of the *esse obiectivum*: among its inmates are, more especially, theoretical systems, problems and problem situations, and, above all, critical arguments, c.q. the state of a critical argument. Not to speak of Popper's intentions, which are quite different from those of the Mediaevals.

However, in one respect I should prefer the Mediaeval approach to Popper's. The adherents of the *esse obiectivum* appear to take the *esse obiectivum* not as a *modus essendi beside* those of real and mental being, but as just a subdivision of the latter[28]:

1 *esse (ens) reale*
 = the physical world

2 *esse (ens) rationis*
 = mental being

    a esse subiectivum
     = mental acts *including* their contents

    b esse obiectivum (solum, tantum)[29]
     = the objective contents *apart from* the corresponding acts

I think, by speaking of *Third* World Popper suggests his tripartition to be an adequate division of entities, which it is no more in his view than in the Mediaevals'[30].

However, at another, more important point the adherents of the *esse obiectivum* are similar to Popper; they stress the certain degree of reality (*esse diminutum*) one must attribute to the *contents* of thought *as such,* which the merely mental being (*ens rationis* taken as mental *acts*) has not.

So a continuous line of development can be shown from Henry of Ghent's *essentiae absolutae* via Scotus' *esse representatum* to the (mainly Scotistic or Franciscan) *esse obiectivum*[31]. Its post-Mediaeval occurrences (e.g. with Descartes, Bolzano, Frege, Popper) show that the thoroughly Platonic problem of the *status* of the Ideas (c.q. the universal concepts) did concern in one way or another many thinkers of the European tradition[32].

[1] Alfred North Whitehead, *Process and Reality. An Essay in Cosmology*. Gifford Lectures delivered in the University of Edinburgh during the session 1927-'28, Cambridge 1929, 53.

[2] See C. J. de Vogel, *Philosophia* I, *Studies in Greek Philosophy*, Assen 1970, 228 f.

[3] See Aristot., *Metaph.* N 4, 1091b13-14; Aristoxenus, *Harmon. elem.* II, p.30 Meibom.

[4] See C. J. de Vogel, *Greek Philosophy. A Collection of Texts*, III, Leiden ²1964, nr. 1326b and the literature mentioned there.

[5] See E. Panofski, *Idea*, Leipzig 1924.

[6] *Platons Gottesbegriff*, in: *La notion du divin depuis Homère jusqu'à Platon*. Entretiens sur l'antiquité classique, Tome I, (241-283), 273. Verdenius' other argument (reference to *Timaeus* 52A) seems not to be conclusive in this regard.

[7] See C. J. de Vogel, *Philosophia* I, 219.

[8] I cannot see how Professor de Vogel (*Greek Philos.* III, nr. 1326b; *Philosophia* I, 182) can take Plato, *Soph.* 249A (and *Timaeus* 31B) for the source of the conception of the Ideas as eternal and immutable thoughts of the Divine Mind. Indeed, the whole Intelligible World is spoken of as a living being (παντελὲς ζῷον, παντελῶς ὄν), and so far this conception may be compared to Aquinas' view of the Ideas as "Living Beings" in God's Mind; but the passages under discussion do not contain anything about the *locus* of the Ideas, and that should have been the very point of comparison.

[9] The decisive point seems to be that the predicative use of θεός does not point at, nor even permits to conclude to, the personification of a Divine Subject. See E. Ehnmark, *The Idea of God in Homer*, Uppsala 1935 and J. Gunning, *De nieuwe Attische Komedie als bron van kennis der Griekse religie*, diss. Amsterdam 1940, 12 ff., quoted by Verdenius, *op.cit.*, 274.

[10] Richard Reitzenstein, *Augustin als antiker und mittelalterlicher Mensch*. Vorträge der Bibliothek Warburg 1922-'23 I (1924).

[11] See e.g. *Enneads* V 1, 4, lines 25-28; cf. VI 2, 18.

[12] *Retract.* I 3, 4: *Nec Plato quidem in hoc erravit quia esse mundum intelligibilem dixit, si non vocabulum, quod ecclesiasticae consuetudini in re illa inusitatum est, sed ipsam rem velimus attendere.*

[13] *De diversis quaestionibus* 83, q. 46; cf. *De Trinitate* VI 10, 11; *De Genesi ad litt.* V 15, 33 and IV 24, 41; *Epist.* 118 (*ad Dioscurum*), 20-21; *De civ. Dei* VIII 4, etc.

[14] *Namque rara visio est et nimis ardua conspicere, Domine, aeternitatem tuam incommutabiliter mutabilia facientem.*

[15] Cf. Djemil Saliba, *Étude sur la métaphysique d'Avicenne*, Paris 1927, 89-92.

[16] That Henry's innovation is due to his Arab sources, may appear from Albert the Great's view of the Ideas during his Neoplatonic period. See Jean Paulus, *Henri de Gand, Essai sur les tendances de sa métaphysique*, Paris 1938 (Unfortunately this brilliant monograph has been out of print for a long time).

[17] *Op. Oxon.* I, d. 35, q.unica, nr. 12 (= I, 553b).

[18] See esp. *Rep. par.* I, d. 36, q. 3, nr. 20 (= XX, 455).

[19] Petrus Thomae, *De esse intelligibili* (only in the manuscripts, e.g. Cambridge, Univ. F. III 23, 222ʳ-237ᵛ). His epistemology, too, includes the acts of the *intellectus creatus*.

[20] *Questio de Ideis*, found in *Vat. Lat. Borgh.* 171, 34ʳᵃ-36ᵛᵃ, edited by A. Maurer in: Mediaeval Studies 23 (1961), 163 ff.; wrongly attributed by Ledoux (edition of William of Alnwick) and others to Henry of Harclay.

[21] See his *Quest. disp.*, q. 1: *Utrum notitia actualis quam habet Deus de creatura posuerit ipsam ab eterno in aliquo esse causato* (*Vat. Lat.* 1012, 60ᵛ-62ᵛ and

212

Florence, Laurenz. *Plut. XXXI, dext. 8*, 34rb) and *Quodlibet*, q. 2: *Utrum perfectiones creaturarum virtualiter contente in essentia divina, secundum quod habent ibi esse proprium et distinctum inter se et ab essentia, precedant rationes ideales* (*Vat. Lat* 1012, 48ra-49ra and Florence, Laurenz. *Plut. XXXI, dext. 8*, 53^r-54^v).

[22] Cf. Sir Karl Popper's Third World theory, *Epistemology without a Knowing Subject* (in: *Objective Knowledge, An Evolutionary Approach*, Oxford ²1973, 106-152) and *On the Theory of the Objective Mind* (*ibid.*, 153-190); see also below, n.27.

[23] Notice, however, that with Ockham the doctrine is no longer restricted to God's knowledge, but concerns all kinds of intellection, whereas those of James of Ascoli and Peter Aureoli even concern sensitive knowledge, too.

[24] Sometimes the question is discussed whether or not the Ideas in God's Mind are identical with the Platonic Ideas. So e.g. Ferrarius Catalaunus O.P., *Quodlibet* (written in 1276), q. 1: *Utrum idee quas theologi ponunt esse in Deo sint eedem cum ideis quas Platonici posuerunt* (Paris, *Arsenal* 379, 225^r-233^v); so an anonymous author in a *Quodlibet* found in Dôle, Ms. 81, 344^r-353^v, q. 2: *Utrum idee quas Plato posuit sint ille quas ponunt in Deo theologi.*

[25] See e.g. James of Ascoli (Florence, Laurenz., *Plut. XXXI, dext. 8*, 34vb: *Id quod est in aliquo solum obiective, impossibele est quod sit totaliter idem cum eo quod est in illo formaliter. Patet, quia tunc idem, et secundum quod idem, esset in aliquo obiective et non esset obiective in ipso; que sunt contradictoria. Sed cognitio qua Deus cognoscit creaturam est in Deo formaliter. Lapis autem cognitus a Deo non est in Deo formaliter, sed solum obiective.*

[26] See above, p. 207.

[27] Frege, *Über Sinn und Bedeutung* in: Zeitschr. f. Philos. und philosoph. Kritik 100 (1892) (25-50), 32. The principle of Popper's Third World (see *op.cit.* 106-190) seems to be nothing but a replica of Frege's universe of objective contents of thought, despite the former's claim that it just "resembles most closely" (Popper, *op.cit.*, 106).

[28] E.g. James of Ascoli as quoted by William of Alnwick (ed. Ledoux, p.3): *esse cognitum alicuius obiecti importat entitatem distinctam a cognitione; ...lapis secundum eius esse cognitum et representatum habet entitatem sibi propriam... et per consequens lapis in esse cognito et representato differt a cognitione et a representante.*

[29] For this addition, see above, p. 210.

[30] As Popper himself clearly shows by speaking of "two different senses of knowledge or of thought: (1) *knowledge or thought in the subjective sense*, consisting of a state of mind or consciousness or a disposition to behave or to react; and (2) *knowledge or thought in an objective sense*, consisting of problems, theories and arguments as such... knowledge in the objective sense is *knowledge without a knower*; it is *knowledge without a knowing subject*" (*op.cit.*, 108-9).

[31] For the similarity of the *esse obiectivum* to Henry's *essentiae absolutae*, see e.g. James of Ascoli, *Florence Ms*, 35ra: *Esse vero intentionale est illud quod convenit rei ut habet esse obiective rel representative in aliquo alio ente reali. Et quia representari in aliquo obiective indifferenter convenit tam universali quam etiam singulari, ideo esse intentionale non magis appropriat sibi universale quam singulare, nec econverso.*

[32] That the occurrence of the *esse objectivum* with Descartes is due to Scotistic influences has successfully been argued by R. Dalbiez, *Les sources scolastiques de la théorie cartésienne de l'être objectif. A propos du "Descartes" de M. Gilson*, in: Revue d'histoire de la philos. 3 (1929), 464-72.

THE INTELLECT IN PLOTINUS
AND THE ARCHETYPES
OF C. G. JUNG

HANS-RUDOLF SCHWYZER

Porphyry tells in his *Life of Plotinus*, 18,10 ff. that the first time he heard Plotinus teaching, he had disagreed with his doctrine that the Intelligibles were not outside the Intellect. Therefore (he goes on) he wrote against the master to show that, on the contrary, the objects of thought existed outside the Intellect. Hereupon, Plotinus charged his intimate pupil Amelius to refute Porphyry. Amelius wrote a lengthy treatise to solve the difficulties of the novice, but at first only provoked a counter-argument. Finally indeed by answering this reply he managed to convince him. Longinus, however, the eminent critic of those times, censured Porphyry for having changed his mind[1].

In the philosophical system of Plotinus this doctrine is a central point which he had touched upon in many of his treatises, especially in *Enn.* V, 9 [5][2], in VI, 4-5 [22-23], and in the first three chapters of V, 5 [32] which Porphyry entitled *That the Intelligibles are not outside the Intellect and on the Good*. On the background of this doctrine, A. H. Armstrong read a paper in the Vandoeuvres-Meeting 1957[3], where he confessed his inability to detect the doctrine in the *Dialogues* of Plato, but admitted that Plotinus and other interpreters in antiquity did find it there. Everybody, however, agrees that the well-known activity of Self-Thinking, which Aristotle attributes to the Intellect[4], must have been a model for Plotinus, the Intellect being to Aristotle a metaphysical reality, whereas, to Plato, it was but an instrument of cognition.

Still, the Aristotelian doctrine was not the only model. Plotinus also relied on the theorem that the Platonic Ideas are the thoughts of God. We read this for the first time in Philo, *De opificio mundi* 5, p.4 M. as an explanation of Plato, *Tim.* 29d-30e. The theorem is hardly Plato's own opinion, but since it is certainly not the invention of Philo, it probably is an interpretation common in the Platonic school long before Philo.

The connexion of these two theorems (the one of the Self-Thinking Intellect, and the other of the Ideas as thoughts of God) appears for the first time in Albinus, *Didasc.* 9, p.163, 17 Hermann, and 10, p.164, 24 ff.[5]

We do not know whether Plotinus read Albinus. If he did not, then, in fact, he had found the connexion in an earlier Platonist. But, surely, he was the first to draw an important conclusion from this connexion: if the Intellect embraces as its unique objects the Intelligibles i.e. the Platonic Ideas, the Intellect is equal to the sum of the Intelligibles. Consequently, it is at the same time One and Many. There cannot be any difference between Intellect and Intelligibles: subject and object of thinking disappear in the whole Intellect (*Enn.* VI, 9 [9] 5, 16); but each of the many Intellects, paradoxically, retains its specific difference (IV, 3 [27] 5, 7). In the Intelligible World, there exists neither place nor time; therefore, all things are always united there in an 'All-Together'[6]. The Intellect is without extension, but nevertheless is not a perfect unity, but embraces all Intelligibles. "All are one there and yet are distinct" (V, 9 [5] 6, 3). The Intellect is manifold, not in place, but in otherness (VI, 4 [22] 4, 25). It is distinct and repugnant to distinction. Every idea is separated from every other, but being intelligible and being included in the whole Intellect, – nay, being identical with it – every idea at the same time is identical with every other, just as in the seed all powers are indistinctly united though of course promising a different development (V, 9, 6, 11).

The sameness of ideas or of Intellects has its parallel in the Souls. The Souls of men, of animals, of plants and anorganic things are different, not only from group to group, but also from individual to individual; nevertheless in that they are Souls they do not differ (VI, 5 [23] 9, 12-13; VI, 7 [38] 8, 27-31). On this theme, Plotinus wrote a particular treatise, viz. IV, 9 [8], where he showed that the so-called differences between Souls were, properly speaking, rather differences between bodies (IV, 9, 3, 13-15; 4, 12-13). In the Intelligible World, there does not exist any difference. But even in our Sensible World, the Souls must be identical. The 'Sympathy', i.e. the Feeling-together of the different parts of the world, and the communication between men imply the identity of Souls.

According to Plotinus, the Intellect thinks the Intelligibles, but its thinking is not comparable to the thinking of any given object by any given subject; for otherwise it would not think at all before thinking its objects, and this, indeed, is inconceivable (V, 9 [5] 5, 7). Certainly, the Intellect is always thinking, and since its objects are identical with itself, it is really thinking itself. Further, the Intellect is conscious of its thinking, for not only do Intellect and Intelligibles coincide, but as the Intellect's only task is to think, also the act of thinking is identical with it (V 3 [49] 5, 39-46). Therefore the Intellect always possesses knowledge of its thinking, but it is by no means necessary to distinguish its Self-Thinking from its thinking that it is thinking (II,9 [33] 1, 50-57).

The thinking of men, however, and the thinking of the Intellect are not the same. Men do not possess clear thinking but only hazy ratiocination. They cannot think all objects at once, but only one after the other, and they forget many of their objects completely. For that, they have but a Discursive Reason. The Intellect, for its part, is always in possession of its thoughts and always seizing all its thoughts at once, and as it is thinking unceasingly, there is no room at all for any subsequent thinking (II, 9 [33] 1, 52-53). The consciousness of the Intellect is continually clear, and its thinking runs without fatigue, for its thinking and being coincide. In this Intellect is comparable to Nature. Nature also is working without fatigue and without rational planning. Nature, according to Plotinus, creates its creatures merely by contemplation. But Nature is not aware that it is creating; it does not work consciously, but it is in harmony with itself like a sleeper who does not dream (III, 8 [30] 4, 19-25).

This unconscious working is admirable. Even for men, sometimes, unconscious processes are better than conscious ones. The healthy man is enjoying his health without consciousness, a handsome man remains handsome even if he does not reflect on his quality, and the wise man exerts his wisdom without being always conscious of it (I, 4 [46] 9, 11-14). Consciousness sometimes is even hindering. The concentrated reader is not aware that he is reading. And the brave fighter does not have the leisure to reflect on his bravery. "Conscious awareness, in fact (says Plotinus, I, 4, 10, 23 ff.), is likely to enfeeble the very activities of which there is consciousness; only when they are alone are they pure and more genuinely active and living; and when good men are in this state their life is increased, when it is not spilt out into perception, but gathered together in one in itself."

A man is conscious of himself as long as he is different from real being and from Intellect. He has to put away sensation and consciousness if he wishes to see real being or, rather, to become real being. The conversion to it brings gain. A man retreating inwards becomes possessor of all; he unites with real Being when he leaves behind all things and also himself. Severing from his self he reaches real self, and this is the real being of Intellect, where all differences are removed, where self-abandonment and self-fulfilment coincide (V, 8, 11, 5-13; VI, 5, 12, 13-25).

According to Plotinus, the Intellect has full consciousness of itself.

Nevertheless, for men, the Intellect is the great collective where human consciousness begins to disappear. It seems daring, but it is perhaps legitimate to compare the Plotinian Intellect with what modern psychologists call the "Collective Unconscious". The conception was named by the well-known psychologist and psychiatrist C. G. Jung (1875-1961). In his book *Transformations and Symbols of the Libido* (first published in German, 1912, translated CW[7], vol. 5, 177, § 258) he wrote: "The Unconscious... is universal: it not only binds individuals together into a nation or race, but unites them with the men of the past and with their psychology. Thus by reason of its supra-individual universality, the Unconscious is the prime object of any real psychology." Later on he replaces the term "Universal Unconscious" by "Collective Unconscious", first in his paper *Instinct and the Unconscious*, British Journal of Psychology 10, 1919, 15-26, reprinted in CW 8, 129-38. Here we read (133, § 270): "The Instinct and the Archetypes together form the Collective Unconscious." In this sentence, he for the first time uses the term 'Archetype', though previously he used to speak of 'Primordial Images', a term borrowed from a letter of Jacob Burckhardt[8].

Jung has developed his theory against Freud for whom the contents of the Unconscious are limited to repressed tendencies, which ought to be removed by analysis, whereas Jung's Unconscious contains plenty of Archetypes below the threshold of consciousness and far beyond the personal sphere. For Freud the Unconscious is an ugly region from which we should emerge, for Jung however the spiritual and intellectual achievements of mankind are based on the Collective Unconscious. "The contents of the Collective Unconscious are invariable Archetypes that were present *a priori*" (In his book *Aion*, published 1951, translated CW, vol. 9, part 2, 8, § 13). They are "the fundamentally analogous forms of perception that are to be found everywhere" (CW 8, 165, § 353, first published 1947).

Jung is quite aware that his Archetypes are akin to the Platonic Ideas. For he writes in the same paper (CW 8, 191, § 388) that the Platonic Ideas stored up in a "supra-celestial place" (Plat. *Phaedrus* 247c) are "a philosophical version" of the Archetypes. And in another paper (published 1935, translated CW, vol. 9, part 1, 4, § 5) Jung said briefly: "Archetype is an explanatory paraphrase of the Platonic *Eidos*." Plato himself uses neither the adjective 'archetypos' nor the noun 'archetypon'; in the passage, however, where the Greek word, in a philosophical sense, occurs first, viz. Philo, *De opificio mundi* 16 (I 4 M.), the author, using the Platonic *Timaeus* 28a ff. in order to describe the biblical creation speaks of the "archetypical and intelligible idea" when rendering the Platonic term 'paradigm'. In the same treatise, 71 (I 16 M.) Philo introduces the pleonasm *archetypon paradeigma* i.e. 'Prototypical Model'. Of course, Philo did not invent the word, but took it from some lost source belonging to the Platonic school.

Plotinus often uses the term *archetypon* for describing the Intellect or the Ideas. In *Enn.* V, 9 [5] 5, 22, he tells us that the maker of the All cannot create anything by looking at what does not yet exist; the objects of this thinking are not outside models, but rather "Archetypes, Primals and the Essence of Intellect". Here by 'Archetypes' we are gripping both the Intellect itself and its content, the Ideas. For Plotinus, as I have pointed out, there does not exist any barrier between the Ideas, each Idea, within the Intellect, being identical to each other Idea. Similarly Jung said in his paper on *The Archetypes and the Collective Unconscious* (Eranos-Jahrbuch 2, 1934, printed 1935, 225): "In the Unconscious the single Archetypes are not isolated from each other, but they are in a state of contamination, of the most complete mutual interpenetration and interfusion."[9]

Within the Plotinian Intellect individuality vanishes, the differences between the single Ideas disappear just as the differences between the single Souls ought to be removed, for otherwise comprehension between men cannot be realized. In Jung's paper we meet a similar thought: "No, the Collective Unconscious is anything but an incapsulated personal system; it is sheer objectivity... There I am the object of every subject... There I am utterly one with the world, so much a part of it that I forget all too easily who I really am" (CW, vol. 9, part 1, 22, § 46). And in his *Psychology of the Transference* (published 1946, translated CW 16, 169, § 354), Jung spoke of a "Non-individual Psyche" and said: "Although this Psyche is innate in every individual it can neither be identified nor possessed by him personally. It is the same in the individual as it is in the crowd and ultimately in everybody. It is the precondition of each individual Psyche, just as the sea is the carrier of the individual wave."

Not earlier than in the second volume of his book on the *Mysterium coniunctionis*, published 1956, translated CW 14, 534, § 761, Jung called Plotinus a witness to the idea of the *mundus unus*. The whole passage runs as follows: "In his fourth *Ennead* (IV, 9 [8] 1 ff.). Plotinus discusses the problem of whether all individuals are merely one Soul, and he believes he has good grounds for affirming this question. I mention Plotinus because he is an earlier witness to the idea of the *unus mundus*. The 'Unity of the Soul' rests empirically on the basic psychic structure common to all Souls, which, though not visible and tangible like the anatomical structure, is just as evident as it." What Jung calls "the basic psychic structure," is for Plotinus rather the unity of the Intelligible World. For, as mentioned above, the pure thinking of the Intellect is, for Plotinus, quite different from the Discursive Reason or Reckoning of men. Similarly Jung says: "The Archetype represents the authentic element of Spirit, but a Spirit which is not to be identified with the human intellect, since it is the latter's *spiritus rector*" (published 1947, translated CW 8, 206, § 406).

Instincts and Archetypes are mutually akin, for they form together the Collective Unconscious, but they are by no means identical. "Just as his Instincts compel man to a specifically human mode of existence, so the Archetypes force his ways of perception and apprehension into specifically human patterns" (first published in English, 1919, reprinted CW 8, 133, § 270). In a later paper (published 1947, translated CW 8, 218, § 423) Jung formulates as follows: "The dominants of the Collective Unconscious fall phenomenologically into two categories: instinctual and archetypal. The first includes the natural impulses, the second the dominants that emerge into consciousness as universal ideas." In Plotinus, the Instinct can easily be compared to that kind of *theoria* which the unreflected nature exerts, whereas the archetypal dominant is comparable to the painless acting of the Intellect. The human consciousness of course is superior to the instincts of beasts, plants or even stones, but it is still inferior to the autarky of the Intellect.

It is not my intention to prove by this paper that Jung was a disciple of Plotinus. On the contrary, in the period of his developing the doctrine of the Archetypes and the Unconscious, his acquaintance with the philosophy of Plotinus was certainly modest. He had heard of him through a book by Arthur Drews, *Plotin und der Untergang der antiken Weltanschauung*, Leipzig 1907, from which he drew a few quotations for his own book *Transformations and Symbols of the Libido* (printed 1912, translated CW 5, 138, § 198). Unfortunately, he became the victim of Drews' errors who compared the Plotinian Trinity (One, Intellect, Soul) with the Christian Trinity, and took Plotinus for a forerunner of the Nicean symbol 'One Being in three Hypostases'. This is obviously mistaken, since in Plotinus' interpretation of Plato, *Republic* 509b, the Good or One is always 'beyond Being'. Jung quoted Plotinus a second time in the book *Aion* (published 1951, translated CW, vol. 9, part 2, 219, § 312), but there he does not deal with the doctrine of the Archetypes and the Unconscious. A third quotation is in the book *Synchronicity*, published 1952, translated

CW 8, 490, § 927. Here he used again the book of Drews and told us, this time misunderstanding both Plotinus and Drews, that the individual Souls originate from the World-Soul. The only important passage Jung is quoting is in his *Mysterium coniunctionis*, cited by me above p. 218. But as Jung published this book only in 1956, i.e. many years after having conceived his ideas, Plotinus cannot be the source of his doctrine. Jung is mentioning him only in search of ancient witnesses to previously articulated ideas.

Perhaps it seems reckless to say that a scholar of such wide learning was but little familiar with Plotinus. Anyhow, he certainly did not know that the term 'Archetype' was often used by Plotinus, and that no ancient philosopher had done more for the elucidation of the Unconscious. For, in his paper in the 'Eranos-Jahrbuch' 2, 1934, printed 1935, 180[10], Jung asserted: "The term 'Archetype' derives from St. Augustine". In fact, St. Augustine did not write the Greek word; he only gave a description of the Platonic Ideas in his paper *De diversis quaestionibus* in the *quaestio* 46, 2 (Patrol. Lat. 40, col. 39) which runs as follows: *sunt namque ideae principales formae*[11] *quaedam vel rationes rerum stabiles atque incommutabiles quae ipsae formatae non sunt ac per hoc aeternae ac semper eodem modo sese habentes quae in divina intelligentia continentur.* In the revised edition of 1954, translated CW, vol. 9, part i, 4, § 5, Jung corrected: "The term 'Archetype' occurs as early as Philo Judaeus"[12]. He also produced some passages from Irenaeus, from the Hermetics and from Dionysius Areopagita, but did not mention Plotinus at all.

Of course, I am far from censuring Jung for his lack of philological knowledge and his ignorance of sources. In fact, my only intention is to show his independence from Plotinus. A modern psychiatrist plagiarizing a Greek philosopher would not be worth speaking of. But it is exciting that an outstanding empiricist of the twentieth century has independently attained, in his researches, results comparable to those of a speculative metaphysician of the third century.

Still, it would be incorrect to conceal the differences between the two thinkers. Plotinus draws a system of values. At the bottom lies Matter, devoid of Value and of Being. Upwards is the Sensible World which has but a derivative Being, then follows the Soul, the lowermost of the three Primary Hypostases, above it the Intellect i.e. the true Being, finally at the top the One or the Good, unrecognizable and beyond the Intellect. Jung of course admits neither Matter in a Plotinian sense nor the One. He is not a metaphysician, he merely tries to take some steps from the sphere of consciousness back to the great realm of the Unconscious. He does not speak of 'above' and 'below' and does not pronounce moral judgments. In a paper first published 1947, translated CW 8, 206, § 406, he declared: "Instinct is not in itself bad any more than Spirit is good". Even to Plotinus Instinct is not bad, but Matter for him is absolute evil. The Intellect however is far above evil, it is perfect and true Being.

Contrary to Plotinus' conviction Jung wrote in his book *Aion*, published 1951, translated CW, vol. 9, part 2, 267, § 423: "We do not know what good and evil are in themselves. It must therefore be supposed that they spring from a need of human consciousness and that for this reason they lose their validity outside the human sphere. That is to say, a Hypostasis of good and evil as metaphysical entities is inadmissible." In this passage, Jung is denying exactly what Plotinus had been proclaiming. To the latter, on one end of the chain, there is the Good in itself, on the other end the Evil in itself. Jung however is remembering his empirical starting-point, for he intends to screen the man of this world, whereas Plotinus tries to surmount the sensible man and to change him into the authentic man and to conduct him to the Intellect and even beyond it to the One.

NOTES

[1] As we are told *Life of Plotinus*, 20, 95, and as we gather from Proclus, *In Tim.* 98c (I, 322, 24 Diehl), who tells us that Longinus asserted the Paradigm (i.e. the Intelligible World) to be posterior to and therefore different from the Demiurge (i.e. the Intellect).

[2] Plotinus is quoted by *Enneads, books, chapters*, and *chapter-lines* of the Budé-Text, ed. E. Bréhier, 1924-38, adopted by Henry and Schwyzer in their edition, 1951-73. If necessary, the place of a book in the chronological order handed down by Porphyry, *Life of Plotinus* 4-6, is added by a chiffre in square-brackets. The translations from *Enn.* I-III are those of A. H. Armstrong, in the Loeb Collection, 1966-67, from *Enn.* IV-VI those in St. MacKenna's fourth edition revised by B. S. Page, 1969, both modified occasionally.

[3] Published in *Entretiens sur l'antiquité classique*, tome 5 (= *Sources de Plotin*), 391-413.

[4] Particularly *Metaph.* 1074b33 ff.

[5] As Armstrong, o.c. 403, pointed out, and long before him W. Theiler, *Die Vorbereitung des Neuplatonismus*, 1931, 16.

[6] This term of Anaxagoras, fr. B 1, is often used by Plotinus when he is depicting the Intellect, e.g. VI, 5 [23], 6, 3; V, 8 [31] 9, 3; VI, 6 [34] 7, 4; V, 3 [49] 15, 21.

[7] Jung is generally quoted after the English *Collected Works* (= CW), Routledge and Kegan Paul, London, 1953 sqq., and Bollingen Series, New York, 1953 sqq. (not yet complete).

[8] Burckhardt's letter to Albert Brenner is printed in English translation in CW 5, 32, note 45.

[9] Quoted according to the first English translation by Stanley M. Dell in *The*

Integration of Personality, New York, 1939, 91. The passage is omitted in the second edition.
[10] Quoted according to the first English translation by Stanley M. Dell in *The Integration of Personality*, 53.
[11] Maybe the term *principales formae* is a translation of the Greek *archetypa*.
[12] The passages are quoted above p.217-8.

LIST OF PUBLICATIONS
BY PROF. DR. C. J. DE VOGEL

Compiled by

J. VAN HEEL

1930

Over de rust, die naar men zegt, het geloof geeft,
    in: Eltheto, monthly of the N.C.S.V., 85 (1930), pp.77-78.

1931

Over de verhouding van geloof en denken. (Komt het verstand in het christelijk geloof tot zijn recht?),
    in: Eltheto 85 (1931), pp.120-140 and pp.148-161.
Levende Steenen, On the reorganisation in the Dutch Reformed Church, Zutphen 1931.
De laatste ernst, Zutphen 1931.
Rijkdom en ontbering,
    in: Eltheto 85 (1931), pp.177-184.

1933

Review of Josepha Kraiger-Porges, *Lebenserinnerungen einer alten Frau,*
    in: Eltheto 87 (1933), pp.253-257.
Zwaard en Kruis, (On Ernest Psichari, Renan's grandson),
    in: De Gids 97 (1933), pp.323-352.

1936

Een keerpunt in Plato's denken. Een historisch-philosophische studie,
    Amsterdam 1936.

1937

De legende van Renan en de twintigste eeuw,
    in: Onder Eigen Vaandel 12 (1937), pp.33-50.

1938

De eigenlijke strekking van Newman's gedachten over de rechtvaardiging,
    in: Onder Eigen Vaandel 13 (1938), pp.219-224.

1939

Newman's gedachten over de rechtvaardiging. Hun zin en recht t.o.v. Luther en het protestantse Christendom, Wageningen 1939.
Review of Schmid, *Epikurs Kritik der platonischen Elementenlehre,*
    in: Museum 46 (1939), p.149 ff.
Review of Schneidewin, *Das sittliche Bewusstsein, eine Gorgiasanalyse,*
    in: Museum 46 (1939), p.171 ff.
Review of Naaykens, *Platons leer over de ziel,*
    in: Museum 47 (1939), p.88 ff.

1940

Review of Van Schilfgaarde, *De Zielkunde van Aristoteles,*
    in: Museum 47 (1940), p.151 ff.
Review of Raeder, *Platons Epinomis,*
    in: Museum 47 (1940), p.230 ff.

Nogmaals de Rechtvaardigingsleer (on Eduard Böhl),
    in: Onder Eigen Vaandel 15 (1940), pp.27-52.

1941

Over beginselen van theologische discussie (on the analogia entis),
    in: Vox Theologica 12 (1941), pp.145-157.
Over de plaats van de theologische faculteit aan onze universiteiten,
    in: Alg. Ned. Tijdschrift voor Wijsbegeerte 34 (1941), pp.141-160.
Review of Brommer, *Eidos en Idea,*
    in: Museum 49 (1941), p.51 ff.
Review of Vink, *Plato's Alcibiades,*
    in: Museum 48 (1941), p.170 ff.

1942

Review of D. Loenen, *Protagoras and the Greek Community,*
    in: Museum 49 (1942), p.104 ff.

1943

Fourth revised edition of B. J. H. Ovink, *Overzicht der Griekse Wijsbegeerte,*
    Zutphen 1943.

1946

Ecclesia catholica. Redelijke verantwoording van een persoonlijke keuze,
    Utrecht 1946, ³1948.
Rechtvaardigmaking bij Katholiek en Protestant,
    in: Ned. Katholieke Stemmen 42 (1946), pp.275-285.
B. J. H. Ovink, Zijn wetenschappelijke en persoonlijke betekenis,
    in: De Gids 109 (1946), pp.31-44.
Review of A. E. Loen, *De Vaste Grond,*
    in: De Gids 1946, pp.52-57.

1947

De ontmoeting van het Wijsgerig Denken met de Christelijke Openbaring,
    in: *Philosophia,* Beknopt handboek voor de geschiedenis van de wijsbe-
    geerte, ed. by H. van Oyen, Utrecht 1947, dl. I, pp.139-181.
Een groot probleem in de antieke wijsbegeerte. Inaugural oration, Utrecht 1947.
Review of Aalders, *Het derde boek van Plato's Leges,*
    in: Museum 52 (1947), p.149 ff.

1948

La dernière Phase du Platonisme et l'Interprétation de M. Robin,
    in: *Studia Vollgraff,* Amsterdam 1948, pp.165-178.
L'Idée de l'Unité de Dieu une Verité rationelle,
    in: *Mélanges philosophiques* (offered to the members of the Xth Inter-
    national Congress of Philosophy held at Amsterdam, 1948), Amsterdam
    1948, pp.24-39.
Athanasius, *Redevoeringen tegen de Arianen* [dated 1943]. Translation, in-
    troduction and notes. Utrecht 1948.
Review of Plumpe, *Mater Ecclesia,*
    in: Museum 53 (1948), p.7 ff.

1949

Problems concerning later Platonism,
    in: Mnemosyne S. IV, 2 (1949), pp.197-216 and 299-318.

1950

Greek Philosophy. Texts with notes and explanations. Vol. I, *Thales to Plato,*
    Leiden 1950, ²1957, ³1963, ⁴1969.
Plato en het moderne denken,
    in: Tijdschrift voor Philosophie 12 (1950), pp.453-476.

De continuïteit van het West-Europese denken,
   in: Alg. Ned. Tijdschrift voor Wijsbegeerte 42 (1950), pp.177-190.
Het R.K. Kerkbegrip (uit een openbare discussie, gehouden voor de Universiteit van Amsterdam),
   in: Vox Theologica 20 (1950), pp.153-159.
Het geloof en zijn redelijke fundering. Bijdrage tot een Congres gehouden door
   de Utrechtse Kath. Studentenvereniging "Veritas".
   in: Geloof en Wetenschap, Utrecht 1950, pp.79-95.
Review of H. Cherniss, Aristotle's Criticism of Plato and the Academy,
   in: Museum 55 (1950), p.72 ff.
Review of O. Gigon, Sokrates, Sein Bild in Dichtung und Geschichte,
   in: Museum 55 (1950), p.168 ff.
Review of G. J. de Vries, Spel bij Plato,
   in: Museum 55 (1950), p.196 ff.

1951

Avicenna en zijn invloed op het West-Europese denken,
   in: Alg. Ned. Tijdschrift voor Wijsbegeerte 44 (1951), pp.3-16.
Examen critique de l'interprétation traditionelle du Platonisme,
   in: Revue de Métaphysique et de Morale 56 (1951), pp.249-268.
Une nouvelle interprétation du problème socratique,
   in: Mnemosyne S. IV, 4 (1951), pp.30-39.
Review of G. Quispel, Ptolemée, Lettre à Flora,
   in: Museum 56 (1951), p.198 ff.

1952

Het probleem van het kwade in de Antieke Wijsbegeerte,
   in: Studia Catholica 27 (1952), pp.20-38.
L'histoire de la philosophie en quel sens fait-elle partie de la philosophie?
   in: Actes du Congrès des Sociétés de Phil. de langue francaise, Strasbourg
   1952, pp.359-362.
Vollenhoven's werk over de Griekse Wijsbegeerte vóór Plato,
   in: Alg. Ned. Tijdschrift voor Wijsbegeerte 44 (1952), pp.223-240.
Het totalitarisme van Plato's Staat en het totalitarisme van de Katholieke Kerk,
   in: Annalen van het Thymgenootschap 40 (1952), pp.173-197.
Review of D. H. Th. Vollenhoven, Geschiedenis der Wijsbegeerte voor Plato en
   Aristoteles,
   in: Mnemosyne S. IV, 5 (1952), pp.155-156.
Review of B. Delfgaauw, Beknopte Geschiedenis der Wijsbegeerte, deel I,
   in: Museum 57 (1952), p.144 ff.

1953

Greek Philosophy. Texts with notes and explanations. Vol. II, Aristotle, the
   Early Peripatetic School and the Early Academy. Leiden 1953, ²1960, ³1967.
Het Christelijk scheppingsbegrip en de Antieke Wijsbegeerte,
   in: Tijdschrift voor Philosophie 15 (1953), pp.409-425.
Platon a-t-il ou n'a-t-il pas introduit le mouvement dans son monde intelligible?,
   in: Actes du XIième Congrès International de Philosophie, (Brussels), Vol.
   XII, Amsterdam-Louvain 1953, pp.61-67.
On the Neoplatonic character of Platonism and the Platonic character of Neo-
   platonism,
   in: Mind 62 (1953), pp.43-64.
Discussie rondom Vollenhoven,
   in: Alg. Ned. Tijdschrift voor Wijsbegeerte 45 (1953), pp. 22-23.
Review of R. Höisted, Cynic Hero and Cynic King,
   in: Mnemosyne S. IV, 6 (1953), pp.243-244.

1954

A la recherche des étapes précises entre Platon et le Néoplatonisme,
   in: Mnemosyne S. IV, 7 (1954), pp.111-122.
De Wijsbegeerte en de Faculteit der Letteren,
   in: Alg. Ned. Tijdschrift voor Wijsbegeerte 46 (1954), pp.186-190.

1955

Waarneming, verstand en intuïtie in de Griekse Wijsbegeerte,
   in: Alg. Ned. Tijdschrift voor Wijsbegeerte 47 (1955), pp.105-120.
The present State of the Socratic Problem,
   in: Phronesis 1 (1955), pp.26-35.
Quelques remarques à propos du Premier chapitre de l'Éthique de Nicomaque,
   in: *Autour d'Aristote*. Recueil d'études de philosophie ancienne et médiévale
   offert à Mgr. A. Mansion. Louvain 1955, pp.307-323.
Conferentie: De Wijsbegeerte in het Hoger Onderwijs,
   in: Universiteit en Hogeschool 1 (1955), pp.128-136.
Chapter XII in: *De kerk die mij boeide,* Utrecht 1955, pp.91-96.
Het Platonisme,
   in: Encyclopedie van het Christendom, Amsterdam-Brussel 1955, p.619.

1956

Eigenaardig Katholicisme,
   in: Te Elfder Ure 3 (1956), pp. 195-196.
Waarheid en onwaarheid aangaande het protestantisme,
   in: Te Elfder Ure 3 (1956), pp.233-247.
Review of R. P. Oliver, *Nicole Perotti's Version of the Enchiridion of Epictetus,*
   in: Museum 61 (1956), p.101 ff.
Du Protestantisme orthodoxe à l'Église catholique. (Les motifs d'une option
   personelle). Trad. par Pierre Brachin. Paris 1956.
   (Translation of *Ecclesia Catholica,* 1946).

1957

Het monisme van Plotinus,
   in: Alg. Ned. Tijdschrift voor Wijsbegeerte 49 (1957), pp.99-112.
Review of O. Gigon, *Kommentar zum ersten Buch von Xenophons Memo-*
   rabilien-Kommentar zum zweiten Buch von Xenophons Memorabilien,
   in: Erasmus 10 (1957), pp. 612-616.
Over de Nieuw Guinea kwestie,
   in: De Tijd, dec. 1957 (4 articles; the 5th published in: Plein, 1958).

1958

Antike Seinsphilosophie und Christentum im Wandel der Jahrhunderte,
   in: *Festgabe J. Lortz,* Baden-Baden 1958, pp.527-548.
   Separate Baden-Baden, 1958.
Het Atomisme bij de Grieken,
   in: Studium Generale. Maandblad voor culturele vorming 4 (1958), **nr. 5,**
   pp.134-136.
Averroës als verklaarder van Aristoteles en zijn invloed op het West-Europese
   denken,
   in: Alg. Ned. Tijdschrift voor Wijsbegeerte 50 (1958), pp.225-240.
Review of Olympiodorus, *Commentary on the first Alcibiades of Plato,* ed.
   L. G. Westerink,
   in: Museum 63 (1958), p.283 ff.
Review of *Sexti Empirici Opera,*
   in: Museum 63 (1958), p.14 ff.
Over de Nieuw Guinea kwestie,
   in: Plein, febr. 1958.

Naar aanleiding van Röling: Nieuw Guinea als wereldprobleem,
　　in: Te Elfder Ure 5 (1958), pp.193-198.
De Academie, Plato, Het Platonisme and *Het Neo-platonisme,*
　　in: Filosofisch Lexicon, samengesteld door J. Grooten en G. J. Steen-
　　bergen, Antwerpen-Amsterdam, 1958, pp.5, 198, 222-223.

1959

Greek Philosophy. Texts with notes and explanations. Vol. III, *The Hellenistic-
Roman Period.* Leiden 1959, ²1968, ³1973.
La théorie de l' ἄπειρον chez Platon et dans la tradition platonicienne,
　　in: Revue Philosophique de la France et de l'Étranger 84 (1959), pp.21-39.
Review of *Histoire de la philosophie et métaphysique.* Aristote, St. Augustin,
St. Thomas, Hegel,
　　in: Gnomon 31 (1959), pp.628-630.
Review of Zeno O.F.M. Cap., *Our way to certitude. An introduction to Newman's
psychological discovery: the illative sense, and his grammar of assent,* Leiden
1957,
　　in: Revue d'Histoire Ecclésiastique 54 (1959), pp.214-216.

1960

The legend of the Platonizing Aristotle,
　　in: *Aristotle and Plato in the Mid-Fourth Century* (First Symposium
　　Aristotelicum, Oxford 1957), ed. Göteborg 1960, pp. 248-256.
Review of E. de Keyser, *La signification de l'art dans les Ennéades de Plotin,*
Leuven 1955,
　　in: Mnemosyne S. IV, 13 (1960), pp.81-82.
Review of G. Huber, *Das Sein und das Absolute,*
　　in: Mnemosyne S. IV, 12 (1960), pp.258-261.

1961

Aristotele e l'ideale della vita contemplativa,
　　in: Giornale di Metafisica 16 (1961), pp.450-466.
What philosophy meant to the Greeks,
　　in: International Philosophical Quarterly 1 (1961), pp.35-57.
"Ego sum qui sum" et sa signification pour une philosophie chrétienne,
　　in: Revue des sciences religieuses, Université de Strasbourg 35 (1961).
La méthode d'Aristote en métaphysique d'après Métaphysique A1-2,
　　in: *Aristote et les problèmes de méthode.* (Symposium Aristotelicum, Louvain
　　1960), ed. Louvain 1961, pp.147-170.
Review of Kesters, *Plaidoyer d'un Socratique,*
　　in: Forum der Letteren 1961, pp.187-193.
Het huidige stadium van de Nieuw Guinea-kwestie,
　　in: De Maand 4 (1961), pp.215-218.

1962

Participatie en Causaliteit,
　　in: Nederlands Theologisch Tijdschrift 17 (1962), pp.122-132.
Review of Rabbow, *Paidagogia,*
　　in: Mnemosyne S. IV, 15 (1962), pp.409-413.

1963

Amor quo caelum regitur,
　　in: Vivarium 1 (1963), pp.2-34.
Who was Socrates?
　　in: Journal of the History of Philosophy 1 (1963), pp.143-161.
The Concept of Personality in Greek and Christian Thought,
　　in: Studies in Philosophy and the History of Philosophy, Washington D.C.,
　　2, 1963, pp.20-60.

The topic of eternal change in Greek and later Western Philosophy compared with Indian Thought,
in: Acts XIII Internat. Congress of Philosophy, Mexico 1963, Vol. IV, pp.375-389.

1964

Review of Ch. Rutten, *Les catégories du monde sensible dans les Ennéades de Plotin* (1961),
in: Mnemosyne S. IV, 17 (1964), pp.314-316.
Review of W. K. C. Runciman, *Plato's later epistemology,*
in: Gymnasium 71 (1964), pp.457-460.
Review of K. Gaiser, *Platon und die Geschichte,*
in: Gymnasium 71 (1964), pp.397-398.

1965

On Iamblichus V.P. 215-219,
in: Mnemosyne S. IV, 18 (1965), pp. 388-396.
Did Aristotle ever accept Plato's theory of transcendent Ideas? Problems around a new edition of the Protrepticus,
in: Archiv für Geschichte der Philosophie 47 (1965), pp.261-298.
Het Godsbegrip bij Plato, I,
in: Acta Classica, Kaapstad, 7 (1965), pp.32-43.
Review of W. K. C. Guthrie, *A History of Greek Philosophy.* Vol. I, *The earlier Presocratics and the Pythagoreans,* Cambridge 1962,
in: Gymnasium 72 (1965), pp.259-261.

1966

Pythagoras and Early Pythagoreanism. An interpretation of neglected evidence on the philosopher Pythagoras, Assen 1966.
Het Godsbegrip bij Plato, II,
in: Acta Classica, Kaapstad, 8 (1966), pp.38-52.
Some reflections on the Liber de Causis,
in: Vivarium 4 (1966), pp.67-82.
Review of E. Berti, *La filosofia del primo Aristotele,* Padova 1962,
in: Mnemosyne S. IV, 19 (1966), pp.187-190.
Review of W. Kamlah, *Platons Selbstkritik im Sophistes,*
in: Gymnasium 72 (1962), pp.301-302.
De Oost-Berlijnse Friedenstagung,
in: Adelbert, maart 1966.

1967

Theoria. Een bundel opstellen over de Griekse Wijsbegeerte, Assen 1967.
Review of H. C. Baldry, *The Unity of Mankind in Greek Thought,*
in: Gymnasium 74 (1967), pp.463-465.
Plato, Aristotle and the ideal of contemplative life,
in: Philippiniana Sacra 2 (1967), Manilla, pp.672-692.
Review of Timpanaro-Cardini, *Pitagorici III,*
in: Mnemosyne S. IV, 20 (1967), pp.319-321.

1968

Het humanisme en zijn historische achtergrond, Assen 1968.
Plato. De filosoof van het transcendente, Baarn 1968.
Aristotle's Attitude to Plato and the Theory of Ideas, according to the Topics,
(Contribution to the third Symposium Aristotelicum, 1963),
in: *Aristotle on Dialectics.* Proceedings of the Third Symposium Aristotelicum, Oxford 1968, pp.91-102.
Review of W. J. Oates, *Aristotle and the Problem of Value,* Princeton University Press, 1963,
in: Mnemosyne S. IV, 21 (1968), pp.305-307.

228

1969

Erasmus and his Attitude towards Church Dogma,
  in: Scrinium Erasmianum, Vol. II, Leiden 1969, pp.101-132.
Girishiya tetsugaku to shūkyō. Fujisawa Reifu, Inagaki Rioten, Katō Noburō
  ta yaku. Tokyo 1969.
Review of W. K. C. Guthrie, *A History of Greek Philosophy.* Vol. II, *The*
  Presocratic Tradition from Parmenides to Democritus, Cambridge 1965,
  in: Gymnasium 76 (1969), pp.90-92.
Review of J. A. Philip, *Pythagoras and Early Pythagoreanism,* (Phoenix,
  Suppl. VII), Toronto 1967,
  in: Journal of Hellenic Studies 89 (1969), pp.163-165.

1970

Philosophia. Part I, *Studies in Greek Philosophy,* Assen 1970.
Wijsgerige aspecten van het vroeg-Christelijk denken. Kleine geschiedenis van de
  Patristische en vroeg-Middeleeuwse wijsbegeerte, Baarn 1970.
Review of *The Cambridge History of Later Greek and Early Medieval Philosophy,*
  edited by A. H. Armstrong, Cambridge University Press, 1967,
  in: Bibliotheca Orientalis 27 (1970), pp.391-6.
Review of W. Burkert, *Weisheit und Wissenschaft. Studien zu Pythagoras,*
  Philolaos und Plato, Nürnberg 1962,
  in: Gymnasium 77 (1970), pp.69-71.

1971

On the character of Aristotle's ethics,
  in: *Philomathes.* Studies and essays in the humanities in memory of Philip
  Merlan, The Hague 1971, pp.116-124.
A propos de quelques aspects dits néoplatonisants du platonisme de Platon,
  in: *Le Néoplatonisme* (Colloque de Royaumont 1909), Paris 1971, ed.
  CNRS, pp.7-16.
Boethiana I,
  in: Vivarium 9 (1971), p.49-66.
Review of W. K. C. Guthrie, *A History of Greek Philosophy.* Vol. III, *The*
  Fifth Century Enlightenment, Cambridge 1969,
  in: Bibliotheca Orientalis 28 (1971), pp.231-233.

1972

De onmisbaarheid van het overbodige, Leiden 1972. (Rede gehouden ter gelegen-
  heid van haar 25-jarig hoogleraarschap aan de Rijksuniversiteit te Utrecht).
Boethiana II,
  in: Vivarium 10 (1972), pp.1-40.
Was Plato a dualist?,
  in: Thêta-Pi 1 (1972), pp.4-60.
A sample of rational theology in XIth century Indian Philosophy. a) A short
  introduction into comparable Greek thought.
  in: Thêta-Pi 1 (1972), pp.140-144.
Probleme der späteren Philosophie Platons,
  in: *Das Problem der ungeschriebenen Lehre Platons,* Beiträge zum Verständnis der platonischen Prinzipienphilosophie, hrsg. von Jürgen Wippern.
  Darmstadt 1972, pp.41-87.
Die Spätphase der Philosophie Platons und ihre Interpretation durch Léon Robin,
  in: ib., pp.201-216.
Review of W. K. C. Guthrie, *A History of Greek Philosophy.* Vol. III, *The Fifth*
  Century Enlightenment, Cambridge 1969,
  in: Gymnasium 79 (1972), pp.108-110.

229

1973

Encore une fois: le Bien dans la République de Platon,
   in: *Zetesis*. Bijdragen op het gebied van de klassieke filologie, filosofie, byzantinistiek, patrologie en theologie door collega's en vrienden aangeboden aan Prof. dr. Emile de Strycker, Antwerpen-Utrecht 1973, pp.40-56.
Two major problems concerning Socrates,
   in: Thêta-Pi 2 (1973), pp.18-39.
Quelques problèmes à propos de l'exposé de M. Berti,
   in: Thêta-Pi 2 (1973), pp.111-113.
Trois questions à M. Wisniewski,
   in: Thêta-Pi 2 (1973), pp.124-125.
Aan de Katholieken van Nederland. Aan allen. Nijmegen 1973.
Plato in de latere en late Oudheid, bij heidenen en christenen,
   in: Lampas 6 (1973), pp.230-253.
The problem of philosophy and Christian faith in Boethius' Consolatio,
   in: *Romanitas et Christianitas*. Studia Iano Henrico Waszink oblata. Amsterdam-London 1973, pp.357-370.

1974

Humanism in the contemporary era,
   in: Thêta-Pi 3 (1971), pp. 109-122.
Aeterna veritas, Utrecht 1974.

Forthcoming:
   L'Éthique d'Aristote offre-t-elle une base appropriée à une éthique chrétienne? Contribution au Congrès Thomiste, Rome 1974.
   Review of M. L. West, *Early Greek Philosophy and the West*, Oxford 1971, in: Bibliotheca Orientalis.

230

TABULA GRATULATORIA

J. A. M. van Amerongen, Winsum (Gr.)
Library St. Anne's College, Oxford, England
Professor A. H. Armstrong
A. J. M. Asselbergs, Nijmegen
Prof. Pierre Aubenque, Université de Paris-Sorbonne, France
Baker Library, Dartmouth College, Hanover N.H., U.S.A.
Werner Beierwaltes, Freiburg, B.R.D.
Bergische Universität Wuppertal, Bibliothek, Wuppertal, B.R.D.
Prof. Enrico Berti, Padova, Italia
Bibliotheek Arnhem, Arnhem
Bibliothèque Cantonale et Universitaire, Fribourg, Suisse
Bibliothèque Centrale, Facultés Universitaires N. D. de la Paix, Bruxelles,
    Belgique
Bibliotheek Filosofisch Instituut Katholieke Universiteit, Nijmegen
Bibliotheek en Leeszalen der Gemeente Rotterdam
Bibliotheek Rijksuniversiteit Leiden
Bibliotheek Katholieke Theologische Hogeschool, Amsterdam
Bibliothèque de l'Université de l'Etat, Mons, Belgique
Bibliotheek der Vrije Universiteit, Amsterdam
The Blegen Library – American School of Classical Studies, Athens,
    Greece
Drs. D. H. Borgers, Oostburg
H. A. G. Braakhuis, Nijmegen
M. D. Bremmer, Amstelveen
Brock University Library, St. Catharines, Ontario, Canada
Brotherton Library, Leeds, England
Buma-Bibliotheek, Leeuwarden
Prof. dr. Walter Burkert, Zürich, Schweiz
Drs. B. M. M. Bijnsdorp, Hulst
Harold Cherniss, Princeton, New Jersey, U.S.A.
Concordia Seminary Library, St. Louis, Mo., U.S.A.

Alfred M. M. Dekker en W. H. M. Dekker-Vos, Utrecht
Prof. dr. B. Delfgaauw, Groningen
Dr. J. P. Th. Deroy, Heemstede
Heinrich Dörrie, Münster/Westfalen, B. R. D.
Prof. dr. H. J. Drossaart Lulofs, Amsterdam
Dr. J. Eekels, Uithoorn
Ir. W. Engelenburg, Doorn
C. W. van Essen-Zeeman, Vinkeveen
David L. Fowler, Trondheim, Norway
Mevr. Franken, Utrecht
Professor David Furley, Princeton, New Jersey, U.S.A.
René A. Gauthier, Grottaferrata (Roma), Italia
Olof Gigon, und das Seminar für klassische Philologie und antike Philo-
    sophie der Universität Bern, Schweiz
Dr. J. W. Groothuyse, Amsterdam
A. C. J. Habets, Utrecht
Fritz-Peter Hager, Bern, Switzerland
J. van Heel, Utrecht
Ds. W. van Herpen, Ned. Herv. Predikant, Hagestein
J. C. A. van Herten, Bilthoven
A. Hilhorst en C. Hilhorst-Boink, Bunnik
J. J. C. van Hoorn-Groneman, Utrecht
Dr. Mr. H. Houwens Post, Former Professor of Portuguese at the Uni-
    versity of Utrecht
Dr. R. Horst, Leersum
B. L. Hijmans en M. M. Hijmans-van Assendelft, Eelde
Institute of Classical Studies, Librarian, London, England
Institute of Mediaeval Studies, Toronto, Ontario, Canada
Istituto per le Scienze Religiose, Bologna, Italia
Johan J. de Iongh, Nijmegen
Dr. L. F. Janssen, Utrecht
Prof. dr. M. Jeuken, Leiden
Prof. dr. Robert Joly, Mons, Belgique
Paulus Kalligas, Athens, Greece
Mr. B. Kolff, Amerongen
W. van der Kraan, Drempt
J. H. M. Krah, Rockanje
Ir. E. Landeweer, Purmerend
Elie Lopes Cardozo, Zeist
F. Losecaat Vermeer, Haarlem

F. Makaliwy, Drachtster Compagnie (Frl.)
Prof. dr. Jaap Mansfeld, Bilthoven (Utrecht)
Prof. S. Mansion, Louvain, Belgique
Mr. J. Mastenbroek, Amsterdam
Monastic Manuscript Microfilm Library, St. John's Abbey & University,
    Collegeville, Minnesota, U.S.A.
Evanghélos A. Moutsopoulos, Athens, Greece
P. G. van der Nat, Den Haag
K. R. Oosterhuis, Den Haag
A. J. B. Olthof, arts, Dordrecht
F. M. Ossewijer, Leek
Drs. H. A. Oude Essink, Bunnik
Professor Joseph Owens, Toronto, Can.
René Palmen, Venlo
A. M. van Paridon, Oegstgeest
Maja Pellikaan-Engel, Aerdenhout
Prof. dr. A. Peperzak, Nijmegen
Philosophy Library, Oxford, England
Provinciale Bibliotheek van Zeeland, Middelburg
Dr. G. Puchinger, Den Haag
I. N. Robins, Cambridge, England
J. M. de Roon Hertoge, Den Haag
John Rylands University, Manchester, England
Prof. dr. L. M. de Rijk, Leiden
H. D. Saffrey, Paris, France
Prof. René Schaerer, Genève, Suisse
D. M. Schenkeveld, Heemstede
G. Schepperle, West-Terschelling
Pierre-Maxime Schulh, Paris
Hans-Rudolf Schwyzer, Zürich, Switzerland
Theo Gerard Sinnige, Nijmegen
Drs. J. Steeg, Heeswijk-Dinther
Modestus van Straaten o.s.a., Groesbeek/Nijmegen
H. J. Straver, Sneek
Prof. dr. Emile de Strycker s.j., Antwerpen, België
Teruo Suzuki, Osaka, Japan
Leonardo Tarán, New York N.Y., U.S.A.
Theol. College of the Canadian Reformed Churches, Hamilton, Ontario,
    Canada
Theologische Hogeschool, Kampen

F. J. E. Tichelman, Alkmaar
Dr. Maria Timpanaro Cardini, Firenze, Italia
Library University of Birmingham, England
University of London Library, London, England
Universitätsbibliothek Basel, Schweiz
Universitätsbibliothek Marburg, B.R.D.
Universitetsbiblioteket, Uppsala, Sweden
Universiteitsbibliotheek v. Amsterdam
University of York Library, Heslington, York, England
Prof. dr. W. C. van Unnik, Bilthoven
Fons van de Veerdonk, Roosendaal
Prof. dr. G. Verbeke, Leuven, België
Prof. dr. W. J. Verdenius, Zeist
Mr. Elisabeth A. Verloop, Den Haag
T. E. Vetter, De Bilt
Winnie F. Villeneuve, Ottawa, Ontario, Canada
Mej. J. W. Visée, Amsterdam
Prof. dr. Elizabeth Visser, Groningen
Prof. dr. G. J. de Vries, Wolfheze
J. H. Waszink, Leiden
Prof. dr. V. Westhoff, Groesbeek
S. Wiersma, Utrecht
Atie Wiersma-Buriks, Paterswolde
E. J. van Wolffelaar, Utrecht
Dr. Cornelia W. Wolfskeel, Utrecht
Centre de Wulf-Mansion, Louvain, Belgique.